C000319819

Walks & Tours
in France

Published by The Automobile Association,
Fanum House, Basingstoke, Hampshire RG21 2EA

Editorial contributors:
Paul Atterbury (The North, The Loire)
Keith Howell (Ile de France)
John Lloyd (Burgundy, The Rhône Valley)
Robin Neillands (Brittany, Normandy)
Tony Oliver (Auvergne and Languedoc, Provence
and the Côte d'Azure)
Ian Powys (Alsace and Lorraine, Franche-Comté)
Mary Ratcliffe (The Atlantic Coast, Périgord and Quercy)
Kev Reynolds (The Pyrenees)
Richard Sale (Auvergne and Languedoc, Provence and the Côte
d'Azure)
Melissa Shales (Berry and Limousin)
John White (The Alps)

Published by AA Publishing
(a trading name of Automobile Association Developments Limited,
whose registered office is Norfolk House, Priestley Road, Basingstoke,
Hampshire RG24 9NY. Registered number 1878835)
© The Automobile Association 1993
Reprinted 1994, 1995

Walk maps extracted from the Institut Géographique National de
France (IGN) 1:25 000 Série Bleue and TOP 25 with the
permission of IGN © 1993.

Tour maps based on IGN 1:250 000 Série Rouge with the permission
of IGN © The Automobile Association and the Insitut Géographique
National de France 1993.

All rights reserved. No part of this publication may be reproduced,
stored in a retrieval system, or transmitted in any form or by any
means – electronic, mechanical, photocopying, recording, or otherwise – unless the written permission of the publishers has been given
beforehand.

A catalogue record for this book is available from the British Library.

ISBN 0 7495 0554 0 (HARDBACK)
ISBN 0 7495 1238 5 (SOFTBACK)

Typesetting by:
Microset Graphics Ltd
Colour Reproduction by:
Fotographics Ltd
Printed and Bound by:
Graphicromo SA

The contents of this publication are believed correct at the time of
printing. Nevertheless the publishers cannot accept responsibility for
errors or omissions, or for changes in detail given.

Page one: Rocamadour, Périgord and Quercy
Pages two and three: St-Gervais-les-Bains, The Alps

Contents

Introducing the Book

The abbey of St-Front in Périgueux, Périgord and Quercy

Most people would agree that France, with its wonderfully diverse scenery, culture, cuisine and architecture, can offer something to suit all tastes – if you know where to go. With this in mind, *Walks and Tours in France* has been designed to help travellers find their way around, either by car or on foot, and to discover its many different faces at their own pace. This combination ensures you will see all the major sights in any given area, but it also enables you to search out the less well-known corners and to reach the heart of the country and its people.

So that a day out can be planned according to time, energy and inclination, the walks and tours are integrated within each region, with the walks starting on or near the routes of the car tours. Each tour (located on the map on page 7) takes in a number of attractions in an area – a château, a seaside resort, a spectacular geological feature, a pretty village – while the walks take you off the beaten track, to explore, at a more leisurely pace, glorious countryside, ancient towns or quiet hamlets.

All the routes have been carefully researched and every effort has been made to ensure accuracy. However, the landscape can change and features mentioned as landmarks may alter or disappear in time. The changing seasons also greatly affect the appearance of the landscape.

The walks should have adequate parking space available at their starting-point, but sometimes this space is limited and thoughtless parking can cause considerable inconvenience to nearby residents, or cause a traffic hazard. Remember, too, that whatever the time of day or year, farm vehicles must always have clear access to field entrances and tracks.

Opening times of places of interest are not given in this book. It is always advisable to check the current details in advance when planning a visit.

4

INSTITUT GEOGRAPHIQUE NATIONAL

The Institut Géographique National de France (IGN-F) is the French national mapping agency, and a world leader in the sourcing and recording of geographic information. In common with the majority of government mapping organisations, it is a product of the requirement for military maps and is a direct descendant of a service launched by Napoleon. In its modern form, employing 2000 staff, it is engaged not only in mapping France but also supplies its services wherever they may be required throughout the world. During the past 40 years IGN-F has operated in over 50 countries.

Modern cartographic institutions now create digital databases of geographic information and maps are just one of the by-products of these activities. Quite

techniques to produce maps of the highest quality, and a total of over ten million copies of 1500 different maps are printed on IGN-F printing machines every year.

Ten per cent of IGN-F's entire budget is spent on research and development, much of which is carried out with external organisations in co-operative ventures. One such venture was with the French National Space Agency, resulting in the SPOT satellites, which produce images of the earth's surface to the highest resolution currently available.

Three new major databases of France are currently in preparation and these will become part of the essential infrastructure of the country. Paper maps will be one of the products, but the major use will be with Geographic Information Systems. These systems will use the data in a wide variety of services, from town planning to forestry, from the optimisation of transportation services and communications to long-term land-use planning.

The maps used in this book for the tours and walks are extracted from two of IGN-F's major series covering France – the 1:250 000 Série Rouge and the 1:25 000 Série Bleue respectively. These sheet maps are available at more than 10,000 retail outlets throughout France, where the distinctive IGN-F badge is displayed.

a formidable range of expertise and equipment is required, and IGN-F has pioneered many of the techniques essential for acquiring geographic information. It is intimately involved in all the processes necessary to produce a modern map, and these include aerial surveys, ground surveys, cartography and printing. Each of these activities requires high levels of skill, organisation and modern equipment. In order to maintain the IGF's flow of expertise, more than 60 students graduate each year from the Ecole Nationale des Sciences Géographiques (French National Geographic Sciences College) to work in IGN-F.

The IGN Aerial Survey Department employs 26 aircrew members and 50 ground-based mechanics to operate its five aircraft. The aerial photographs produced by this team are not only used to make maps, but are freely available for a multiplicity of other uses. Ground surveys are necessary to add detail, such as place names, administrative boundaries and road conditions, which cannot be extracted from photographs. IGN-F has developed special cartographic

INSTITUT GEOGRA PHIQUE NATIONAL

IGN

Finding the Walks and Tours

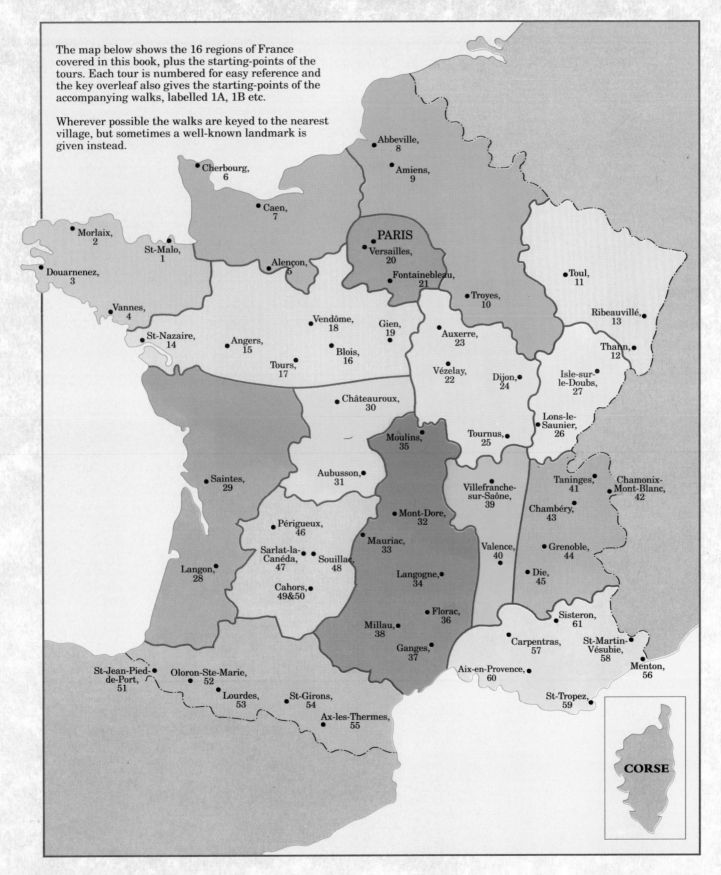

The map below shows the 16 regions of France covered in this book, plus the starting-points of the tours. Each tour is numbered for easy reference and the key overleaf also gives the starting-points of the accompanying walks, labelled 1A, 1B etc.

Wherever possible the walks are keyed to the nearest village, but sometimes a well-known landmark is given instead.

Cherbourg, 6

Abbeville, 8

Amiens, 9

Caen, 7

Morlaix, 2

St-Malo, 1

PARIS

Versailles, 20

Alençon, 5

Fontainebleau, 21

Toul, 11

Douarnenez, 3

Troyes, 10

Ribeauvillé, 13

Vannes, 4

Vendôme, 18

Gien, 19

Auxerre, 23

Thann, 12

St-Nazaire, 14

Angers, 15

Blois, 16

Vézelay, 22

Dijon, 24

Isle-sur-le-Doubs, 27

Tours, 17

Châteauroux, 30

Tournus, 25

Lons-le-Saunier, 26

Moulins, 35

Saintes, 29

Aubusson, 31

Taninges, 41

Chamonix-Mont-Blanc, 42

Villefranche-sur-Saône, 39

Chambéry, 43

Mont-Dore, 32

Périgueux, 46

Mauriac, 33

Valence, 40

Grenoble, 44

Sarlat-la-Canéda, 47

Souillac, 48

Langon, 28

Langogne, 34

Die, 45

Cahors, 49&50

Florac, 36

Sisteron, 61

Millau, 38

Carpentras, 57

St-Martin-Vésubie, 58

Ganges, 37

Menton, 56

St-Jean-Pied-de-Port, 51

Oloron-Ste-Marie, 52

Aix-en-Provence, 60

Lourdes, 53

St-Girons, 54

St-Tropez, 59

Ax-les-Thermes, 55

CORSE

La Roque-Gageac, Périgord and Quercy

Map Legend

RENSEIGNEMENTS TOURISTIQUES *TOURIST INFORMATION*

GR   autre sentier

Itinéraire balisé sur sentier (GR, autre sentier) (1), hors sentier (2)
Signposted route along footpath (GR, other) (1), out of footpath (2)

Itinéraire non balisé intéressant sur sentier (1), hors sentier (2)
Interesting unsignposted route along footpath (1), out of footpath (2)

Itinéraire de ski, de randonnée ou de raid
Cross-country or high mountain skiing route

Passage délicat
Hard part of hiking trail

Remontée mécanique en service en été
Ski-lift and chair-lift to be used in summer

Limite de zone réglementée
Boundary of restricted area

Refuge ou gîte d'étape gardés, non gardés. Abri
Refuge or overnight stopping place with keeper, without keeper. Shelter

Camping. Centre équestre. Site d'escalade équipé. Aire de départ de vol libre
Camping. Riding centre. Climbing site with facilities. Hang-gliding area

Aire de détente. Tennis. Golf
Leisure area. Tennis. Golf

Centre de ski de fond. Port de plaisance. Mouillage. Sports nautiques
Cross-country skiing centre. Yachting harbour. Anchorage. Sailing sports

Canoë-kayak (point de mise à l'eau). Piscine. Baignade
Canoeing (launching place). Swimming-pool. Bathing-place

Station classée
Resort with tourist interest

MENTON

Ville d'art. Station thermale, verte, de sports d'hiver, balnéaire
City of artistic interest. Spa, openair, winter sports, seaside resort

Agglomération touristique, centre d'activité, site ou détail remarquables
Town of tourist interest, activity centre, notable site or building

Gorges de la Vésubie

Édifices remarquables. Curiosités diverses. Informations tourisme
Notable monuments. Divers places of interest. Tourist information centre

Gare ou point d'arrêt ouvert au trafic voyageurs   *Gare*   *Arrêt*
Station or stopping-place open to passenger traffic

Voie interdite aux véhicules à moteur. Aire de stationnement
Prohibited road for motor vehicles. Parking area

Bouée. Bouée lumineuse
Buoy. Light buoy

Moyens de sécurité civile (permanents ou saisonniers) - *Means of civil security (perennial or seasonal)*
Poste de police ou de gendarmerie. Téléphone isolé
Police station. Isolated telephone station.

Canot de sauvetage. Surveillance de plage
Lifeboat. Beach patrol.

Secours en mer : coordination assurée par CROSS
Sea rescue : coordination ensured by CROSS

Point de départ de la promenade
Start point of walk

Ligne de la promenade
Line of walk

Direction de la promenade
Direction of walk

Parcours alternatif
Alternative route

③ Lieu d'intérêt (promenade)
Walk map point of interest

Ligne de l'itinéraire
Line of tour

③ Lieu d'intérêt (itinéraire)
Tour map point of interest

Pages nine and ten: The Rhône Valley

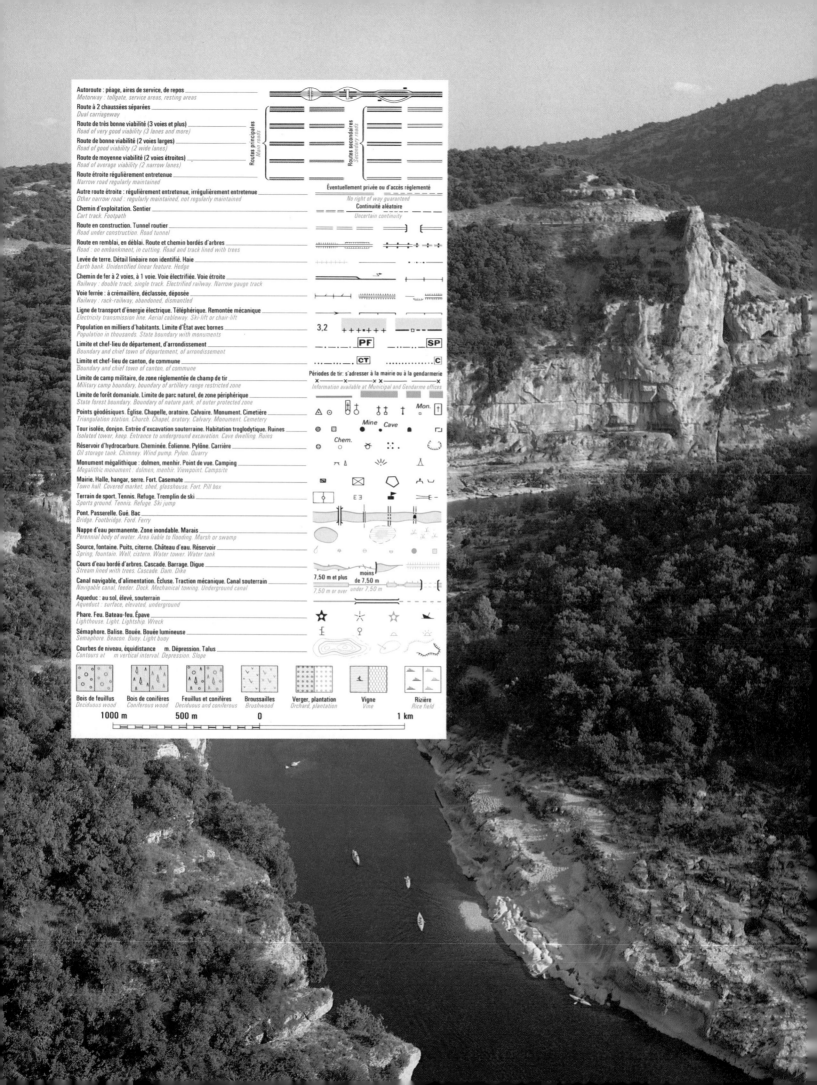

Autoroute : péage, aires de service, de repos
Motorway : tollgate, service areas, resting areas

Route à 2 chaussées séparées
Dual carriageway

Route de très bonne viabilité (3 voies et plus)
Road of very good viability (3 lanes and more)

Route de bonne viabilité (2 voies larges)
Road of good viability (2 wide lanes)

Route de moyenne viabilité (2 voies étroites)
Road of average viability (2 narrow lanes)

Route étroite régulièrement entretenue
Narrow road regularly maintained

Routes principales / *Main roads*
Routes secondaires / *Secondary roads*

Éventuellement privée ou d'accès réglementé
No right of way guaranteed

Autre route étroite : régulièrement entretenue, irrégulièrement entretenue
Other narrow road : regularly maintained, not regularly maintained

Chemin d'exploitation. Sentier
Cart track. Footpath

Continuité aléatoire
Uncertain continuity

Route en construction. Tunnel routier
Road under construction. Road tunnel

Route en remblai, en déblai. Route et chemin bordés d'arbres
Road : on an embankment, in cutting. Road and track lined with trees

Levée de terre. Détail linéaire non identifié. Haie
Earth bank. Unidentified linear feature. Hedge

Chemin de fer à 2 voies, à 1 voie. Voie électrifiée. Voie étroite
Railway : double track, single track. Electrified railway. Narrow gauge track

Voie ferrée : à crémaillère, déclassée, déposée
Railway : rack-railway, abandoned, dismantled

Ligne de transport d'énergie électrique. Téléphérique. Remontée mécanique
Electricity transmission line. Aerial cableway. Ski-lift or chair-lift

Population en milliers d'habitants. Limite d'État avec bornes
Population in thousands. State boundary with monuments

3,2

Limite et chef-lieu de département, d'arrondissement
Boundary and chief town of département, of arrondissement

PF   SP

Limite et chef-lieu de canton, de commune
Boundary and chief town of canton, of commune

CT   C

Limite de camp militaire, de zone réglementée de champ de tir
Military camp boundary, boundary of artillery range restricted zone

Périodes de tir: s'adresser à la mairie ou à la gendarmerie
Information available at Municipal and Gendarme offices

Limite de forêt domaniale. Limite de parc naturel, de zone périphérique
State forest boundary. Boundary of nature park, of outer protected zone

Points géodésiques. Église. Chapelle, oratoire. Calvaire. Monument. Cimetière
Triangulation station. Church. Chapel, oratory. Calvary. Monument. Cemetery

Mon.

Tour isolée, donjon. Entrée d'excavation souterraine. Habitation troglodytique. Ruines
Isolated tower, keep. Entrance to underground excavation. Cave dwelling. Ruins

Mine   Cave
Chem.

Réservoir d'hydrocarbure. Cheminée. Éolienne. Pylône. Carrière
Oil storage tank. Chimney. Wind pump. Pylon. Quarry

Monument mégalithique : dolmen, menhir. Point de vue. Camping
Megalithic monument : dolmen, menhir. Viewpoint. Campsite

Mairie. Halle, hangar, serre. Fort. Casemate
Town hall. Covered market, shed, glasshouse. Fort. Pill box

Terrain de sport. Tennis. Refuge. Tremplin de ski
Sports ground. Tennis. Refuge. Ski jump

Pont. Passerelle. Gué. Bac
Bridge. Footbridge. Ford. Ferry

Nappe d'eau permanente. Zone inondable. Marais
Perennial body of water. Area liable to flooding. Marsh or swamp

Source, fontaine. Puits, citerne. Château d'eau. Réservoir
Spring, fountain. Well, cistern. Water tower. Water tank

Cours d'eau bordé d'arbres. Cascade. Barrage. Digue
Stream lined with trees. Cascade. Dam. Dike

Canal navigable, d'alimentation. Écluse. Traction mécanique. Canal souterrain
Navigable canal, feeder. Dock. Mechanical towing. Underground canal

7,50 m et plus   moins de 7,50 m
7,50 m or over   under 7,50 m

Aqueduc : au sol, élevé, souterrain
Aqueduct : surface, elevated, underground

Phare. Feu. Bateau-feu. Épave
Lighthouse. Light. Lightship. Wreck

Sémaphore. Balise. Bouée. Bouée lumineuse
Semaphore. Beacon. Buoy. Light buoy

Courbes de niveau, équidistance   m. Dépression. Talus
Contours at   m vertical interval. Depression. Slope

Bois de feuillus	Bois de conifères	Feuillus et conifères	Broussailles	Verger, plantation	Vigne	Rizière
Deciduous wood	*Coniferous wood*	*Deciduous and coniferous*	*Brushwood*	*Orchard, plantation*	*Vine*	*Rice field*

1000 m   500 m   0   1 km

Walking

France's magnificent scenic variety has something for every walker, from casual strolls along gentle coastlines and forest tracks to more challenging routes in the Alps and Pyrenees. The country is endowed with an excellent network of 40,000km of long-distance footpaths known as *Grandes Randonnées* (GRs). *Sentiers de Pays* (or GRs de Pays) are mostly one or two-day routes. *Petites Randonnées* (PRs) are day or half-day walks, typically following circular routes.

While much land is privately owned, most landowners are tolerant towards walkers; you will generally be welcome on any path or track, providing you observe the country code (in particular close gates, do not leave litter and do not pick flowers or fruit), and respect *privé* (private) and *réserve de chasse* (hunting reserve) signs.

Finding the way

Walkers' paths are marked on 1:25 000 scale IGN (Institut Géographique National) maps; these are the maps used in this book and are indispensable if you are planning your own walks. Also useful are maps at 1:50 000 scale, which cover a larger area in slightly less detail. Maps and footpath guides can be hard to obtain in out-of-the-way places, but tourist offices *(syndicats d'initiative)* often stock a selection.

GRs are generally well indicated with signposts and paint-marks (a white stripe over a red one), but some 'paths' are no more than undefined routes across wild country and waymarking is occasionally erratic. *Sentiers de Pays* are usually marked in yellow and red, *Petites Randonnées* generally in yellow or blue. When the route changes direction, four stripes are painted together with an arrow; side paths to avoid are sometimes marked with a painted X.

What to wear

Stout shoes or walking boots make walking less tiring, protect your feet and assist your balance. Shorts and a T-shirt are fine in high summer, and a hat may help keep off the sun. Carry enough clothing to enable you to adapt to temperature variations including waterproofs.

Checklist: what to carry

Rucksack, water-bottle (keep it topped up; French heat can make walking thirsty work), compass, map, waterproofs, spare clothing, waterproof gloves, first-aid kit (plasters for blisters, ointment for cramp, antiseptic cream), sun screen lotion, insect repellent, French dictionary or phrasebook, plenty of food, whistle (six blasts every minute is the international distress signal), torch and (if you are really venturing into the wilds) survival bag. Optional extras might include lightweight binoculars, a walking stick (useful for fending off menacing dogs), a towel (for foot or body bathing in streams) and a pocket lens and field guide (for wild flower enthusiasts).

When to go

The far south is too hot for lengthy walks in much of July and August, but fine in spring and autumn. The Dordogne is best between April and October. June to mid-September is the time for walking in the major mountain areas – the Alps, Pyrenees, Franche-Comté, and the Massif Central. Northern France, including Brittany and Normandy, is best between May and September.

Useful addresses

The Fédération Française de la Randonnée Pédestre, 8 Avenue Marceaux, 75008 Paris (tel 010-331 47236232) can advise on specific paths. UK bookshops with a wide range of French maps and guides include McCarta Ltd, 15 Highway Place, London N5 1QP and Edward Stanford, 12 Long Acre, London WC2E 9LP.

Driving

Before you leave

To drive abroad a full driving licence is sufficient; an international driver's licence is not required. Most UK insurance companies cover travel within EC countries, but this is usually only for third party cover. To extend this to a comprehensive (all-risks) policy, obtain a Green Card from your insurers two weeks before travelling. AA Five Star insurance (also available to non-members) covers breakdown and repair, garage bills, hotel vouchers, repatriation and cost of hire car. The AA (24-hour telephone in the UK) will contact the nearest mechanic for you when needed. Right-hand drive cars can be adjusted for headlight beam by using clip-on 'beambenders' (reusable) or by sticking black tape over the 7-9 o'clock area of the headlights. A GB sticker, given free by the ferry companies, must be displayed. Also pack a first-aid kit, hazard warning triangle (compulsory), spare bulbs, jump lead, points, spark plugs, fire extinguisher, torch, tow rope.

In France

Speed limits are 50kph (37mph) in built-up areas, 90kph (56mph) on country roads, 110kph (68mph) on dual carriageways and toll-free motorways, and 130kph (80mph) on toll motorways. In the wet, limits are lowered to 110kph (68mph) on toll motorways and 80kph (50mph) on other roads. The minimum age for front-seat passengers is ten. Seat belts must be worn (in the back too if you have them). Priority is given to traffic coming from the right, unless there are yellow diamond-shaped signs, which give you automatic priority (these are the rule on most country roads); a black line across the sign means you no longer have priority. On roundabouts, traffic on approach roads gives way as in the UK.

Emergency numbers

Police and ambulance, tel 17; fire, tel 18.

Fuel

Leaded fuel (*super*), unleaded (*sans plomb*) and diesel (*gazole*) are widely available.

Roads

Autoroutes, or motorways, are numbered with the suffix A; the toll autoroutes (*péage*) are often remarkably empty by British standards; tolls are quite high, but for long-distance journeys these save much time. Toll-free autoroutes (*sans péage*) are appreciably busier. N roads (national roads) are the equivalent of British A roads, while D roads (departmental roads) are usually much quieter and more suited to touring. In mountain regions, beware of underestimating journey time.

St-Malo to Dinan

No visitor to Brittany should miss two towns which lie on the north coast, the port of St-Malo and the medieval town of Dinan. Both are beautiful, although they are very different in character. A link between the two is the River Rance, which flows past Dinan and out to sea at St-Malo, and is barred on the way by a great tidal dam. Dinan and St-Malo in particular enable the visitor to conjure up the colourful and violent past of Brittany.

Route Directions

The tour starts from St-Malo ①.

Follow signs for Rennes through the suburb of St-Servan-sur-Mer and, keeping the estuary of the Rance on your right, carry on past the Tour Solidor ②.

Follow signs for Dinard, crossing the top of a huge dam, the Barrage de Rance ③.

Turn right on to the D 266 into Dinard ④.

From the promenade here there are fine views across the harbour to the walled city of St-Malo.

Return to the D 266, following signs for Dinan and Pleurtuit. Pass the aerodrome on the right and stay on this road, which becomes the D 766, all the way into the centre of Dinan ⑤.

Dinan is usually crowded, but there are plenty of car parks and it is normally possible to park in the Champ-Clos in the centre, close to all the sights.

From Dinan, follow signs for Mont-St-Michel and Caen, to pick up the N 176 over the Rance bridge, following signs for Dol-de-Bretagne. After 6km fork left on to the D 29, signposted Cancale, and continue north via the D 74 and the D 76, following signs for 'Le Port' as you come into Cancale ⑥.

From Cancale harbour, follow signs for Pointe du Grouin or 'St- Malo par la Côte', on to the D 201 for Pointe du Grouin (7km) ⑦.

Continue along the picturesque coast road past the Baie du Guesclin and through the suburb of Rothéneuf ⑧.

Pass through Paramé, and then along the seafront to the main gateway into the walled town of St-Malo.

The 14th-century Tour Solidor in St-Servan, built to protect French shipping from English pirates, now houses a museum devoted to sailing ships ▶

Points of Interest

① St-Malo is a ferry port for Brittany Ferries, a yachting centre and a commercial port. The modern town has spread far outside the walls of the old town, but it is the latter which draws the visitors. Although old St-Malo is completely walled and protected by a great castle which is now the town hall, the impression of age, though beautiful in the clear Channel light, is an illusion, for St-Malo was almost totally destroyed in 1944, when the German garrison refused to surrender, and was pounded into submission by artillery and naval gunfire. The restoration has been very successful, healing the scars of war.

Wise visitors will begin their tour with a walk around the ramparts, which are dotted with statues of Malouin seafarers such as Surcouf and Duguay-Trouin. From here there are views to Dinard, to the offshore rocks, over the town and to the Ile du Grand Bé, just offshore and in reach at low tide, where the writer François-René de Chateaubriand lies buried. Other recommended sights are the Quic en Groigne tower, which contains a waxwork museum, the town museum in the castle keep which records the exploits of Malouin corsairs, and the Vauban fort, which can only be reached at low tide.

The inner walls of the old town are lined with cafés and restaurants and St-Malo as a whole has plenty of good hotels.

② The medieval Tour Solidor in St-Malo's suburb of St-Servan was built in the late 14th century to protect shipping in the Rance from English pirates and Malouin corsairs from the vengeance of English mariners. It is an evocative building which was once the town jail and now houses a museum devoted to fully rigged clippers.

③ The Barrage de Rance, which spans the river above St-Malo, creates electricity by harnessing the tidal current flowing upstream. When the tide is flowing the sluices are opened and it turns the turbines. The sluices are then closed to contain the water and during the ebb this is

13

BERTRAND DU GUESCLIN

Every visitor to Brittany should know something about the life and times of Bertrand du Guesclin, the great Breton warrior and hero. Bertrand was born about 1320 in the castle of La Motte Broons near Dinan and knighted in 1356, the year of the Battle of Poitiers. In 1359 he captured Dinan and held it against an English army commanded by John of Gaunt, Duke of Lancaster, and during the siege fought a famous duel with Thomas Canterbury.

Bertrand fought the English for the next 20 years and rose to be Constable of France to Charles V. His tactics were not to meet the English in battle, where their archers were invincible, but to wear the English armies down on long marches and pick off their soldiers in guerrilla fighting. When he was not at war with them, Bertrand was on friendly terms with the English; indeed the English Constable, Sir John Chandos, who captured Bertrand twice, at Auray and at Nájera in Spain, was Bertrand's best friend.

By 1380 Bertrand's Fabian tactics had almost driven the English out of France. He died in 1380 while besieging the castle at Châteauneuf-de-Randon. The castle surrendered the next day, and the English governor came and placed the keys in the dead Bertrand's hands.

▲ *Dinard's elegant promenades and gracious hotels are reminders of its fashionable past*

let out over the turbines to produce a continuous flow of electricity into the national grid.

④ Dinard is a gracious and fashionable seaside town with fine promenades and many good hotels, a resort of the smart set since the turn of the century, when Edward VII, the Prince of Wales, used to come here with his cronies. It was developed during the 1850s by an American entrepreneur, and before that was a fishing port. There are good views over a forest of yacht masts to the walls of St-Malo. The Promenade du Clair de Lune is adorned with flower-beds and palm trees and the finest hotels and the casino can be found on the Plage de l'Ecluse. From Dinard there are excursions by boat up the Rance to Dinan and to Fort la Latte on Cap Fréhel, and also to Jersey.

⑤ Dinan has so much to see and do that it is hard to know where to begin. A good place to do so is the Tourist Office in the Rue de Léhon, which offers visitors a town plan and a walking guide to all the sights. A little further up the road lies the school where the writer Chateaubriand began his education. The Champ-Clos in the town centre is now a car park but contains the equestrian statue of Dinan's and Brittany's hero Bertrand du Guesclin, who was Constable of France to Charles V and defeated the English to end the first phase of the Hundred Years War. In 1359 Bertrand fought and killed an English knight, Sir Thomas Canterbury, in the Champ-

Clos and on his death in 1380 he instructed that his heart should be returned to his native town of Dinan, where it still lies in the Basilique St-Sauveur.

Dinan is a place to park the car and stroll down to the banks of the Rance by the Rue du Jerzual, a steep street lined with medieval houses. The riverside is lined with pleasant restaurants and is the perfect place for lunch or dinner. Alternatively, visit the Jardin Anglais near St-Sauveur or explore the fascinating streets of the town, many of which are lined with timber-framed houses. The castle of the dukes of Brittany is splendid and parts of it are open to visitors. There are more fine houses in the Rue de Léhon, which leads to the quiet riverside hamlet of Léhon. Few tourists visit Léhon, but it is very attractive.

The clock tower in the Rue de Léhon was a gift to the town from the Duchesse Anne, the last ruler of an independent Brittany at the end of the 15th century, and there are more medieval houses in Place des Merciers.

⑥ Cancale is an oyster port and seaside resort, a busy little gem of a place tucked into a corner of the Baie du Mont-St-Michel, from which there is a view of the Mont itself on the far side of the bay. Oysters have made Cancale famous. They are bred out in the bay and gathered from the flat-bottomed boats that sit on the harbour sands at low tide.

Trawlers are lashed to the mole and yachts come in to shelter, so that Cancale is always full of life. There are several good hotels by the harbour and lots of small restaurants along the quay, where the first course on any menu is a plate of Cancale oysters.

From Cancale there are good walks and excursions to Pointe du Grouin and the beaches of the north coast.

⑦ Pointe du Grouin is a nature reserve and a bird sanctuary, with marvellous views over the bay to the island of Mont-St-Michel and, away to the south, to the great hump of Mont-Dol near Dol-de-Bretagne.

From the parking place there is a footpath up to the tip of the Pointe and from there another footpath leads along the coast to St-Malo. The first walk on this tour takes in Pointe du Grouin.

⑧ Rothéneuf is a pleasant suburb of St-Malo, adjoining a wide beach. Sights to see here include the coastal rocks carved by the Abbé Foure in the last century and the manor house lived in by the 16th-century explorer and discoverer of Canada, Jacques Cartier.

Dinan's strategic position guarding the River Rance now makes it one of the prettiest towns in Brittany ▼

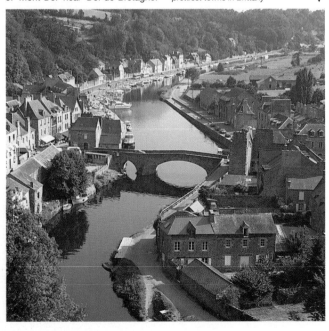

Around Pointe du Grouin

BRITTANY

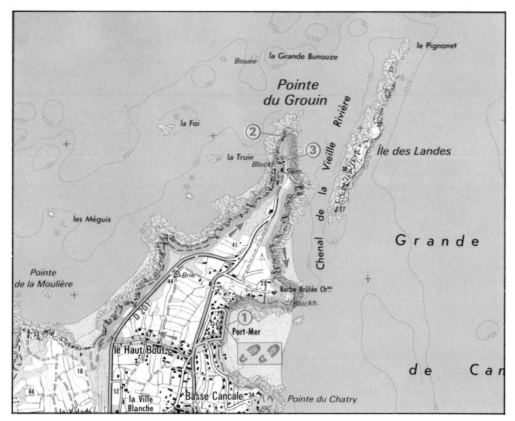

▲ *Rock plants at Pointe du Grouin*

This walk follows the coastal footpath round from the Baie du Mont-St-Michel over to the far (western) side of Pointe du Grouin. The Sentier du Littoral is easy to follow as it winds through the bracken, but the cliffs are steep and small children should be kept under control.

Route Directions

Start from the beach at Port-Mer ①.

Climb the short steep hill to the D 201. Cross over and at the fork take the minor road right for le Haut Bout, signposted Basse-Cancale, but almost immediately turn right up a lane between the houses which leads across the neck of the peninsula to the D 201 again.

Cross the road and take the rough track left, down towards the bay and the coastal footpath. The views along the coast from here towards St-Malo are superb. Here you can rest or paddle on the beach before picking up the path again and following it north towards Pointe du

Grouin. Halfway to the Pointe a small headland juts out to sea.

From here there is a good view of the offshore rocks and Pointe du Grouin. The path leads on through the bracken by the cliff edge, past the signal station and up to the Pointe ②.

Return along the footpath, from where there are good views across the narrow channel of the Vieille

Rivière to the Ile des Landes, a breeding ground for gulls, terns, cormorants and, from time to time, puffins. Here there are many World War II German blockhouses ③.

Carry on south, round the next headland, and past another blockhouse, descending to the beach in front of Port-Mer.

From the cliffs there are magnificent views of the windswept Breton coastline ▼

Points of Interest

① Port-Mer is a small, pretty seaside resort with a sandy beach set in a tiny cove between two green headlands. There is a short promenade and several friendly hotels and restaurants.

② Pointe du Grouin is a nature reserve and one of the long islands just offshore is a bird sanctuary. Stay on the path because efforts are being made to reduce the erosion caused by visitors and restore the rock plants. From the Pointe there are good views over the Baie du Mont-St-Michel.

③ Most of the World War II blockhouses of the German 'Atlantic Wall' have long since disappeared but those here are in fine condition and are often used by birdwatchers studying gulls on the Ile des Landes just offshore. There is a café nearby.

1B

Dinan and the River Rance

This walk covers the old parts of Dinan, but also quiet stretches of the River Rance, which runs just below the town ramparts. The town's streets may be busy but the Rance towpath will not be. There is only one steep section on the walk.

Route Directions

Start from the tourist office in the centre of Dinan. Turn left and walk down the Rue de Léhon, stopping to visit the Basilique St-Sauveur in a square to your left ①.

The Rue de Léhon also contains the school attended by the local writer Chateaubriand ②.

Continue down the Rue de Léhon to the gateway in the medieval curtain wall ③.

Pause here to look right to the great tower of the ducal castle. Then pass through the gateway and along the Rue Beaumanoir, which leads into a lane and then, via some steps, into the beautiful hamlet of Léhon ④.

Stop here to see the old houses, the streets full of flowers and the abbey. Cross the old bridge ⑤.

Follow both the red and yellow GR de Pays waymarks, along the towpath and past the lock, under the road viaduct, and after half an hour reach another bridge ⑥.

This links the village of Lanvallay with the quayside restaurants and shops of Dinan. A stop here is recommended and the walk can be shortened by going over the bridge and up the narrow medieval Rue du Petit Fort back into the town centre. To continue the walk, turn right along the quay to where the road forks. Follow the signs left along the valley, climbing slightly with a stream beside the road to the left, past the Auberge de Jeunesse. The road crosses a bridge and turns right, with the iron railway viaduct now in sight on the right.

Leave the road here, turning left into the woods, then slightly right on to a steep, winding footpath that climbs up a slope and comes out at the top into a large housing estate. Follow the waymarks and 'Centre Ville' signs back to the town centre.

Points of Interest

① The Basilique St-Sauveur was built and rebuilt between the 12th and 18th centuries and contains relics from every period, including the heart of Bertrand du Guesclin. The rear of the church juts into the Jardin Anglais, while the square in front is full of small restaurants.

② François-René de Chateaubriand, the 19th-century writer, was born in Combourg, and had his schooling at this *lycée*. He died in 1848 and is buried on the Ile du Grand Bé, just off St-Malo.

③ The great castle of the dukes of Brittany has served as a fortress and a prison and is now a museum. This gateway leading down to Léhon was once part of Dinan's fortifications.

④ Léhon, 15 minutes' walk from the centre of Dinan, is a beautiful hamlet built in golden stone and full of flowers. It grew up around the priory of St-Magloire, which still stands here beside the Rance.

⑤ The old packhorse bridge leads walkers over to the towpath.

⑥ The suburb of Lanvallay is on the east bank of the Rance, but the west bank just across the bridge is more interesting. It has a narrow medieval street leading up to the centre of Dinan, and quayside restaurants.

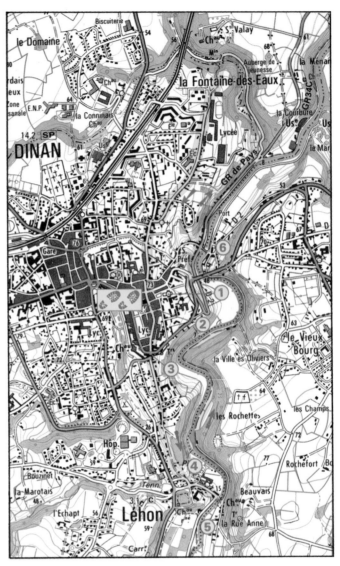

◀ *The old houses overlooking the Rance at Dinan present a picturesque mixture of local architectural styles*

The towpath that runs alongside the Rance at Léhon ▶

The Montagnes d'Arrée

BRITTANY

This figure-of-eight tour covers the rolling moors of the Montagnes d'Arrée and the walking centre at Huelgoat, and follows scenic routes across some of the most attractive country in western Brittany. It takes in Morlaix, Carhaix-Plouguer and the pleasant town of Châteauneuf-du-Faou, and passes close to the great calvary and parish close (*enclos paroissial*) at St-Thégonnec, which is well worth a visit.

Route Directions

Start from Morlaix ①.

Follow the 'Toutes Directions' signs to the D 769 for Carhaix-Plouguer. (Those interested in walking around St-Thégonnec should pick up the N 12 at Morlaix Nord.)

The D 769 is a picturesque route rising and falling for 24km, before turning right into Berrien (to where the tour returns later) and following the D 14 down into Huelgoat ②.

Leave Huelgoat on the D 14, cutting across open rolling country for 16km, before turning right on to the D 21, signposted Brasparts ③.

Follow the D 785, signposted Pleyben ④.

From here pick up the N 164, signposted Châteauneuf-du-Faou and Carhaix-Plouguer, and follow this for 16km, past Ty-Blaise, to Châteauneuf-du-Faou ⑤.

Return to the N 164 and follow this very attractive road beside the River Aulne to Carhaix-Plouguer ⑥.

Leave Carhaix-Plouguer on the D 764, signposted Huelgoat, and fork right after 3km on to the minor road, signposted Poullaouen, and then join the D 769 and carry on past Locmaria Berrien, travelling beside the River Argent and following the road round to the right to arrive at Berrien ⑦.

Follow the road through woods, and at the D 769-D 42 crossroads take the D 42 right, signposted Scrignac and Guerlesquin.

The D 42 runs across fields and patches of heather-dotted moorland, with wide views to the south-east, and through Scrignac. Then bear left on the D 54 to join the D 9 to Plougonven ⑧.

Stay on the D 9 to return to Morlaix.

Points of Interest

① Morlaix is a port, though it lies some 16km inland from the sea. The most striking feature of the town is the great 19th-century railway viaduct, 70m high, towering over the rooftops. Morlaix stands on the frontier between the Côtes d'Armor and Finistère, and the river divides the two. The town centre is always busy and quite attractive, with good shopping and several agreeable restaurants.

▼ *The impressive railway viaduct at Morlaix*

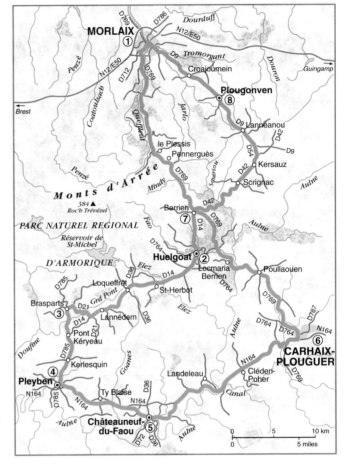

② Huelgoat can lay some claim to the title of the capital of the Argoat, the 'Country of Wood'. It is a resort town famous for good walks on waymarked trails into the woods and in particular for the short walk from the lake at the foot of the town to the 100-ton Roche Tremblante, which every visitor tries to move. The exceptionally beautiful woods are full of fine trees, pretty streams and huge granite boulders covered with moss, and those who like to fish can find plenty of sport in the lake.

③ At Brasparts there is a parish close and a calvary which shows, among other scenes, St Michel killing the dragon. The church was rebuilt in the 18th century but retains a very fine 16th-century Virgin of Pity and some excellent stained glass from the original building. The village itself is pretty and stands in beautiful countryside.

④ Pleyben has a magnificent parish close and an annual *pardon* (pilgrimage procession) which takes place on the first Sunday in August. The calvary dates from the middle of the 16th century and was remodelled and extended in 1743, when more figures were added. The church has two belfries and is heavily decorated inside and out. With the ossuary, which also dates from the 16th century, the parish close of Pleyben presents a delightfully coherent scene.

⑤ The agreeable little town of Châteauneuf-du-Faou stands on the River Aulne and is a centre for salmon fishing, though it lies a good way up river from the sea and well upstream from the major salmon fishing centre of Châteaulin. Those who do not fish will still find the setting attractive, for the town occupies the slope of a hill and there are fine views over the river and the surrounding countryside. Another popular attraction is the chapel of Notre-Dame des Portes, which, like many Breton churches, is the scene of a *pardon,* held each year here on the third Sunday in August. The Aulne is very pretty and there are pleasant walks along its banks.

⑥ Carhaix-Plouguer is a large town at the junction of several roads and is often too full of traffic. It is the market town for the local dairy farmers, and visitors will find it a good touring centre, well supplied with hotels.

The pretty town of Châteauneuf-du-Faou is a centre for salmon fishing ▼

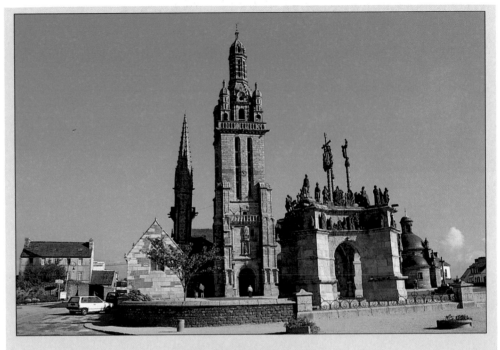

THE PARISH CLOSE

The parish close (*enclos paroissial*) is much less common in Brittany than the tourist posters might lead you to suppose, and the best examples lie to the west of the route covered by this tour in the villages of St-Thégonnec, Guimiliau and Lampaul-Guimiliau, all south-west of Morlaix. These splendid churches were erected as part of the Counter-Reformation at the end of the 16th and the start of the 17th centuries.

The typical parish close consists of three elements: the church, which is generally large and well cared for, with lots of stained glass and statues; the ossuary, where the bones of the long dead were kept after removal from the cemetery to make room for more; and, most striking of all, the great carved calvary in the churchyard showing the Crucifixion and scenes from the Old and New Testaments. Together these elements bear witness to the strong religious convictions of the Breton people and act as a statement of local pride.

▲ *A traditional carved calvary*

Sites to see in Carhaix-Plouguer include the church of Plouguer, which has Romanesque foundations and a 16th-century nave, and the Maison du Sénéchal, which houses the tourist office and is full of information on the town and the district.

⑦ A small village in the Parc d'Armorique, close to the moors of the Montagnes d'Arrée, Berrien is a good touring centre for the surrounding district and the walks around Huelgoat. Just to the west of here lies the course of the old Roman road that links Carhaix with the coast; traces of it can still be seen.

⑧ Plougonven is a sizeable but beautiful village in an area full of pretty villages. However, it is special because of its parish close. The calvary is said to be one of the oldest in Brittany, dating from 1554. The carvings show a number of scenes, including the Descent from the Cross and the Entombment. The church is even earlier and was consecrated in 1523.

Le Sentier Pittoresque, Huelgoat

One of the most enjoyable walks in Brittany, this passes through a dense, mysterious wood, around and over moss-covered rocks, and beside a rushing stream. Good footwear is advisable, without slippery leather soles, but this attractive walk is not difficult.

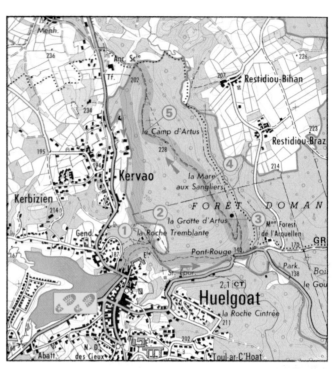

Route Directions

Start from a large signboard and a notice board, detailing local walks and the sights *en route*, beside the great lake which lies at the foot of the town. Take the narrow path beside the stream and past the old mill on the far bank to the first rock chaos, the Grotte du Diable ①.

Continue down over steps and rocks, then climb up and over the far slope to the Roche Tremblante ②.

Descend the slope from the Roche Tremblante, past the café, and pick up the path, the Allée Violette, for the Pont Rouge.

The path turns north through the woods, past more large, moss-covered rocks and beside a number of pools to the Grotte d'Artus ③.

Continue past the Mare aux Sangliers ④.

The path then veers off left to the Camp d'Artus ⑤ and the far end of the wood. Turn back here, along the Chemin du Louarn, to the café by the Roche Tremblante. Retrace your steps to the start.

The Grotte d'Artus ▶
The route of 'Le Sentier Pittoresque' ▼

Points of Interest

① The Grotte du Diable is just one cave among many in this moss-covered jumble of great rocks set on and above the rushing stream. The path here leads under the rocks and through a short tunnel and can be slippery, but the setting is sublime.

② The Roche Tremblante is a rocking stone weighing over 100 tons which everyone tries to move. You need to apply the shoulder to just the right spot, but since this is unmarked even by the thousands who have tried, very few people have succeeded.

③ and ⑤ This part of Brittany is as full of the Arthurian legends as Cornwall, and in addition to the Grotte d'Artus (Arthur's Cave) there is a small clearing a little further into the wood marked by two great rocks. This is thought to be the site of the Camp d'Artus, but is more probably the remains of a Gallo-Roman fortress.

④ The Mare aux Sangliers is a marshy pond to which wild boar used to come to drink. It is now surrounded by large stones, and it is possible to take another path from here back to the start of the walk.

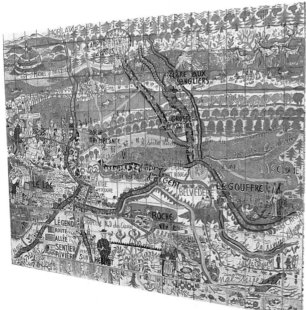

A walk from the parish close of St-Thégonnec

This walk is fairly long, but easy to follow. It begins and ends by the handsome parish close of St-Thégonnec, and the way is marked at every turn by granite Breton crosses, some of considerable age.

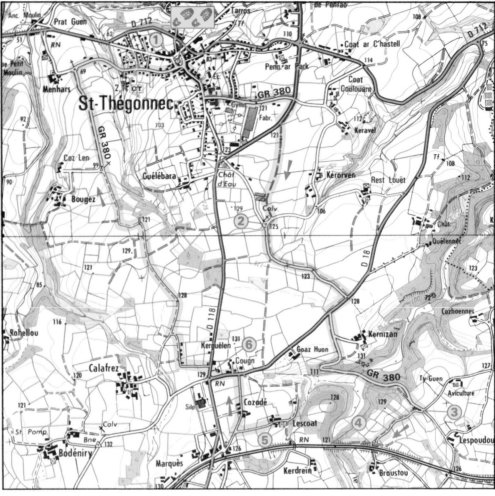

Route Directions

Start from the great church and parish close of St-Thégonnec ①.

Walk along the Rue de la Gare, opposite the entrance to the calvary, to the first main turning to the left, following the red-and-white waymarks of the GR 380. Keep to this until the main road, the D 118, and turn right for 200m before forking left on to a narrow track, which emerges after about 400m on to a lane. Turn right, then fork left for the first stone cross, the Croix Goarnisson ②.

Follow the GR waymarks down into the steep-sided green valley of the River Coat Toulzac'h. Climb the far side to reach the Croix de Broustou ③.

Leave the lane here, turning sharp right to descend the hill on a narrow track, still following the waymarks, until a railway bridge appears ahead. The waymarks lead under the bridge to the abandoned hamlet of Broustou, but the walk turns sharp right, picking up yellow waymarks for the Pont-Hir ④.

Follow the river round, climbing up through the woods to the *lavoir* or wash-house in the pretty hamlet of Lescoat ⑤.

Follow the lane out of Lescoat to the first road junction. (There is another interesting cross 100m beyond the turn, on the outskirts of Marquès.) Turn right through the farm at Cozodé, then left at the D 18, then right again on to the D 118.

◄ *The exceptionally fine parish close at St-Thégonnec is dominated by its grandiose church tower, built in Renaissance style*

(Those who wish to shorten the walk can follow the D 118 into St-Thégonnec.) Turn left at the first house and follow the lane into another hamlet, Kerguélen ⑥.

Here the lane becomes a track. Follow it through woods and fields to another cross, where the GR 380 comes in from the left. Walk straight ahead, following the GR 380 waymarks to yet another cross, where the path turns right uphill, and back into St-Thégonnec.

Points of Interest

① The parish close of St-Thégonnec is one of the finest and most famous in Brittany. It was erected in 1610 and the base is covered with carved figures, including one of St Thégonnec with the wolf he harnessed to his cart after his donkey had been devoured. The ossuary dates from 1676 and the church from the 16th century.

② Like most of the tall Breton crosses, the Croix Goarnisson was erected at the end of the 17th century and, like many others hereabouts, it was probably intended to help pilgrims find the church at St-Thégonnec.

③ Like the previous cross, the Croix de Broustou is 17th-century, and although recently restored it has been precisely dated to 1662.

④ The Pont-Hir aqueduct was built at the same time as the great railway viaduct at Morlaix. It is 100m long and built of brick.

⑤ Lescoat consists of a few houses draped with flowers but it retains the ancient *lavoir* where clothes were washed by the women of the village until recent times.

⑥ Kerguélen is a hamlet, partly on the main road, partly on the side track that soon becomes a footpath and leads back to St-Thégonnec.

Cornouaille and Pointe du Raz

BRITTANY

This is a picturesque and exciting tour, taking in some of the finest places in the entire province; beautiful granite towns like Locronan, attractive fishing ports such as Douarnenez and Audierne, centres of culture like Pont-l'Abbé, spectacular natural wonders such as Pointe du Raz and famous calvaries like the one at Notre-Dame de Tronoan. In summer the road to Pointe du Raz can be crowded, but there are no difficulties other than parking.

Route Directions

Start from Douarnenez ①.

Follow the coast, heading first for the beach at les Sables Blancs, and then following the minor coast road signposted Pont-Croix for 7km to the D 407. Turn left at Lescogan for the D 7, then turn right and follow the D 7 to Pointe du Van and around the Baie des Trépassés to Pointe du Raz ②.

From Pointe du Raz take the D 784 to Audierne ③.

Continue on the D 784 to Plozévet, from where the D 2, signposted Pont-l'Abbé, leads south for 25km to Plonéour-Lanvern. In the town centre follow the 'Autres Directions' signs and pick up the D 57, signposted Plomeur. Follow the D 57 for 3km and at a crossroads take a right turn, signposted la Chapelle de Tronoan. Follow this road until the distinctive belfry of the chapel appears ahead ④.

Follow the signs to St-Jean-Trolimon on to the D 57 for Plomeur. Turn right and follow the D 785 for Penmarc'h and the great Eckmühl lighthouse ⑤.

Return along the D 785 through Penmarc'h to the right fork with the D 53, and then follow the D 53 to Loctudy ⑥.

From Loctudy take the D 2 for Pont-l'Abbé ⑦.

Leave Pont-l'Abbé on the D 785 for Quimper, forking left after 3km on to the D 240, signposted Treméoc and Plogastel-St-Germain. Continue into Plogastel-St-Germain, then follow the D 57 north, across the D 784 and up to the D 765. Turn left and continue for 4.5km before turning right on to the D 39 for Plogonnec. Here turn left in the village to join the D 63 for Locronan ⑧.

To visit the town turn right off the D 63. From Locronan follow the D 7 for 4km to return to Douarnenez.

Locronan's beautiful silver granite Renaissance houses bear witness to its prosperous past ▶

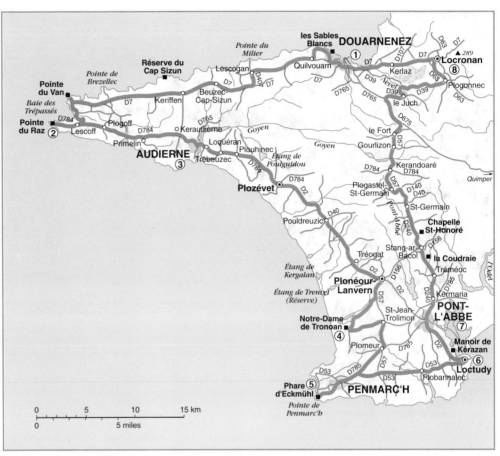

▲ *For centuries lighthouses and beacons were the only protection for sailors against the treacherous seas of Pointe du Raz*

Points of Interest

① Douarnenez is now a holiday centre as well as a successful fishing port sprawling around the shores of the bay, and the combination makes it an enjoyable and interesting place to visit. The fishing boats are painted in bright reds, blues and greens and glitter in the sun, tied up in rows along the quay. The daily fish market at the Port du Rosmeur is well worth visiting, and a boat trip around the bay is also recommended. There are two good sandy beaches flanking the town, and good views of the bay from Boulevard Jean Richepin.

SEA BIRDS

Brittany is a marvellous place for birds and in particular for sea birds, with great colonies of gulls nesting on the cliffs and offshore islands. The diversity of habitats, with deep estuaries, tall cliffs, a great tidal range and a litter of offshore islands to provide secure nesting sites, means that a variety of sea birds and waders can be seen at any time of the year.

On this tour there is a good sea-bird sanctuary at the Réserve du Cap Sizun on the north side of the peninsula. The nesting time starts in late March and is over by July, but a great number of birds can be seen at any time. Auks and guillemots, various types of gull and cormorants all come regularly to Cap Sizun. Although their numbers have declined in recent years, puffins can still be seen from time to time on the offshore islands, and the general bird population is increasing. The offshore islands in the Raz de Sein are also popular with birdwatchers and can be reached from the port at Audierne.

② Pointe du Raz is one of the famous sights of Brittany and is therefore rather spoiled by the rash of cafés and shops which have opened up by the lighthouse. It ought to be a wild and lonely spot of sea and rock and sky, and often is in winter, when great westerly gales pound the rocks and fill the air with spray. There are marvellous views out to sea, and the place is worth a visit for that reason alone.

③ Audierne is a small and popular fishing port, rather pretty, set at the foot of a green hill on the Goyen estuary. Ferry boats ply from here to the Ile de Sein, and there is a good beach nearby at Ste-Evette. Several restaurants offer good seafood, and there is an annual *pardon* on the last Sunday in August.

④ The calvary at Notre-Dame de Tronoan stands in open country by a large chapel. The carvings have been severely eroded but the overall effect is still magnificent. The chapel is very large and has its bell tower in the centre of the roof rather than at the end.

⑤ The Phare d'Eckmühl stands on land at the end of the village of Penmarc'h and is open to visitors. The views from the lighthouse are superb and it is a most imposing building, towering over the beach and the rooftops of the town.

⑥ Loctudy is a small, out-of-the-way resort combined with a fishing port. It stands at the mouth of the bay that leads to Pont-l'Abbé, and apart from being a very good place to stay in while visiting this corner of Brittany it also has a fine 12th-century church, as well as good boat trips to the peninsula known as the Ile-Tudy and the Iles de Glénan.

⑦ Pont-l'Abbé is the capital of the Bigouden. This region is famous for the most spectacular of Breton coiffes, tall and distinctive, which is still worn hereabouts at *pardons* and weddings, and sometimes on Sundays and at markets. Examples can be seen in the Musée Bigouden, which occupies the 14th-century castle. Other sights include the abbey church of Notre-Dame des Carmes, which has some medieval glass, the ruined church at Lambour and the memorial to the local people massacred in the 17th century for refusing to pay a tax on paper. Two local *pardons* commemorate this event, on the first Sunday in August and the last Sunday in September.

⑧ Locronan is a gem in silver granite, one of the most beautiful places in France, and one which no visitor should miss. As a result, it can be very crowded indeed in July and August. The town also holds distinctive local *pardons* called Troménies, which are held on the hill outside the town on the second Sunday in July, though the Grande Troménie takes place only every six years. Locronan is an artists' centre and the many *ateliers* are open to visitors, who can watch weavers and potters at their craft. There are two fine granite churches, St-Ronan and Notre-Dame de Bonne Nouvelle, a museum, and a good walk up to Locronan mountain, which is 289m high and offers fine views. But the real attraction lies in the beautiful granite houses, built in the 16th century and well preserved.

Locronan is a thriving tourist centre ▼

A walk around Pointe du Raz

BRITTANY

Pointe du Raz is the most spectacular section of Brittany's coast, a great finger of rock probing the Atlantic. This is a walk on well-trodden paths, but children should be kept under control and rubber-soled footwear is essential.

Route Directions

Start from the car park at Pointe du Raz. This is at the end of the road, by the little square of shops and cafés. For a good view of the coast and the offshore rocks, walk forward to the viewpoint ①.

Then turn right and follow the footpath that runs along the cleft above the Baie des Trépassés ②.

Descend this footpath to the sandy beach. Then follow the road up to the D 784 and cross over into the village of Lescoff ③.

Pick up the path by the campsite and follow it back west, along the cliff, where there are glorious sea views, and then drop down to the little port of Bestrée ④.

From here it is possible to return up the road to the D 784, but the full walk continues along the well-trodden path back to the café and car park at Pointe du Raz.

Points of Interest

① Pointe du Raz is occupied by a lighthouse, some small shops and restaurants in a hollow square, and some memorials to shipwrecks. On a clear day there are views out to the Raz de Sein and the Ile de Sein. When there are gales the Pointe offers a wonderful prospect of great waves crashing on to the offshore rocks.

② The Baie des Trépassés, the Bay of the Dead, is where onshore currents bring bodies ashore from ships sunk out in the Raz de Sein. In spite of the name it is a pleasant spot with a small hotel at one end and a great sweep of warm sand.

③ Lescoff is a typical village of western Brittany: a huddle of whitewashed cottages tucked away in the green folds of the headland, out of the wind but always within sight and sound of the sea. This is the place to stop for refreshment during the walk.

④ Only bold fishermen use the tiny harbour at Bestrée, reached by a steep track from the main road high above. A high concrete wall acts as a breakwater but the shelter is minimal and waves break right over it when the inevitable gale comes in behind a high tide. There are good views along Pointe du Raz, and usually some small boats to provide a little colour.

Bays and coves provide welcome shelter ▼

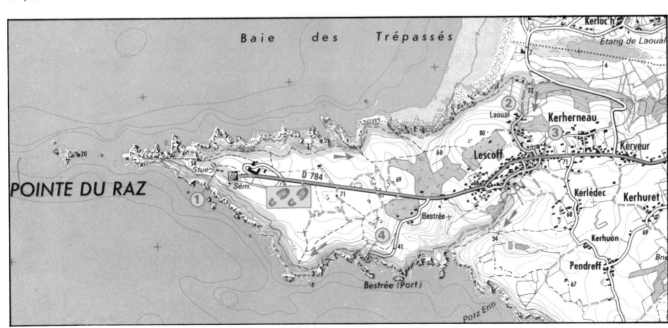

A four-chapel walk on Cap Sizun

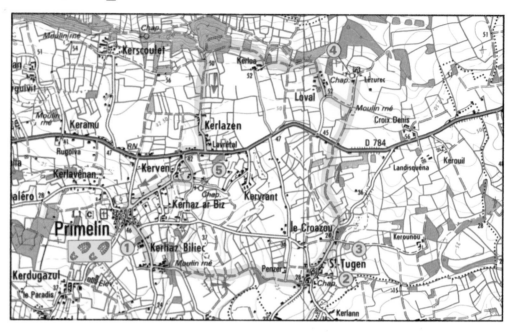

Though is an easy but interesting walk suitable for the entire family, along lanes and over tracks, linking four attractive but very different Breton chapels. It begins in the small village of Primelin, between Esquibien and Plogoff.

Route Directions

Start from the church in the centre of Primelin, where there is parking ①.

Turn down the lane towards Kerhaz Biliec, turning left at the crossroads on to a track which leads through the fields towards the tall square tower of the church at St-Tugen ②.

Just 30m further down the road is the well of St Tugen ③.

From the well follow small signs to le Croazou, on to a track and across the D 784 and then slightly right on to a footpath across the fields and through bracken to the manorial chapel at Lézurec ④.

From here return to the lane and follow it round to the farm and hamlet at Loval, picking up another track there for Kerloa. Continue past a track junction to Kerscoulet and Kerlazen, on to a metalled lane and to the D 784. Turn right, crossing the road, and then left to the small wayside chapel at the first road junction ⑤.

From here it is a short, easy walk back to the centre of Primelin.

Points of Interest

① Primelin is an agreeable and peaceful village, with an attractive late-medieval church right in the centre. Typically Breton, the granite church has an openwork belfry with a wide balcony, and the inside is very clean and bright, with a flagstone floor.

② St Tugen is a popular 6th-century Breton saint whose help is said to be invoked against rabies. The church is very attractive and full of interesting artefacts, such as a catafalque cover used to drape coffins at funerals and numerous votive relics and banners which the congregation carry at the local *pardon*, including a wooden model of a ship. There is some good stained glass.

③ One of the symptoms of rabies is hydrophobia, or fear of water, and those who need help for this go to the well of St Tugen, which contains a small statue of the saint set above a stone basin full of fresh spring water. The basin is usually full of coins.

④ The chapel in Lézurec belongs to the manor house and is reached by the drive, but it is not always open. The building is in local granite and very attractive, and the outside of the manor house is also well worth a brief inspection.

◀ *The little chapel at Lézurec is attached to the manor house*

⑤ The wayside chapel at Kerlazen is small and very pretty and set on a triangle of grass beside the road, where it is washed by the sound of the sea beating in. Its façade has been eroded by the salt air, but the simplicity of the building is very appealing.

The clear spring water in the well of St Tugen was traditionally believed to offer a cure for those unfortunate enough to be suffering from rabies, a symptom of which is fear of water. Brittany is associated with numerous saints, of whom St Tugen is among the most popular ▼

Vannes to the Landes de Lanvaux

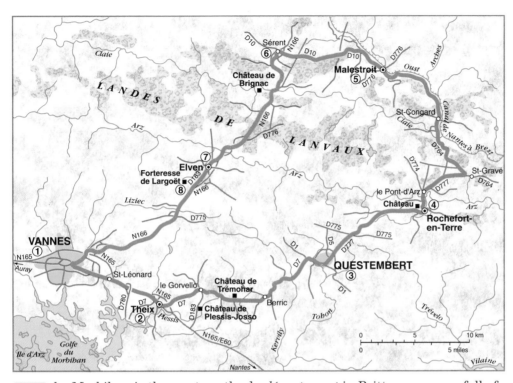

The Morbihan is the most southerly *département* in Brittany, an area full of interesting towns, pretty villages, fine countryside and rare sights. The most popular attraction of the region is the Golfe du Morbihan, whose islands can be visited on boat trips from Vannes. But this tour heads inland, away from the Golfe, to explore a selection of lesser-known places, slightly off the beaten track but nevertheless well worth visiting.

Route Directions

Leave Vannes ① on the main road east to join the ringroad, the N 165, which is a dual carriageway, before leaving it for the village of Theix ②.

Pick up the D 7 here, signposted Questembert ③.

From the centre of Questembert follow the 'Toutes Directions' signs on to the ringroad, and then take the D 777 for 10km to the pretty town of Rochefort-en-Terre ④.

From Rochefort-en-Terre stay on the D 777 to St-Gravé, turning left 1km before the village of St-Gravé for Malestroit ⑤.

The road out of Malestroit, the D 10, follows the River Oust for a short distance before veering off towards Sérent ⑥.

From Sérent follow the N 166 south for 14km to Elven ⑦.

After another 3km turn right to the Forteresse de Largoët ⑧.

Return to the main road, the N 166, and continue back into Vannes.

◀ *The lavoir or wash-house in Vannes, for centuries one of the hubs of town life*

Points of Interest

① Vannes is a splendid medieval town still largely within its original fortified walls, which now overlook attractive public gardens. It stands at the head of the great Golfe du Morbihan and is the departure point for cruises and ferry boats visiting the islands out in the gulf, such as the picturesque Ile aux Moines. The town was founded in the 9th century, though the walls are much later. They completely surround the old quarter near the great Cathédrale St-Pierre, which contains the tomb of the saint and mystic St Vincent Ferrier. St Vincent was born in Vannes and died there in 1419.

One of the most popular sights in Vannes is the house called the Maison de Vannes, which bears two grinning gargoyles known as Vannes

THE GOLFE DU MORBIHAN

The Golfe du Morbihan is virtually an inland sea, cut off from the Atlantic by the narrow peninsula of the Presqu'île de Rhuys. The sea flows into the Golfe through a narrow channel just a few metres wide between Port-Navalo and Locmariaquer, flooding across a great expanse of sand flats and small islands covering an area of some 300 square km. There are hundreds of islands in the Golfe, of which about 40 are inhabited. The two largest, the Ile aux Moines, or Monks' Island, and the Ile d'Arz, have hotels and restaurants. They are popular destinations for excursions by people visiting Vannes and other places round the shore, such as Auray, and boats full of visitors ply the Golfe throughout the summer.

The Presqu'île de Rhuys has two places that are particularly worth visiting, the great castle at Suscinio, which was the summer home of the dukes of Brittany and is a splendid moated building, and the abbey at St-Gildas-de-Rhuys, where Abelard, the lover of Héloïse, was once the abbot.

and his Wife. The Promenade de la Garenne is occupied by a large public garden and gives good views of the ramparts, especially from the corner by the old *lavoir* or wash-house at the Frères Jolivel alley. Vannes has so many beautiful corners that the whole town is well worth exploring, especially on a Saturday, when a great market occupies much of the town centre.

Vannes is also a good touring base. Apart from the Golfe, the Landes de Lanvaux, Ile Conleau, the port of Conleau and the Forteresse de Largoët are all worth visiting.

② Theix is small but there is a lot to see. In the centre is the Chapelle de la Dame Blanche, built in 1239 and one of the oldest in the province, though restored several times. The Château de Plessis-Josso, dating from the 13th century to the 18th, has a lot to offer, and the village itself is very attractive.

③ Questembert is a market town and displays the fact with its main attraction, a great market hall with three broad bays and a wide timber roof on tall pillars, originally built in 1552 but with later restorations. It remains in fine condition. The market square which surrounds it is composed of medieval houses, one of them bearing a pair of figures known as Questembert and his Wife. The town is a noted gastronomic centre.

④ Rochefort-en-Terre is the capital of the moorlands of the Landes de Lanvaux and a very pretty place. It is full of old houses and narrow cobbled streets, and the inhabitants make it even more attractive by filling the streets and the fronts of their houses with flowers, in great beds and large tubs and small window-boxes. There are flowers everywhere in Rochefort as well as a great many antique shops, hotels and restaurants, and all this brings tourists flooding in.

The town occupies a ridge above the River Arz and most of it is medieval or dates from the 16th or 17th century, with hardly a sign of anything later. The church is dated between the 12th and 16th centuries and there is a small calvary in the town square.

⑤ The small town of Malestroit is comfortably situated between the winding River Oust, on which it stands, and the moors of the Landes de Lanvaux to the west. The streets and squares are very picturesque and full of half-timbered houses. The handsome church of St-Gilles has good carvings on its porch and doors. A little to the west of Malestroit, in the village of St-Marcel, is a museum which tells the story of the Morbihan Maquis during World War II.

⑥ Sérent, a little village on the northern edge of the Landes de Lanvaux, has a number of fine houses and a church in the Flamboyant Gothic style, but is notable chiefly as a touring centre for the moorlands and woods that lie to the south.

⑦ A small market town just off the road to Vannes, Elven has a church with a 16th-century choir. The town centre is pleasant enough but the great attraction is that to the north lies the Château de Kerfily, set in a park beside the River Arz, while just to the south lies the great Forteresse de Largoët.

⑧ The Forteresse de Largoët, or Tours d'Elven, is an impressive sight, set in the woods some 5km west of Elven. With a height of 44m, the main tower or *donjon* of Largoët is the tallest medieval tower in France, with supporting walls 6-9m thick. The castle was erected and enlarged in the 13th and 14th centuries, and in the 15th century was the retreat of Henry Tudor, Earl of Richmond, who lived here from 1474 to 1476, before returning to England in 1485 to defeat Richard III at Bosworth and become Henry VII. A few years later Charles VIII of France swept through Brittany with an army and half destroyed Largoët, which later became a hunting lodge, but large parts of the castle are still intact and become the venue for *son et lumière* shows in summer.

◀ *The Forteresse de Largoët, or Tours d'Elven*

A forest tour in southern Normandy

This tour circles the southern part of Normandy, passing through some of its great forests and the Parc Naturel Régional Normandie-Maine, a place of great natural beauty, full of small villages and historic towns. Apart from in the major towns and the area around the famous spa at Bagnoles-de-l'Orne, the roads are quiet and the countryside gently rolling, falling away south of Domfront to the great plain of the Sarthe.

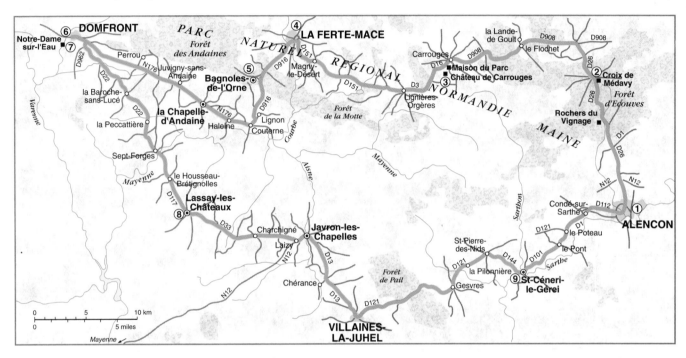

Route Directions

Start from the town centre in Alençon ①.

Follow the 'Autres Directions' sign for Mortrée and Argentan. This road becomes the D 26. Cross the N 12 and continue across the plain into the Forêt d'Ecouves and to the Croix de Médavy. This spot is marked by a World War II Sherman tank ②.

Press on north out of the forest to the D 908 and turn left here for Carrouges. (One kilometre south of Carrouges lies its great château ③.)

Leave Carrouges on the D 16, which becomes the D 3 after 3km. From Lignières-Orgères follow the D 151 to Magny-le-Désert and then continue on the same road until you arrive at la Ferté-Macé ④.

From la Ferté-Macé take the main D 916 to Bagnoles-de-l'Orne ⑤. (The first walk on this tour begins on the bridge over the lake by the Casino in Bagnoles-de-l'Orne.)

Leave Bagnoles on the D 916, signposted Couterne, then turn right on to the N 176, through Haleine and Juvigny-sans-Andaine, to Domfront ⑥.

Two kilometres from the town, beside the river in Domfront-Gare, stands the beautiful Romanesque church of Notre-Dame-sur-l'Eau ⑦.

(The second walk begins at the cemetery gates at la Croix des Landes.)

Leave Domfront on the N 176, signposted Alençon, turn right on to the D 962, then left on to the D 22 and so briefly into the Sarthe, where the road becomes the D 117, to Lassay-les-Châteaux. Worth inspection in the centre of Lassay is the 13th-century *château-fort* ⑧.

Leave Lassay on the D 33, signposted Javron-les-Chapelles. Turn left on to the N 12 into the town centre, then right on to the D 13 for Villaines-la-Juhel. Turn left on to the ring road and pick up the D 121 for Gesvres and St-Pierre-des-Nids. Turn right here on to the D 144 for St Céneri-le-Gérei ⑨.

Leave on the D 101, turning right on to the D 1 at le Poteau. Turn right on to the D 112 for Alençon.

The massive 16th-century château of Carrouges was built to guard the border between Normandy and Maine ▼

▲ *The remarkable roofscape of the castle of the dukes of Alençon*

THE PARC NORMANDIE-MAINE

France has many parks, some national, and some regional, such as the Parc Normandie-Maine, which spans the border between Normandy and Maine. The Parc Normandie-Maine was created in 1975 and covers 230,000 hectares. It has as its main feature the two great forests of Ecouves, north of Alençon, and Andaines, which runs from east of Domfront to east of the spa town of Bagnoles-de-l'Orne.

People live and work in the park and commercial development is not forbidden provided it is in keeping. The park authorities aim to develop an understanding of the region among residents and visitors by establishing museums devoted to the local ecology and rural life, and by encouraging traditional crafts and activities such as forestry and farming.

Visitors can get a great deal of information about the park and about the activities that take place there by visiting the Maison du Parc in the château at Carrouges. Leisure activities in the park include walking on waymarked trails, horse-riding, birdwatching and cycling.

Points of Interest

① Situated on the River Sarthe, Alençon was the seat of the great dukes of Alençon, who ruled here in the Middle Ages, and their 14th-15th-century castle still stands in the city centre. Alençon is also famous for lacemaking and examples of *'point d'Alençon'* can be inspected in the Musée de la Dentelle. Other sights include the Halle au Blé, once the grain market, now used for concerts and shows, and the excellent Musée des Beaux-Arts.

② The Sherman tank was the main Allied battle tank of World War II. The one displayed at the Croix de Médavy served with the French 2nd Demi Brigade under General LeClerc at the battle of the Falaise Pocket in August 1944, which destroyed most of the German armour in Normandy. It was present when LeClerc's men entered Alençon in triumph on 12 August 1944.

③ The gatehouse of the château of Carrouges dates from the 16th century and gives access to the château, a vast and sprawling building which stands on the site of a medieval *château-fort* but dates from the time of Henri de Navarre, at the end of the 16th century. The château is well furnished and can be visited. The stable block contains the Maison du Parc Régional Normandie-Maine and the orchard a great variety of apple and pear trees.

④ La Ferté-Macé is a small market town most famous for its tripe, which is sold, grilled on skewers, at the Thursday market. The church is chiefly notable for the Romanesque belfry, while the town museum contains work by a local artist, Charles Léandre.

⑤ Bagnoles-de-l'Orne is a pretty spa town, with lots of hotels, a lake, a casino, fine public gardens, some elegant shops and many walks in the surrounding woods. The waters of the spa are said to be efficacious for circulation problems, and this quality has given the town its nickname 'the capital of veins'. While many people still come to take the waters, Bagnoles is now best known as an excursion centre for the Orne *département* and the valley of the River Vée. The tourist office in the main street will supply information and maps of all the nearby attractions.

⑥ Domfront is a very picturesque hill town, with the remnants of encircling walls and a medieval *château-fort*. Thirteen of the original towers still stand and the castle dominates the public gardens just to the west of the town centre and gives excellent views over the country to the south. The town centre, much of which is pedestrianised, is a maze of narrow cobbled streets and old houses, some of which date from the 16th century.

⑦ The church of Notre-Dame-sur-l'Eau stands on the banks of the River Varenne at Domfront-Gare, below the town ramparts. The church was partly dismantled in the last century and nearly destroyed in the fighting of 1944, but has been well restored and is a beautiful Romanesque building.

⑧ The castle at Lassay is a splendid example of a 15th-century *château-fort*, a real medieval castle with battlements and turrets and a moat, all in a fine state of preservation. The castle was built in the reign of Charles VII in 1458, at the end of the Hundred Years War, and is notable for having cannon loops in the drum turrets.

⑨ St-Céneri-le-Gérei would not look out of place in Provence, with its fine houses and a riot of flowers in every garden and window-box. But the architecture is pure Norman – even the hilltop church above the river, which is a fine example of the Romanesque. The best view of the church and the village can be had from the bridge over the River Sarthe, just below the town centre. This is said, with reason, to be the prettiest village in France and should not be missed during any tour of Normandy.

▼ *The* château-fort *at Lassay*

A walk through the forest around Bagnoles-de-l'Orne

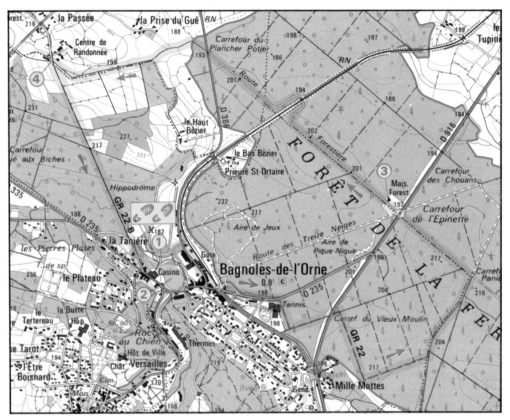

plentiful and easy to follow, leading through woodland and northwards to the Carrefour Panier. Turn left here for the Carrefour de l'Epinette and the Maison Forestière ③.

Follow the Route Forestière straight ahead, over the level crossing to the Carrefour du Plancher Potier, which has tables and a picnic site.

Leave the forest track here, crossing to a footpath which, after 50m, arrives at a stream. This may be crossed with ease in good weather but when the stream is high it is necessary to walk over a footbridge made out of two concrete telephone poles laid across the gap – not easy. From here the footpath leads on to the Village du Cheval ④.

At this point the GR 22B comes in from the west and can be followed south and through the forest to emerge on to the road by the Casino du Lac.

This is an easy walk in the woods north of Bagnoles-de-l'Orne, on footpaths and forest rides. It can be muddy after rain but good trainers are perfectly adequate and the walk is suitable for families with small children but not toddlers. Parts of the route follow the GR 22 footpath.

Route Directions

Start from the attractive bridge over the boating lake by the Casino du Lac in the centre of Bagnoles-de-l'Orne ① and ②.

Skirt the north edge of the lake, go through the public gardens, pass the railway station, turn left at the roundabout and follow the side of the D 235 for 200m, picking up GR 22 waymarks. These take you into the wood by the back of the indoor tennis court. The waymarks are

Points of Interest

① The lake at Bagnoles-de-l'Orne, spanned here by a small bridge leading across to the public gardens, was formed by damming the River Vée for the thermal baths. The Casino du Lac stands beside the bridge and the Allée du Dante leads from the bridge to the thermal baths.

② While the origins of Bagnoles owe everything to the spa, the modern town is chiefly notable as an excursion centre and resort, with a great range of sporting activities available. These include indoor and outdoor tennis courts, as well as shops, restaurants and hotels.

③ The Maison Forestière, set at the foot of two open rides and beside the main road, is an information centre for the Forêt des Andaines, and will supply details on forest activities and wildlife.

④ A useful spot to find at the end of a long walk is this small activity centre, the Village du Cheval. It is a centre for horse and pony rides as well as for carriage driving, and has a small restaurant and café.

29

5B

A ridge walk from Domfront

This gentle walk begins on the eastern outskirts of Domfront at la Croix des Landes and continues along a ridge with great views to the south, dipping down into the valley and passing through a number of pretty villages.

Route Directions

Park in the car park by the cemetery at la Croix des Landes, and follow the GR 22 waymarks across the road and up a lane opposite ①.

There are fine views south from here across the great plain of southern Normandy. Follow the lane until it turns into a track that goes past a number of attractive houses and farms to the turning left to la Fieffe. Turn right here, picking up yellow waymarks and arrows on to a footpath to la Bunelière ②.

Follow this footpath along the ridge to the east, passing another track on the right, down the track to the hamlet of le Saut Gautier. All these places are waymarked with yellow slashes and one place leads naturally to another.

From the Parc Turpin, take the track on the left as far as the cross to Paul Vivien ③.

Continue down to the small camp site and fishing centre by the lake at la Géraumière ④.

The lane then climbs up to the hamlet of le Frêne, then down the hill by a narrow lane to la Poucherie. Take the footpath right here for la Torillère. From there take the back lanes along the ridge to la Hélonnière, where a footpath to the right crosses the stream and climbs to the hamlets of la Guillerie and la Touche. Turn left here and follow the lane to the track to les Toutinières, on the right. Take this back on to the GR 22, and then turn left again into Domfront.

Points of Interest

① This lane from the crossroads at la Croix des Landes is a very pretty walk and provides great views to the south across the flatlands of Mayenne. Parts of it follow the GR 22 footpath.

② This walk takes in a number of attractive hamlets and small villages, all notable for their cottages and cottage gardens, which in summer are full of flowers, particularly roses. La Bunelière is one of the prettiest of all, a quiet hamlet surrounded by copses and orchards.

A stone-built cottage near Domfront ▼

③ This sort of memorial is all too common in France, whose countryside is littered with memorials to those gallant men and women of the Maquis – the French Resistance fighters of World War II – who fought the Germans and perished in a thousand nameless, hopeless struggles. Nearly 50 years after Paul Vivien was taken away, to die in a concentration camp, the local people still leave flowers on his memorial.

④ Those in need of refreshment by this stage of the walk must find it here at the camp site and fishing centre at la Géraumière, where there is a small café and a shop used mainly by campers and caravanners.

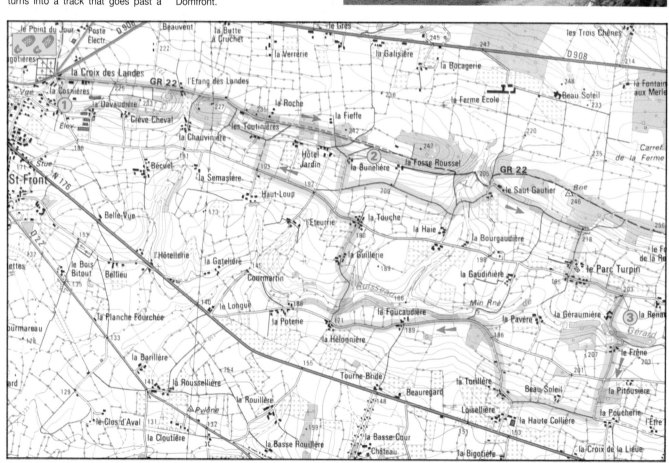

The north coast of the Cotentin

T his tour will take the traveller through one of the most attractive parts of Normandy, mostly on minor roads which are largely free of traffic, winding along the coast or across the hinterland to some very pretty places. Cherbourg is the only large town, but the way out is well signposted and this route should avoid any unduly heavy traffic or large lorries.

▲ The harbour at Barfleur, overlooked by the mariners' church

▲ The little Chapelle des Marins at St-Vaast is all that remains – the nave and choir – of a Romanesque church demolished in the 19th century

Route Directions

Leave Cherbourg's harbour front, following the signs to the Val de Saire. After 2km turn left for le Béquet ①.

Pick up the coast road, the D 116 signposted Barfleur, and follow it along the coast to Gatteville-le-Phare, before taking the D 10 to the lighthouse. There are wonderful views along the coast and out to the rocks of the Raz de Barfleur ②.

Return to Gatteville and then go left on the D 116 to Barfleur ③.

Turn left out of the harbour, pick up the D 1 and go along the coast to Réville and St-Vaast-la-Hougue, which surrounds a marina ④.

At the end of a sandspit stands the Fort de la Hougue ⑤.

From St-Vaast it is a short drive (1km) down the D 1 to Quettehou. (The first walk of this tour begins in the centre of Quettehou, or can be picked up by the 13th-century church ⑥.)

Leave Quettehou on the D 902, signposted Barfleur, and turn left after 1km for le Vast on the D 26, a very pretty village. From le Vast take the D 25 beside the River Saire, then the D 120, signposted Digosville, through the village of Valognes. At the T-junction turn left on to the D 24 and after 4km turn right on to the D 56, signposted Délasse. Continue on

the D 56 over the N 13 towards St-Martin-le-Gréard.

Go straight ahead, across the D 900, heading now for Couville. Bear right on to the D 22, pass under the D 904 and continue on the D 22 for 8km before turning left on to the D 64 for Vasteville. Turn right here on to the D 37, signposted Beaumont. Turn left on to the D 901 and stay on this road to reach the church at Jobourg. Turn left here for Nez de Jobourg on the D 202 and follow this road to the point, which is actually on the Nez de Voidries, overlooking the Nez de Jobourg. (The second walk on this tour starts here, heading south along the GR 223 footpath.)

Return to Dannery on the D 202 and turn left on to the D 401, following this to Auderville and Goury. From Goury return to Auderville and turn left in to the main street on to the D 45, signposted St-Germain-des-Vaux and Port Racine ⑦.

Follow the D 45 along the coast to Gréville-Hague and Urville-Nacqueville. Turn right in the town centre, along the D 22, signposted Ste-Croix-Hague, and continue on the D 22 for another 5km to a crossroads with the D 64. Turn left here and pass through Octeville to return to Cherbourg.

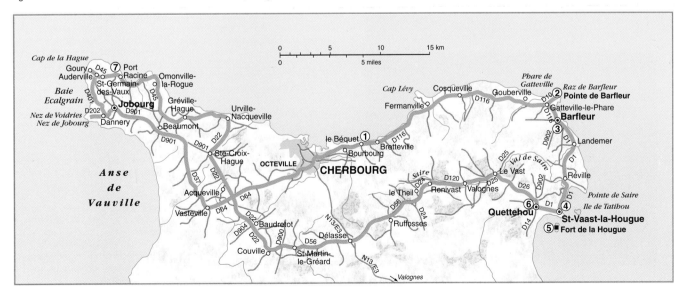

FISHING PORTS

The fishing ports of the Cotentin are among the most attractive in Normandy: sprawling villages built in the local granite, with a great church towering over the rooftops. The harbours are still full of life, and since the fishermen are good gardeners the streets behind the port are always full of flowers, in gardens and window-boxes, in small beds beside the road and in hanging baskets, their colours set off by the glinting granite of the buildings.

The fleets, or at least the boats that remain (for the local fishing industry has declined greatly in recent years), are largely inshore trawlers devoted to Channel fishing for sole and sea bass, or for those lobsters, crabs and langoustines that feature so often in local dishes. A high proportion of the catch, certainly in the smaller places such as Barfleur, St-Vaast, Port Racine and le Béquet, is sold to local restaurants and to local people, who come to the quayside when the boats come in to get the pick of the catch. There is also good angling from most of the quays and harbour moles, and the rocks are regularly scoured for shellfish.

With the decline of the fishing industry, most of the ports have developed a secondary trade as yachting harbours. There are large marinas in Cherbourg and St-Vaast and most of the other ports have facilities for cruising yachts, which come in here throughout the summer from the UK and French ports up and down the coast.

Fishing boats and pleasure craft in the harbour at St-Vaast-la-Hougue ▼

▲ *The Cour Ste-Catherine, near the harbour at Barfleur*

Points of Interest

① The coast road from Cherbourg runs right beside the quiet little fishing village of le Béquet, less well known than Barfleur or St-Vaast. It has a small but solid harbour, built against the Channel gales in round local stones. The harbour contains an assortment of fishing craft and the houses look out towards the sea. This can be an exciting spot to visit in a gale when the waves sweep over the sea wall.

② The lighthouse on Pointe de Barfleur, which warns shipping to avoid the rocks and the race off the Pointe, is at 71m one of the tallest lighthouses in France. The church in the village of Gatteville-le-Phare has a 12th-century bell tower, and the Chapelle des Marins, the Sailors' Chapel, in the centre is partly Romanesque.

③ Barfleur is a very attractive port, with its harbour overlooked by a great marine church. Note the bronze memorial, on a great rock by the breakwater, to William the Conqueror's expedition of 1066. (Several other Norman ports claim that it was from there, not Barfleur, that the Conqueror set sail.) It was in the wild waters off Barfleur in 1120 that the Conqueror's only grandson was drowned in the wreck of the 'White Ship', an event which brought the Plantagenets to the throne of England. Barfleur today is also a yachting centre and a touring base, with several good hotels and restaurants.

④ The small town of St-Vaast-la-Hougue (pronounced St Va' locally), is now a well-known yachting port for Channel sailors, and therefore equipped with a vast marina. It is also a notable place for oysters and has a number of popular hotels and restaurants. The town is close to the beautiful Val de Saire, one of the most attractive and less visited corners of the Cotentin.

⑤ The great Fort de la Hougue was built in the 17th century by Vauban, Louis XIV's military architect, to protect the shipping in the St-Vaast roads from English warships and privateers. It is still in excellent condition and can be reached from the town along a narrow causeway.

⑥ The best sea views around Quettehou can be obtained from the cemetery of the church outside the town centre. Quettehou is an attractive excursion centre, close to the Val de Saire, and a good place to stay in when visiting the D-Day beaches and parachute-drop zones which lie just to the south.

⑦ Few ports in France are as charming as the little harbour of Port Racine on the north coast of the Cotentin. About the size of two tennis courts, it is said to be the smallest harbour in France. It contains a surprising number of small craft and is very popular with anglers, who fish from the high wall, and with artists, who like to include it in their paintings.

A walk around Quettehou

NORMANDY

This is a walk the whole family can enjoy, on clear tracks and without any undue difficulties other than one or two short, steep climbs. It begins on the outskirts of Quettehou, and has been waymarked by the local walking group, who recommend it to visitors for the good views out to sea.

Route Directions

This circular walk takes in parts of two waymarked local walks, the Circuit du Tronquet, signposted with white waymarks, and the Circuit de la Frégère, signposted with rust-red waymarks. It is possible to pick up the walk in the centre of Quettehou ①.

(Alternatively, you can start at the large car park by the 13th-century church ②.)

If you park in the town centre, walk the 300m to the church up the Allée de l'Eglise. From the church, go through the gate at the back of the graveyard and take the left fork,

following the occasional white stripes of the Circuit du Tronquet. From this path there are glimpses out to sea ③.

The path leads through sunken lanes and along the edge of the Bois du Rabey to the hamlet at le Tronquet, with its farm and duckpond.

Shortly after leaving le Tronquet the path veers off right into more woods and round a ridge to Fanoville. Continue on a footpath or farm tracks, which can be muddy, to the hamlet of la Frégère ④.

Here the track leads off left at the bottom of the hill and follows the path along the valley floor into the hamlet of le Frestin. The house beside the path here was once a water-mill and still has a working water-wheel ⑤.

Follow the path through the hamlet. Just before the road, pick up the rust-red waymarks to the right and follow these uphill on to the Circuit de la Frégère. These waymarks are more frequent but less accurate than the white ones, as they continue beyond the left turn shown on the 1:25 000 map, terminating at le Rouard. Walkers should turn left on to the road before this, down to le Valvachet, and then up the track to the left, which climbs steadily back to the ridge and the church.

Points of Interest

① Quettehou is the chief town of this canton, though really little more than a large village with a population of around 1300 people. The countryside around here is devoted to farming, and most of the local fishermen live in nearby St-Vaast. Walkers can stock up on provisions here before walking up to the church.

② There are good views of Vauban's impressive Fort de la Hougue and the Pointe de Saire from the cemetery of this late-Norman church which, with its 15th-century bell tower, dominates the town below and the surrounding country-side. The entire building is very attractive and the views are superb.

③ From this first section of the footpath the views out to sea, to Vauban's Fort de la Hougue and the jagged rocks of the Barfleur race, are magnificent.

④ This walk leads in and out of a number of small hamlets, but this one at la Frégère is the most attractive and the most typical, with granite cottages and flower-filled gardens, and surrounded by small fields and apple orchards.

The water-mill at le Frestin ▶

⑤ Water-mills are becoming rarer, even in France, so the attractive example at le Frestin is well worth a look, though it dates only from the last century and has recently been restored.

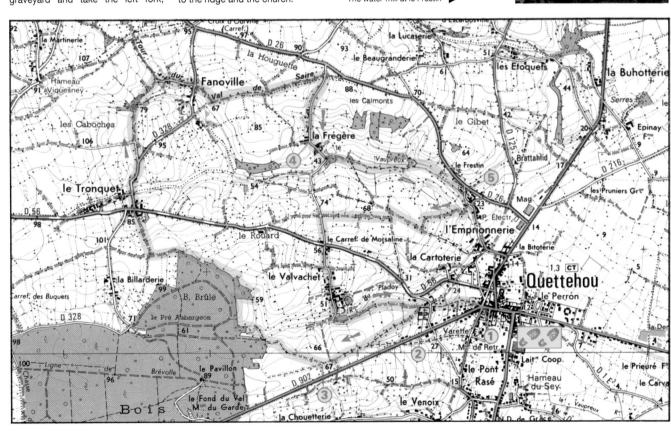

6B

A coastal walk from the Nez de Voidries

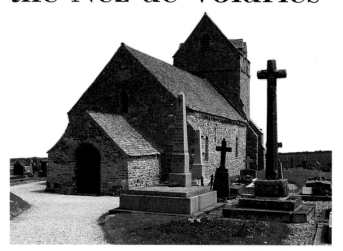

◀ *The 12th-century church at Jobourg*

Although this part of the coast is dominated by the unlovely nuclear power station at la Hague, this beautiful walk gives only the occasional glimpse of it. The walk is not suitable for small children.

Route Directions

Start from the car park by the café at the Nez de Voidries ①.

Pick up the red-and-white GR 223 waymarks here and follow the path east. It is well defined and easy to follow, **but avoid the cliff edge.** The whole route is highly scenic and there are excellent views of the cliffs below Gravelette from Moncanval, and of the Anse de Pivette ②.

Follow the path around the headlands, with some climbing and descending, past the track up to le Thiébot, until the path reaches a gate in a chain-link fence, above the Anse des Moulinets ③.

From here, steep steps with green railings lead down to the bay and up

again. Walkers should *not* go through the gate. Instead, turn left, uphill, keeping to the path beside the chain-link fence, which will bring the Lac des Moulinets into view ④.

The path, wider now, runs above the dam wall and round to the north-west, becoming a farm track. Follow this along flower-lined walls and hedges into the pretty hamlet of le Thiébot ⑤.

From le Thiébot it is an easy walk of 2km along a beautiful lane through the pretty hamlets of Dannery and Mouchel, and along the D 202 for 1km back to the car park.

▲ *The spectacular west coast of the Cotentin*
Village houses at Dannery ▶

Points of Interest

① There is a café and a car park at the Nez de Voidries, which is a fine viewpoint looking down on the Nez de Jobourg and offering marvellous sea views along the coast in both directions.

② This northern part of the western Cotentin coast is a mixture of cliffs and coves, and few spots are more picturesque than the little beach and bay at the Anse de Pivette.

③ Be wary of the state of the sea and the tide should you decide to venture down the steps to the sheltered bay of the Anse des Moulinets, where, because of off-shore currents, swimming out to sea is not advisable. The best view of this delightful sheltered cove is from the cliff path above and to the north.

④ The Lac des Moulinets is actually a reservoir, but a very pretty one, surrounded by woods and set just above the cliffs. It is a popular spot for sea birds and warblers, especially on a summer's evening.

⑤ Le Thiébot is a little dream of a village, all in yellow stone with red geraniums glowing everywhere in summer in flowerpots and window-boxes, a typical example of the pretty hamlets that lie above the cliffs in this part of the Cotentin.

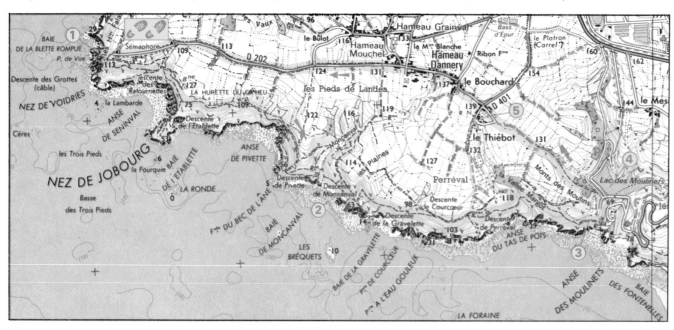

The Suisse Normande and the Orne valley

This is a varied tour through constantly changing countryside, taking in some of the high points of the Suisse Normande, a charming hilly region south of Caen and bounded by the River Orne, which runs beside the road for much of this tour. The roads are narrow, single-track in places, always winding and sometimes steep, so high speeds are not advisable. The route takes in a number of attractive small towns, many pretty villages and some splendid viewpoints.

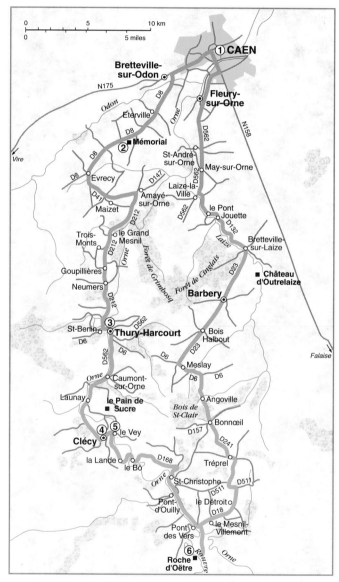

Route Directions

The tour starts from Caen ①.

Leave from below the castle in the centre and follow the 'Toutes Directions' signs, then pick up signs for Rennes-Granville as far as the racecourse at la Prairie. From there pick up the D 8, signposted Evrecy and Aunay-sur-Odon, and follow this to Evrecy, passing a World War II memorial on the left ②.

Turn left at the church in Evrecy on to the D 41. At Amayé-sur-Orne turn sharp right at the outskirts of the village on to the D 212, signposted Thury-Harcourt, and turn left into the town at the hamlet of le Hom, and then cross the River Orne into Thury-Harcourt.

Thury-Harcourt is the 'Gateway to the Suisse Normande'. Stop by the gates of the château ③.

(This is the start of the first walk and a good place from which to explore the ruined château.)

◄ Evrecy
▼ Pont d'Ouilly

From here follow the D 562 beside the Orne for 13km to Clécy ④.

(The second walk, to the Pain de Sucre, begins by the church in Clécy.)

On leaving Clécy turn right by the church, and descend to the river again, following the signs to the Pont du Vey ⑤.

From here follow the river upstream to St-Christophe and Pont-d'Ouilly. Keeping the river on your right, pass through le Bateau, turn left on to the D 18, then immediately right under the viaduct on to the road which leads up to the viewpoint at the Roche d'Oëtre ⑥.

From here, return to the D 18 and turn right, following the D 511 for 5km. At a T-junction turn left and then right after 100m for Tréprel. Take the D 241 from here north to Bonnoeil and Angoville and on to the T-junction with the D 6. Turn left here and go downhill for 1km through Meslay, then right on to the D 23 to Bretteville-sur-Laize. Cross the River Laize and turn left on to the D 132 along the Laize valley to the D 562. Turn right here to return to Caen.

THE SUISSE NORMANDE

The Suisse Normande is an area of forested hills, deep, steep-sided valleys and, flowing through the centre, the River Orne. This has carved out a beautiful valley, which is the most direct route south from the Calvados coast and the Caen plain to the open country of the Sarthe and Maine, which begins some 80km to the south.

The Suisse Normande forms part of the Armorican massif, a region of shale and sandstone rocks seamed by granite outcrops. In spite of its name, however, it does not provide the highest points in Normandy, an honour reserved for Mont Avaloirs and the Signal d'Ecouves, which both soar to 417m.

The region was once quite industrial and there are still the crumbling remains of old factories and iron works along the banks of the Orne near Pont-d'Ouilly. The iron-ore quarries at St-Rémy, north of Clécy, closed down in 1967. Today the region lives by farming and tourism, and in particular 'green' tourism, offering scope to walkers, horse-riders and cyclists, climbers and canoeists, as well as providing a good choice of camp sites and *gîtes*.

▲ The Musée de la Paix (Peace Museum) in Caen
The spectacular viewpoint at the Roche d'Oëtre ▶

Points of Interest

① The ancient capital of the Norman dukes, Caen is full of interest. Sights to see are the castle, the new and splendid Musée de la Paix, or Peace Museum, and the two abbeys, the Abbaye aux Hommes, built by William the Conqueror, and the Abbaye aux Dames, built by his wife Matilda, as well as some of the churches. The Tourist Office just opposite the castle will provide much useful information on what else to see and do in Caen.

② The countryside around Caen is full of memorials to the bitter fighting of 1944, and this memorial to the men of the 43rd (Welsh) Division is a good example. There are also many military cemeteries, each of which has a book outlining the battles that took place in the vicinity in the summer of 1944.

③ Thury-Harcourt is a market town and tourist centre for the Suisse Normande and the Orne valley. It is a pretty and prosperous town with a ruined château, destroyed by the Germans on the night before they evacuated the town in 1944, and a number of good small hotels and restaurants down by the river. The railway which runs along the valley is no longer in operation, though from time to time plans are mooted to restore it as a tourist attraction.

④ Clécy, the 'capital' of the Suisse Normande, is set in one of the most attractive parts of the Orne valley, at a point where the river is overlooked by high cliffs. The town is therefore best known as a walking and touring centre, for excursions into the surrounding hills and south along the valley towards the southern heartland of Normandy. There are a number of good hotels and restaurants.

⑤ There are fine views and walks along the Orne valley from the bridge over the river at the Pont du Vey just below Clécy. The best way to see the river is from the footpath or the road which runs alongside it, overlooking the riverside hotels, the canoeists, and the climbers who scramble on the cliffs by the old viaduct.

⑥ The viewpoint at the Roche d'Oëtre overlooks the River Rouvre, not the Orne, but is none the less spectacular for that. The cliff edge is screened by gorse and rocks and the drop is sheer, so children should be kept under control. Buzzards circle over the trees far below where the river sparkles and the views, especially in the spring and autumn, are quite superb.

A circular walk from Thury-Harcourt

NORMANDY

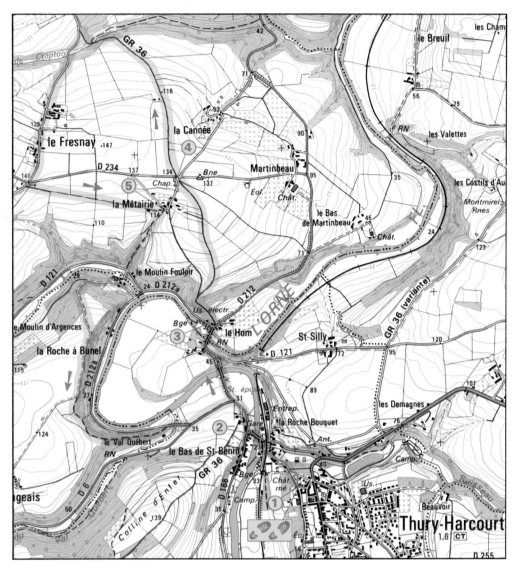

This walk takes in sections of two longer walks, the GR 36 and the Tour de la Suisse Normande, both of which are well waymarked and easy to follow. It is not difficult and the whole family will enjoy it.

Points of Interest

① Like many Norman towns, Thury-Harcourt was badly damaged in the fighting of 1944, when the château was burned, so that only the façade remains. The town is now the principal centre for visitors to the Suisse Normande and has good hotels and restaurants.

② The River Orne carves a path just below the streets of Thury-Harcourt and makes several bends here as it skirts the town. Most of the hotels and restaurants as well as the abandoned railway line and station are here by the river.

③ Le Hom has two notable features: the great cleft in the rock by which the road crosses an island in the river, and the fishing weir and salmon ladder just past the crossroads in the centre.

④ Little wayside chapels, usually containing a statue of the Virgin or of St Roch, the patron saint of pilgrims, are very common in France. This little shrine also stands at a spot where there are good views back across Thury-Harcourt.

⑤ The farm at la Métairie is a typical small Norman farm. It has apple orchards for the production of cider and Calvados and pens for pigs and poultry. The fields contain speckled Norman cattle, kept for the butter and cream used in the rich Norman cuisine.

Route Directions

Start from the gates of the ruined château in Thury-Harcourt, where there is parking ①.

Pick up the red-and-white waymarks of the GR 36 as the way descends, crossing the railway line, then turning right and left to cross the River Orne ②.

Keep bearing right, picking up signs to Goupillières and St-Silly, crossing the Orne again after 200m, then passing through a cleft in the rocks, along the road and over two more arms of the Orne to the hamlet of le Hom. Bear left here for the weir and salmon ladder ③.

Return to the D 212-D 212a corner and pick up the GR 36 again. The start of the path is well waymarked and the route begins with a stiff uphill climb through the woods above the Orne to the point where the paths divide. The one coming in from the left is the GR de Pays (Tour de la Suisse Normande). Take the GR 36, the right-hand path, and follow it out into open fields up to a small chapel beside the D 234 ④.

Cross the road, keeping half left, and pick up a track leading north across open fields. This path leads to a steep and sudden descent through more woodland and down into the valley of the Ruisseau du Val de Cropton. The path crosses the stream and climbs uphill to come out on to the road 100m before the hamlet of Cropton. Turn left on reaching the road and walk down into the valley again and up to the straggling hamlet of le Fresnay.

Continue to a junction with several roads and with the GR de Pays, which can be picked up behind the small stone bus shelter. Follow this footpath east, through apple orchards, to the farm at la Métairie ⑤.

Turn right on the track and follow the red-and-yellow markers down through the woods to the D 121. Cross over to the houses and factory buildings, following waymarks around a path on to a footpath and away through the woods and over la Roche à Bunel for about 2km, until the path comes out on the D 212a. Turn right up to a road junction and turn left to a T-junction, then right again over the river and past the railway station, and back to the château.

A courtyard at Thury-Harcourt ▶

A walk to the Pain de Sucre from Clécy

Clécy, the 'capital' of the Suisse Normande, is a popular walking centre with many long way-marked trails. This walk is fairly short, however, with marvellous views over a great loop of the river and the cliffs of the Orne valley. Some steep climbs are involved but the walk is not difficult.

Route Directions

Start from the church in the centre of Clécy or in the car park by the post office ①.

Take the road past the post office, signposted the Orne and le Vey, down the hill to the elbow bend by the Manoir de Placy ②.

Here pick up the signboard and blue waymarks for the Circuit du Pain de Sucre. Walk to the gates of the Manoir de Placy, and take the right fork down to the river and through the hamlet until the track becomes a footpath. Follow this beside the Orne and, keeping to the blue waymarks leading to the bridge, cross the river at Cantepie. The bare front of the Pain de Sucre should be plainly in sight ahead for most of the way. Pick up the distinctive red-and-white GR 36 waymarks on the bridge ③.

Follow these up the road to the left, then round to the right and through a farmyard, the path ascending through the woods, narrow in places but with plenty of waymarks. The path circles the rear of the Pain de Sucre, and a good view of the Orne valley can be had from beside the hang-glider launching ramp at the Rochers de la Houle ④.

From here follow the path along the hillside to the south, then descend slowly to come out on to a minor road by the small church at le Vey ⑤.

Turn down the road under the railway bridge and go straight on across the river bridge at le Vey to the crossroads on the D 168, from where the steps directly ahead lead up to the centre of Clécy.

The bridge over the Vey at Clécy
▼ *Clécy from the Pain de Sucre* ▶

Points of Interest

① Clécy is a good walking centre and a spot to stay in while exploring the Suisse Normande. The village is constructed of grey granite, relieved by plenty of flowers in gardens and window-boxes, but the main attraction is the surrounding countryside.

② The Manoir de Placy is now an hotel, but it contains a number of interesting artefacts and these make it well worth a visit. The house is a typical Norman manor house of the 16th century and has fine gardens overlooking the river.

③ The bridge over the Orne at Cantepie gives some of the best views of the cliffs surrounding the valley near Clécy.

④ The woods that screen the cliffs give way for a while at the Rochers de la Houle, where the rocks drop sheer into the valley and provide both a fine view over the great loop of the river and a superb launching spot for hang gliders, which circle above the river during the summer and at weekends.

⑤ The riverside hamlet of le Vey is a pretty spot, with a couple of fine hotels, some good views over the river from the bridge and the little chapel of le Vey behind the railway embankment. The riverside here is popular with visitors, especially on summer evenings, when swifts and swallows dart over the water.

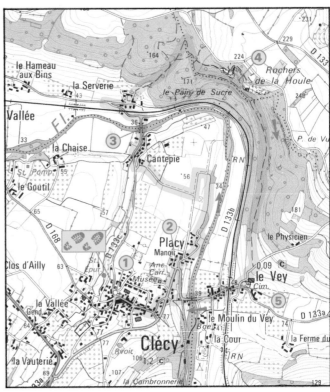

Abbeville to Le Touquet

This tour explores the area between the Rivers Somme and Canche, which includes the marshlands of the Bay of the Somme, the river valleys of the Authie and the Canche, undulating farmland pleasantly broken by woodland, and the natural forest of Crécy. It follows a route rich in history, from William the Conqueror to World War II, and along the way are great churches and abbeys, fortifications, old seaports, famous resorts and a variety of typically French villages.

Route Directions

The tour starts from Abbeville ①.

From the town centre follow the D 925 to Eu and Dieppe as far as Cambron. Turn right here on to the D 3, a pretty, tree-lined road which winds its way alongside the canalised Somme. At a major roundabout go straight on into St-Valéry-sur-Somme ②.

Return along the D 3, and at the roundabout turn left on to the D 940. Cross the Somme and follow the road as it curves round the bay. (To the right is Noyelles, the starting point for the first walk on this tour.) Turn left into le Crotoy ③.

Leave by the same route, following signs to Rue and Berck. Turn right off the main road to enter Rue ④.

To the left of the main road is a turning to the Parc Ornithologique du Marquenterre ⑤.

Continue along the D 940 to Waben and then turn left, towards Berck and le Touquet, still on the D 940. Follow this road past Berck, the Bagatelle amusement park and a number of other resorts. At the next major intersection turn left into le Touquet on the N 39 ⑥.

Leave by the same road, cross the Canche and enter Etaples ⑦.

(Turn left on the D 940 for the military cemetery.) Turn right on to the N 39 to follow the Canche towards Montreuil. At the junction with the N 1, turn right for Montreuil ⑧.

From Montreuil, take the N 39 Hesdin road along the southern side of the Canche valley and after 10km turn right on to a minor road towards Campagne-lès-Hesdins. Follow this past Campagne to Maintenay on the D 130 and the D 139. In the village turn right, pass the town hall, and then turn left at a roundabout. Cross the Authie by a lovely mill, then turn left to Valloires ⑨.

After the abbey at Valloires follow the river valley on the D 192 and the D 224 to Argoules, Dominois, Estruval, Ponches and Dompierre-sur-Authie. (To see the ruined abbey of Dommartin turn left at Dompierre-sur-Authie.) Turn right on to the D 111 at Dompierre-sur-Authie towards Crécy. Just before Crécy is the site of the battle. Go straight through Crécy, and then continue through the forest to Forest-l'Abbaye. (Here is the starting point for a walk.) In Forest-l'Abbaye bear left to Lamotte-Buleux and then turn left on to the D 32 towards St-Riquier ⑩.

Follow the D 925 back to Abbeville.

Pleasure craft at St-Valéry-sur-Somme ▶

▼ *The 18th-century Cistercian abbey at Valloires*

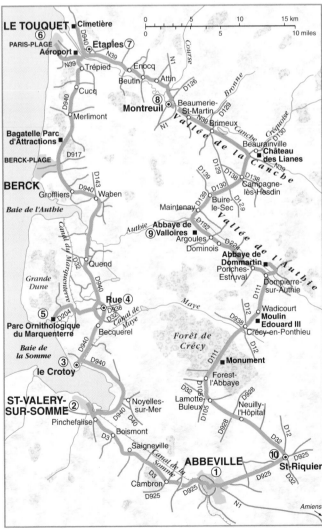

▲ *One of the graceful 18th-century rococo interiors at the Château de Bagatelle*

THE IMPACT OF WAR

Although a long way from the fighting, the coastal region that runs north from the Somme towards the Channel ports was deeply involved in World War I. Boulogne and Calais were the major ports for the handling of men and materials, but other harbours played their part. During this period St-Valéry-sur-Somme was busier than it had ever been, despite the limitations imposed by tides and sandbanks, and all kinds of stores were unloaded here for onward transport to the Front Line, by rail or on barges along the Canal de la Somme. Many of the Chinese labourers who are buried at Noyelles were part of the huge labour force employed in the port.

Also important was Etaples, first for its military hospitals, and second for its stores depot and training camp. This notorious establishment was widely feared for its harsh regime and bullying instructors, who were widely believed to have sparked off the mutiny of 1917, when troops led by Percy Topless, the 'monocled mutineer', rampaged through the town in pursuit of officers and military police.

Another key town in the region was Montreuil. Field Marshal Haig lived in the château at Beaurepaire to the south of the town from 1916 to 1919, and in Montreuil's main square there is a fine statue by Paul Landowski of Haig on his horse, Miss Ypres.

Points of Interest

① Devastated by the Germans in 1940 and regularly ignored by visitors, Abbeville is actually a town of considerable interest. It sits pleasantly beside the Somme, with old quays flanking the river, and at its heart is the great cathedral of St-Vulfran, with its notable Flamboyant Gothic façade. Houses dating from the Middle Ages to the 18th century add atmosphere, and just outside the town is the delightful miniature Château de Bagatelle.

② In 1066 William the Conqueror's invasion fleet set sail from St-Valéry (although other north-coast ports claim the honour), and this port at the mouth of the Somme is full of history and charm. Fishing boats and yachts still fill the quays and *fin-de-siècle* villas overlook the beaches. Behind is the old town, its attractive narrow streets contained within ancient fortified walls whose great gateways are still in use. There are memorable views out over the bay of the Somme.

③ Across the bay of the Somme and looking back towards St-Valéry is le Crotoy, an old-fashioned fishing village and resort surrounded by acres of salt-marsh populated by wild birds and *pré-salé* sheep. Famous for its seafood and its literary and artistic associations, le Crotoy is also the end of the line for

the Chemin de Fer de la Baie de Somme, the steam railway from St-Valéry.

④ In the Middle Ages Rue was a seaport but it now lies well inland. A small town of great charm, Rue is made memorable by the 15th- and 16th- century Chapelle du St-Esprit, a masterpiece of decorative Flamboyant Gothic architecture. Nearby are timber-framed buildings and the massive medieval belfry.

⑤ The bay of the Somme is one of the best sites in Europe for sea birds and migratory species, and a good place to spend a day birdwatching is the Parc Ornithologique du Marquenterre, a huge reserve with parking, a restaurant and picnic facilities.

⑥ Built by the English as a smart resort at the end of the 19th century, and a famous social centre between the wars, le Touquet still has plenty of period charm, with its streets of art nouveau seaside villas, its grand church, town hall and covered market and its smart restaurants. Postwar developments around the fine beach have compromised the town's gentility, but there is still plenty to enjoy in this thriving resort.

⑦ Across the Canche estuary from le Touquet is the fishing port of Etaples, popular with artists in the 19th century, and still home to a busy fishing fleet and fish market.

Just to the north, and on a sloping site overlooking the sea, is the magnificent World War I military cemetery designed by Sir Edwin Lutyens, the final resting place for hundreds of soldiers who died in the local military hospitals.

⑧ In the Middle Ages Montreuil had a busy port, a fortress, a monastery and 40,000 inhabitants. Today it is well inland and a much quieter place, a walled hilltop town of great appeal. Winding cobbled streets lined with 17th- and 18th-century houses, fine squares, an old citadel surrounded by 3km of ramparts, an abbey church and plenty of good hotels and restaurants make Montreuil one of the most attractive small towns in the north of France.

⑨ In a lovely wooded setting in the

▼ *The peaceful harbour at le Crotoy, a fishing village and resort*

Authie valley stands the Abbaye de Valloires, a rich range of 18th-century buildings in soft-coloured stone surrounded by attractive gardens. Founded in the 11th century, the abbey was a burial place for many of the French knights killed at Crécy. To be enjoyed today are the 16th-century dovecot and the rococo interiors designed by the Viennese artist Pfaff von Pfaffenhoffen.

⑩ Set on the side of a steep hill, St-Riquier is a notably attractive small town. Its main features are a 16th-century belfry, the early-18th-century Hôtel-Dieu, or hospital, and a little house whose roof is shaped like a Napoleonic tricorn. However, the great triumph is the Benedictine abbey, a marvellous composition in luminous stone at the end of a little square. Its wonderfully ornate 16th-century tower and façade make it one of the finest examples of the Flamboyant Gothic style.

Noyelles-sur-Mer

THE NORTH

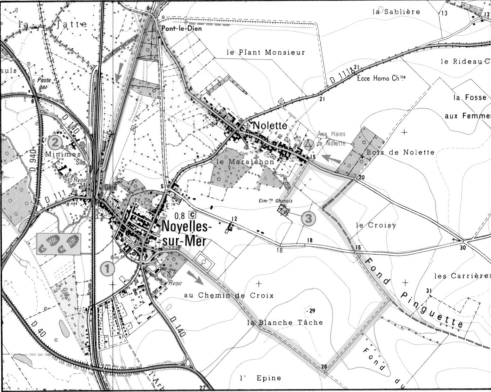

The poplar-lined River Dien ▼

Fine views across a landscape that once adjoined the sea, wide open fields and little wooded river valleys, quiet villages, an enchanting narrow-gauge steam railway and an unusual World War I memorial are all features of this pleasant, undemanding walk.

Route Directions

Start from the level crossing in Noyelles ① and ②.

Walk up the main street, pausing at the château, with an art gallery on the left. After the boulangerie, turn right into Rue de l'Eglise. The church is on the right, before the junction with the main road. Turn right, cross the road and take the first turning on the left, Rue du 8 mai.

Leaving the village behind, walk past the sports ground and keep straight on along a path through open fields to reach a path branching to the left at right angles. Follow this gently downhill, pass an old quarry on the right and at a junction take the main track to the left. This leads straight

across a minor road and soon you will see to the left the gateway of the Chinese cemetery ③.

Follow the path round to the right, away from the cemetery and up to a road. Turn left, and soon there is a track to the left leading directly to the cemetery. After visiting it, return to the road and continue down into the village of Nolette. Pass the lions on the left, and at the main road go straight across and take the road towards Ponthoile.

Continue to the picnic area on the right, cross the river and turn immediately left along a poplar-lined track beside the River Dien. Follow the track through the trees, which soon give way to open fields on the left, to reach the first cottages of Noyelles. The track becomes a road which leads back to the level crossing.

Points of Interest

① With its cafés and shops, Noyelles is a typical French farming village, made more attractive by the River Dien which flows through it. The church, dedicated to the Assumption of the Virgin Mary, is a simple 16th-century structure in brick and stone. With its centre set to the east of the main Boulogne-Abbeville railway line, the village

marks the transition from rolling agricultural plains and woodland in the east to marshland in the west, reclaimed from the Somme bay.

② Noyelles is the central point of a narrow-gauge steam railway, the Chemin de Fer de la Baie de Somme, that runs round the bay from St-Valéry to le Crotoy. Tourist services with old locomotives and vintage verandahed coaches operate on summer weekends and on some weekdays during the holiday season. This line, and another running westwards to the resort of Cayeux, are the remains of a large narrow-gauge network, the Réseau de la Somme, opened between 1887 and 1892. The trackbed of another branch, which ran eastwards to Canchy, on the edge of the Forêt de Crécy, can be seen on the walk where it crossed the Dien on a small iron bridge.

③ Set among the fields and copses at the edge of the hamlet of Nolette is the unexpected sight of the Cimetière Chinois. Here are the tombs of 900 members of the huge Chinese Labour Corps attached to the British army during World War I. Most of them died during the Spanish influenza epidemic in 1919. The Chinese did not fight, but worked in many ways to support the army. Today the cemetery, with its Chinese-style gateway and its rows of immaculately maintained graves, each marked with a Chinese inscription, is a quiet reminder of the worldwide impact of the war.

Historical links between Nolette and the Far East are underlined by the two marble lions that stand by the crossroads, gifts to the community from Taiwan.

▼ *Charollais cattle near Noyelles*

Crécy Forest

The huge Forêt de Crécy, north of Forest-l'Abbaye, 4500 hectares of natural beech, oak and other broad-leaved trees, is crossed by generous numbers of roads, tracks, bridleways and footpaths. Walking through the colourful yet tranquil forest is particularly pleasurable in the spring and autumn.

Route Directions

Start from Forest-l'Abbaye.

Leave the village by the D 111 to Crécy-en-Ponthieu ①.

Look immediately for a sign marking the start of the Forêt de Crécy. A car park is on the right, among the trees, and nearby are a picnic site and information board. From the car park follow the track to the right marked Promenade du Hallot. This leads towards the sports field.

Just before the gate into the field bear left and follow a path that runs along the edge of the forest. The route is marked by yellow circles painted on trees. Keep straight on, flanking the forest, and ignoring all turnings to the left until a major fork is reached, where one path is higher

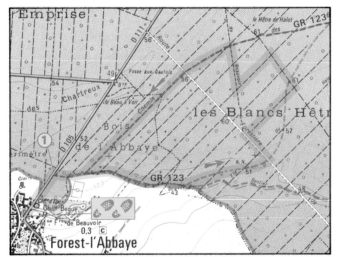

than the other.

Take the left, or upper, fork into the forest, clearly marked by a yellow arrow. This path carries on more or less straight through the huge beech trees until it meets a wide, well-defined track. Turn left along the track into a clearing and after 150m

turn right into the forest again along a well-marked track.

This path leads to the Mare du Hallot, a marshy pond hidden in the forest's heart.

Just before the pond take a sharp left turn, also well marked, and follow this path through the forest. At the second crossing of paths, turn left on to another clearly arrowed path. This leads to the magnificent old oak, one of the largest in the forest, known as the Beau Seigneur. Bear left here, and after 200m bear right on to a wider path. Keep straight on, crossing the well-defined track again, and the path leads back to the sports field and the car park.

Points of Interest

① Set on the eastern flank of the forest a short drive from the Promenade du Hallot, Crécy-en-Ponthieu is a pleasant small town with a lively main square and a handsome medieval church. At its

▲ *The forest still shelters deer, pheasant and wild boar*

heart are two monuments. One, of brick and stone, was apparently put up by Eleanor of Aquitaine to celebrate the safe return from the Crusades of her two sons, Richard Lionheart and John Lackland. The other, erected in 1905, commemorates Jean, the blind King of Bohemia, who perished with his son in the battle of August 1346. Crécy's name will always be associated with this battle, in which the English under Edward III inflicted a severe defeat on the much larger armies of Philippe VI, thanks largely to the English archers. At the end of the day 20,000 Frenchmen lay dead, including 1300 knights and 11 princes, and English dominance over much of France was assured.

Today a wooden tower stands on the site of the windmill used by Edward as a look-out post, and from the top there is a sweeping view over the battlefield. The tower displays information panels to explain the events of that dreadful day.

Amiens, the Somme and the battlefields

This tour follows the valley of the Somme eastwards from Amiens, where extensive water-meadows, lined with poplars and pockets of woodland, form a landscape of great variety and appeal. Turning north across a more open and undulating countryside, the tour crosses the battlefields of World War I to visit the towns, villages, memorials and cemeteries whose names tell the story of that conflict.

The magnificent Gothic vaulting of Amiens cathedral ▼

Route Directions

The tour starts from Amiens ①.

From the city centre turn north and cross the Somme and then turn right on to the D 1. Continue through Daours to Fouilloy. (Turn right on the D 23 to Villers-Bretonneux to visit the Australian National War Memorial ②.)

Return to Fouilloy and turn right towards Corbie, crossing the river again ③.

From the town centre take the minor road to Vaux, and follow it through the woods that line the Somme's northern bank. To see the river at its best, turn right in Vaux. From Vaux continue on the D 42e straight on through Sailly-Laurette to Chipilly, and then turn left towards Etinehem, by a moving memorial that depicts a soldier tending a wounded horse. From Etinehem take the D 1e to Bray-sur-Somme. (From Bray a short detour south on the D 329 leads to Froissy and the narrow-gauge steam railway that runs beside the river towards Cappy.)

Leave Bray on the D 329 towards Albert and immediately after the town turn right on to the D 147 towards Fricourt. At a major cross-roads just south of Fricourt turn left on to the D 938 to Albert ④.

Take the D 929, signposted Cambrai, out of Albert to Pozières ⑤.

Turn left to Thiepval ⑥.

Turn left at the crossroads for Lutyens' Somme memorial. From the crossroads take the road to the left that passes the Ulster tower before dropping down into the valley of the Ancre. Cross the river and the railway and then turn left and immediately right, passing the Newfoundland Memorial Park on the right, towards Mailly-Maillet ⑦.

By Mailly church turn left, and then soon take the D 176 signposted Bertrancourt and Thièvres. As it approaches the Authie valley the road becomes attractively wooded.

At a junction just outside the village of Authie turn left and then right through the woods to Pas-en-Artois on the D 124 ⑧.

Leave Pas-en-Artois by the same road, and then bear right to Thièvres on the D 1. In the village take a small, unmarked road to the right before the church. This leads along the pretty valley of the Authie to Amplier and Doullens ⑨.

From Doullens take the main N 25 south towards Villers-Bocage and Amiens, with short detours to the right to Naours with its vast network of underground caves, and to the fine 18th-century Château de Bertangles with its grand gates, sculpted pediment, dovecot and attractive old church in banded brick and stone.

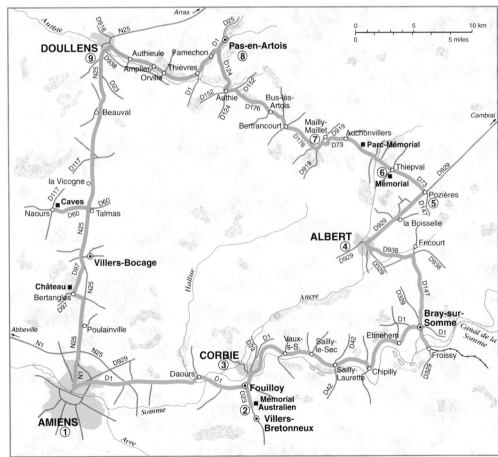

▲ *Sir Edwin Lutyens' moving and imposing war memorial at Thiepval commemorates 73,367 British soldiers killed on the Somme who have no known grave*

Points of Interest

① The capital of Picardy, and a city famous since the Middle Ages for its textiles, Amiens has at its heart the largest and one of the most splendid of all France's Gothic cathedrals. Remarkable both for its scale and for the unity of its architecture and sculpture, the Cathédrale Notre-Dame dates largely from the first half of the 13th century. It stands high above the Somme, which was for centuries the city's trade route and link to the sea, and spread out below it is the old riverside quarter of St-Leu, with its narrow streets and old timber-framed cottages now in process of restoration.

A thriving and busy city with good shops and restaurants, Amiens has an excellent museum and a great deal of interesting architecture, ranging from Renaissance mansions to a modern concrete tower by the architect Auguste Perret. To the east of the city are the Hortillonnages, acres of market gardens set in the water-meadows of the Somme and accessible only by small boats.

② See 2 on page 45.

③ See 3 on page 45.

④ Famous in the annals of World War I, Albert was largely destroyed between 1915 and 1918. Rebuilt in the 1920s, the town retains many echoes of the pre-war era. Its most famous building is the pilgrim church of Notre-Dame-de-Brébières, a precise replica of the 1880s original, complete with gilded Virgin on top of the tower. Shell damage in 1915 caused the figure to hang precariously from the ruined tower and many legends became associated with Albert's leaning

Virgin, an event still recorded by postcards on sale in the town. Also notable are the grand town hall of 1931, with its sculptural panels and stained glass, and the art deco railway station.

⑤ Right by the main road in Pozières is the great classical portico and flanking screen walls of the Memorial to the Missing of the 5th Army, a formal architectural composition in the familiar white stone. Nearby is a more unusual memorial, an obelisk surrounded by four bronze models of tanks, commemorating the first use of tanks in battle by the British in September 1916.

⑥ Visible from afar in every direction as it rides the horizon like a great cathedral brooding over the landscape of the Somme and the Ancre, Thiepval is Sir Edwin Lutyens' finest war memorial. This is the British Memorial to the Missing of the Somme, a commemoration of the 73,367 soldiers killed in the Somme campaigns who have no known grave. A complex pyramidal structure of brick and stone, conceived as a series of intersecting and pierced arches, Thiepval is both architecture and sculpture, a masterpiece of symbolism conveying by its scale a lasting sense of tragedy.

⑦ An unexpected treasure among the memorials and cemeteries, Mailly-Maillet's church of St-Pierre has on its exterior a wonderfully decorative sculptured portal depicting the banishment of Adam and Eve from the Garden of Eden. Begun in 1509, this important example of Flamboyant Gothic was saved from the ravages of World War I by the local *curé,* who protected it beneath layers of sacking.

THE SOMME

Inevitably overshadowed by the battles of 1916-18, the Somme is actually a remarkably attractive and relatively unknown river. It winds its way from its source at Fonsommes, east of St-Quentin, to join the English Channel at St-Valéry-sur-Somme, flowing for much of its length through a broad valley of ponds and water-meadows flanked by poplars and denser woodland. Along its banks are abbeys and churches, châteaux, traditional Picardy villages and three sizeable cities, St-Quentin, Amiens and Abbeville. Several centuries of history have left their mark, but for many people the Somme and its tributary, the Ancre, are synonymous with World War I. The Somme's gentle route is marked by names famous in the history of that conflict, and today memorials and

military cemeteries keep the memory alive. Extensively fought over in 1916, and again during the German offensive and breakthrough in the spring of 1918, the Somme was also an important transport artery for the Allied forces. Made navigable by the 1840s for 156km from its estuary at St-Valéry to a junction with the Canal de St-Quentin, the Somme was probably at its busiest during World War I, when all kinds of materials and supplies were transported to the Front by barges. Since then it has seen quieter days, and few boats now use its 25 locks, one of which can be seen in the centre of Corbie.

Today the Somme is a river of secret pleasures, its banks popular with fishermen, and its tree-lined course easily explored by car or on foot.

⑧ Set in the wooded hills and valleys that surround the headwaters of the Authie, Pas-en-Artois is a delightful small town full of 17th- and 18th-century brick and stone houses. At its heart, and standing in rolling parkland, is a formal little 18th-century château.

⑨ It was in Doullens on 26 March 1918 that Field Marshal Haig accepted the appointment of General Foch as Supreme Commander of the Allied Forces, a decision that helped to secure an Allied victory. A stained-glass window in the town hall depicts this historic meeting.

▼ *A market stall at Doullens, a traditional Picardy town*

A traditional Picardy town, Doullens also reflects the turbulent history of earlier centuries. The old streets are overlooked by the bulky ruins of the 17th-century citadel, set on a hilltop to the south-west. Also notable is the small belfry of 1613, while in the church of Notre-Dame is a memorable Entombment of 1583; seven life-size figures all carved from startlingly white limestone, in a style blending Gothic and Renaissance details. A comparable Entombment, equally expressive but in a more primitive style, can be seen in the church at Villers-Bocage, to the south of Doullens and just off the road back to Amiens.

Aspects of the Somme

This walk explores the Somme, its landscape, its architecture and the memorials of World War I, crossing rolling agricultural plains before descending into the wooded river valley. The field tracks can be muddy in wet weather.

Route Directions

Start from Place de la République, behind the modern church in Fouilloy ①.

Cross the main road and walk up Rue Thiers, opposite the large concrete granary. Pass the school and at the end of the road turn right. At the main road, the D 23, turn left and walk up the hill away from the town. At the first fork bear left, keeping a large garage and lorry park on the right, and walk up towards the tower of the Australian National War Memorial ②.

The road quickly becomes a track, which leads up the side of the hill to pass well to the left of the tower. Look back for fine views of the abbey, the Somme valley and Corbie ③.

At the first junction turn right along a track that runs beside the memorial's boundary fence, and follow this until it meets the road. From the memorial, turn right again along the road and immediately turn left along a track that goes straight across the fields. There are good views back to the memorial and across to the church of Villers-Bretonneux.

Where the track meets a road (the D 168e) turn left down the hill to the crossroads and then turn right. Take the first track on the left, clearly visible from the crossroads, and follow this until it meets another track. Turn right. This is a bit of a dog-leg, but it avoids the road. Keep on this track across the fields, dropping steadily down into the valley. Eventually this joins the road. Bear left along the road, which is quite busy. Cross the D 1 to go straight on into Aubigny, passing on the left a small military cemetery holding mostly Australian soldiers killed in the spring of 1918. Continue to the village centre and then turn right by a large crucifix, along Rue de l'Abbaye. This leads down to the canalised Somme. Turn right along the towpath, and follow it past the

poplars back to Fouilloy. Stay beside the river until the path meets Rue Emile Zola. This leads directly back into Place de la République.

Points of Interest

① Fouilloy, a small town on the Somme, is virtually a suburb of Corbie, but it is not without interest. At its centre is an unusual church. Built in 1958, this has a façade decorated with a series of modernist sculptures depicting the life of St Martin.

② Dominating the valley of the Somme for miles is the tall white tower of the Australian National Memorial and Cemetery. Designed by Sir Edwin Lutyens and incorporating many of his favourite motifs – the classical entrance pavilions, the furled flags in cut stone, the inspired blend of architecture and landscape – the Memorial is placed high above the

Somme where the Australians, at great cost, halted the German breakthrough of the spring of 1918.

The setting, the architecture, the immaculately-kept cemetery ranged up the slope and, at its climax, the tall tower with its screen wall carrying the names of the dead, all combine to provide a moving experience.

③ A busy town set beside the canalised Somme, Corbie is best known for its abbey. Founded in 657, and housing 300 monks at the time of Charlemagne, the abbey flourished until the Revolution, when much of it was destroyed. What remains is the 16th-century abbey church, an impressively solid building in the town centre. Just west of Corbie, and on the Ancre, is la Neuville, where the 16th-century church has a most unusual portal in the form of a lively bas-relief, full of primitive detail, depicting Christ's Entry into Jerusalem.

Lutyens' Australian National Memorial ▼

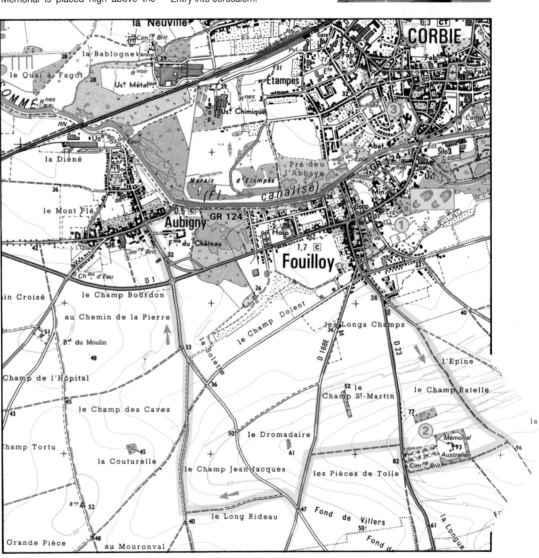

Around Naours

Near Naours the plains of Picardy are broken by winding valleys whose steep, chalky sides are in places thickly wooded. This walk, largely along field paths and woodland tracks, offers a wide variety of views. Paths are sometimes steep, and sections can be muddy in wet weather.

▼ *Naours' broken-pot mosaic*

Route Directions

Start from the post office by the crossroads in the centre of Naours ①.

Turn right, and walk along Rue de la Croix. Take the first road on the right, signposted the Grottes de Naours ②.

This road passes the entrance to the caves and then meets the D 60. Go straight across and up Rue Malmontée, which leads out of the town. At a fork bear left along a well-defined track offering good views back over the town and the two windmills. Follow this track across the fields and then, just after the power line, turn right on to a grassy track.

At the next junction take the track to the right, across the fields towards the power line. Just before the power line there is a crossing of tracks. Turn left towards the trees and follow this track steeply down into the valley. At the edge of the woods it meets another, smaller path. Turn left and keep along the winding, and sometimes muddy, path sunken in the valley bottom between fields and woods. At a fork by a wind-pump keep straight on.

This narrow and uneven path soon widens and swings to the left along the base of a steep escarpment, and then winds its way along the valley until it meets a road. Turn right and follow the road up the hill. When the road bears away to the right, take a track to the left before the power line. This track makes its way along the crest of the hill, passing holiday chalets and then opening out to give views of two windmills ③.

Drop down to pass close behind them to rejoin Rue de la Croix just by the house with the broken-pot mosaic.

Points of Interest

① With its grand church and range of typical Picardy architecture, Naours is a handsome little town, nestled in a valley beneath steep chalk hills.

② The Grottes de Naours are a huge network of underground caves, known locally as *muches, cruettes* or *boves*. Probably dating from the 9th century, the caves were certainly well established in the Middle Ages, and were used extensively during the religious upheavals of the 17th century, by which time an entire underground town had been created, with streets, squares, chapels, shops, stables, a bakery and accommodation for 3000 people. Abandoned in the 18th century, the network was rediscovered in 1887 by the local priest and, apart from a period in 1942 when it was occupied by the Germans, it has been accessible to the public ever since. Now part of a pleasantly old-fashioned kind of theme park, the caves can be visited, along with a local folk museum.

③ The windmills stand in the grounds of the caves and can be visited. There is no access to them from the track.

One of the well-restored windmills in the grounds of the Grottes de Naours ▼

Troyes and the Forêt d'Orient

This tour explores the landscape of woods, lakes and farmland that lies to the east of Troyes, the former capital of Champagne. Following initially the wooded valley of the Seine, the route then turns away from the river and into the hills before dropping down to the Parc Naturel Régional de la Forêt d'Orient, whose lakes, rivers, natural woodland and reservoirs famous for sailing and birdwatching enrich a countryside devoted to agriculture.

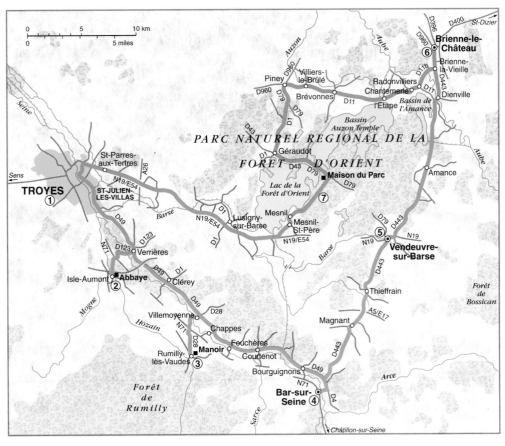

▲ *Lac de la Forêt d'Orient is popular among water-sports enthusiasts*
A field of sunflowers in a farming area near Troyes (above right) ▶

Return to Verrières and pass through it, noting the timber-framed buildings characteristic of the region and then in Clérey turn right, towards Clérey Sud. The road drops steeply down towards the river but at the cross-roads before the river turn left for Villemoyenne and Chappes, a pretty village with a grand church and a big weir by the bridge. (From here a short detour can be made south on the D 28 to Rumilly-lès-Vaudes ③.)

From Chappes follow the D 49 on to Courtenot and Bourguignons and, at a major junction, bear right into Bar-sur-Seine ④.

Leave the town by the same road and at the junction keep right on the D 443 towards Vendeuvre-sur-Barse ⑤.

This is an attractive road, climbing into the wooded hills before descending again into Vendeuvre. From the town centre take the Bar-sur-Aube road and turn left on to the D 443 towards Amance and Brienne-le-Château ⑥.

With lakes and reservoirs to the left, turn right and cross the Aube into Dienville and carry straight on into Brienne. Leave the town by the same road and at Brienne-la-Vieille turn sharp right on to the D 11b towards Piney. Pass through the farming village of Radonvilliers, now on the D 11, with the Aube reservoir to the south, and just outside Piney turn left on to the D 79 at the main junction. Take the right fork, the D 1, to Géraudot and Lusigny-sur-Barse. Follow this road through open countryside towards Géraudot. Here turn left along the D 43 and the D 79 alongside the lake in the Parc Naturel Régional de la Forêt d'Orient ⑦.

The lake is largely hidden by trees but there are viewpoints and picnic sites with ample parking. Continue through the forest, with the bird reserve to the south, and at the Maison du Parc turn right along the lakeside towards Mesnil-St-Père.

From Mesnil follow the signs for the N 19, and at the N 19-E 54 turn right to return to Troyes.

Route Directions

The tour starts from Troyes ①.

From the city centre take the road that runs beside the old quays, the Bassin de la Préfecture, and follow it to the south-east. Pick up signs for St-Julien-les-Villas and the D 49. Cross the waterway and from then on keep it to the right. At St-Julien the waterway joins the Seine and as the suburbs are left behind the road winds its way through the woods and fields that flank the river valley. (At Verrières divert south across the Seine on the D 123 to the abbey at Isle-Aumont ②.)

▲ *Renaissance half-timbering and architectural details in Bar-sur-Seine and Troyes*

Points of Interest

① In 1420 Henry V of England married Catherine of France in the church of St-Jean in Troyes, a marriage planned to ensure English dominance of much of France. In the event the plan went wrong, and nine years later the English were driven from the city by Joan of Arc. Although rebuilt later, the church still stands, one of a number of medieval churches in Troyes that mark the various stages of the Gothic style.

In the heart of the old city is the Cathédrale St-Pierre-et-St-Paul, dominating an area contained within a loop of the Seine and noted above all for its stained glass. Famous since the Middle Ages for hosiery and *andouillettes,* small sausages made of pig's intestines, Troyes still gives the impression of a medieval city, its narrow streets lined with timber-framed buildings whose upper storeys are cantilevered out over the street on carved supports, a distinctive local architectural style. Lively and a pleasure to explore, Troyes also has a remarkable modern art museum, with fine works by Derain and the Fauves, and by Braque, Modigliani, Delaunay and other outstanding 20th-century artists.

② Set on a high promontory of land to the south of the Seine, Isle-Aumont has been settled at least since neolithic times, its powerful position supporting a series of strongholds, castles and religious buildings. The abbey was founded by the Benedictines in 1097, but the buildings date from the 12th century, and have examples of both Romanesque and Gothic details.

③ Rumilly-lès-Vaudes, set on the edge of woodland to the south of the Seine, is worth a visit for its 16th-century manor house and church, the latter notable for its fine sculpted doorway and its altarpiece in coloured stone.

④ Spread along the southern shore of the Seine and contained by its surrounding woodland, Bar-sur-Seine is a pleasantly old-fashioned town marking the boundary between Champagne and Burgundy. Renaissance mansions and huge riverside mills recall its prosperity in the 16th and 17th centuries.

⑤ Vendeuvre-sur-Barse is approached along a dramatic road that winds its way across the surrounding woodland. It has a 16th-century church with interesting carved details and a massive château of a slightly later date, built on the site of an earlier stronghold. The château is best seen from its large and attractive park.

⑥ Another château, this time a formal structure of the 18th-century set on a hill to the west of the town, can be seen at Brienne-le-Château, best known for its Napoleonic associations.

Brienne still has a military academy, and this makes its mark on a traditional town whose features include a wooden covered market and a church with fine Renaissance stained glass.

⑦ The Parc Naturel Régional de la Forêt d'Orient, designated in 1970, is a protected area of natural forest, low-lying marshland and rich agricultural land. Situated within the park, the artificial Lac de la Forêt d'Orient covers nearly 2300 hectares. It has an ornithological reserve where visitors can enjoy the many varieties of bird drawn to the lakes and their surroundings. There are opportunities for seeing wild boar and deer in their natural environment and at Mesnil-St Père there is a lakeside resort with beaches, sailing and water-sport facilities. The information centre is in the Maison du Parc, a traditional Champenoise building re-erected in the heart of the park between the two lakes.

NAPOLEON AND BRIENNE

At the age of nine, and fresh from Corsica, the young Napoleon entered the military school at Brienne-le-Château as an *élève du roi,* or King's scholar. Small and by no means fluent in French, Napoleon probably suffered at the hands of his fellow students, who numbered about 100. But his pride and determination kept him going, and he passed out successfully in 1784, with excellent reports for mathematics and military studies. A statue of Napoleon wearing the distinctive uniform of the school stands outside Brienne's town hall.

Throughout his life Napoleon retained fond memories of his time at Brienne, seeing the period as an important formative stage in his career. In January 1814 he returned to Brienne for the last time, at the head of an untrained conscript army that was able, thanks to his leadership and inspiration, to drive a far larger and better equipped Prussian and Russian force back towards Bar-sur-Aube.

At his death Napoleon repaid his debt to the town with a legacy that went towards the building of the town hall, completed in 1859. A small museum in the old military school is devoted to his memory. Brienne today has a much larger military academy and a military airfield which keep alive the Napoleonic tradition.

Toul and Lac de Madine

From Toul this tour leads through the vines and mirabelle orchards of the Côtes du Toul, to St-Mihiel, where the first major American battle of World War I is commemorated in a rotunda at Montsec, high above Lac de Madine. Passing through part of the Parc Naturel Régional de Lorraine, and after visiting a tiny Renaissance hilltop village, you return to Toul.

Route Directions

The tour starts from Toul.

Leave Toul, heading north-west, by the D 908, signposted St-Mihiel. The main villages in this wine-growing area are Lagney and Lucey ①.

From Lucey follow the D 908 to Lagney, then on to Boucq. Continue through agricultural land and the Forêt de la Reine to Corniéville. Orchards line the road into Gironville, where the route crosses the D 958. From Gironville-sous-les-Côtes, a long, straight, tree-lined road leads to Apremont-la-Forêt. From here take the D 907 to St-Mihiel ②.

Take the D 901 out of St-Mihiel, signposted Hattonchâtel. Turn left on the D 908 to reach Hattonchâtel ③.

Retrace your steps on the D 908 and go to Woinville. At Woinville, turn left on to the D 119, signposted Montsec ④.

From Montsec the road runs through Richecourt. Turn left on the D 33 to St-Baussant. Here a detour may be made, via the D 28, the D 904 and the D 48, to visit Nonsard-Lamarche, one of the marinas and camp sites on Lac de Madine ⑤.

From St-Baussant turn left on a minor road to Flirey. Turn left by the war memorials and church, on to the D 958, and at Limey-Remenauville turn right on to the D 100, signposted Lironville and Martincourt.

From Martincourt the tiny D 106 passes through a little valley and leads into Griscourt. After the village of Saizerais continue on the D 90b. As the road approaches the Moselle valley the surroundings become somewhat industrial. High above the loop in the river sits the village of Liverdun ⑥.

From Liverdun take the D 90 back into Toul.

Dismantled by order of Cardinal Richelieu in 1634, the Château de Hattonchâtel was rebuilt after World War I in the style of the 15th century. The work was carried out between 1924 and 1928 on behalf of Belle Skinner, an American, who was captivated by the ruined château ▶

Points of Interest

① Situated to the left of the D 908, Lucey is one of the larger producers of both wine and the mirabelle, a small yellow plum much used for distilling a distinctively flavoured liqueur. Lucey is a typical Lorraine village, with houses terraced and set well back from the road. Each is about four times as deep as it is wide, with an arched gateway for wagons into a stable area, and to one side the door leading into the living quarters. A great stone fireplace with a bread oven to one side forms the back wall of this room and at one time helped to heat the smaller room behind. Behind the stable and living quarters is an open courtyard for farm implements and the family pig. Beyond is the distillery area, under a lean-to cover, with a kitchen garden stretching up the slope behind.

In just such a Lorraine farmhouse is the Maison Lorraine de Polyculture, a record of local life from the 18th century to the beginning of the 20th. One local grower brings his grapes here after the *vendange* – so in October the visitor may perhaps see the living side of this museum. The local *vin gris de Toul* is a sharp, refreshing, slightly rosé wine, pressed immediately after the grapes are picked. Rival viticulturists say that *gris de Toul* needs to be drunk using two hands – one to hold the glass, the other to hold on to the table. Blending with other grape varieties, notably Auxerrois, can reduce the sharp acidity of some of the wines.

② Works by the sculptor Ligier Richier, born in St-Mihiel around 1500, are to be found all over Lorraine. His *Laying of Christ in the Tomb* is in the church of St-Etienne here, and another, the *Skeleton*, in Bar-le-Duc's church dedicated to the same saint. Hattonchâtel also boasts a disputed Ligier Richier in its tiny church.

If your visit coincides with the infrequent opening times, do not miss the Benedictine library, with its beautiful woodwork and ceiling from the reign of Louis XIV, and a spectacular wrought-iron staircase and banisters.

③ An American, Belle Skinner, came to Hattonchâtel at the end of World War I and fell in love with the village. As well as rebuilding the Mairie-Ecole, she laid on water and provided vine stocks to replace those destroyed during the war. A plaque outside the château records her part in its rebuilding. The interior stonework patterning in alternate red

and white squares, reminiscent of Normandy, presents a much less forbidding aspect than the pseudo-medieval exterior. A large formal pool stands in the wide courtyard surrounded by trees, and there is a fine reconstructed baronial hall.

④ At Montsec a road leads around the hill, to the bottom of wide steps leading up to the white stone rotunda. Impressive columns support a circular plinth, open to the sky, with a bronze relief map of the progress of the 1918 battle. Benches along the edge of the parking space allow you to look out and enjoy the view. Others are set on their own, in trimly kept grassed areas, for quiet contemplation and remembrance. Four thousand of the 10,000 American dead lie in the cemetery at nearby Thiaucourt-Regniéville, where the war memorial has a statue of a French *poilu* shaking hands with an American soldier.

⑤ From both Hattonchâtel and Montsec you have looked down on Lac de Madine. Created about 15 years ago, to provide much-needed extra water for Metz and Nancy, it covers 1100 hectares, with boating, sailing and many other sporting facilities. The two main camp sites are at Heudicourt and Nonsard.

⑥ Liverdun owes its name in part to the Celtic word *dun*, meaning a hilltop fort. The road winds up and through the old Porte Haute into the village. In the church are unusual tomb inscriptions, from the 1380s to 1400, cut deeply into the pillars of the nave and chapels. Each has a delicately carved hand, in ruffed sleeve, its finger pointing down towards the actual tomb in the floor. The tomb of St Euchaire, patron saint of the church beheaded in nearby Pompey in 362, shows him in full episcopal robes, his crozier

JOAN OF ARC

Domrémy and Vaucouleurs, villages for ever associated with the name of 'La Pucelle', the Maid, lie just to the south. This young girl led the dispirited forces of France to victory against the English in 1429.

But where did she come from? Many believe her to have been a half-sister of the Dauphin, Charles VII, whom she took to Reims to be crowned. There is strong evidence that her father was the king's brother, Louis, Duc d'Orléans, her mother being the queen, by then long estranged from her often insane husband, Charles VI.

Such a background would make sense of the many otherwise inexplicable episodes in Joan's life. How did a young shepherd girl, however inspired by her 'voices', manage to convince a chauvinistic feudal court and a king doubtful of his own legitimacy?

Outside the cathedral at Toul is a plaque commemorating Joan's appearance before the Bishop's Court to answer a charge of breach of promise.

Who lies in the tomb in the church at Pulligny, south of Nancy? Until the 19th century it was marked as the resting place of Joan and her husband, Robert des Armoises, whom she married in Metz in September 1436.

Once Joan's mission was complete, she was an embarrassment as an illegitimate half-sister to the king, who nonetheless could not let her die at the stake. A condemned heretic was substituted for her. Records at Rouen show the executioner's wages and the cost of wood for burning five unfortunate women between 1430 and 1432. They name the women, but there is no Jeanne d'Arc among them.

But whoever Joan was, however she was used by politicians of the day, the fact remains that her actions enabled France to stand united and ended the Hundred Years War. She will for ever be synonymous with the national pride of France.

under his left arm and his head, still wearing the mitre, cradled on his chest.

In Place de la Fontaine are arcaded entrances, not unlike those found in the *bastide* towns of the Dordogne.

Little statues of saints and protectors stand in niches on the corners and over the doorways of several houses.

The beautiful 17th-century library of the Benedictine abbey at St-Mihiel ▼

Hattonchâtel – a hilltop village

A choice of walks is offered here: a stroll round an interesting hilltop village and its countryside, vineyards and orchards, or a longer route around the same village.

Route Directions

Start from the Salle des Gardes in Hattonchâtel ①.

For a waymarked circular walk around the village, following the Sentier de Ronde ②.

The longer walk starts from the same spot. Follow the orchard path towards Vigneulles-lès-Hattonchâtel. At the top of a rise, near a shrine to the right of the road, a path leads to the right across the top of a mirabelle orchard. Soon afterwards fork left towards the village then on to a surfaced road. At the T-junction with the D 901 turn right: from here the route is signposted with yellow-and-blue discs. Pass an educational establishment *(Maison familiale rurale)* on your left and continue uphill, turning left after 500m on to a narrow woodland trail.

Where this emerges on to a vine-covered slope there is a view across the valley and, on clear days, as far as Nancy. The path continues into woodland and passes a well-head ③.

Continue down the steep slope and into open country, following clear arrows on trees. As you skirt some orchards you will see the church tower of Creuë ④.

Follow the marked path out of Creuë to the right, take the right fork, and climb past sandy cliffs into mixed woodland, and then bear round to the right.

After 1km this path reaches the source of the Loussot ⑤.

The track climbs out of woods and on to open tilled fields. This is a rough stretch of about 500m. At the top of this path, turn right and head back towards Vigneulles. From there retrace your steps back up the slope to Hattonchâtel.

From Hattonchâtel, the highest village in the Meuse, there are superb views over the plain below. The chief glory of Hattonchâtel is the château, originally built in the 9th century for Hatton, the Bishop of Verdun, destroyed in 1634 and rebuilt in the 1920s ▶

Points of Interest

① All that remains of the 14th-century Porte Notre-Dame, in a niche in the Salle des Gardes, is a statue of the Virgin, a replica of the original which stood over this gateway.

② The Sentier de Ronde follows the base of the fortifications which used to surround the village (which takes its name from the 9th-century château of Bishop Hatton). At 400m Hattonchâtel is the highest village in the Meuse *département,* and there are splendid views out across the vineyards and plain below.

③ This square, stone-block well-head is believed to be Roman in origin. The well is dry now, but as it is still 8m deep it has been covered with a metal grille for safety.

④ Below the church in Creuë is a cross of timber brought back from Jerusalem by pilgrims in 1936. The church belfry is said to date back to the days of Charlemagne, but most of what is seen today is 15th-century, with additions made in 1862. These include the carved likenesses of the stonemason, architect and contractor on the first pillars and vault.

⑤ To the left of the road, down a few stone steps, is a dank, square, stone-lined enclosure. Open the metal door covering the spring and you would think the place was bone dry – until you put your hand in and feel the astonishingly clear and still water. This is the source of the Loussot.

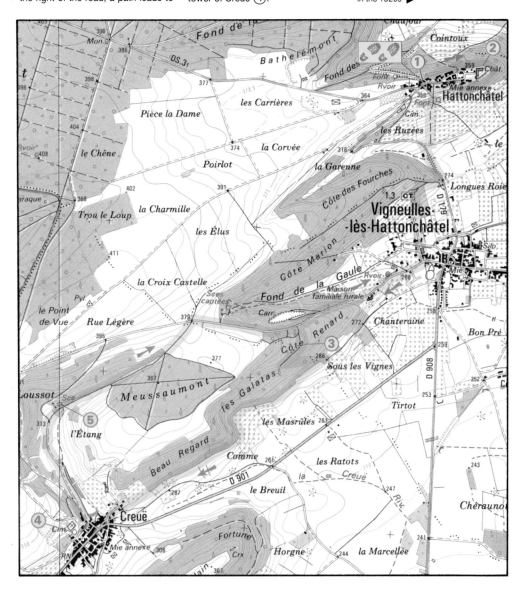

WALK 11B: 10KM/ALLOW 2½ HOURS

The Côtes de Toul

Every other Sunday during the summer, the Randonnées Touloises organise group walks. It can be fun walking and talking with local enthusiasts. Walks are signposted with a time to the next goal rather than a distance, and the walking speed is a comfortable 4km an hour. This walk is the Circuit de la Linotte, the Linnet Walk.

Route Directions

Start from the village of Trondes ①.

Go down Rue des Thermes and cross the main street. Turn right in front of the village fountain and church, along Rue de la Neuveville. On leaving the village, on the D 192, pass a walkers' noticeboard with a map of the immediate surroundings and all the local signposted walks. The path carries on beside a wood, marked with a linnet sign on a post.

At the foot of Bois de Raumont turn left. The path rejoins the D 192 for a few hundred metres then continues through pine and beech woods to reach Laneuveville-derrière-Foug ②.

Leave the village along the road leading straight down from the café. Turn left at Rue des Paquis and out into open fields. Round a small hill there is a view of Boucq on its hillside. Take the track to the right, past Faux Moulin farm and on to Renard Moulin. Pass Renard Moulin farm to reach a sharp bend in a road, where an arrow directs you to the left. Follow the road (the D 101) through la Tuilerie de Trondes back to Trondes.

Points of Interest

① Trondes is a typical small agricultural village, on the 'Route du Vin'. The church is basically 15th-

century and the fountain just outside is still supplied by the conduit which the Gauls laid to bring water to their community.

② Laneuveville-derrière-Foug is a Gallo-Roman settlement, like Trondes, but no traces remain and the church dates from around 1825. There is, however, the Fontaine des Soeurs, near the church, one of many such drinking fountains to be found all over Lorraine. The Café du Centre is a good spot to stop for a rest. In a corner of the geranium-bedecked courtyard is a deep stone-lined pond, with a fountain and trout. On the foundations of the 13th-century château in Boucq there are still

▲ *A view of Trondes*

two 14th-century towers, dominating the little village, its church and vineyards. The church, too, has a fortified tower, from the third floor of which a footbridge used to lead directly into the castle. The doorway is still visible, though now bricked up.

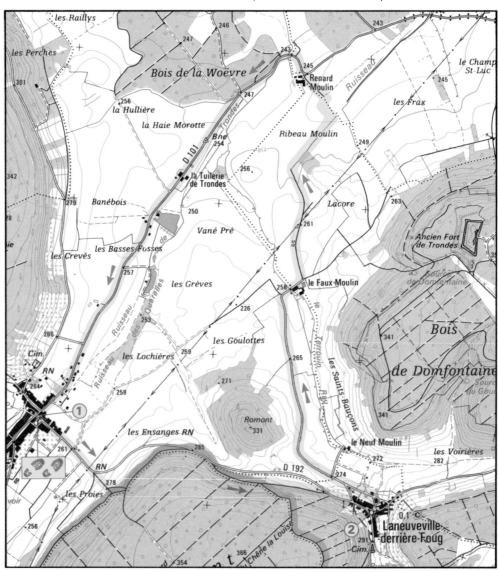

Thann and the Ballons des Vosges

H ere in the Vosges, expect to have to climb a bit – both in the car and on foot. On this tour the views that can be gained by leaving the car and walking up to the peaks and cols amply reward the energetic. The route takes in Grand Ballon (1424m), the highest peak in the Vosges.

Route Directions

The tour starts from Thann ①.

Leave Thann on the N 66, which runs along a broad valley towards Willer-sur-Thur. Turn right on to the D 13 *bis*, signposted Goldbach-Altenbach and Grand Ballon. The road climbs out of Willer-sur-Thur, with a small stream in woodland down to the right. (At Col Amic, a 5km detour to the right leads to Hartmannswillerkopf) ②.

Turn left at Col Amic, on to the D 431, the Route des Crêtes, a forested road signposted Grand Ballon and Markstein. The road twists and climbs up to Grand Ballon ③.

From the lay-by car park at the foot of Grand Ballon an easy 30-minute walk takes you to the summit. Return to your car and continue towards the hotel, restaurant, café and souvenir shops. Most of the downhill and cross-country ski trails are also usable in the summer. Carry on along the Route des Crêtes, towards le Markstein ④.

Down to the right is Lac de la Lauch. At le Markstein the road becomes the D 430 and is signposted le Hohneck ⑤.

At Rainkopf the road crosses from Haut-Rhin to Vosges and, carrying on towards the Col de la Schlucht, passes the source of two rivers – the Vologne and the Meurthe. Just by the former, there is an interesting alpine garden, at Haut-Chitelet ⑥.

Before reaching the Col de la Schlucht turn back southwards along the D 34d and a short detour along the D 67 will take you to Lac de Retournemer ⑦.

The D 34c along the Chajoux valley is the more scenic route to la Bresse, through pine woods and past small lakes and houses, each on its own hillock. At la Bresse join the D 486 to le Thillot via Cornimont. Once through the textile town of le Thillot turn on to the N 66, signposted St-Maurice-sur-Moselle. Another textile town, this is also a base for exploring, summer or

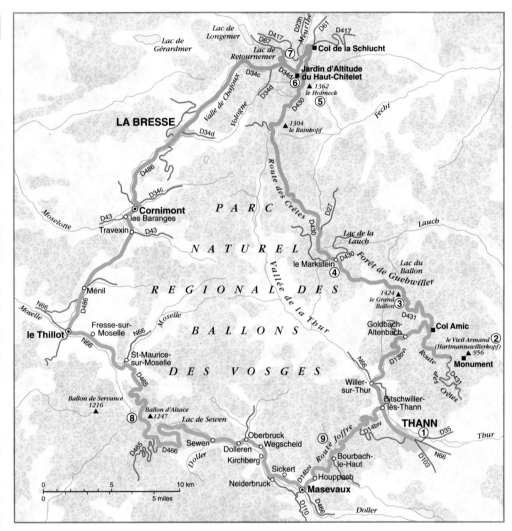

winter, the whole area around the Ballon d'Alsace ⑧.

To continue the tour turn right on to the D 465 just before St-Maurice, and turn left after the Ballon d'Alsace on to the D 466, which winds down the valley of the Doller, signposted Masevaux, after Lac de Sewen. At Masevaux, take the D 14 bIV – a twisting mountain road known as the 'Route Joffre' ⑨.

This road is signposted Bitschwiller. Here rejoin the N 66 and turn right back into Thann.

Dramatic prospects of pine-clad peaks receding into the mist and reflected in still waters are characteristic sights on the Route des Crêtes ▶

Points of Interest

The views from Grand Ballon are stupendous – stretching even to Mont-Blanc on a clear day ▶

① Thann is situated at the entrance to the Thur valley, which was an important medieval trade route between Italy and the Netherlands. In 1160 Bishop Thiébaut died in Gubbio, Italy. He had promised his episcopal ring to his servant who, unable to loosen it, pulled off the bishop's thumb. He kept it as a relic and on his way home, as he rested by the river bank, his staff took root and bright lights shone above the fir trees in the forest. Taking this as a divine sign, the local Count of Ferrette built a chapel on the spot: hence the name Thann, the Germanic word for a fir tree. There was certainly a church here in 1287, dedicated to St Thiébaut and attracting pilgrims. On 30 June each year three pine trees are burned in front of the church.

A picturesque example of Flamboyant Gothic, built of red sandstone from Soultz and yellow sandstone from Rouffach, the Collégiate St-Thiébaut was finished in 1495 and the steeple added in 1516. The carved oak choir-stalls and misericords are the finest in Alsace. Among the figures and caricatures are a scholar, a fiddler and a quaint gentleman in 15th-century spectacles.

Try to visit the nearby Engelbourg. The Oeil de la Sorcière, the Witch's Eye, up on the hill is the base of the circular keep, which fell on its side after a bungled demolition attempt in 1673. It does indeed look like an eye peering down on the town.

② Alsace was German territory at the start of World War I. Thirty thousand men died on Hartmannswillerkopf, a small group of hilltops overlooking the Rhine plain, between August 1914 and Christmas 1915. On 5 January 1916 the French Minister for War, Galliéni, ordered that 'isolated operations such as that at Hartmannswillerkopf must cease, in order to spare men's lives'. There is a mausoleum on a hilltop and long rows of crosses, the tricolour for ever flying above – a place for reflection.

In the museum photographs of the troops of both sides show that even in the worst sector of the front, the *Hexenküche*, or Witches' Kitchen as the Germans named it, camaraderie in adversity overcame some of the horror, some of the time.

③ At Grand Ballon there is a car park just to the right of the road and the summit is visible, half an hour's easy walk away. The path winds up to the monument to the Chasseurs Alpins, the 'Blue Devils'.

④ Le Markstein is a favourite place for hang-gliding enthusiasts. You can also hire mountain bikes here and there are many marked and signposted routes available for all skills and ages. The wildly convoluted plastic channels are packed with snow in winter to create bob-sleigh runs.

⑤ At a parking place at Hohneck, where there are stupendous views, is the Fontaine de la Duchesse, the source of the River Moselotte and site of a picnic held in the 1550s by Christine of Denmark and friends.

⑥ In the Jardin d'Altitude at Haut-Chitelet there are more than 3000 specimens of South American, Himalayan and Scandinavian high-altitude flora as well as a peat bog. Similar gardens may be seen at Samoëns (Savoie) and Lautaret (Hautes-Alpes).

⑦ A 2km detour through pine woods along the D 67 leads to the tranquil Lac de Retournemer, nestling in a hollow at the head of a valley. In spring it is surrounded by a carpet of wild daffodils.

⑧ A path leads up to the orientation table on the Ballon d'Alsace, from where, at 1250m, there are splendid all-round views. From here the D 465 snakes up to the Col du Ballon, passing on the right the Ballon de Servance (1216m).

Here were quarried the green porphyry for the base of Napoleon's tomb at the Invalides in Paris, and the lovely rose-coloured porphyry used for the columns of the Opéra.

⑨ The Route Joffre is a tortuous mountain road built in World War I to supply the troops at Hartmannswillerkopf. Negotiating its hairpin bends gives some idea of the problems the French faced, whereas a direct rail link from Mulhouse supplied the German forces.

The monument to the Chasseurs Alpins, the 'Blue Devils', on Grand Ballon ▼

ECOMUSEE

Near Ungersheim, off the N 83 10km north of Mulhouse, in the unlikely setting of an abandoned potassium mine, is the Ecomusée. This is dedicated to the saving of the fast-disappearing architectural heritage of Alsace. Some 50 traditional houses and barns, dating from the 14th century to the 20th, have been re-erected, having been saved from demolition in their original sites.

Dominating the 'village' is a 12th-century *château-fort,* rescued from near Mulhouse. Some houses have been left unfinished for a better understanding of the techniques involved in half-timbered building, a feature of all Alsatian villages. Many are furnished with authentic pieces, giving a good idea of the life of the period. There is always something of interest going on here during the summer, though it is best to telephone to check opening times. There are regular demonstrations of crafts and skills and special festivals to mark the midsummer feast of St John, harvest time and the *vendange* – the grape harvest.

Happily, many people are becoming more conscious of the need for preservation of their heritage. Barns which would have been demolished as useless not so long ago are now offered to the Ecomusée. There are dozens of buildings stored ready for re-erection when funds become available.

Encouraged by the success of the stork–rehabilitation programme at Hunawihr, the Ecomusée also has a stork-breeding enclosure, protecting both the half-timbered houses and the storks which nest on their roofs.

Lachtelweiher and Baerenkopf

ALSACE AND
LORRAINE

From a quiet lake-side this walk leads to the summit of the Baeren-kopf (1074m) and back. The path goes through mixed woodland and open alpine meadows.

◀ *In summer walkers should be prepared for high temperatures as well as high altitudes in this region of wooded peaks and alpine meadows*

Route Directions

Start from the Auberge du Lachtelweiher at the lake of Lachtelweiher, about 5km from the village.

The path is marked with a blue rectangle and leads through beech woods and then up across meadowland to the Auberge du Lochberg ①.

Continue to reach the signpost marked Col de la Fennematt ②.

The track to the Baerenkopf is clearly indicated, turning sharp left back up a meadowland path towards beech woods. At the top of the pasture, through a coppice of beech, a red rectangle sign marks the way to the small shrine at the Col du Lochberg ③.

Here a three-way signpost points to the left through pine woods, to the Baerenkopf ④.

Continue down the path, still marked with a red rectangle, and signposted Masevaux-Sudel. It is rocky and descends very steeply, following a drystone wall ⑤.

Bear left, the path becoming smoother and wider as it dives into pine woods. Here it meets a path marked with a red-and-white rectangle. Follow this, and after about 200m, at a T-junction, take the path signposted Brückenwald/Kirchberg. Cross a small stream and a few hundred metres further on, out of the woodland, take a hairpin bend back before continuing in the original direction. The signs to follow from here are red-white-red rectangles. At the next junction carry straight on, following the red-white-red rectangles. After a gate in a wire fence the path joins a forestry road. Turn left by a blue rectangle sign on a large beech tree. The farm above the lake is now visible to the left; and the path joins a narrow gravel roadway. Return to the Auberge where there is a memorial ⑥.

Points of Interest

① Just behind the Auberge du Lochberg is a bronze plaque in memory of Francis Dolfuss, who died here, in an accident with a broken ski, on 13 January 1935.

② From the Col de la Fennematt there is an excellent view across to the Ballon d'Alsace. One path leads over the col, past the source of the River Doller, which you crossed at Masevaux, and on to another auberge.

③ The Col du Lochberg is high, open meadowland with bilberries and blackberries and views across the tops of the Vosges massif.

④ On the Baerenkopf there is a chalet refuge erected by the Club Alpin. From here a rocky path leads through beech woods to the summit at 1074m. This is an open area, but there is shade if needed.

⑤ You walk down the 'German' side of a low double drystone wall, which from 1870 to 1918 was the Franco-German frontier. Now it marks the boundary between the *départements* of Haut-Rhin and Territoire de Belfort.

⑥ At the Auberge du Lachtelweiher another cross commemorates Bernard Eugène, who died here in an accident on 1 March 1923.

The Col de la Fennematt ▼

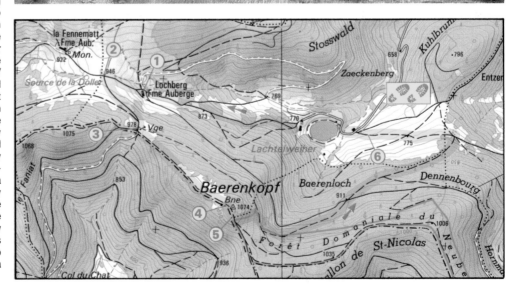

ALSACE AND
LORRAINE

Lac du Ballon

This forest trail, rocky and wild but well marked, leads to a trout-filled lake beneath the summit of Grand Ballon, at 1424m the highest peak in the Vosges.

▲ *A log footbridge is used to cross the stream at the Cascades du Seebach, which are a picturesque jumble of rocks*

Route Directions

Start from the parking space by a right-hand bend in the single-track road that leads off the D 430 le Markstein-Sengern road at the sign for Auberge Gustiberg.

An orange cross-country-skiing sign points up the track to Dauvillers: this is the track by which you return. Cross the road on to another track, leading right, dropping below the level of the road and marked with a red-white-red rectangle.

Cross a stream shortly and follow the arrow and the red-white-red marker pointing to the right, which indicate the way to the Cascades du Seebach and Lac du Ballon. This is the lowest part of the walk, so it is uphill all the way to the lake from now on. Clear markers and directional arrows help along a very overgrown path which could be slippery in wet conditions. Continue to arrive at the Cascades du Seebach ①.

Carry on across a log footbridge and along a path up to the right which leads through woods to a few rocks arranged as steps leading up on to a broad forestry road. Turn right where a sign indicates Lac du Ballon. Go up this broad forestry road and as you leave the forest there is a splendid view of Grand Ballon and its hotel ahead. Take the next fork left, marked with a red-white-red sign, which leads to steps up on to the dam wall and Lac du Ballon ②.

Cross the dam wall, past a car park, and turn sharp right, along a road signposted Lac de la Lauch – the way is marked with both a red-white-red rectangle and a blue Latin cross on a white ground. At the top of a rise, follow the Lac de la Lauch route ahead. At the next clearing leave the blue-cross sign and double back to the right, along a ski track marked with an orange sign and signposted Lac de la Lauch. A stream chatters along beside you in the forest to your left. A short way down this slope, the path turns sharply back on itself to the left. Two blue-cross signs are visible where, soon after this, the path turns right and crosses the stream. Follow a forestry road to continue gently downhill.

At a T-junction, turn right along another forestry road. There are no Club Vosgien signs on this section of the walk, but it leads straight back to the start.

Points of Interest

① The Cascades du Seebach are a slide of convoluted rocks, with little water in a dry season, but with a restraining metal barrier to stop the foolhardy risking their lives.

② Lac du Ballon lies in a small glacial hollow surrounded by pine forest. Every now and then its mirror-like calm is ruffled by leaping trout breaking the surface. As they do so they shatter the perfect image in the lake's waters of the wooded slopes of Grand Ballon, looming above (the name Ballon is derived from the Alsatian word *bolong*, meaning 'long wood'). A walk right round the lake on the sandy shingle beach takes about 20 minutes – time enough to absorb the tranquil atmosphere.

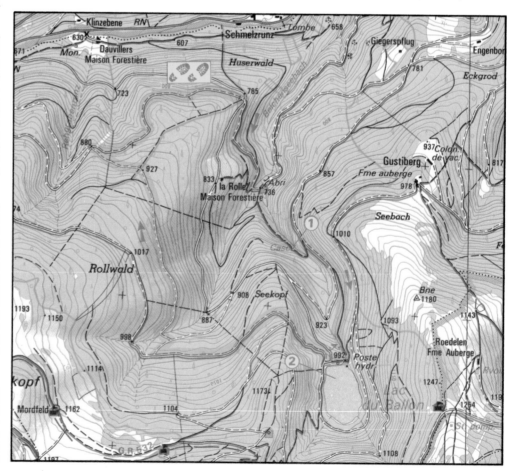

Castles and wines of Alsace

Drivers should swap over occasionally on the mountain roads of this circuit to allow each other a chance to enjoy the scenery. There are tales of silver-mining at Ste-Marie-aux-Mines and a grim reminder of the Nazis at Natzwiller/Struthof. Mont-Ste-Odile and Haut-Koenigsbourg should not be missed, and along the Route du Vin you will have to decide who drives and who enjoys the wines.

Points of Interest

① Ribeauvillé is the centre of the Alsace wine-growing region. On 'Pfiffertag', the Sunday nearest to 8 September, wine is dispensed freely at the town hall fountain during one of the largest tourist festivals in Alsace. The 'Pfifferhüs', the meeting place of the *confrérie*, founded on 31 August 1481, has an intricately carved wooden frontage. Many other houses have exquisite carvings, in both stone and wood. The 14th-century door of the church of St-Grégoire still has its original intricate wrought-ironwork and the museum houses some magnificent silver-gilt chalices. These, with the spacious ruins of the Château de St-Ulrich, bear witness to the luxurious life led by the counts of Ribeaupierre.

Do not miss Hunawihr, just south of Ribeauvillé, with its fortified church – used by both Catholic and Protestant congregations – and its

storks. A captive breeding programme was started just in time to prevent the extinction of the bird which is the emblem of Alsace.

② Silver, copper and lead have been mined at Ste-Marie-aux-Mines since the 9th century. The museum at St-Barthélémy, with its galleries and mineral collection, tells the story.

③ By a roadside stream at Noirceux is a tiny chapel, each of its modern stained-glass windows the gift of two or three local families.

④ Ample parking surrounds the observation tower at the Champ du Feu. One hundred and fifteen narrow steps lead to an equally narrow platform with room for a dozen people at a time. An orientation panel around the edge of the railing identifies the many features to be seen from this 1100m vantage point.

◄ *Vineyards at Hunawihr, one of the prettiest villages in Alsace*

Route Directions

The tour starts from Ribeauvillé ①.

Leave the town by the D 416, sign-posted Ste-Marie-aux-Mines. The road climbs up into birch and beech woods, with darker pines on the higher slopes. From the Col du Haut de Ribeauvillé the road dips down to Ste-Marie-aux-Mines ②.

Go on to the N 59, heading east along the Val d'Argent, signposted Lièpvre. Turn left on leaving the village on to the D 48 towards Rombach-le-Franc and continue on the D 48 towards the Col de Fouchy. The road passes Noirceux ③.

Continue through Villé on the D 39. At Villé turn left on to the D 424 and at St-Martin turn right on to the D 425 through Breitenbach, up towards the Col du Kreuzweg. Turn left on to the D 57 towards the Col de la Charbonnière and take the D 214 to the Champ du Feu ④.

Carry on along the D 214 towards la Rotlach, and at Croix Rouge turn left on to the D 130, signposted Natzwiller/Struthof ⑤.

Return to the D 214 and turn left

towards Klingenthal. At Klingenthal turn left on to the D 204 and soon afterwards right on to the D 216 to Boersch ⑥.

From Boersch take the D 35 to Ottrott, signposted Heiligenstein and Barr ⑦.

Continue to Mittelbergheim and turn right on to the D 425 to Andlau ⑧.

Return to the D 35 and continue to Itterswiller. Continue to Nothalten, turning right out of the village, still on the D 35, and left by the fountain towards Dambach-la-Ville ⑨.

On leaving the southern gateway of Dambach, turn right on to the D 35 towards Dieffenthal. Ortenbourg and Ramstein castles are up on the hill to your right. Continue southwards on the D 35, signposted Haut-Koenigsbourg and Ribeauvillé. Pass through Scherwiller and Châtenois. At Kintzheim take the D 159 up to Haut-Koenigsbourg ⑪.

Return to the Route du Vin, and turn right for Ribeauvillé and Bergheim ⑫.

From Bergheim the road leads back into Ribeauvillé.

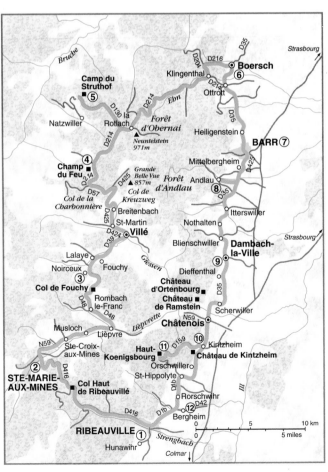

▲ *A pretty, flower-filled Renaissance well-head can be seen at Boersch*

WINES OF ALSACE

Bordeaux wines are known by the prestigious names of the châteaux which grow and bottle them. Champagne has its *marques*. Burgundy and Beaujolais take their names from villages. Alsace wines tell you from which variety of grape they are pressed – Riesling, Muscat, Sylvaner, Gewürztraminer, Tokay and the Pinots, Blanc and Noir. Six are white and the last a dry rosé or red. A Tokay or a Riesling may come from anywhere along the 120km 'Route du Vin', which extends from near Thann in the south to Marlenheim, north of Strasbourg. Individual villages have built up a reputation for producing a very high quality of wine from one or other of the grape varieties.

Alsace has the advantage that its vineyards along the Route du Vin are sheltered by the Vosges from westerly winds and enjoy a warm, dry climate with a low rainfall.

There is a wide variety of soil types, each best suited to a specific variety of grape. Of the grapes used to produce *appellation contrôlée* wines, Sylvaner yields a light, often slightly sparkling wine, the best of these grapes being grown in the light, sandy soils around Barr and Rouffach.

Pinot Blanc, or Klevner, accounts for about 10 per cent of the area under vines. Pinot Noir (1 per cent), produces the only rosé to light-red wine in Alsace. Riesling is the favourite among Alsatian wine drinkers. The oldest grape variety grown here, it marries well with *choucroute*. It grows best around Riquewihr, Ribeauvillé and Dambach-la-Ville.

Muscat is another old-established variety, producing a dry white wine not at all like the sweeter Muscat varieties grown in warmer southern vineyards. Tokay came from Hungary in the

16th century and produces a rich yellow wine, excellently suited to foie gras and red meats. Gewürztraminer has a splendid bouquet and is well suited to cheeses and some of the rich Alsatian desserts.

If in doubt in a restaurant, ask for Edelzwicker, a blend of wines which, although they might not individually have aspired to *appellation contrôlée* status, are in many cases remarkably fine in combination.

⑤ A truncated hollow white column marks the site of the only Nazi extermination camp in France, at Natzwiller/Struthof. The barrack blocks and fences have been retained as a memorial to the 10,000 who died here. Today deer browse in the forest edge nearby.

⑥ Boersch is a 14th-century walled *bourg*, its two fortified gates still the only way into the cluster of houses within the ramparts. Outside the 16th-century town hall is a Renaissance well-head, now filled with plants and flowers. In summer every village along the Route du Vin vies with its neighbours to have the most spectacular display of geraniums, begonias and petunias.

Nearby Klingenthal was the site in the 1730s of the Royal Armaments Factory, where many of the swords, bayonets and pikes were produced for the French armies.

⑦ Barr is a pleasant small town, with many traditional houses and a Renaissance town hall of 1640 in red Vosges sandstone. The Folie Marco is still as it was built in 1763, the pride but financial ruin of Félix Marco, the bailiff who built it. Now a museum, it displays local and 'Rhenish' furnishings from 1610 to 1830, and you can try the local wine in the *winstub* cellar.

⑧ The abbey at Andlau was founded around 880 by Richarde, wife of Charles le Gros, who had fled

his court after wrongfully being accused of adultery. The naïve stone frieze around the outside dates from the 1130s, and is one of the earliest examples of high-relief carving. The humour and cryptic stories can best be appreciated through binoculars – mermaids ride fish, dragons and serpents writhe, the Devil has a rope around the neck of a fraudulent wine merchant and a knight rides a dromedary.

⑨ The medieval ditch and walls still surround Dambach-la-Ville, and three gateways have survived. There are many picturesque half-timbered houses, with the wrought-iron shop signs typical of Alsace. Dambach, the largest vineyard in Alsace, is especially noted for its fine wine, and has its very own 'wine circuit' for pedestrians.

⑩ In Kintzheim's Volerie des Aigles, eagles, vultures, owls, condors and other birds of prey live and fly at liberty against the backdrop of the ruined medieval castle's courtyard.

⑪ A citadel has occupied the heights where Haut-Koenigsbourg now stands since the 12th century. The huge fortress built in 1479 was destroyed during the Thirty Years War. The ruins commanded the plain

like a romantic folly and attracted the attention of the great 19th-century restorer, Viollet-le-Duc. But in 1899 the site was presented to Kaiser Wilhelm II by the people of Sélestat. His architect, Bobo Ebhardt, restored Haut-Koenigsbourg to his own vision of a 15th-century stronghold. Some of his fantasies may not be in the best of taste, but the final result is vastly impressive. There is nothing of the theme park here – all is solid timber, Vosges sandstone and

granite, brooding over dark Teutonic forests.

⑫ After the massive bulk of Haut-Koenigsbourg, Bergheim is a tiny village, still walled, its dry moat now serving as back gardens to the wine-growers' multicoloured houses, whose courtyards front the narrow streets. The village gate, dated 1300, is still the main entrance and beside it stands a lime tree which has seen 600 years of festival and laughter, war and terror.

▼ *Haut-Koenigsbourg: a grandiose folly brooding over the forests of the Vosges*

Ortenbourg and Ramstein

Ramstein is to the right but the dangerous state of the stonework means public access is forbidden. Soon after, reach a flight of railway-sleeper steps up to the base of Ortenbourg's walls, rising sheer from the bedrock ①.

After visiting the castle ruins, return to the gateway and walk straight ahead. The path leads between hedges, signposted with a white cross to Scherwiller, and a red triangle to Dieffenthal. The path drops gently down, through oak woods, and after a quarter of an hour meets an unsignposted path. Take this path, a rocky and steeper descent, to the right. Coming out of the forest, on to a path above a vineyard, you will pick up a white-cross sign on practically the last tree on the right. Turn right. The path soon joins a surfaced road through the vines which runs along beneath the forest, turning to the left. Continue into more woodland to return to Huehnelmuehl.

Points of Interest

① A wooden fort was built at Ortenbourg around 1000, but it was rebuilt in stone around 1258 by Rudolf of Habsburg, Holy Roman Emperor. Held by Charles le Téméraire, Duke of Burgundy, from 1470 to 1474, it was burnt by the Swedes on 1 April 1633 and became the property of Scherwiller in 1920.

These are the ruins before you. Go round to the left of the castle, noting the rock faces from which much of the stone must have been quarried. A gateway with a cross-shaped arrow slit leads to a wooden staircase and bridge into the inner bailey. The massive keep, still 30m high, is surrounded by a tall curtain wall with arrow slits at each of four floor levels.

There is a magnificent view across the plain below, with Dambach-la-Ville and its church steeple, the vineyards and, away in the distance, the Black Forest.

The keep of Ramstein, built originally as a base for a siege of Ortenbourg in 1293, is visible through the arrow slits of the Ortenbourg bailey.

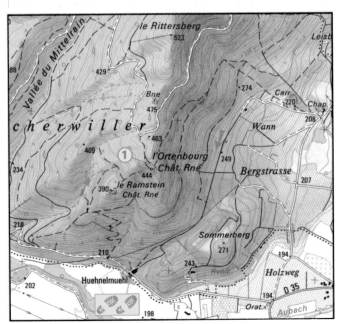

For 400 years Ortenbourg has defended the entrance to the valleys of Villé and Ste-Marie-aux-Mines. The impressive ruins and the view make this easy climb well worth while.

Route Directions

Start from the car park at the *auberge* in Huehnelmuehl.

The path through the woods is signposted Ortenbourg. It zig-zags upwards, through beech, sweet chestnut and oak woods, with rails and steps where necessary. The path passes a small Gothic building, before reaching a plateau by a signpost pointing left to Ortenbourg.

13B

ALSACE AND LORRAINE

Dreistein and the Pagan Wall

This is an easy walk along forest tracks. Best enjoyed on a bright sunny day, it passes the ruins of a 13th- and a 14th-century castle and part of the mysterious 'Pagan Wall', built by Celts some 600 years before Christ.

Route Directions

Start from the parking place by the wide S-bend on the D 426 5km south of Klingenthal.

A red X-shaped cross at the start of the path is signposted to 'Hertzthal – Dreistein: ³/₄ hour'. The path crosses a stream and climbs up through tall pine trees. At Hertzthal swing round to the left and after a few metres climb straight up the earth bank and into the forest. The track here is very steep and rugged but well marked with two X-shaped red crosses. This 'staircase' of rocks and tree roots is only 200m long, but it may feel like more! Carry straight on across the Badstube – St-Valentine path, to a signpost announcing 'Dreistein : 10 minutes' ①.

After visiting the ruins return to the path, following the red cross up into the forest to the right. At the next path crossing, take the left-hand fork

up a natural sandstone staircase towards Stollhafen ②.

The sign to follow from here is a plain red Latin cross, changing after Stollhafen to a yellow X-shaped cross. Soon afterwards, reach the Pagan Wall ③.

Carry on, with the wall to your right, to a seat at the highest point of the walk – Rocher St-Nicolas. A hundred metres further along the wall is a postern gate ④.

The path follows the course of the wall. Follow the yellow X-shaped cross to the Sentier Valentine, marked with a red Latin cross and a blue triangle. Here the path leads downwards for the first time, crossing a forestry road, to the Badstube ⑤.

From the Badstube a wide forestry road drops down to Hertzthal and the steep track back to the car park.

▼ The mysterious Pagan Wall, built out of massive blocks of solid rock

Points of Interest

① The two 13th-century castles at Dreistein belonged to the seigneurs of nearby Ratzenhausen in the 15th century and were abandoned in the 17th. Today, nature has all but reclaimed the ruins.

② Seven trails cross at Stollhafen, and there is a seat and a multiple signpost. A strangely shaped rock, looking like a cauldron on two legs, lies beside one of the paths.

③ Large, rough-hewn blocks, well over 1m in length, some with mortise joints cut into them where oak wooden tenons were used, make up the massive Pagan Wall. It runs for 10km around the top of the spur on the end of which is built Mont-Ste-Odile, following the top of steep slopes which alone would daunt many would-be attackers. It has now blended into the hillside, an enigma over which historians and archaeologists still argue.

▲ Built on a spur, Mont-Ste-Odile affords spectacular views

④ The Celts, Gauls or hermits who used the steep track leading from this postern gate down to the Badstube spring had a long, hard climb back up with their water.

⑤ In a pretty clearing to the right of the path is a stone-lined basin, still fed by the Badstube spring.

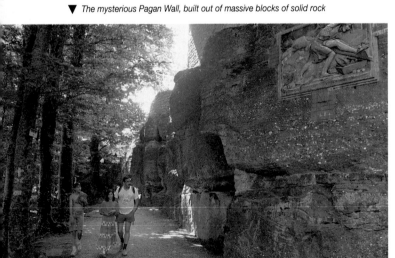

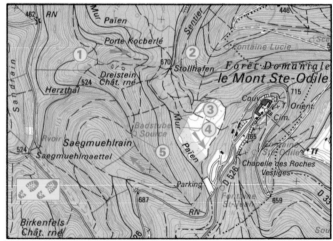

The Loire Atlantique

T he port of St-Nazaire guards the mouth of the Loire, and from here the wild Atlantic coast spreads westwards. This tour explores the rocky coastline, with its fine beaches, resorts and fishing villages, as well as the remote landscape of the salt-marshes and the Parc Naturel Régional de Brière.

Route Directions

The drive starts from the centre of St-Nazaire ①.

From the town centre follow the D 92 westwards along the coast, signposted Ville-ès-Martin and St-Marc. Then bear left on the D 292 to wind along beside the sea, passing little bays, lighthouses and holiday villas, towards Ste-Marguerite and Pornichet, where the road rejoins the D 92 ②.

From Pornichet the road skirts the bay to enter the large resort of la Baule-Escoublac ③.

Follow the road briefly inland, cross the harbour and then turn left towards le Pouliguen ④.

Leave le Pouliguen and continue round the rocky Pointe de Penchâteau, following signs for 'Le Croisic par la Côte'. The next town along this dramatic coastline is Batz-sur-Mer ⑤.

The centre of Batz is nearer the peninsula's northern shore. Fine beaches, caves and a huge German blockhouse mark the route. Follow the D 45, which rounds the peninsula, to enter le Croisic ⑥.

Blessed with a sheltered position, le Croisic is both a resort and a fishing port with a fish market ▼

Continue along the northern shore back into Batz and then, just east of the town, take a minor road to the left, signposted Kervalet ⑦.

Cross the railway and follow the road into the heart of the village. Leaving Kervalet, take the D 92 northwards across the salt-marshes towards la Turballe. At the northern edge of the marshes turn right to the old walled town of Guérande ⑧.

Turn back towards la Turballe, via le Grand Trescallan, with its calvary and marshland views. From la Turballe follow the D 99 round Pointe du Castelli to Piriac-sur-Mer ⑨.

Continue along the coast to Quimiac on the D 452 before looping south to Kercabellec and Mesquer. From Mesquer the D 52 runs inland to St-Molf and St-Lyphard ⑩.

Leave St-Lyphard on the D 47 towards Herbignac, and then at a fork either bear right on the D 51 towards la Chapelle-des-Marais ⑪, or take the left fork to Herbignac and the ruins of the 12th-century château at

▲ *A formerly isolated salt-marsh village, still largely undeveloped, Kervalet retains much of its traditional character*

Ranrouet. Leave la Chapelle to the south, taking the D 50 to cut across the Parc Naturel Régional de Brière to St-Joachim ⑫. (Turn right here for picturesque Ile de Fédrun.)

Continue south to Montoir-de-Bretagne, and turn right on the N171 to return to St-Nazaire via Trignac.

Points of Interest

① Built in the mid-19th century as a port for Nantes, which could no longer handle the largest ships, St-Nazaire developed rapidly as a shipping centre. Famous warships and passenger liners have been built here, notably the *France* and the *Normandie*. Used by the Germans during World War II as a major submarine base, the town was virtually destroyed by bombing and by the fighting in 1945. Rebuilt after the war, St-Nazaire is an interesting example of modern town planning, with spacious squares and avenues and an excellent 1957 church decorated with mosaics and stained glass. A legacy of the war is the huge concrete submarine pen, covering some 38,000 square metres and linked to the river by a covered lock, which enabled submarines to come and go safe from aerial detection.

The large port of St-Nazaire has an American war memorial of 1917 ▼

② The former salt-marsh village of Pornichet became a popular resort in the 1860s thanks to its fine beach, the start of the 8km of sand that flank the Côte d'Amour. The old town, to the south, is now hard to distinguish from the extensive modern development that has spread round the bay, although large villas hint at a smarter past.

③ Developed from nothing in the late 19th century, la Baule is now one of Brittany's top seaside resorts. Several kilometres of beach, towering modern hotels, a casino, a huge pleasure-boat harbour and a naturally mild climate due to its

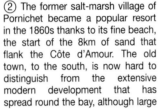

▲ *The harbour at le Croisic*

position have enabled the town to maintain its popularity.

④ Separated from la Baule by a wide navigation channel, and with its own beach and harbour, le Pouliguen retains echoes of its origins as a fishing village. Smart restaurants and shops now fill the narrow streets and the old quays, but its simpler past is underlined by the calvary and the old church with its sculpture and stained glass. Stretching westwards to le Croisic, the rocky shore, famous for its caves, is broken by little beaches.

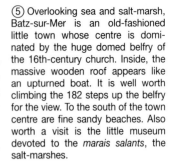

⑤ Overlooking sea and salt-marsh, Batz-sur-Mer is an old-fashioned little town whose centre is dominated by the huge domed belfry of the 16th-century church. Inside, the massive wooden roof appears like an upturned boat. It is well worth climbing the 182 steps up the belfry for the view. To the south of the town centre are fine sandy beaches. Also worth a visit is the little museum devoted to the *marais salants*, the salt-marshes.

⑥ Renowned for its setting and its views, le Croisic is a decorative and traditional fishing village which seems to cope well with its summer visitors. Terraces of old granite cottages overlook the quays and the harbour, filled with pleasure boats in summer and fishing boats out of season. Nearby are the fish market and the tall tower of the 15th- and 16th-century church, while the 17th-century town hall houses a maritime museum.

⑦ Set on a mound that rises from the flat landscape of the salt-pans, Kervalet is a traditional and largely undeveloped salt-marsh village. Little streets of old stone cottages surround the chapel, making it easy to imagine the isolated and self-contained lifestyle of the salt-marsh workers in earlier times. Tourism has made little mark here, or at Saillé, the former capital of the salt-marshes, set on an island a few kilometres to the north-east.

⑧ Built on a plateau high above the salt-marshes, the medieval town of Guérande still has its containing walls and ramparts, pierced by four fortified gateways. Streets of grey stone buildings encircle the imposing church, built between the 12th and the 16th centuries and full of Romanesque and Gothic detail. The best way to see the town is to walk round it on the walls, overlooking the narrow streets, and enjoying the views over the salt-marshes.

⑪ Housed in a typical Briéron cottage at la Chapelle-des-Marais is a museum devoted to clog making, formerly a major local industry, along with information about the Parc Naturel Régional de Brière.

⑫ St-Joachim, set at the heart of the Parc Naturel Régional de Brière, is a typical marshland village. Originally an island approachable only by boat, the village retains the atmosphere of its isolated past. There is a church with a tall spire and a calvary inside. To the west, and still accessible only via two narrow bridges, is Ile de Fédrun. This attractive island village surrounded by marshland and canals has traditional thatched cottages, some of which can be visited.

SALT-MARSHES

In Roman times the land between the le Croisic peninsula and the walled town of Guérande was covered by the sea, but changes in the water level gradually transformed this wide gulf into a huge area of salt-marsh. At the marshes' western rim this takes the form of mud-flats on which oysters, clams and other

shellfish are cultivated. However, the main local industry at least since the Middle Ages has been salt making.

The whole area is divided into a series of shallow tidal reservoirs, surrounded by clay banks and fed by the high tides via an intricate network of canals. The reservoirs are in turn divided into a chequer-board of *oeillets*, salt-pans. It is in these that the salt is formed as the sea water evaporates in the hot summer sun.

Throughout the summer and autumn the dried salt is collected from the pans and carefully raked into large mounds ready for collection.

Each pan can supply up to about 80kg of pure white salt, which is gathered from the surface, and up to about 1800kg of the more basic grey salt.

After collection, the salt is stored in warehouses or under cover in the open, and then packed for distribution. The narrow roads that cross the salt-marsh give a wonderful view of this arduous industry, particularly during the autumn when the salt is raked from the dried pans by hand. It is an extraordinary landscape of unexpected colour, filled with wild flowers, marshland birds, and there are ample opportunities to buy salt from roadside stalls.

Angers to Saumur

Through the heart of this tour runs the broad valley of the Loire, and it is the river that has determined the history of the towns, villages, castles and abbeys that line its banks. The scenery is delightfully varied, from the flat farmland of the north bank to the wooded hills and vineyards of the south, and everywhere is the decorative elegance of the carved white tufa stone.

Route Directions

The drive starts from Angers ①.

From the town centre turn south, and follow signs to Cholet along a broad dual carriageway, the N260. Cross the Rivers Authion and Loire and then turn left on to the D 748, signposted Brissac-Quincé. Soon after leaving the main road turn left on the D 751 towards Juigné-sur-Loire. From Juigné carry straight on through St-Jean-des-Mauvrets and St-Saturnin and then turn left on the D 55 towards St-Mathurin. From St-Saturnin a detour of 10km leads to the château at Brissac-Quincé ②.

Before reaching the Loire turn right on the D 132 towards St-Rémy-la-Varenne and drive through the village, following the D 952 to the abbey at St-Maur-de-Glanfeuil ③.

Here the road comes out of the woods to run beside the Loire, through le Thoureil, the starting point for the first walk, to Gennes ④.

From Gennes take the Saumur road, the D 751, along the Loire, passing through Cunault ⑤.

Go on to St-Hilaire-St-Florent ⑥.

▲ *Flower gardens adorn Angers' castle of red schist and white stone*

Carry on to Saumur ⑦.

From Saumur take the D 947 to Chinon along the south bank of the Loire, passing through the wine villages of Souzay-Champigny and Parnay, to Montsoreau ⑧.

This is the starting point for the second walk, and from here a detour of 9km can be made to the abbey at Fontevraud-l'Abbaye ⑨.

Continue beside the Loire to Candes-St-Martin.

Turn left to cross the River Vienne on the D 7, heading for Tours. The road flanks the Loire to a junction by the nuclear power station. Turn left, cross the Loire and continue north on the D 749 to Bourgueil. From Bourgueil take the Angers road, the D 35, pass through Allonnes and then at a major roundabout turn left on the N147 towards Saumur. Go straight on to the Loire and turn right to drive along the D 952, the raised embankment that borders the north shore. Do not take the N347, the newer ring road that passes to the west of Saumur. Follow the road to St-Martin-de-la-Place ⑩.

At St-Martin turn right on the D 214 towards Longué-Jumelles, cross the Authion and immediately turn left along a minor road that runs beside the river. At the second bridge turn left on the D 79 to les Rosiers ⑪.

Leave les Rosiers by the same road and then bear left on the D 59 towards Beaufort-en-Vallée. At Beaufort turn left along the N147 towards Angers and then turn right on the D 74 to Mazé and the Château de Montgeoffroy ⑫.

Rejoin the main road and continue along it to Angers.

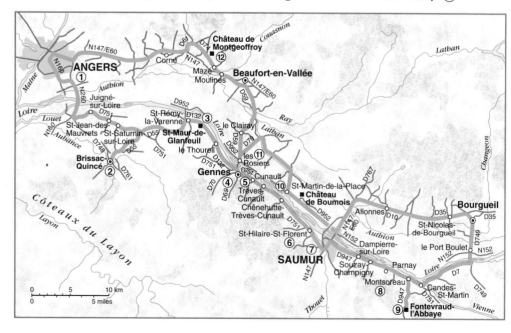

▲ *Gennes' fine Romanesque church*

Points of Interest

① Sandwiched between the Maine and the Loire, Angers is a handsome and compact city. At its heart is the great 17-towered 13th-century castle, around which are streets lined with buildings dating from the Middle Ages to the 19th century. A centre for tapestries and the wine trade, Angers is a city of white stone and grey slate, enlivened by parks and gardens.

② One of the most distinctive and yet least known of the Loire châteaux, Brissac-Quincé is a 17th-century mansion squeezed between

WINES OF THE LOIRE

The Loire is one of the great wine regions of France, producing every kind of wine from ordinary table varieties to fine *appellation contrôlée* vintages. The Loire valley from Angers to Saumur and from Saumur to Chinon is the heart of this region, with vineyards spread over the hills of the river's southern shore and across the flat plains of the north. Most Loire wines are based on Gamay, Cabernet, Sauvignon, Chenin Blanc, Breton and Pineau vines, but the constantly varying soil conditions ensure an infinite variety of results.

Passing through the heart of the vine-growing region, this tour gives ample opportunities for *dégustation,* sampling, at the many

roadside vineyards and warehouses. Among the many varieties available for tasting are the light rosés and whites of Anjou, the Saumur and Anjou reds made around Angers, the richer reds of the Bourgueil region and Chinon, the sparkling wines of Saumur and its surrounding villages, produced by the *méthode champenoise,* the dry white of St-Cyr-en-Bourg and the light red of Champigny.

Many vineyards can be visited, and the well-known makers of Saumur sparkling wine have regular tours for visitors. There is a signposted 'Route du Vin' around the region, but good starting points are the Maisons du Vin in Angers and Saumur, centres for information about the wines of the Loire.

two 15th-century towers, the remains of an earlier fortified castle. Unusually, it is still inhabited by descendants of the family that built it, and so the interiors are particularly interesting.

◀ *Left and above: Saumur's castle overlooking the Loire and the 17th-century Notre-Dame des Ardilliers*

③ Overlooking the Loire, the abbey of St-Maur is a grand classical building largely of the 17th century. Built for the Benedictines on a site that has been valued since Roman times, it incorporates important work of the 11th and 13th centuries.

④ A quiet riverside resort, Gennes has one remarkable feature, the

ruined Romanesque church set in the woods high above the town. Here is the moving memorial to the cadets of the Saumur Cavalry School who died holding the Loire against the Germans in 1940.

⑤ This flowery little village of Cunault is built around the magnificent Romanesque church, one of the best in France, and notable for its grand vaulted nave and its wealth of carved capitals, keystones and arcades. A much simpler church of the same period can be seen at Chênehutte-Trèves-Cunault.

⑥ At St-Hilaire is a mushroom museum, housed in an underground network of old tufa caves.

⑦ Traditionally a Protestant stronghold, Saumur still has a feeling of the 17th century. The famous pinnacled castle dominates the landscape and overshadows the narrow streets that run back from the handsome, tree-lined river front. Famous for its sparkling wines, its Cavalry School, its town hall and its range of museums, which include displays of horses and tanks, Saumur has great appeal.

⑧ Montsoreau's rather severe castle is the main feature of this attractive river side village. On the hills to the south extensive vineyards overlook the confluence of the Loire and the Vienne.

⑨ With its Plantagenet tombs, its Romanesque kitchen and its dramatic abbey buildings, Fontevraud is an essential place to visit for anyone wanting to appreciate the historical links between France and England.

⑩ Formerly a major Loire port, St-Martin-de-la-Place is typical of the villages on the north bank of the Loire, with old houses sheltering behind the raised embankment. There is an unusual memorial to Admiral Dupetit-Thouars, who died fighting Nelson at the Battle of Aboukir. His family owned the nearby Château de Boumois, a decorative 16th-century building marking the transition from medieval fortress to Renaissance mansion.

⑪ Les Rosiers is a pleasant riverside resort with tree-lined streets around a church whose unusual Renaissance belfry dominates the flat landscape of the northern shore.

⑫ Completed in 1779 and unaltered since, the Château de Montgeoffroy is set in attractive parkland, its classical elegance combining with its range of period interiors to express the spirit of pre-Revolutionary France.

Le Thoureil

THE LOIRE

This varied walk starts from le Thoureil, climbs gently into hills which give fine views across the vines and farmland of the Loire valley, and then passes through natural woodland before descending back down to the river.

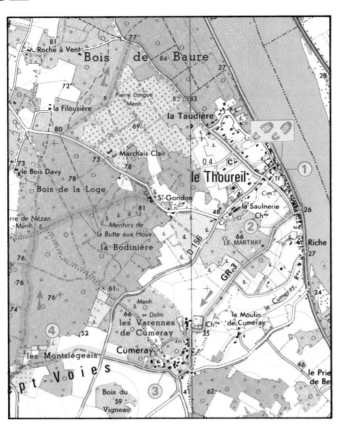

▲ Le Thoureil has a simple Romanesque church with a handsome interior

Route Directions

Start from the church, behind which there is a square with parking space, in le Thoureil ①.

Turn right and walk along the Loire. Opposite a slipway turn right up a narrow little road called Creuse Rue. This climbs quite steeply, and soon offers excellent views eastwards along the river ②.

The road drops down into a valley, passing through fields to the delightful village of Cumeray ③.

Follow the road through the village. At a T-junction turn right, leaving on the left a newish house with a standing stone in its garden. At the next junction fork left. Do not go up the branch marked with a road sign. Follow the road out of the village and up to its junction with a larger road, the D 156. Go straight on, along a track across the fields and towards some woods. Enter the woods briefly, then turn sharp right along a track that runs beside a vineyard before re-entering the woods ④.

Look out for the yellow marks painted on trees and follow the track through the woods for some distance. At the second well-defined

crossing of paths, take the right turning, marked by parallel yellow lines. After a while the path leaves the woods, to join a minor road by a house. Turn left and follow the road for some time, passing on the right a fruit farm. Where the road enters the woods, turn right on to a track indicated in yellow on a telegraph pole. This track runs along the edge of the woods and then meets a much better-defined track. This is the long-distance footpath GR 3. Turn right and follow this track, which soon becomes a road, back down to le Thoureil. At a crossroads turn left along Rue de l'Eglise, which leads back to the church.

Points of Interest

① Traditionally a port from which wines and apples were shipped to Paris, le Thoureil is now a delightfully quiet riverside village whose former significance is marked by the series of fine white stone mansions, many with carved Renaissance details, that face the Loire. In the heart of the village is the simple church with its Romanesque tower. Inside are 16th-century carvings of saints which came originally from the nearby abbey of St-Maur.

② As the road climbs above le Thoureil the broad course of the Loire valley comes into view. To the east can be seen the Ile de Gennes,

the suspension bridge that links Gennes and les Rosiers and, rising high above the woods of the southern shore, the spire of Gennes' ruined Romanesque church.

③ With its handsome white stone farmhouses, walled gardens and surrounding vineyards, Cumeray is a fine example of the attractive hidden hamlets of the Loire. Notable is the big square dovecot, with fine classical detail and an iron weathercock. Everywhere in the hamlet are gardens filled with flowers and fruit, and in the valley cattle graze beneath the poplars.

④ This walk is remarkable for its agricultural diversity. At different times of the year the tracks and roads are flanked by vines, sunflowers, fruit trees, maize, cereals and artichokes.

Charming Cumeray is a secluded and peaceful Loire valley hamlet ▼

15B

THE LOIRE

Montsoreau

Fine views, old windmills and huge expanses of vines characterise this walk, which starts and finishes in the famous Loire village of Montsoreau. The route, while it is steep in parts, mostly follows well-defined tracks, although some sections are on minor roads.

Route Directions

Start from the main square in Montsoreau ①.

Turn away from the Loire and at the end of the square take the first left, Haute Rue. Follow this for a short distance as it climbs above the village and then turn right up the steep Ruelle de la Motte. Pass on the right the farm buildings of la Motte, and at the top of the hill turn right, following a sign to the Moulin

Montsoreau's dramatic château, built in the mid-15th century, towers over the Loire and is best seen from the north bank ▶

de la Tranchée. The old windmill can be clearly seen, surrounded by a huge sea of vines ②.

Walk along the track to the mill, then follow it through the vines. At a well-defined junction take the right fork, which winds away down a hill dotted with caves ③.

This track drops down into the valley, passes the local rubbish dump and then joins the main road to Fontevraud-l'Abbaye. This is a busy road, so take care. Turn left, walk briefly along the road and then take the first right, towards an old water-mill, along a minor road signposted Fabrique de Savon. Follow the road uphill, forking right by the Fabrique de Savon, housed in a handsome old farmhouse and open to visitors. Take the road signposted Turquant, which leads up to the Moulin de la Herpinière ④.

The windmill stands at a crossroads. Turn right and then immediately leave the road to follow a track that bears left through the vineyards. (Those wanting a slightly shorter walk can stay on the road, which goes directly back to Montsoreau.) Follow the track, which curves round towards a farm marked by the base of a ruined windmill, and then turn right along a path which leads steeply downhill beside a substantial stone wall. When the track joins a minor road turn left towards Montsoreau church, and then follow the road back to the main square.

Points of Interest

① The 15th-century Château de Montsoreau, which now houses a museum devoted to the Goums (French Moroccan cavalry) and the Moroccan campaigns, dominates

▲ *One of Montsoreau's two windmills*

both the pretty village and the fine views over the village and the Loire which can be enjoyed from the hills to the south. The contrasting materials of the region, white stone and grey slate, are seen at their best in Montsoreau, where decorative architectural details enrich both the castle and the narrow streets around it. Alexandre Dumas made the château famous with his novel *La Dame de Montsoreau.*

② Montsoreau is an ideal base for the wine lover, for vineyards surround the village and to the west are a series of riverside villages famous all over the world for their wine – Parnay, Souzay, Champigny and St-Cyr-en-Bourg.

③ Scattered over the hillsides are caves formed by the excavation of white tufa stone, and the route of the walk passes a number of typical examples. Some are now used for the cultivation of mushrooms, or as wine cellars, many of which offer *dégustation,* or agricultural stores, while others lie overgrown and abandoned. Visitors must not enter these underground caves for they can be highly dangerous and in any case are private.

④ There are two windmills on this walk, both post mills, meaning that the whole body of the mill can be turned on a central post to take advantage of the wind direction. The Moulin de la Tranchée, raised high above the surrounding vines, is derelict but still has the main parts of its sails. Further on is the famous Moulin de la Herpinière, which dates back to the 15th century. Completely restored, it is open to visitors, and in the tufa cave below it is a museum of old tools and local crafts.

The Loire and the Cher, royal rivers

This tour explores the Loire and the Cher, one of the Loire's major tributaries, both of them grand rivers whose banks have witnessed the progress of history since Roman times. Châteaux dominate the route, from famous royal palaces to manor houses, representing the flowering of French architecture from the Middle Ages to the 18th century. Also exciting is the varied landscape of forest, vineyards and farmland watered by attractive little rivers such as the Beuvron and the Bavet.

Route Directions

The drive starts from Blois ①.

From the town centre head south, crossing the Loire by the old bridge and following the D 956 in the direction of Châteauroux. At a major roundabout continue on the same road towards Cellettes. From Cellettes a short diversion to the left leads to the Château de Beauregard ②.

Continue through the town, cross the River Beuvron and then turn left on the D 77 towards Cheverny. At a junction turn right on the D 765 into Cour-Cheverny. Leaving the town, follow signs to the Château de Cheverny ③.

After passing the château take the D 52 to Troussay, whose little château is set to the right of the road ④.

From Troussay continue to Cormeray, and then turn left on to the D 956 again to Contres. In the town centre turn right on to the D 30 towards Thenay and Pontlevoy ⑤.

(From Pontlevoy the D 85 leads south-east to the D 176, which in turn leads to the Roman ruins at Thésée and to Monthou-sur-Cher, the starting-point for the second walk, a tour along the Bavet valley to the Château du Gué-Péan) ⑥.

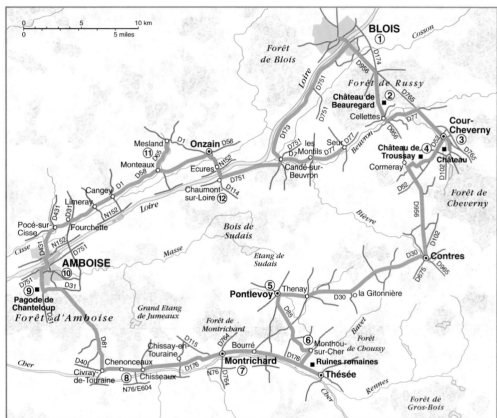

From Thésée take the D 176 along the north bank of the Cher to Montrichard ⑦, Chissay-en-Touraine, Chisseaux and Chenonceaux ⑧.

Leave Chenonceaux on the same road to Civray-de-Touraine and turn right in the village on to the D 81, a minor road that runs through the forest towards Amboise ⑨.

When this joins a main road, the D 31 turn left, first following signs to the Pagode de Chanteloup ⑩.

Drop down into Amboise. Leaving Amboise, cross the river and turn sharp right to follow the N152 along the north bank of the Loire and then immediately bear left on the D 431 towards Pocé-sur-Cisse. From Pocé

◀ *Blois, with its fine church and cathedral, occupies a formerly strategic position on the Loire*

take the D 1, following the Cisse valley to Limeray, with its interesting church, Cangey with its free-range duck farms, Monteaux, the starting point for the second walk, and Onzain. A short diversion north from Monteaux on the D 65 leads to the vineyards of the Mesland region ⑪.

At Onzain turn right and cross the Loire to Chaumont ⑫.

At the junction the château and village lie to the right. From Chaumont turn left on the D 751 to Candé-sur-Beuvron. From Candé an attractive diversion leads along the Beuvron valley on the D 7 and D 77 to les Montils and Seur. In Candé turn left and take the D 173 through the village, which leads directly to the Loire. Follow this and the D 751 along the river's south bank back to Blois.

Points of Interest

① Set high on the Loire's north bank and overlooking the fine 18th-century bridge, Blois is clearly a town with a regal tradition. Built around a square at the town's heart is the great château, a study in French architecture from the Middle Ages to the 17th century. For over a century from 1500 Blois was the centre of political and artistic life in France, and today the town retains echoes of that time. The narrow streets that run back from the river are busy, lively and full of interesting buildings of many periods, but paramount is the legacy of the Renaissance.

Busy Amboise has a château that was a royal palace until 1560 ▼

② Hidden in trees near the valley of the Beuvron, the Château de Beauregard is one of the lesser known and so more enjoyable of the Loire châteaux. Dating from the 16th and 17th centuries, it has a good Renaissance atmosphere with both royal and artistic associations. It is still lived in, and the interiors are well worth seeing.

③ Formerly a smart little hunting town on the edge of the Sologne forest, Cour-Cheverny is now devoted to the needs of tourists, who come to try the local wine and to visit the château. Dating from the 17th century, elegantly classical in white stone, and set in a rather English park, the château is atypical of the Loire region, both in its unity of style and in its fine interiors, the latter reflecting continuous owner-ship by one family to the present day. A hunting museum and a pack of hounds add to the interest of a château whose greatest virtue is its sense of grace.

④ The little fortified manor house at Troussay, somewhat overshadowed by its grand neighbour at Cheverny, is a delightful reflection of 15th- and 16th-century domestic architecture. Extensively restored in the 19th century, it is set in woodland, and its appeal is increased by a museum devoted to the vanished traditional way of life of the Sologne.

⑤ The small and peaceful town of Pontlevoy owes its existence to the grand Benedictine abbey whose buildings still fill its heart. Founded in the 11th century, and greatly expanded in later centuries, the buildings later housed a royal military academy. What remains today dates largely from the 17th and 18th centuries: huge classical façades in white stone. However, earlier work can be seen in the abbey church. There is a lorry museum in part of the abbey, and the local museum contains interesting advertisements and old photographs.

⑥ See 1 and 2 on page 70.

⑦ With its enjoyably old-world atmosphere and splendid river front, Montrichard is a fine town. The dramatic ruins of a medieval fortress stand high above it, overlooking the placid Cher and the 17th-century bridge. The town's old streets contain good shops, old houses and several interesting churches, including the tiny chapel in 1476 witnessed the marriage of the future Louis XII and the deformed Jeanne de France. In the hills behind the town are tufa caves now used as wine cellars.

⑧ Visually the most exciting and the most romantic of all the Loire châteaux, Chenonceau is uniquely the creation of three women. The first was Katherine Briçonnet, the wife of the royal financier Thomas Bohier, who masterminded the construction of the original elegant Renaissance château between 1512 and 1521. The second was Diane de Poitiers, Henri II's mistress, inspiration and business manager, who was given the château by Henri in 1547, it having passed to the royal family as payment for some of Bohier's debts. It was she who extended the building on a series of arches over the Cher, a daring architectural device, and developed the gardens.

On Henri's death the queen, Catherine de Medici, took over Chenonceau, forcing Diane to exchange her mansion for the gloomy fortress at Chaumont. Catherine added the upper storeys to the bridge, greatly expanded the parks and gardens, and left the château much as it is today.

⑨ Perhaps the most typical, and thus the most popular of all Loire towns, Amboise is packed tightly around the mound that supports the still massive remains of the château. Built at the end of the 15th century as a royal palace, Amboise represented the transition from fortress to mansion. It remained in royal hands until 1560, but from then on its decline was steady and inexorable. What remains, including the royal apartments and the Tour des Minimes, with its ramp up which horsemen could ride, is still a splendid testimony to royal ambition. The town, busy and full of visitors for much of the year, has plenty of narrow streets lined with interesting buildings, a museum of postal

▲ *The François I staircase at Blois*

history and the house in which Leonardo da Vinci spent his last years.

⑩ Set high on a wooded hill south of Amboise, the 18th-century oriental fantasy of the Pagode de Chanteloup is all that remains of a large château and park created by the Duc de Choiseul. Exiled from Versailles, Choiseul created at Chanteloup a rival centre of artistic and intellectual life, and when he returned to court he created the pagoda in appreciation of all those who had remained loyal to him during his exile. Magnificent views of the Loire valley can be had from the top of the tapered, 44m-tall pagoda.

⑪ See 3 on page 69.

⑫ Seen from the north, the Château de Chaumont looks impressive, a powerful and severe fortress set high above the river and its surrounding village, its military form only lightly softened by Renaissance detail. It was for this that Diane de Poitiers was compelled by Catherine de Medici to exchange her beloved Chenonceau.

WORTHY CITIZENS

Royal connections apart, Blois can claim several citizens of stature, two of whom are commemorated by statues in the town. Standing proudly at the head of the grand flight of steps that bears his name, and surveying the town spread below, is the statue of Denis Papin. Born near Blois in 1647, Papin fled to England to escape religious persecution, following the revocation of the Edict of Nantes in 1685. It was while in exile that he published the results of his experiments with steam cooking, work that lead directly to the development of the pressure cooker. His statue incorporates a large and complicated version of this now familiar piece of kitchen equipment. Later he carried out pioneering experiments in the use of steam as a motive force, but died unrecognised and in poverty in 1714.
Another statue in the town commemorates Robert Houdin (1805-71), scientist, writer and clockmaker, whose memory is also preserved by a room devoted to his life and work in the archaeological museum at Blois. Highly regarded for his experiments in precision timekeeping, Houdin made a number of electrical clocks that were widely exhibited in the 1850s and 1860s, along with a series of mystery clocks. An example of the latter can be seen in the château at Cheverny.

The work of a third distinguished citizen is commemorated not by a statue but by the delicious aroma of chocolate that drifts across the western part of the town. Auguste Poulain was born in Pontlevoy in 1825 and as a young man went to Paris to train in the luxury grocery trade. Later he bought a shop in Blois and set up in business as a *chocolatier artisan*. In 1848 he opened his own factory, and today this famous establishment employs a substantial workforce in the production of 33,000 tonnes of chocolate a year.

The vineyards and woods of Monteaux

THE LOIRE

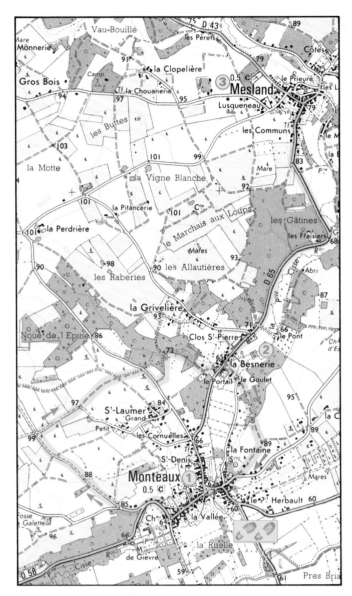

▼ *A winery near the attractive hamlet of la Besnerie*

Monteaux stands on the Cisse, and this walk explores the varied landscape of this attractive river valley, including vineyards, open farmland, old farm buildings and delightful chestnut woods. The route is partly on minor roads and partly on tracks. There are no route markers.

Route Directions

Start from the centre of Monteaux ①.

Head for Cangey, to the west, keeping the town hall and the church on the right. On reaching the château, now a winery, follow the road round to the right and then round to the left. Take the first turning on the right into Rue Marius Denis. At the first fork bear right, keeping the vineyard on the right. The road climbs up towards open fields and vineyards, becoming a track as it leaves the houses behind. Continue along the track until it meets a minor road, and then turn right. Follow the road until it bears right, and at this point carry straight on along a grassy track, keeping the poplars on the right. Walk towards the woods across the fields and when the track meets a minor road, just before the woods, turn right. After 150m take the first track on the left. This curves round to the left and then drops down into the chestnut woods. At a fork bear right, following the stream that runs through the woods. After coming out of the woods follow the track down past farm buildings and join the D 65 by the entrance to a winery. An old wine press stands on the lawn. Turn left into the hamlet of la Besnerie ②.

At this point a diversion of 2km to the north up the D 65 leads to Mesland ③.

After passing the château on the right take a track on the right, opposite a barn with two pairs of doors. The track leads past the château, offering a view of its gateway, and then crosses the Petite Cisse on a bridge, with an adjacent ford for vehicles. Continue on the track, straight up the hill and into woods, keeping the buildings on the right, to emerge from the woods high above the village. At a junction bear right towards a water-tower. The track now becomes a road which joins the D 58 and drops steeply down towards Monteaux, giving good views of the village's grey slate roofs and the woods of the Loire valley beyond. Follow this road back to the village centre.

▲ *La Besnerie boasts a small but handsome château*

Points of Interest

① A traditional farming village made the more attractive by the course through its centre of the Cisse with its series of little bridges, Monteaux is notable for its vineyards, which share the Mesland *appellation contrôlée*. Around the village are farms and wineries where the distinctive wines of the region can be purchased, one of which is in Monteaux's château.

② The hamlet of la Besnerie, with its old houses and winery, is dominated by its château, a small but elegant structure with an impressive carved stone gateway. The château is private, but a path runs beside it.

③ The small town of Mesland, famous for its wines and the carved Romanesque doorway of its church, lies 3km north of Monteaux, along the pretty Petite Cisse, and high in the hills above the Loire. The doorway of the otherwise plain church has an arch of primitive stone heads, each carved with a different style of beard, including one that is plaited. These reflect the pagan traditions associated with the village, where it used to be believed that storms could be averted by the ringing of the church bells by scantily dressed village maidens.

69

Monthou and the Château du Gué-Péan

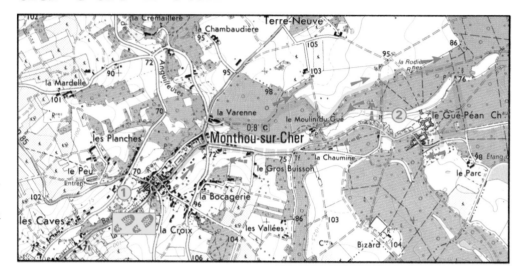

The Bavet, a tributary of the Cher, forms the backbone of this walk, which explores the woodland paths that surround the river between Monthou-sur-Cher and the Château du Gué-Péan. Most of the walk follows woodland and field paths.

Route Directions

Start from the square behind the church in Monthou-sur-Cher ①.

Turn left by the war memorial, along the Route du Château. Pass the cemetery and at the first crossroads turn left into the Route de Blois. Cross the River Bavet, and then take the first path to the right, which leads into the woods, keeping an old farm on the right. At the first fork take the left-hand, climbing path. (The right fork follows the winding course of the river to a series of bubbling ponds that mark the source of the St-Lyé stream, a pleasant spot for a picnic.) The path climbs through the woods and then drops sharply. At the edge of the woods turn right and follow a steeply descending track beside the trees, and then turn left on to a narrow track that leads back into the woods before reaching a farm set in a clearing. This farm and its riverside garden are private. The track widens as it climbs up through the woods, cutting into the hillside below the level of the fields. Follow it up until it emerges into an open field, bear right and then walk along the edge of the field. The path here is not very well defined. After about 400m, where the field edge turns to the left, go straight on into the woods, following a narrow and rather overgrown path that soon passes a ruined house on the left. The path soon becomes clearer. Follow it straight through the woods until it comes out into a clearing planted with saplings. Keep to the left edge of the clearing and then, at a junction with a larger path, take a right turn, indicated by two parallel yellow strips on a tree. Continue

▲ Gué-Péan is a fine late-Renaissance château with a secluded setting

across the clearing and cross the river on a wooden bridge. Now well-defined, the path runs straight through the woods. Keep straight on for 500m, cross over a larger track and then after another 100m turn right on to a smaller and initially overgrown path. The turning is again marked by two parallel yellow strips on a tree. The path quickly widens and passes a modern stable complex set in the woods to the left. Keep straight on and the château

comes into view. Follow the road which passes the Château du Gué-Péan ②.

This road then winds through the old stables. Keep along this road, enjoying the views of the château, and then take a track that bears right opposite a small white stone lodge. There are now two alternative routes. To follow the first, turn immediately right on to a yellow marked path that drops down into the valley, crosses the river on a rather precarious wooden bridge, and then climbs up into the woods. Where this meets the path walked along at the start, turn left back to Monthou. Alternatively, continue along the track that follows the valley. This soon joins a road that leads straight back to Monthou.

Points of Interest

① Set well back from the Cher, in the wooded hills of the river valley, Monthou-sur-Cher is a pleasant small town with many traditional buildings and a large church with a central tower, a good example of the local Romanesque style.

② Attractively situated in a wooded valley, Gué-Péan is one of the Loire's least-known treasures. It is a late-Renaissance château, elegantly built from white stone in a slightly archaic fortress style, with a grand tower that commands the valley. The interiors contain a rich variety of 17th- and 18th-century furniture and paintings, and are regularly open to visitors during the season. Another way to see the château is to stay as a bed-and-breakfast guest, a privilege rarely offered by a building of such quality.

A landscape of châteaux and rivers

This tour explores four rivers, the Loire, the Cher, the Indre and the Vienne, and the delightfully varied landscape that lies between them. It is a journey of gardens, rich farmland, vineyards and forest, and along the route are Roman remains, old ports, formidable medieval fortresses and some of the most decorative châteaux of the Loire region, such as Azay-le-Rideau, Ussé and Villandry, with its magnificent formal gardens.

Route Directions

The drive starts from Tours ①.

From the city centre take the N152 west towards Angers. After 10km turn right into Luynes ②.

Leave Luynes on the D 76 to St-Etienne-de-Chigny and make a brief diversion to the right to admire the splendid 16th-century church in the Vieux Bourg. After St-Etienne, rejoin the N152 and follow it to Cinq-Mars-la-Pile ③.

Continue to Langeais ④.

The first walk begins in Langeais. Here, cross the Loire on the big suspension bridge and then immediately turn right on to the D 16, which runs along the embankment on the Loire's south side. This leads to Bréhémont and Ile St-Martin. Just before Ile St-Martin turn left and, after crossing the Indre, drive straight on towards the fairy-tale pinnacles of the château of Ussé ⑤.

At Ussé turn right on to the D 7 and after 3km turn left on to the D 16 towards Huismes and Chinon ⑥.

This road follows the edge of the forest to Chinon, to enter the town beside the château. Leave Chinon on the D 749 to the south, crossing the Vienne, and by the railway turn left towards Richelieu. At a fork bear right towards Champigny-sur-Veude ⑦.

Before reaching Champigny a short detour to the left leads to the Château du Rivau. Continue to Richelieu ⑧.

From Richelieu take the D 757 towards l'Ile-Bouchard ⑨.

From here, a short detour west on the D 760 along the Vienne leads to the famous wall paintings in Tavant's little church. From l'Ile-Bouchard continue northwards on the D 757. A short detour can be taken to the right, on the D 21, to visit the picturesque medieval village of Crissay-sur-Manse, before rejoining the D 757 to Azay-le-Rideau ⑩.

From Azay-le-Rideau take the D 39 through Vallères to join the D 7 to Villandry ⑪.

From Villandry continue east beside the Cher to Savonnières ⑫.

Here the second walk starts. Return to Villandry and turn left on to the D 121 towards la Bernassière. Continue on this road until it meets the main Azay to Tours road, the D 751. Turn

◀ Azay-le-Rideau

left and then first right, crossing the Indre shortly before entering Saché ⑬.

From Saché a detour of 10km can be made to the picturesque basket-making village of Villaines-les-Rochers. Leave Saché on the D 17, following the valley of the Indre through Pont de Ruan, Artannes-sur-Indre and Monts. At Monts, turn left on to the D 86, which crosses the Indre. This leads straight back to Tours, entering the city from the south via Joué-lès-Tours and the Cher.

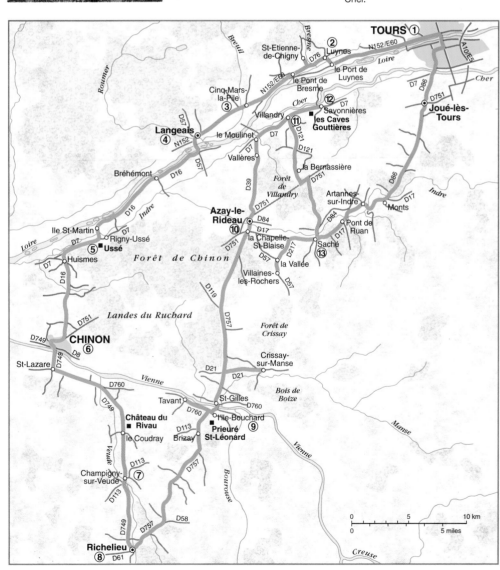

BASKETRY

Villaines-les-Rochers lies a few kilometres to the south of the Indre, midway between Azay-le-Rideau and Saché. It is a particularly attractive village, with old houses spread along a valley with gardens running down to a little river, and a good selection of troglodyte dwellings and caverns hollowed out of the flanking hillsides. However, there is more to Villaines than soft stone, flowers and an old-fashioned atmosphere, for the village has been since the 1840s a centre of basketry and wickerwork.

Much of the village is given over to this traditional craft industry, and over 50 families are actively involved. Scattered throughout the village are small workshops and studios, but the major centre of manufacturing is the large cooperative. This is a complex of workshops and warehouses with a large shop and display area and a video presentation explaining the processes. The technique, unchanged since Balzac described it in the 19th century, requires the cutting in winter of the osiers, which are stood in water until May and then stripped and prepared for working.

Skills that have been handed down within the families for generations are reflected in the variety of wares on sale, ranging from a baby's rattle to garden furniture, and every conceivable type of basket. Styles traditional and modern are well represented, both in the large cooperative shop and in the small family workshops. Villaines-les-Rochers is a perfect example of a working village, drawing its livelihood from one particular activity.

Points of Interest

① A big, bustling, commercial city, Tours is the dynamic heart of the Loire. Strategically important since Roman times, Tours later became a great religious centre and, in the 16th century, a major producer of silk. However, its real growth as an industrial centre came in the 19th century, with the railways, and much of its architecture dates from that period, notably the grand baroque-style railway station, and the town hall.

The old city is sandwiched between the Loire and the Cher, and this is the most rewarding area to explore on foot. There can be seen the cathedral, a complex Gothic structure built between the 13th and 16th centuries, with fine stained glass, the Musée des Beaux-Arts, one of the best in France, and the medieval quarter, old narrow streets of timber-framed buildings now full of interesting shops and restaurants. A lively provincial capital, Tours offers the visitor all those features of city life that are so rare elsewhere in the Loire region.

② A pleasant, old-fashioned town clustered below the severe ramparts of the 13th-century château, Luynes benefits from being off the major tourist track. Owned by the same family since the 17th century, and closed to visitors, the château is best seen from across the vineyards to the west of the town. Medieval and Renaissance houses, a wooden-roofed market and a relaxed atmosphere add to the town's appeal. In the hills to the north-east is a ruined Roman aqueduct, whose history and purpose have never been fully resolved.

③ The village of Cinq-Mars-la-Pile takes its name from the strange monument that stands on its eastern edge. This tower, 30m high, brick clad and crowned by four pinnacles, is claimed by some to be Roman and by others to be later. However, its purpose, its builder and what or whom it commemorates remain a mystery. To the north is a ruined medieval fortress, complete with towers and moat.

④ See 1 on page 73.

⑤ Set against the dark green of a steeply wooded hillside, Ussé is a romantic château of glowing white stone turrets and spires, whose decorative magnificence inspired Perrault to write *The Sleeping Beauty*. Built in the 15th century on the site of a former fortress and greatly altered in later periods, the château still has a remarkable sense of unity. Formal gardens and terraces reach down towards the Indre, and in the park is a pretty Renaissance chapel. Furniture, paintings and a collection of arms and armour make the interior worth a visit.

⑥ Famous for its history and its wine, Chinon is one of the Loire's most popular towns. In appearance it is still a medieval fortress town guarding the northernmost crossing point on the Vienne, a role it has fulfilled since Roman times. Towering above the narrow streets is the great fortress that became the seat of the royal court in 1428. Really two fortresses linked by a bridge, Chinon is a prime example of medieval military architecture, bringing to life the struggles between the French royal houses, and completely dominating its town and the 12th-century bridge it guards.

Even apart from the château Chinon is full of interest, with its medieval streets, secret courtyards, Renaissance houses, a chapel cut from the rock on which the château stands, a barrel-making museum and many festivals during the season.

⑦ Champigny-sur-Veude, a pleasant village in the wooded valley of the Veude, is totally overshadowed by the extraordinary Sainte-Chapelle, a wealth of 16th-century Renaissance decoration in white stone. A carefully balanced sense of proportion make it a delight to contemplate, while inside is a remarkable collection of 16th-century stained glass. The chapel and the buildings near it are all that remain of a magnificent 16th-century château demolished on the orders of Richelieu, who did not want his own nearby palace to be rivalled in splendour.

⑧ A remarkable example of classical town planning and a memorial to the worldly ambitions of Cardinal Richelieu, whose mighty palace stood near by, Richelieu was built from scratch early in the 17th century. Laid out on a strict grid, with grand houses in the centre and smaller ones near the perimeter for the artisans, the town has its own walls and surrounding moat, with elegant entrance gates. Of Cardinal Richelieu's great mansion only the park and a few outbuildings remain, overlooked by the great man's statue.

The best way to visit Richelieu and Champigny-sur-Veude is by steam train, along the Veude valley from Chinon.

⑨ First developed as a fortress on an island in the Vienne, l'Ile-Bouchard later became a busy trading port. Today it is a quiet provincial town, seen at its best from the river. Old houses, a church with a good tower and a 16th-century bishop's throne add to its interest, but the town's best feature is hidden to the south, by the old railway station. This is the ruined apse of the Romanesque Prieuré de St-Léonard, with remarkable carved capitals, a picturesque ruin surrounded by old farm buildings.

⑩ The Renaissance elegance of Azay-le-Rideau, half hidden by trees and rising from the waters of the Indre, must be one of the most familiar images of the Loire, and its appeal is understandable. It is a lovely, highly romantic building, an early-16th-century gem, whose small scale and careful proportions make it outstanding among châteaux that tend in many cases to be grandiose and even vulgar.

⑪ Originally a medieval fortress, the château at Villandry was first developed as a mansion in the 16th century. However, its outstanding feature is its garden. During the 19th century the owner, Dr Carvallo, created at Villandry a formal Renaissance garden marrying French and Italian styles, and nowhere can a better example of this style of garden be seen. There are three parts, a water garden, an ornamental garden and a vegetable garden, all planted in formal Renaissance patterns, their outlines formed by box arabesques, canals and paths. It is a particular pleasure to survey the formal terraces of this great masterpiece against the more natural landscape of the river valley behind.

⑫ See 1 on page 74.

⑬ The small village of Saché, set above the gentle valley of the Indre, has two claims to fame. First, it was the home for many years of the American sculptor Alexander Calder, and one of his large colourful mobiles stands in the main square. Second, the château, really a 16th-century manor house delightfully sited by the river, was owned by Balzac. Here he wrote *Le Père Goriot* and other novels. The interior has been left as Balzac knew it and houses a museum devoted to the great 19th-century writer.

The course of the Indre from Azay-le-Rideau eastwards to Montbazon is particularly attractive, the river winding its way through a lovely wooded valley, its banks dotted with mills, farms and old-fashioned villages. One of the prettiest of these is Monts, set on a hill to the south, with steep narrow streets, a main square out of an old French film and some interesting shops, including a butcher's shop with a rich art-deco-tiled façade.

Around Langeais

This short walk is a pleasant tour of Langeais and the valley of the River Roumer. The route, marked in yellow, follows minor roads, tracks and footpaths and the going is easy, but there is some gentle hill climbing.

Route Directions

Start from the château in Langeais ① and ②.

Cross the Roumer and walk up Rue Charles VIII to the church. Pass the church and climb a flight of steps. At the top turn right and after 50m turn left up another flight, the Chemin de Paradis. At the top carry straight on into the park, and turn left in the middle. There is no clear path – just head across the grass among the trees to the park's western perimeter. Turn left and walk down towards the cemetery. At the cemetery gates turn right along the road. At the crossroads go straight on, along a lane marked ominously Mortvouzet which runs along the side of a hill. There are troglodyte houses and pleasant views over the river valley, with its allotments and gardens, and the church of St-Laurent. Follow this lane as it drops down to the D 57. Here, divert to the

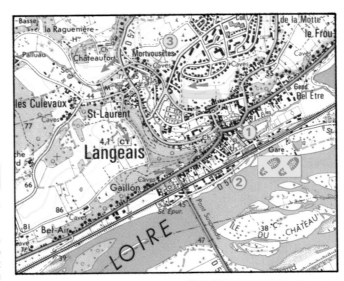

left, to visit a museum of tools and traditional crafts ③.

Cross the main road, the D 57, and follow a track that runs parallel to the Roumer. At the first junction turn left along a sandy track. Cross the river and continue to the stone bridge. Turn left at the bridge along a lane and then take the first right, la Cueille aux Prêtres. This climbs steeply uphill towards the woods, running beside the stone wall that marks the boundary of the château park. Continue to the top, where there is a junction backed by a screen of pine woods. Turn left, and follow the path as it winds down

The forbidding exterior of the château at Langeais, built between 1465 and 1469, conceals a well-furnished mansion ▼

in its centre. Close at hand are a Renaissance mansion and the church, whose tall Renaissance tower adds interest to the skyline. The fast-flowing, flower-lined Roumer runs through the centre of the town, on its way to join the Loire.

② Despite its rather severe appearance, the Château de Langeais is a domestic and delightful château, built, unusually for Loire châteaux, in just four years,

▲ *Langeais was formerly a town of some strategic importance*

through the woods. At the next junction a short detour to the right down a steep path between stone walls allows a good view of the suspension bridge and the Loire. The main path carries straight on, with more views of the Loire through the trees, and then ends at the top of some steps. Turn right down these, and follow the path as it winds down among the troglodyte houses to join the main road, Rue Anne de Bretagne. Turn left to return to the château.

Points of Interest

① Best approached from the south, across the huge Gothic-style suspension bridge, Langeais is a compact town with its château right

at the end of the 15th century. A much earlier fortress had stood on the site, and its ruined keep, still to be seen, is thought to be one of the oldest in France. Seen at its best from its inner courtyard, the château is well furnished, bringing to life the time of Charles VIII, whose marriage to Anne de Bretagne was celebrated here in 1491 and, heralded an era of peace in the Loire region.

③ Housed in the former church of St-Laurent, on the outskirts of Langeais, this museum commemorates the rural crafts of the past, with displays devoted to agriculture, barrel making, iron forging, woodwork, leather working, shoemaking and other skills. Tools, machines, relics and costumes bring to life the Loire's pre-industrial past.

THE LOIRE

17B

Around Savonnières

This varied walk explores the landscape around Savonnières, and features woodland sections, views over the valley of the Cher, pretty farming villages and a long stretch along the river bank with plenty of time for bird-watching. Except for the long flights of steps at the start of the walk, the going is easy, with much of the route on tracks and paths. Yellow markers indicate the route.

passing an old well on the left. At the next junction bear right and then at a fork take the road to the right, signposted la Bretonnière. Follow this road, keeping the water-tower on the right, to la Bretonnière. At the centre of this hamlet is a junction, next to an old well surrounded by grass and trees, much of which is on private land. Turn right and walk to the end of the houses for views across the Cher valley, and then return to the well and go straight on, following a track which borders the woods on the right.

Follow this gradually narrowing track beside the wood to the first junction, and then turn right on to a path that descends through the woods towards the river. This path ends where it meets the main road, the D 7. Cross the road and bear right to follow a track down to a flat area of grass beside the river. Cross this and take a narrow path to the right that runs through the woods bordering the Cher. Overgrown in places, this path follows the water's edge through the woods and out into open fields. Walk towards the circular pumping

▲ *Calcified stuffed animals can be seen at the complex of caves just to the west of Savonnières*

station and then follow the yellow-marked path away from the river to pass between the pumping stations, loop inland and then curve back to the river bank. The path now runs directly towards Savonnières, giving good views of the town and the river. After passing a farm full of chickens and geese it joins the main road. Turn right for the petrified grottos ②.

Turn left to return to the town and the car park.

Route Directions

Start from the stone steps at the end of the church in Savonnières ①.

Climb the steps up to the wooded hills that flank the Cher's south shore. At the top, follow the path as it bears away to the right into the woods. Keep the house on the left. After 50m, at the next junction turn left, flanking the house. This path leads out of the woods and then bears to the right, along the edge of the woods to the corner of the cemetery wall, where it meets a well-defined track. Follow this past the houses and then bear left to join a lane. Keep straight on to a junction with a larger road and turn right. At the next fork bear right towards la Boissière. At the entry to the hamlet, take the right fork, keeping the old barn on the left. Follow the road through the centre of the hamlet,

▲ *Stalactites and a preserved animal in the Savonnières caves*

Points of Interest

① Pleasantly situated beside the Cher, Savonnières dates back at least to the 5th century, although nothing remains from that time. Its oldest building is the church, whose best feature is a fine Romanesque doorway carved with animals and birds. At a later period the hills behind the town were quarried for the white tufa stone, some of which would have been transported on barges on the Cher. This river navigation ended long ago, but the remains of a lock can still be traced opposite the church. With its hotels and restaurants, Savonnières is a convenient base for visits to Villandry, Luynes and the Loire valley.

② Situated just west of Savonnières, this huge complex of caves was discovered during quarrying. There are underground rivers, lakes and waterfalls, and a fine collection of stalagmites and stalactites formed by the action of the water. The displays show the effects of petrification, along with fossils, lithographic stones and the remains of a Gallo-Roman burial ground.

The valley of the Loir

One of the least known yet most attractive of the Loire's tributaries is the Loir, whose route winds its way through woods and quiet, undulating farmland, overlooked by ruined castles and picturesque towns and villages famous for their troglodyte houses carved out of the rocky cliffs. Leaving the Loir valley, with its associations with Ronsard, the tour also explores the rich arable plains of the Gâtine Vendômois.

Route Directions

The drive starts from Vendôme ①.

Leave the town centre towards the north, cross the main course of the Loir and turn left towards Montoire-sur-le-Loir. Follow at first the D 957 along the river's north bank and then continue along the D 5 as it swings away towards Villiers-sur-Loir ②.

Continue to le Gué-du-Loir ③.

After le Gué bear left on the D 24 towards les Roches-l'Evêque ④.

For the first walk, turn left on to the D 917 in les Roches, cross the river and follow signs to Houssay, 5km to the east. Otherwise, carry on to Montoire ⑤.

From Montoire take the road south from the main square towards the château. Cross the river, turn left and drive through the woods of the Loir's south bank to Lavardin ⑥.

Leaving Lavardin, cross the river and return to Montoire along the more open north bank, enjoying the sight of Lavardin's château above the trees. Continue on this road, the D 108, straight through Montoire, and follow the D 917 to Trôo ⑦.

The road up to the old hill town is clearly signposted soon after leaving Trôo's more recent riverside part. From Trôo follow the same road, the D 917, through Sougé, and at Pont de Braye turn left on to the D 305 towards Poncé-sur-le-Loir ⑧.

This is a lovely stretch of road flanked by steep, wooded hills that can be followed as far as la Chartre-sur-le-Loir. After visiting Poncé and its château return along the same road for 1.5km and then turn right to cross the railway and the river on the D 57 towards Couture-sur-Loir ⑨.

In Couture, where the second walk starts, make a short diversion to Ronsard's birthplace, la Possonnière ⑩.

Leave Couture on the D 10 towards Artins. After passing Artins turn right at a crossroads on to the D 8 towards Ternay. (Alternatively, make

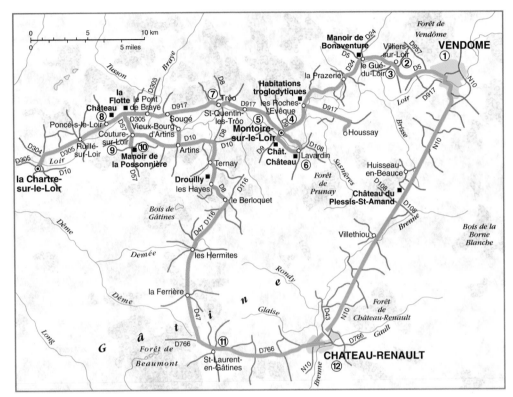

▲ *Vendôme is a handsome town on the Loir with origins dating back to before the time of the Romans*

a short detour to the left at Artins, to the pretty village of Vieux-Bourg-d'Artins, which straddles the Loir.) Ternay's unusual church with its detached tower sits in a flowery garden. Continue on the D 8 to le Berloquet and then at a junction turn right on the D 116 to les Hermites. Follow this road and the D 47 to la Ferrière. In the village turn right, then left and follow signs to St-Laurent-en-Gâtines ⑪.

At the junction with the main road turn left on to D 766, with St-Laurent's extraordinary church already in sight. Continue to Château-Renault ⑫.

Leaving Château-Renault, cross the railway and turn right along the main road, the N10, which leads straight back to Vendôme across the plains of the Gâtine Vendômois.

Points of Interest

① Famous for good food and wine, and for its fishing, Vendôme is a delightful town spread over the several branches of the Loir. Its streets are full of bridges, attractive vistas and old buildings, and high on a hill above the town is the huge ruined château, worth the climb for the views. Vendôme is the town of the 16th-century poet Ronsard and of Rochambeau, the leader of the French forces during the American War of Independence. The latter's statue in the main square is overlooked by two great towers, the 15th-century clock tower and the Romanesque belfry, which is part of, but stands separate from, the abbey of La Trinité, notable for its sculpture.

② Surrounded by fields and vineyards, Villiers is a pleasant little

◀ *Lavardin is an excellent example of a medieval village, with its twisting streets, Romanesque church of St-Genest and ruined fortress*

century detail. The large central square, complete with bandstand, leads naturally down to the river, which follows a flowery route through the town, overlooked by the ruins of the robust medieval château. Old shops, a lively market and the Chapelle de St-Gilles, with its remarkable wall paintings, all contribute to Montoire's distinctive qualities. This is provincial France at its best.

⑥ Delightfully situated by the Loir and surrounded by woods, Lavardin is a classic medieval village, complete with winding streets of old houses, a splendid Romanesque church with wall paintings to match and, crowning it all, the spectacular ruins of a château that in the 12th century resisted attacks by two English kings, Henry II and Richard Lionheart.

⑧ A typically attractive Loir village, Poncé is also blessed with a fine and richly decorative Renaissance château, whose great glory is its vaulted staircase, six flights of decorative white stonework which constitute a catalogue of Renaissance motifs. Formal gardens and a large dovecot add to the pleasures.

⑨ See 1 on page 78.

⑩ See 3 on page 78.

⑪ A remote village buried in the plains of the Gâtine Vendômois, St-Laurent-en-Gâtines is notable for its church, formerly a huge 15th-century manor, brick-built in a commanding style.

⑫ Set on a promontory overlooking the confluence of the Brenne and the Gault, Château-Renault is a pleasantly old-fashioned town with a ruined medieval castle, old riverside mills, a leather museum, a handsome main square and plenty of traditional shops and restaurants.

Montoire-sur-le-Loir benefits from an attractive setting on the river, a good view of which can be gained from the town bridge ▼

MURALS

A characteristic feature of the Loire region as a whole, and the Loir valley in particular, is the tradition of wall painting. Many churches are still decorated with murals and frescos, colourful images and scenes painted between the 12th and the 16th centuries whose survival has been helped by the gentle climate. Some of the most striking examples can be seen in the Chapelle de St-Gilles beside the Loir in Montoire, where the apses carry powerful images of Christ. Painted in the 12th and 13th centuries, these reflect the change from a formalised Byzantine-inspired design to the lively and colourful style associated with the region.

Another important series of murals can be seen in the church of St-Genest at Lavardin. Ranging in date from the 12th to the 16th century, these depict Christ's baptism and passion, heaven and hell, a tree of Jesse, St Christopher and St Margaret. Another St Christopher, of an immense size and painted in the 16th century, can be seen in the church at Villiers-sur-Loir. Other examples dating from the Romanesque period can be seen in St-Jacques-des-Guérets, directly across the river from Trôo, and at Areines, just east of Vendôme.

village whose main claim to fame is the nearby Château de Rochambeau. Set on a cliff overlooking troglodyte houses, this was the home of the marshal whose statue stands in Vendôme. He is buried in the nearby village of Thoré.

③ Built at the confluence of the Loir and the Boulon, the pretty village of le Gué-du-Loir is surrounded by water-meadows and poplars. Just to the north is the manor of la Bonaventure, with poetic associations from the Middle Ages

to the 19th-century poet Alfred de Musset.

④ Famous for its troglodyte houses, les Roches-l'Evêque is little more than a group of old houses, packed tightly against the wooded cliffs that line the Loir's north bank and surrounded by flowers.

⑤ An elegant and busy small town, Montoire-sur-le-Loir is full of decorative white stone buildings rich in Gothic, Renaissance and 17th-

⑦ Trôo is really two villages, the first a pleasant riverside settlement, and the second something much more extraordinary set on top of the hills to the north. Here are an old castle mound, with fine views over the Loir valley, a fine Romanesque church, the remains of fortifications and gateways, ancient stone houses and a speaking well. Linking the two villages are a precipitous staircase down the cliff and a mass of narrow, rocky passages that connect the houses of one of France's greatest troglodyte settlements.

An imposing square tower dominates Trôo's former collegiate church of St-Martin, which was built in 1050 and modified a century later ▶

Around Houssay

▲ *Houssay is a typical small farming community of the Loir valley*

Houssay is set on a minor tributary of the Loir, and this walk explores the farmland and gentle hills south of the river. It passes through the vineyards, open fields and patches of natural woodland that surround the village. Partly on minor roads and partly on well-defined tracks, the route is irregularly marked with red arrows.

Route Directions

Start from the town hall in Houssay ①.

Turn left up a steep lane that leads past the church. At a fork bear left. Walk towards the concrete water-tower, enjoying the good views to the west and down into the valley ahead. Pass the tower, keeping it on the right. At a path crossing turn left, flanking a copse, descend into the valley, with a view of la Soëtiverie ②.

Here the path is surfaced. At a junction turn right, and then at the next crossroads climb straight up a bumpy track, passing on the right a wooden crucifix. Continue on this track up through the woods and out through vineyards and at a crossing turn left, bordering the vineyard. Houssay church can now be seen to the left, through the trees. When the track meets a minor road turn left, and after 200m turn right along a lane marked la Serrerie. Follow this down past an old farm and when it joins another road go straight on.

(Those wanting a shorter walk can now turn left along the road back down to Houssay.) The track crosses open fields and then meets the D 67. Turn right and after 50m turn left on to another track. When this track becomes a surfaced lane go straight on, keeping the farm on the right, and then follow the track across the fields towards the stream and the woods. Before reaching the stream the track crosses another one. Turn left here, and follow the path parallel to the edge of the woods as it winds gently down into the valley,

becoming better-defined. By a cream-coloured house it joins a lane. Turn right and then immediately left before the bridge over the stream at Cran ③.

This lane leads back to Houssay, passing farms and houses, and then enters the village from the east.

Points of Interest

① Houssay is a traditional farming village, with a variety of houses of all periods and a little 19th-century church with a tall spire. Features to look out for include old bread ovens, either attached to the houses or standing by outbuildings in the garden, cellars and store-rooms excavated from the hillsides, and the precisely stacked logs, stored in readiness for the cold, damp winters.

② La Soëtiverie is a tiny farming hamlet set attractively against the steep wooded side of the valley. It is seen at its best from the path that drops down into the valley from the

▲ *An orderly log store in Houssay*

water-tower. With their squat profile and colourful woodwork, the houses are typical of the region. Some of the old barns, cut into the hillside, were formerly troglodyte dwellings.

③ A traditional group of stone-built farmhouses and barns stands by the stream at Cran, with walls covered with vines and gardens filled with flowers. In places the walls have been stained a soft purple by many years of vine spraying.

18B

In the steps of Ronsard

This walk starts in Couture-sur-Loir, in the broad river valley, and then explores the wooded hills and farmland that surround la Possonnière, Ronsard's birthplace. It is a walk with good views, and ample opportunity to see this fertile region's varied crops, farm animals, wild flowers and birds. The walk is mainly gentle but there are some hills. The route is marked erratically in blue.

▲ A bust of Ronsard (1524-85), born at la Possonnière, honours the poet's memory in Couture-sur-Loir

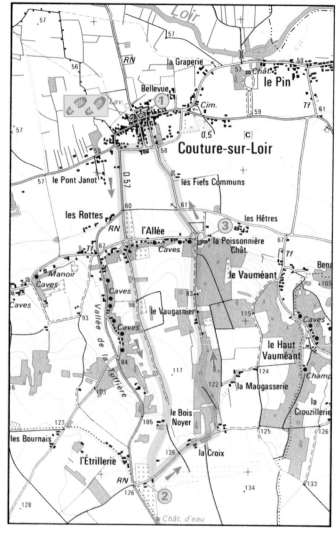

Route Directions

Start from the church in the main square in Couture-sur-Loir ①.

Turn away from the church and head south along Rue Ronsard. At the end of this road turn right opposite the town hall and pause to admire Ronsard's bust on the right. At the next road junction turn left. Follow this road, the D 57, until it bears away to the right, and then go straight on, along the edge of an apple orchard. At the next crossing go straight on uphill towards some woods, taking the left of the two lanes and keeping the stone barn on the right. The lane quickly becomes

a track, and climbs steadily. Look back for good views of the Loir valley, with the two châteaux of Poncé and la Flotte clearly visible. At the next junction continue straight on, passing on the right a painter's studio, which is open to visitors during the season. When the track meets a minor road turn left. In season, fruit can be bought from the farm on the right ②.

Follow the road to the next junction and then bear left, along the larger road, keeping the houses on the right. After 100m turn left on to a track that leads steeply down into the woods. This track drops down through the woods and then widens into a lane that leads directly to the château de la Possonnière ③.

Leaving la Possonnière, take the lane that goes straight across the fields towards Couture. At a junction go straight across the road and follow a little track, Ruelle des Petits Jardins, which passes a tennis court

and then twists and turns through the houses and backyards before emerging just by the church. Turn left back to the main square.

Points of Interest

① Set among fields well to the south of the river, Couture-sur-Loir is a pleasant farming village of quiet streets and old houses, its position framed by the distant wooded slopes of the river valley. At its centre is the church, a typical rural blend of Gothic and earlier styles. Inside are Ronsard family effigies.

② This walk is memorable for the diversity of its farming and its natural flora. At different times of year walkers can expect to see pigs, sheep, cattle, chickens, apples, vines, sunflowers, cereals, chestnuts, blackberries and a wealth of wild flowers.

③ Full of the echoes of its romantic past, la Possonnière is quite simply one of the most appealing of all the houses and châteaux of the Loire. Small and intimate, it is a lovely Renaissance manor house richly decorated with carved details and inscriptions and set in a pretty garden surrounded by picturesque barns and outbuildings. Here Pierre de Ronsard was born in 1524, and it was the fine Loir landscape in which he grew up that helped to shape his poetic vision. The house is open to visitors from time to time.

◄ Orchards bursting with splendid apples like these at Couture-sur-Loir are a frequent sight in the farming country of the Loir valley

The Sologne and the Forêt d'Orléans

E ast of Orléans the Loire winds its way through a low-lying landscape, a dividing line between the remote woods, lakes and heathland of the Sologne, which spreads far to the south, and the Forêt d'Orléans to the north. This tour explores this varied landscape, with its fine châteaux and historic churches marking the eastern limits of the Loire region.

Route Directions

The drive starts from Gien ①.

From the town centre turn south and cross the Loire, and then turn left immediately on to the D 951 which runs along the south bank, enjoying the view of Gien's waterfront. Soon the towers and spires of the château at St-Brisson-sur-Loire come into sight, ranged along the steep valley side to the south. The road passes under a canal aqueduct, and the canal then accompanies it to Châtillon-sur-Loire ②.

In Châtillon turn left, cross the canal and the Loire, and turn left again along a minor road that follows the river's north bank to Briare ③.

Climbing steeply out of the town to the north, leave Briare on the D 47 to Ouzouer-sur-Trézée ④.

At Ouzouer turn left across the canal and pass through the village on the D 45 to la Bussière ⑤.

A short detour on the D 122 to the left leads to Pont-Chevron and the Roman mosaics. From la Bussière follow signs to Montargis and Nogent and leave the town with the château on the right. Join the N7 and continue northwards towards

Much of Gien was carefully restored after it was bombed in World War II ▼

les Bézards. Turn left on to the D 56 to les Choux and Dampierre-en-Burly. In les Choux take a left turn towards Dampierre. Follow this road for 6km and at the first major crossroads turn right on to the D 44 to Montereau and Lorris ⑥.

The first walk starts from Grignon, 5km west of Lorris.

Leaving Lorris take the Sully-sur-Loire road, the D 961 south through the forest to les Bordes, and turn right along the D 952 to Châteauneuf-sur-Loire ⑦.

Bear left off the main road to reach the centre of Châteauneuf. The second walk starts here. Leave the town by the same road and immediately take a right turn on to the D 60 to Germigny-des-Prés ⑧.

Continue to St-Benoît-sur-Loire ⑨.

A turning to the right before entering the town leads to St-Benoît's old port. From St-Benoît continue along beside the Loire towards Sully ⑩.

Turn right at a crossroads on to the long bridge over the Loire, enjoying the view of Sully's château. In Sully turn left on to the Gien road, the D 951, and follow it through a low-lying Sologne landscape, passing St-Aignan-le-Jaillard, Lion-en-Sullias and St-Gondon to enter Gien from the south, passing beneath a lengthy disused railway viaduct.

Points of Interest

① Built against the steep side of a hill and ranged along the Loire, Gien looks splendid when seen from the south. A huddle of decorative buildings rise above the humpback bridge, and are crowned by the church and the château. This, the last of the Loire châteaux, dates from the 15th century and its walls feature the patterned brickwork characteristic of the region. A closer inspection of the town reveals that much of its centre, including the church, was rebuilt in the 1950s, following destruction by bombing in 1944. It is a sensitive reconstruction that retains Gien's distinctive atmosphere. Since the 1820s the town has been known as a centre for decorative ceramics, and pottery is much in evidence, both in the tourist shops and in the colourful tiled street names. The largest factory, to the west of the town, can be visited, and there is a museum with over 400 examples of the local product. Housed in the château is an international hunting museum.

② With its streets of old houses, interesting shops, little bathing beach and suspension bridge, Châtillon-sur-Loire is a pleasant riverside town. Built, like Gien, against the side of a hill, it is a town worth exploring on foot. Just to the west are the old locks that linked the canal to the Loire before the Briare aqueduct was built.

CANALS OF THE LOIRE

From prehistoric times the Loire was used as a navigation channel, but traffic and trade were always hampered by the river's currents, shifting sandbanks and changing water levels. As trade increased, the need grew for a reliable waterway link between the Loire and the Seine. The first stage in this network, the Canal de Briare, was planned by Henri IV and the Duc de Sully, and in 1605 work started on what was to be Europe's first modern canal. With its 35 locks, many constructed in pairs or even flights, and its summit level on the watershed between two rivers, it established the pattern followed by all subsequent canal engineers. The canal was opened in 1642 and its success was immediate. A steady stream of barges, hauled by teams of men, carried to Paris cargoes of wine, wood, coal, iron, fruit and vegetables and pottery.

The next canal was that opened in 1692 to link Orléans with Montargis, and so bypass a difficult stretch of the Loire navigation. Financed by the Duc d'Orléans, this was never to rival Sully's great waterway commercially, and it finally closed in 1954. More important was the Canal du Loing, built in the early 1720s to bypass the equally difficult River Loing navigation that carried barges from Montargis to the Seine. When it opened in 1723 the journey time between the Loire at Briare and Paris was reduced from several weeks to a few days.

The final link was the Canal Latéral à la Loire, completed in 1838, which carried the route southwards to Digoin, bypassing the Loire completely. This canal is remarkable for its great aqueducts, the most impressive of which is the one at Briare. Designed by Eiffel, and built in decorative iron carried on 15 masonry supports, this aqueduct was opened in 1896, replacing a former crossing of the Loire on the level. Just over 660m long, it is the largest aqueduct in the world, and its art nouveau details and decorative lamp standards make it a splendid sight, particularly after dark.

▲ *The château at Sully was built in the 17th century within the shell of a medieval fortress*

③ Briare grew up in the 17th century to serve the new canals opened since 1642 to link the Loire and the Seine. Today these waterways carry little traffic, but the series of basins and quays near the town centre is still the focus of interest. The main feature is the huge iron aqueduct that carries the canal over the Loire, an elegant structure by Eiffel that is one of the waterway wonders of the world.

④ Ouzouer-sur-Loire is an attractive farming village built on the side of a hill that rises steeply from the canal. It has a variety of early houses and a 16th-century church. Just to the north, at Pont-Chevron, is a large and austere château, a monument to 19th-century classicism. Finely furnished in a style not found commonly in the Loire, the château is also famed for the 2nd-century Roman mosaics found on the site.

⑤ Set in a flat and lightly wooded landscape, la Bussière is a pleasant small town completely dominated by its château. Colourful brickwork and decorative 17th- and 18th-century architecture distinguish the château, which stands dramatically by a lake and park created by Le Nôtre. The most famous feature of the interior is the museum of freshwater fishing.

⑥ In the days of the Capetian kings Lorris was a royal town and hunting centre, and today it is still a small town of considerable elegance. There are two handsome squares, overlooked by a Renaissance town hall and a variety of other attractive buildings, including an oak-roofed market dating from 1542. The church, a fine 12th- and 13th-century building, contains remarkable carved choir-stalls, a Renaissance organ case and other unusual fittings. To the south-west is the Etang des Bois, a woodland lake developed as a mini resort, with beaches, cafés, restaurants, picnic sites and water-sports facilities.

⑦ Although it lost the château that gave it its name two centuries ago, Châteauneuf-sur-Loire is still a handsome market town. At its heart is the 16th-century church, truncated by fire in 1940, but still containing a fine organ and an imposing Baroque mausoleum to Louis XIV's Secretary of State, Louis de la Vrillière, the builder of the château, who died in 1681. Well equipped with shops, Châteauneuf also boasts two covered markets, one a former timber boat-house converted into a market in 1854 and the other in delicate cast iron.

⑧ Visitors are drawn to the village of Germigny-des-Prés to see its church, reputedly one of the oldest in France. The first church on the site was indeed built in about 800, but what stands today is largely a 19th-century reconstruction. There is one remarkable and original feature, a 9th-century mosaic on the ceiling of the apse. Byzantine in style and representing archangels guarding the Ark of the Covenant, it probably came from Ravenna, and it survived in the building because it was hidden under layers of whitewash until its rediscovery in the 1840s. This alone makes the visit worthwhile; the rest is an exercise in academic fantasy.

⑨ St-Benoît-sur-Loire's abbey is one of the foremost Romanesque religious buildings in France. Founded in 651, the present abbey dates mostly from the 10th and 11th centuries. Originally a large and influential institution, the abbey was virtually derelict after the Revolution. Over the last hundred years it has been carefully brought back to life, and the Benedictine monks returned in 1944. Extensive restoration has not affected its remarkable Romanesque features, which include the multi-columned porch with its splendid carved capitals. Set at the end of a tree-lined avenue, the abbey is a memorable sight in a quiet little town well away from the main tourist routes.

⑩ Approached across the river from the north, Sully-sur-Loire is a magnificent sight. The château, seemingly floating in its moat, is a prime example of a decorative mansion inserted into a medieval fortress. Built by the Duc de Sully in the 17th century, it is a delight in colour and architectural detail, completely dominating the little town. Three periods of history are revealed by the interior. The first is the Middle Ages, with its Joan of Arc associations, the second the rebuilding from 1602 by Sully, and the third the 18th century, when Voltaire, in exile here, turned it into a cultural centre. The strongest link with medieval times is the Great Hall, whose chestnut roof, dating from 1363, is one of the finest to have survived in good condition from the Middle Ages.

The Canal d'Orléans

This walk follows the course of the disused Canal d'Orléans through a varied landscape of farmland, woodland and lakes and then explores the eastern fringes of the Forêt d'Orléans. Much of the route is along well-defined tracks and forest paths, large parts of which are sections of the long-distance footpath GR 3. These are marked in red and white. The going is generally easy and level.

left that runs through the woods along the lakeside. For this section, follow the red-and-white markers as the path skirts the lake for some distance and then bears left into the forest. When the path meets a road turn left. This road, which has good grassy verges, runs straight through the forest, leading back to the little bridge crossed earlier. Cross the bridge again, and turn immediately left along the raised grassy bank of the waterway, the Rigole de Courpalette. When this meets the canal turn right along the towpath. At the lock and bridge cross the canal, pass the towpath on the other side and take the first track on the right, away from the road but parallel to the canal. Follow this track as it bears away from the canal and into a more open landscape. Cross the

fields with a good view of the raised, tree-lined route of the canal on the right. The track then becomes a road and enters the village, passing old farms and cottages. At the crossroads turn right to the lock and the centre of Grignon.

Points of Interest

① The attractive village of Grignon is well situated beside a lake that was incorporated into the Canal d'Orléans when it was being built. The canal at this point makes a right-angled turn to the north-west, climbing through the lake via a series of three locks, its major engineering feature. Old lock-side cottages and restaurants add to the atmosphere and in the summer

▲ *The canalside village of Grignon*

fishermen and visitors bring this quiet farming village to life.

② Completed in 1692 and built by the Duc d'Orléans to provide a reliable link between the Loire near Orléans and the Canal de Briare, the Canal d'Orléans was part of an extensive network of 17th- and early-18th-century waterways connecting the Seine and the Loire. Barges using the 79km route, with its 28 locks, carried timber, building materials, agricultural produce and other cargoes, but traffic was never heavy, particularly after the Loire itself had ceased to be used as a river navigation in the early 19th century. Never modernised, the canal decayed quietly until its final closure in 1954. Today its quiet, rural route is enjoyed by walkers and fishermen, while its broken locks recall busier times.

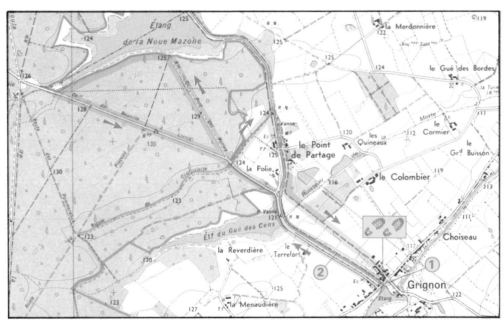

Route Directions

The 17th-century Canal d'Orléans, built as part of the canal system linking the Seine and the Loire, flows through the pleasant farming village of Grignon ▼

Start from the lock in the centre of Grignon ①.

Walk north along the towpath ②.

Running parallel to the Châtenoy road, the towpath is grassy and pleasantly shady. Follow the canal as it curves past the Étang du Gué des Cens and then, where the road divides, take the left fork away from the canal. The road enters the edge of the forest and then crosses a little bridge. Soon after the bridge there is another fork. Bear right on to a forest track, signposted Étang de la Noue Mazone and well marked with red-and-white GR (Grande Randonnée) bars. Follow this track through the forest to the lake's edge and then take a smaller path to the

19B

THE LOIRE

Around Châteauneuf-sur-Loire

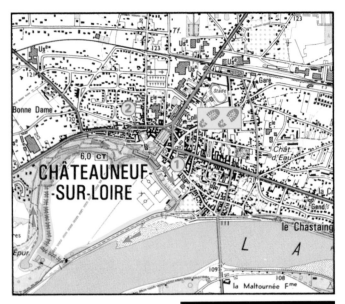

Châteauneuf-sur-Loire is the centre of a series of well-signposted walks that explore the town and its parks, the banks of the Loire and the surrounding woodland, ranging in length from 3km to 19km. The shortest, the Circuit de l'Herbe Vertex, is an easy-going tour of Châteauneuf, its château park and its river-bank, with enjoyable views and ample opportunities for a peaceful picnic.

the last bridge before the moat and follow a path that slopes up to the top of the walls and on to the lawns of the town hall and the maritime museum ②.)

Points of Interest

① Dating originally from the 10th century and at one time a royal residence, the château fell into ruins during the 16th century. It was bought in 1646 by Louis de la Vrillière, Louis XIV's Secretary of State, and extravagantly rebuilt to rival Versailles, only to be destroyed again after the Revolution. The orangery, stables and other outbuildings survived and these now house the town hall and the maritime museum. In the 1820s the grounds were landscaped in the English manner, with rhododendrons and other exotic trees and shrubs, and today these decorative woodlands and riverside paths form a delightful haven for wildlife, and a contrast to the formal grandeur of the remains of the château.

② Housed in the former rotunda of the château, the Musée de la Marine de Loire tells the history of navigation on the Loire and its connecting rivers from prehistoric times to the early steamboats of the 1830s. Models, drawings and artefacts bring to life the heyday of Loire navigation and the people involved in this major industry, which died out in the 1840s.

Informal gardens, landscaped in the English style, complement the remains of the château at Châteauneuf-sur-Loire ▼

Route Directions

Start from the iron gates of the former château in Châteauneuf-sur-Loire ①.

Walk up the formal drive, passing the Resistance memorial on the left and the town hall on the right. Descend the grand flight of steps that crosses the moat and then turn left along a tree-lined path that passes the sports field. At the gates turn right down to the Loire, and then turn right along the river bank. This is a broad riverside walk lined with grass and trees and supplied with picnic tables and children's play equipment. It is backed by an old wall which hides the town, but there are excellent river views. At the first fork bear right away from the river. (Keep straight on beside the river for two longer walks, the Circuit du Grand Val, 6.5km, and the Circuit de Gavereau, 9km.) Follow the track away from the river and up on to the raised embankment with its fine views of the town and church across the fields. To the left are woods and hidden ponds. At the next fork bear right back towards the town, the path now winding its way through the trees beside the streams and ponds. Follow the path straight on. To the left, across a bridge, is a children's play area. The path leads back to the château park, the moat and the grand steps. (For a route that avoids the steps, turn left over

Versailles and the Forêt de Rambouillet

The fertile open countryside east of Versailles contrasts with the richly wooded Forêt de Rambouillet on this tour. The route passes not only several of the historic buildings in the area, including royal residences and an ancient abbey, but also some of its charming rustic sights.

The South Parterre gives a splendid view of Versailles

turning right at the main junction. After a further 3km fork left on to the D 91 and descend the winding road into les Vaux de Cernay ⑤.

Continue along the D 91 to the Château de Dampierre ⑥.

Continue along the same road and turn left after 7km on to a tree shaded road signposted Abbaye de Port-Royal-des-Champs ⑦.

Rejoin the D 91 and turn left to return to Versailles.

Points of Interest

① Louis XIV's grandiose palace of Versailles, along with its spacious gardens and extensive grounds, its an essential stop on any tourist itinerary. A comprehensive programme of restoration, carried out over the past century, has restored the building and its

Marsy's Bassin de Latone was, in 1670, the first marble sculpture to adorn Versailles' formal gardens ▶

contents to much of its original glory. The adjoining town, with its imposing avenues and regular streets, has also undergone extensive renovation.

② Montfort-l'Amaury is a charming and picturesque fortified town dating back to the 11th century, with cobbled streets and some hlstoric buildings. These include a 15th-century prison in Rue de Paris, the

Route Directions

The drive starts from Versailles ①.

From Versailles town centre take the D 91, turning right on to the N286 before joining the N12, signposted Houdan and Dreux. After 18km turn left on to a small country road, the D 76, bordered by open fields and signposted Montfort-l'Amaury ②.

From Montfort follow signs for St-Léger-en-Yvelines on the D 138 through the Forêt de Rambouillet. Take the D 936 to Rambouillet ③.

From the town follow 'Toutes Directions' signs, and take the N306 for 6km before turning right on to the D 27, signposted Clairefontaine-en-Yvelines. After 5km turn left on to the D 72 to reach la Celle-les-Bordes ④.

At the edge of the village bear left on to the D 61. Rejoin the N306 by

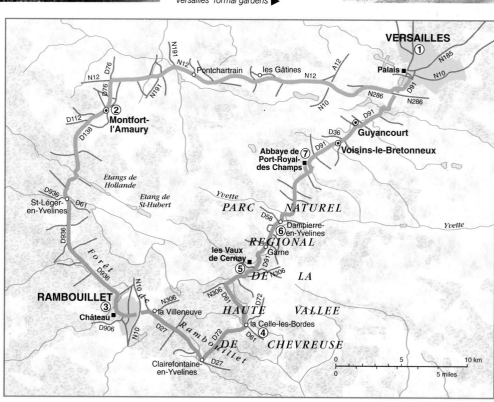

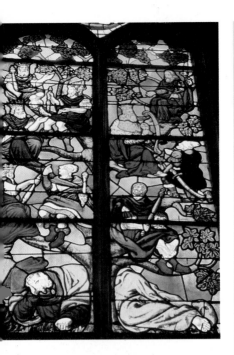

▲ *Renaissance stained-glass windows adorn Montfort-l'Amaury's church*

VERSAILLES AND THE FORET DE RAMBOUILLET

Like most other capital cities, Paris has long since expanded beyond its original boundaries. Thanks to the ever-growing network of motorways and railways which now radiate from its centre, even the small towns and villages of the adjoining region have been drawn under its influence. Many of the hamlets which less than 100 years ago were relatively isolated from events in the capital, and depended on local industries and agriculture for their livelihood, have since undergone a dramatic transformation, largely as the result of the recent development of transport.

In many villages only a comparatively small number of permanent residents are still engaged in providing locally made goods and services. The majority now commute into central Paris each day on the excellent system of public transport. Others, based in the city, own small properties in these more attractive areas of the countryside, to which they travel at weekends and on public holidays.

As a result, some of the smaller villages no longer boast amenities which would be considered essential by other communities. Local shops have been replaced by mobile shops carrying groceries and supplies, and the formerly ubiquitous bar-restaurant no longer exists. Although the village church still stands intact, services are conducted at intervals by a priest who visits each on a rota system.

main road now crosses the embankment of the tranquil millpond of the Moulin des Roches.

⑥ The elegant red-brick and stone château at Dampierre-en-Yvelines was commissioned by the Duc de Chevreuse, and built by Hardouin-Mansart during the closing years of the 17th century, in tribute to Versailles. The château and its formal ornamental gardens by Le Nôtre stand out dramatically against the densely wooded slopes behind. The building contains beautifully preserved examples of both 17th- and 18th-century furnishings.

⑦ The famous Cistercian abbey of Port-Royal-des-Champs was founded in 1204. During the 17th century its Jansenist nuns became involved in a bitter 60-year struggle with the Jesuits, at whose instigation in 1710 Louis XIV ordered the nuns' eviction and the destruction of the abbey buildings. Only the dovecot survives intact, along with the base of the pillars and walls of the abbey church. A small oratory stands on the former site of the chancel, and a nearby 17th-century barn is now a museum of artefacts relating to the abbey's history.

former home of the composer Maurice Ravel (now a museum), and the turreted ruins of the original fortress on a hill overlooking the town, from where there are panoramic views of the surrounding forest.

③ Architecturally unadorned, and dwarfed in size by its offices and stables, the royal château at Rambouillet was owned from the 14th to the 18th century by the d'Angennes family. In 1783 it was purchased by Louis XVI as a base for hunting in the surrounding forest. To please Marie-Antoinette he arranged for the construction of the Laiterie de la Reine, the Queen's Dairy, in the park and also established the National Sheep Farm nearby. These, along with the Chaumière des Coquillages, Seashell Cottage, and the tranquil lakes and islands adjoining the formal gardens, offer ample reward for a gentle stroll around the grounds. The château itself was used recently as the setting for the French soap opera *Châteauvallon,* and since 1897 has been the official summer residence of the Presidents of France.

④ La Celle-les-Bordes is a delightful hamlet set in the heart of the Forêt de Rambouillet and the Celle valley. It boasts a brick and stone manor house that dates from 1610 and was occupied in the early part of the present century by the Duchesse d'Uzès. Until her death in 1933 she indulged her passion for hunting in the area, and the interior of the building is decorated with 2400 sets of antlers from deer killed by her hounds.

⑤ The Vaux de Cernay is one of the most attractive parts of the area. This narrow, wooded valley with its clear stream and rock-strewn cascades has long been a favourite spot for landscape painters. The monks of the nearby abbey, which was founded in the 12th century, created a vivarium by damming the waters further up the valley, and the

The château at Rambouillet is set in attractive formal gardens incorporating a landscaped garden, an avenue of swamp cypresses and a water garden ▶

Rambouillet is unusual among French former royal residences, for it is comparatively modest in size. Originally built in the 14th century, it was substantially enlarged by Louis XVI ▼

Montfort-l'Amaury

ILE DE FRANCE

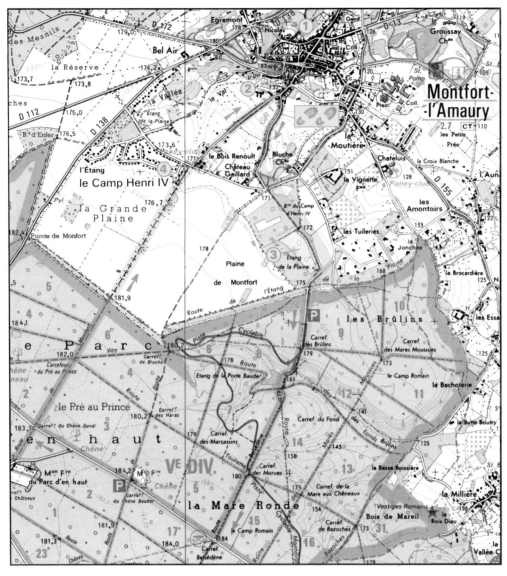

▲ *The Tour de la Duchesse Anne gives a good view of Montfort-l'Amaury*

Cross the road directly into Route du Bois Renoult and return to Place de la Libération via Rue de Sance.

Points of Interest

① This small villa, La Belvédère, was the home of the composer Maurice Ravel between 1920 and 1937, and was altered structurally to suit his small stature. It was here that he wrote several major works, including *Boléro* and *Daphnis et Chloé.*

② Two segments of stone wall are all that remain of the keep of the original 11th-century fortress, while the ruined tower dates from the 15th-century building commissioned by Duchesse Anne de Bretagne. The château ruins provided Victor Hugo with the inspiration for the *Ode aux Ruines de Montfort,* written in 1825.

③ This peaceful lake is one of more than 20 similar expanses of water scattered across the Forêt de Rambouillet. Popular with anglers, they also provide sustenance for the deer and other small mammals and birds who inhabit these woodlands.

④ Henry IV, the first of the Bourbon kings of France, and his army camped briefly on the plain below Montfort-l'Amaury during his unsuccessful siege of Paris in 1589, towards the end of the bitter Wars of Religion.

This circular walk starts in the delightful medieval fortress town of Montfort-l'Amaury and passes through attractive deciduous woodland. It skirts on the way two of the tranquil natural lakes which are part of the attraction of the Forêt de Rambouillet. The lakes of which there are more than 20, attract a variety of wildlife.

Route Directions

Start from Place de la Libération in Montfort-l'Amaury.

Facing away from the church's main entrance, ascend the hill and bear left towards the Musée Maurice-Ravel ①.
Enter the gardens surrounding the Tour de la Duchesse Anne de Bretagne and climb the winding path to reach the tower ②.

After viewing the surrounding area, retrace the path to the entrance to the gardens and follow for 100m the road signposted Houdan. Just before the Musée Maurice-Ravel, turn down the winding, steep and unpaved Rue Boutel, which emerges in the square at the foot of the hill. Turn left and follow the Chemin du Château Gaillard, taking the first turning on the left, which runs alongside the grounds of the Château Bluche. At the junction with Rue Bertrand du Guesclin go straight across and pass through the wooden barrier on to the bridle-path, which bears red-and-white GR 1

markings. After a few hundred metres the path runs alongside the attractive shores of Etang de la Plaine ③.

It then joins a narrow road leading to the right, which peters out into a sloping, sandy path still bearing GR 1 markings. Follow these signs past the Etang de la Porte Baudet and continue along the straight bridle-path into the forest for 1km. At the signposted Carrefour Belsédène, with its leisure area, turn right along the straight gravelled road for 1.5km to the Carrefour du Chêne Duval and its junction with Route de Montfort. Turn right and follow this straight track for 2km, emerging from the woodland and on to the gently sloping plain. The track passes a new housing development and ends at Rue du Vert Galant. Look out for a stone on the opposite side of the road, a few metres to the left, which marks the campsite of Henri IV ④.

Château de Rambouillet

This walk is a pleasant and undemanding stroll around the water gardens and beautifully maintained park of the Château de Rambouillet, set in the historic forest of the same name. The wide expanses of water and the densely wooded landscape form a pleasing contrast with the château and its fine classical gardens.

Route Directions

Start from the car park in front of the town hall in Rambouillet.

After entering the ornamental gardens of the château, approach the terrace bordering the lake and turn left, taking the gravelled path which leads to the round-ended basin, le Rondeau. Follow the path around the basin and along the lake, leaving the château

behind you. At the corner of the lake carry straight on up the gentle slope bordering the D 906. After 600m the path turns sharp right and after another 100m reaches the Tapis Vert, to give a splendid view of the château on the other side of the lake. Continue along the path and bear right after 650m, descending the slope to the edge of the winding rivulet which feeds the lake and runs alongside the Jardin Anglais ①.

Cross a small bridge to the Chaumière des Coquillages ②.

Continue along the path to the edge of the lake and turn left to reach the edge of the Jardin Anglais, passing the Grotte des Deux Amants ③.

Cross the road and follow the signposted route to the Laiterie de la Reine ④.

On emerging past the gatehouse turn left and climb the slope along the bridle-path to the Etang de la Faisanderie. To the left can be seen the Bergerie Nationale ⑤.

Turn sharp right along Route de la Ferme, which runs through the wooded Grand Parc and back to the lake. Turn left and, keeping the water on the right, return to the château gardens and the car park.

Seashells adorn the walls of one room in the Chaumière des Coquillages, built by Penthièvre in Rambouillet's landscape garden for the Princesse de Lamballe ▶

Points of Interest

① Created for the widowed Princesse de Lamballe, a close friend of Marie-Antoinette, this area to the south-west of the château was remodelled to become a 'natural' landscape of winding rivulets and follies.

② One of the few remaining follies in the grounds, the tiny Sea-shell Cottage contains one room entirely encrusted with a remarkable variety of sea-shells and mother-of-pearl, an undertaking which took 10 years to complete. The adjoining boudoir has panelling decorated with delicate paintings of birds and flowers.

③ It is hard to imagine that this shallow cave could ever have been a trysting place for aristocratic lovers, but the shaded paths leading to it and the nearby Jardin Anglais

certainly lend a romantic aura to this part of the château's grounds.

④ One of the last great garden pavilions to be built at the end of the 18th century, the Queen's Dairy was designed in the style of a classical temple. In the central rotunda Marie-Antoinette, in her make-believe role of milkmaid, made cheeses in Sèvres porcelain containers on the marble slab. The adjoining room is a grotto, with fountains to cool the milk churns. A small statue by Pierre Julien, *La Chevrière (The Goat Girl)*, stands in a niche.

⑤ The National Sheep Farm was founded here by Louis XVI, initially with a flock of 42 Merino rams and 334 ewes, which were purchased in Spain and herded here on foot by their own shepherds in a journey taking more than four months. Their less footsore descendants can still be seen thriving here.

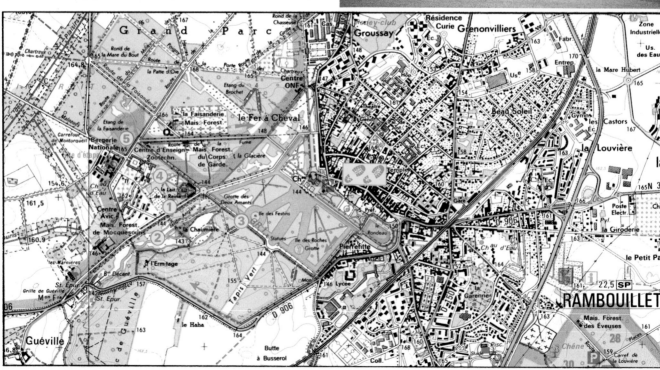

TOUR 21: 116KM

The Forêt de Fontainebleau

ILE DE FRANCE

The rich woodland of the Forêt de Fontainebleau provides a constant leafy backdrop to this tour. The route embraces some of the outstanding châteaux of the area, including the Renaissance palace of François I, as well as the small towns and villages which adorn the outskirts of the forest.

Route Directions

The drive starts from Fontainebleau ①.

From Place du Général de Gaulle take the N7, signposted Paris. Turn left along the D 64, following signs for Barbizon ②.

Barbizon's Auberge du Père Ganne ▼

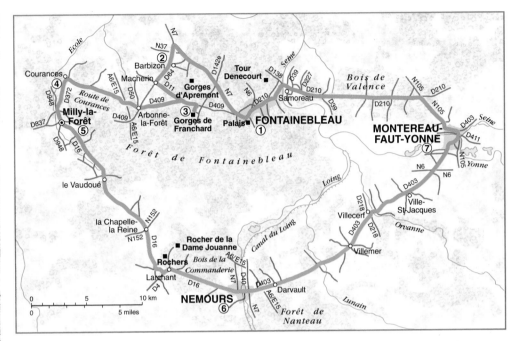

The grandeur of Fontainebleau can be appreciated from the Cour des Adieux, formerly used for parades and tournaments because of its spaciousness ▼

From the village turn left back on to the D 64 signposted Arbonne-la-Forêt. After 2km, at the junction in the hamlet of Macherin, turn left on to the D 11, signposted Fontaine-bleau. Continue along this road for approximately 4.5km and then turn right on to the forest track and follow signs to the car park for the Gorges de Franchard ③.

On returning to the D 409, turn left towards Arbonne-la-Forêt. On reaching Arbonne turn right on to the D 50, signposted Melun, and after 150m turn left into Route de Courances. This wooded lane leads, after 8km, to the privately owned château ④.

Leave the village on the D 372, signposted Milly-la-Forêt ⑤.

From Milly follow the D 16 to Nemours ⑥.

Leaving Nemours, take the D 403, signposted Montereau-Faut-Yonne ⑦.

Leaving Montereau, cross the bridge and bear left on to the N105, signposted Melun. After 5km turn left on to the D 210, signposted Fontainebleau, and return to the starting-point.

87

Points of Interest

① Fontainebleau, François I's beautiful Renaissance palace, lies at the heart of the Forêt de Fontainebleau, and shares its charm and tranquility. The graceful and elegant frontage, with its sweeping horseshoe-shaped staircase, stands at the end of one of five courtyards which divide the original palace from buildings added by succeeding monarchs. The surrounding formal gardens, laid out by Le Nôtre, are carefully maintained, and their colourful displays are complemented by the plumage of a flock of tame peacocks.

② The long main street of Barbizon is lined with houses, villas, restaurants and hotels that nearly all bear a plaque commemorating the painters and writers who stayed here during the 19th century. The Barbizon School of painters, the most famous of whom are Théodore Rousseau and Jean-François Millet, drew their inspiration from the natural landscapes of the surrounding forest. They also left their mark on the Auberge du Père Ganne. This former grocer's shop, which offered cheap lodgings and became an informal meeting place for the artists, still boasts items of furniture decorated by them.

③ Weathering of the underlying sand and limestone of this part of the Forêt de Fontainebleau has produced a number of wooded, rocky outcrops, topped by oddly shaped boulders and caves, and overlooking the deep Gorges de Franchard. Clearly marked paths provide a link between the most interesting sites and panoramic viewpoints from which the countryside can be surveyed.

④ The approach to the Château de Courances is spectacular: a long, straight drive between two

▲ *A fine Renaissance doorway adorns the church of Notre-Dame et St-Loup in Montereau-Faut-Yonne*

canals and avenues of 200-year-old plane trees. The handsome brick and stone building, with its horseshoe-shaped staircase copied from the one at Fontainebleau, was built in the 16th century and remodelled later by Le Nôtre, who also laid out the spacious gardens.

⑤ The fashionable little village of Milly-la-Forêt has numbered Christian Dior and Jean Cocteau among its residents, but is equally renowned for the cultivation of medicinal herbs, including peppermint and other aromatic plants. The covered market hall, constructed entirely of oak and chestnut, dates back to the end of the Hundred Years War and was built to encourage a resurgence of trade following the upheavals of the period.

⑥ In its pleasant setting on the River Loing and surrounded by the woods from which it derived its name in Roman times, Nemours was fortified in the Middle Ages. The imposing château dates back to the 12th century, with additional architectural decoration from the 15th century, and houses a museum containing archaeological exhibits from the town's earliest history to medieval times.

⑦ Situated at the confluence of the Seine and the Yonne, Montereau-Faut-Yonne, an important and formerly fortified town, was the site of Napoleon's final assaults on the Austro-Prussian armies in 1814. The doorway of the collegiate church of Notre-Dame et St-Loup, beside the bridge, displays some fine carved Renaissance panels. Across the road, the former main post office now houses an exhibition of the pottery for which Montereau was famed in the 18th century.

FORET DE FONTAINEBLEAU

The tranquillity of the great forests near Paris conceals the tremendous efforts of foresters over many decades to ensure their preservation and health. Left to

themselves, the forests would inevitably deteriorate, but a long-term rotational process of felling for commercial purposes, followed by careful replanting, enables selected areas to be regenerated.

First conifers, usually Scots pines, are planted, their roots acting as a barrier against erosion of the sandy soil during periods of heavy rainfall. The needles they shed also provide a basis for the subsequent planting of deciduous seedlings, when the fully grown pines have been cut down and removed. The resulting groves of beech, birch, hornbeam and chestnut in turn increase the fertility of the soil, and are then similarly exploited to provide room for the magnificent oak trees which are an outstanding feature of both

the Fontainebleau and Rambouillet forests. At their prime, they can reach a height of 40m, with a diameter of 1m at their base.

Travelling across this region by car, or walking through the woodlands, it is possible to see this gradual and lengthy process of reafforestation taking place, under the direction and control of the French Forestry Commission (ONF), which has been responsible for the management of these state forests for the past three decades.

The Gorges d'Apremont

ILE DE FRANCE

This is a fairly easy walk along part of the Gorges d'Apremont, followed by a steep climb to a wooded plateau with curiously shaped boulders, from where there are extensive views of the surrounding unspoiled Forêt de Fontainebleau.

Route Directions

Start from the east end of Grande Rue in Barbizon.

Parking is available here, on the outskirts of the village, by the entrance to the Club Bizas. Turn right and enter the forest on the wide, sandy path, following the blue signs on the trees. The path slopes gently downwards and reaches a water-tower by a small paddock. Turn left along the path which is signposted to indicate the division between sections 720 and 721 of the forest. After 500m bear left and continue for another 600m along the foot of an escarpment before turning left and climbing the steep slope to the top of the plateau. At the top bear right, and, following the path, pass through an area of weathered boulders to the viewpoint ①.

Continue along the path, which is marked with red-and-white signs, to reach the signposted Lavabo du Diable ②.

The Gorges d'Apremont is a picturesque rock formation near the edge of the Forêt de Fontainebleau ▼

▲ *A small pond on the plateau above the Gorges d'Apremont is known as the Devil's Wash-basin*

The marked path continues around the rim of the plateau, weaving between the smooth boulders and giving extensive views of the surrounding forest. Signposted on the north side of the plateau, and hidden among trees, is the Caverne des Brigands ③.

The clearly defined path then descends the slope to a refreshment chalet and parking area. Bear left and walk through coniferous woodland, parallel to the straight Route de Barbizon, for 1km, to return to the starting-point.

Points of Interest

① This weathered outcrop rises from the sandy forest floor to provide spectacular views of the woodlands, with their mixture of oak, birch, beech and conifers. The viewpoint overlooks the ravine which the route followed earlier, as well as the Bière plain, which stretches away to the west.

② The top of the plateau is covered with an accumulation of sandstone boulders, many of which have weathered into remarkable shapes. The hollowed surface of the Lavabo du Diable, or Devil's Wash-basin, contains a small, stagnant pond which is periodically replenished by rainfall.

③ The Caverne des Brigands, or Robbers' Cave, is tucked away in a clump of pine and acacia trees. This again is the result of the weathering of the stone by frost and rain. Although its position on the top of the plateau would have provided adequate warning of any approach by intruders, there is no evidence that the cave was ever used by brigands who roamed the forest.

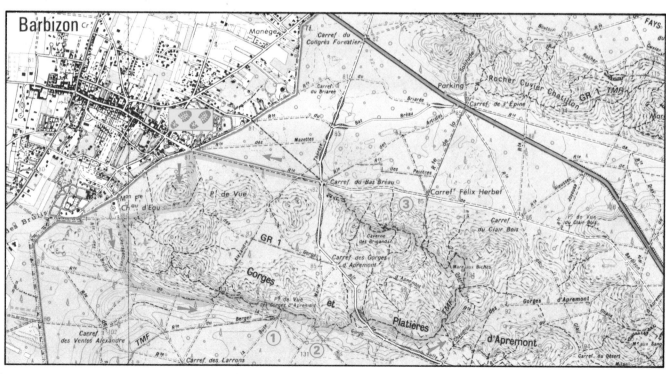

WALK 21B: 3KM/ALLOW 1½ HOURS

The Gorges de Franchard

▲ *A woodland trail through the Gorges de Franchard*

This is a moderately demanding walk across the slopes of the Gorges de Franchard, offering some superb open vistas of the countryside to the south of the woodlands.

Route Directions

Start from the signposted car park, just off the Carrefour de l'Ermitage de Franchard on the D 301e.

Cross the bridle-path to the Franchard hermitage ①.

Pass this, keeping the sandy fire-break on the left. Climb gradually towards the rocks without changing direction, to emerge on to another sandy path, Route de Tavannes. After 300m a prominent mushroom-shaped rock will be seen on the right. On reaching this, bear to the left to a bench overlooking the ravine. This is the Grand Point de Vue ②.

Descend the three steps and bear right, following the blue signs on the trees and rocks. These lead into a

The Gorges de Franchard is a popular area for walking, owing to its combination of pretty woods and open, rocky landscape. Near by is the former hermitage of Franchard, whose grounds give welcome shade in summer. Only the walls of the hermitage have survived ▼

small declivity and a sandy path marking the division between sections 762 and 763 of the forest. Cross the path, and ascend into the rocks, still following the signs, which will bring you to another signposted viewpoint. Continue along the edge of the plateau until you reach the viewpoint of the Antre des Druides (the Druids' Cave), and then continue along the signposted lane below. At the foot of the ravine, turn right on to Route Amédée, and at

the next junction turn left on to Route du Carnage. This winding path, after another 300m, emerges on to Route de l'Ermitage. Turn right along this track to return to the car park.

Points of Interest

① This site was occupied by a religious community in the 13th century. After the community was

dissolved, an annual country fair took place here on Whit Tuesday until the early part of the last century. The walls of the original hermitage are now incorporated into the present forest rangers' cabin.

② A breathtaking panorama of the Forêt de Fontainebleau can be had from this point. This view extends to the Bière plain in the far distance, beyond the villages of Ury and Recloses.

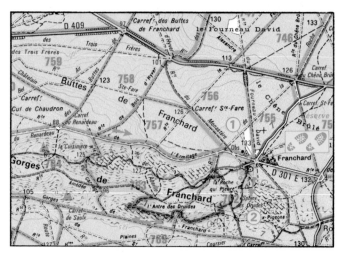

The Morvan

S tarting from one of the most famous towns in Burgundy, this tour passes through the lightly wooded Yonne valley before winding its way through the forested hills of the Parc Naturel Régional du Morvan. Though natural sights such as rivers, lakes and viewpoints predominate here, there are also several châteaux, churches and villages to attract the attention. The roads can be a little slow, but traffic is normally extremely light.

Route Directions

The drive starts from Vézelay ①.

Follow the D 951 towards Clamecy to reach Chamoux and the Cardo-Land theme park ②.

Continue on the D 951 to Dornecy and in the village take the second left on to the D 985, signposted Brèves, Corbigny and Tannay.

Turn right on to the D 165 and enter Tannay ③.

Leave Tannay on the D 119 and at Cuzy turn right on to the D 985 towards Monceaux-le-Comte and Corbigny ④.

In Corbigny turn left by the town hall, on to a road signposted Lormes and Montsauche-les-Settons, and after a few metres turn right on to the D 977 *bis* towards Montsauche. Continue through Cervon and at the Carrefour de Vauclaix go straight ahead. At la Roche fork left, still on the D 977 *bis*, and continue for another 16km on the winding road to Montsauche ⑤.

Go through Montsauche on the D 977 *bis*, signposted Dun-les-Places ⑥.

Turn left on to the D 236 towards Dun-les-Places and Quarré-les-Tombes. Turn left on to the D 6 and enter Dun-les-Places.

Pass through Dun-les-Places on the D 6, heading towards Brassy and Lormes. Just after Brassy pass the southern end of the Réservoir de Chaumeçon ⑦.

Continue to Lormes ⑧.

Leave Lormes on the D 944, signposted Vézelay, Avallon and Clamecy, and where the road forks on the edge of the town continue straight ahead on the D 944 towards St-Martin-du-Puy and Avallon. A short diversion to the right after St-Martin leads to the Château de Vésigneux ⑨.

Some way further on, the D 944 passes the Château de Chastellux on the left ⑩.

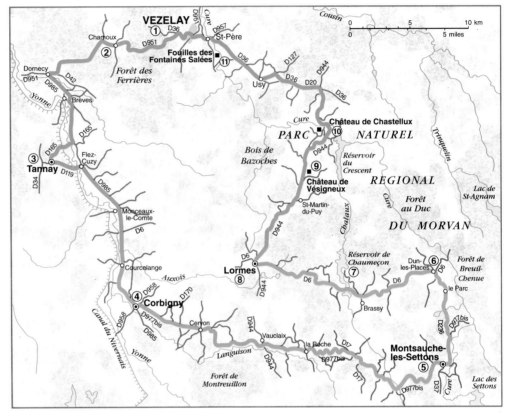

▲ The village of Tannay, formerly walled, overlooks the Yonne

After Chastellux turn left on to the D 20, and then the D 36, signposted Vézelay, St-Père and Usy. Note that the D 36 changes to the D 20 and then back to the D 36 again, but to save confusion just follow the signs towards Vézelay and St-Père. At Usy watch for a small sign to Vézelay to the right, as this road avoids making a loop through the village. Within 100m rejoin the D 36 and turn right, following signs to St-Père, Pierre-Perthuis and Vézelay. Continue to St-Père ⑪.

At the T-junction in St-Père turn left on to the D 957 to return to Vézelay.

Points of Interest

① One of the great pilgrimage centres of France, Vézelay is an attractive small town spilling down its hillside and overlooked by the magnificent Basilique Ste-Madeleine. Restored in the 19th century after considerable damage during the Revolution, the basilica has an outstanding tympanum and capitals.

② Situated in woodland on the outskirts of Chamoux, Cardo-Land is a small park with a prehistoric theme. Several millions of years are covered and there are some spectacular models of dinosaurs.

③ Built on slopes overlooking the River Yonne, Tannay was once a walled village. Gateways still exist

Notre-Dame church, in the village of St-Père, below Vézelay, stands on the site of a 9th-century monastery sacked by the Vikings. It has a handsome porch ▼

and there are several medieval houses. The church contains a beautiful bas-relief of scenes from the life of St Hubert.

④ Corbigny, a busy little market town, lies on the pretty River Anguison, a tributary of the Yonne. Its Abbaye de St-Léonard has been rebuilt several times since it was founded in 864.

⑤ The highest resort in the Parc Naturel Régional du Morvan, Montsauche-les-Settons was rebuilt after it was totally destroyed by the Germans in 1944. Nearby is les Settons, a popular holiday centre.

⑥ Dun-les-Places, one of the Morvan's many quiet villages, has a distinctive church, built in the mid-19th century with the financial

The beautiful Lac des Settons is a popular holiday centre offering water sports and fishing. It hosts regattas in summer

assistance of a former corsair.

⑦ An artificial lake created by damming the River Chalaux, the Réservoir de Chaumeçon is very popular with anglers and sailors. The Chalaux is used several times a year for wild-water canoeing competitions.

⑧ Lormes is a large and lively village at the main crossroads in the Morvan and has good access to all the lakes of the region. From the church there is an excellent panorama over wooded hills.

⑨ The medieval Château de Vésigneux was partially rebuilt in the

The Basilique Ste-Madeleine enjoys a fine position overlooking Vézelay ▼

16th and 17th centuries. It was once owned by Prince Louis II, who because of his arrogance was known as the Grand Condé.

⑩ Built on a granite escarpment surrounded by woods, the Château de Chastellux has been the seat of the Chastellux family for more than 900 years. Several towers were added in the 15th century and the castle was restored in the early 19th century.

⑪ Being at the foot of Vézelay's famous hill, St-Père has always been in the shadow of the famous basilica in more ways than one. Yet it has an outstanding church of its own, with a beautifully sculpted porch and a fine belfry. Nearby are the Roman remains of Fontaines Salées.

RESISTANCE FIGHTERS

With its extensive forests and mountainous terrain, the Morvan was an ideal hiding place during World War II. The Resistance (or *Maquis*) established several strongholds in the area and kept up a campaign that frustrated the Germans between 1942 and 1944 and especially during the months following the Normandy invasion.

Around 15 groups were set up to ambush and harass the enemy, assist British agents and maintain escape routes for prisoners of war. Later they fought bravely to link up with the invasion forces as they headed east and south through France.

Today visitors can see several memorials to them around the Morvan. One of the most poignant is a small cemetery beside a track deep in the forest near the village of Savelot. It contains the graves of 21 Resistance fighters and the seven-man crew of an RAF bomber.

As the Resistance became more successful, the Germans shot many civilians in the Morvan and burned several villages, among them Montsauche-les-Settons, Dun-les-Places and Planchez. These were later rebuilt.

A museum to the Resistance in the Morvan is located at the Maison du Parc near St-Brisson.

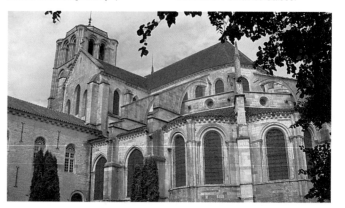

Around Corbigny

This easy walk to the north-west of Corbigny explores the varied countryside between the Yonne and Anguison valleys. Extensive views over open countryside are followed by woodland scenery which provides welcome shade in the heat of summer.

▲ *A peaceful rural landscape near the village of Chitry-les-Mines*

Route Directions

Start from the car park at Corbigny's Jardin Public at the junction of Rue de l'Anguison and Rue des Essais. Turn left out of the Jardin Public, following 'Toutes Directions' sign, and at the junction with the main road turn right towards Brinon-sur-Beuvron and Nevers. Cross the level crossing and after 300m fork right along a minor road opposite a large grain silo. After about 150m the road becomes a track, once a Roman road ①.

The track climbs easily between hedgerows for about 500m and then begins to descend, after 1km becoming a surfaced road again on reaching Chitry-les-Mines ②.

Follow the road as it curves to the left through the village and when it meets the main road turn right. After about 125m turn right on to a minor road just before the Chez Paulette café, pass the church and after 500m turn right on to a wide, leafy footpath immediately after a small cemetery on your right. After about 250m the path breaks into the open again and after another 250m enters the Bois du Moulin ③.

Continue straight on through the woods for 500m until a fence appears across the path ahead. Just before the fence a minor path branches off through the trees to the left and after about 25m meets another clearly defined footpath. Turn right here, following the path through the woods, along the top of a railway embankment.

After about 800m the path bears left and crosses the railway, bearing right along the opposite embankment. After 250m the track becomes a surfaced road. After another 400m fork left along Rue de la Cave into Corbigny ④.

At the end of the road turn left to return to the car park.

Points of Interest

① The former Roman road, which in places still shows signs of cobbles, offers some fine views over the arable land of the Yonne valley. There is a calvary beside the path just before the road enters Chitry-les-Mines.

② Chitry-les-Mines was a lead-mining village in the 15th and 16th centuries, but is now a picturesque place beside the Yonne and the Canal du Nivernais, with among its features a château and an old water-mill. The village was the home of the writer Jules Renard, whose bust can be seen in front of the church.

▲ *The River Anguison at Corbigny*

③ The Bois du Moulin is a large and dense wood of broad-leaved trees where at most times of the year a wide variety of fungi can be seen.

④ The walk into Corbigny provides good views of the town where it sprawls across the valley of the River Anguison. The river forms an attractive border to the shaded Jardin Public.

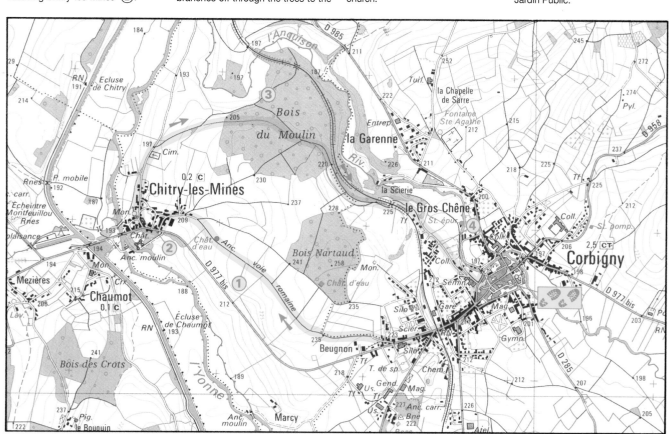

22B

BURGUNDY

Around Bonnetré

This walk in the heart of the Parc Naturel Régional du Morvan encompasses typical landscapes of the area – forests, lakes and an occasional field of Charollais cattle. As much of the walk is in thick forest it is best to carry a compass.

Points of Interest

① From the farm here there is a good view over the Réservoir de Chaumeçon to the woodland beyond. The reservoir, 4.5km long, is one of the six main lakes of the Morvan.

② Vaussegrois is a tiny group of cottages and farm buildings occupying a charming spot by the Réservoir de Chaumeçon. The hedgerows leading into the hamlet are lined with hazel trees, and the ripe nuts are a good source of sustenance for autumn walkers.

③ At this point the path heads deep into the Bois de Bonnetré, part of the vast forests that make up the Morvan. The trees in this area are mainly firs or beech and birch. There are also many varieties of fungi.

④ The pretty Etang Poitreau is a small, artificially dammed lake in a tranquil forest setting. Although it is beside the road from Brassy to Chalaux it attracts few cars.

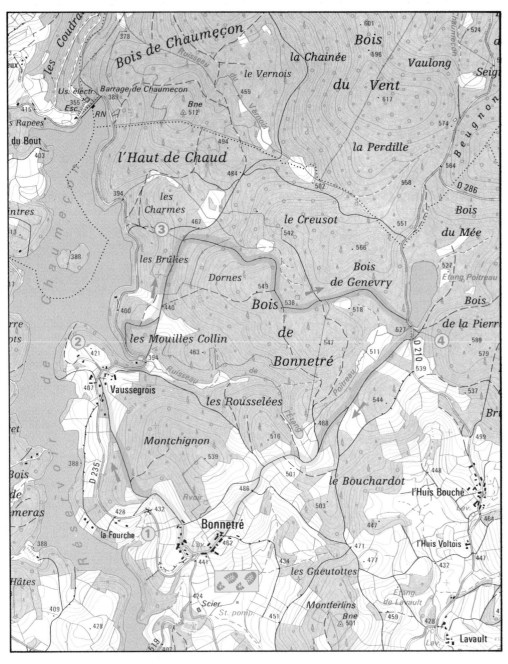

Route Directions

Start from Bonnetré's wash-house.

Walk along the minor road away from the village and fork right uphill past a small wooden shelter. Turn right at the T-junction by a farm and after 125m take a track that forks left of another farm ①.

The track descends for 250m, after which fork right, ascending through woods. Soon the path begins to descend again and in just under 1km reaches Vaussegrois ②.

At the end of the track turn right on to the road, which winds round an inlet of the Réservoir de Chaumeçon, and after a little more than 500m take a track that climbs steeply through woods to the right (indicated by a red-and-yellow marker). After 400m the path reaches a clearing.

Beyond the clearing follow the red-and-yellow markers for another 500m to a fork in the path. Bear right here, ignoring the red-and-yellow-marked path ahead, and follow a gently climbing path which gradually steepens ③.

Follow this slightly overgrown path for about 1km and take the first distinct turning to the left, which after 1km descends to the road by the Etang Poitreau ④.

Turn right on to the road for 200m, then take another path to the right along a hedge at the edge of the forest. Continue along this path for 1km, more or less following the edge of the forest. Continue between hedges for another 1km to Bonnetré. Walk through the village to return to the wash-house and the car.

North of Auxerre

This tour passes through gently undulating countryside mainly comprising fields of cereal crops punctuated by copses. By contrast around Chablis the slopes are covered by the vines that produce one of Burgundy's most famous white wines. The roads are not at all busy, though delays could be encountered at peak times where the route uses the N6: briefly at Auxerre and Joigny, and at Migennes.

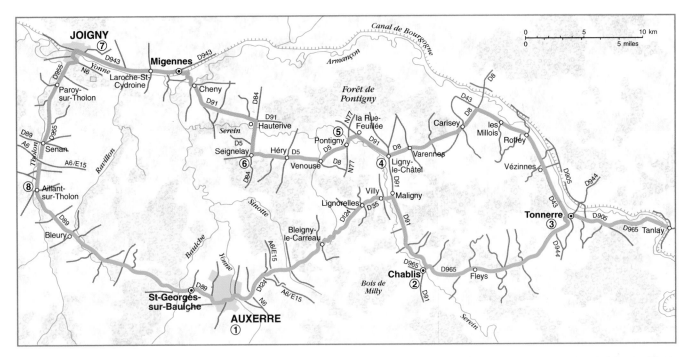

Route Directions

The drive starts from Auxerre ①.

Leave Auxerre by crossing the River Yonne and following signs for 'A 6 (Sud)'. Just after crossing the railway on the outskirts of the town turn left on to the D 124, signposted Ligny-le-Châtel. Continue to Lignorelles and leave the village on the D 35, signposted Villy and Tonnerre. Pass through Villy to Maligny, then turn right at the T-junction in the village and take the D 91 to Chablis ②.

Take the D 965 from Chablis to Tonnerre ③.

For the second walk leave Tonnerre on the D 905 towards Dijon and after 3.5km turn left on to the D 965 to Tanlay.

Just after the church of Notre-Dame in Tonnerre take Rue de l'Hôpital to the left, signposted Paris and Troyes, and after 300m, having crossed an arm of the River Armançon, take the D 43 to the left, signposted Junay. Continue through Junay to Vézinnes and Roffey and about 2km after les Millois turn left at the crossroads on to the D 8, signposted Carisey, Varennes and Auxerre. Pass through

Carisey, following signs for Auxerre, then pass through Varennes to Ligny-le-Châtel ④.

In the village turn right on to the D 91, signposted les Baudières, Migennes and Joigny. At la Rue-Feuillée turn left on to the D 5 towards Pontigny and after 400m turn left at the junction with the N77, signposted Montigny-la-Resle and Auxerre, to arrive in Pontigny, with its abbey ⑤.

Just after the Abbaye de Pontigny turn right on to the D 5, signposted Venouse and Seignelay. After about 1.5km bear right at an unsigned fork

Joigny is an attractive little town on the northern edge of Burgundy. It has some fine 15th- and 16th-century half-timbered houses, restored in recent years ▼

and follow the D 5 through Venouse, Rouvray and Héry to Seignelay ⑥.

In the centre of Seignelay turn right on to the D 84 towards Hauterive and Brienon-sur-Armançon. After about 3km, at the crossroads by the Auberge de Hauterive, turn left on to the D 91 towards Cheny and Migennes. Pass through Cheny and then follow 'Toutes Directions' signs into Migennes. At the T-junction with the D 943 turn left on to a road signposted Migennes Centre and Joigny ⑦.

▲ *Auxerre's 13th-century abbey church of St-Germain*

The first walk starts from Joigny.

Leave Joigny by the N6, signposted Auxerre. On the outskirts of the town turn right, after crossing the railway, on to the D 955 to Aillant-sur-Tholon ⑧.

In the centre of Aillant go straight ahead (left of the church) at the crossroads, where the D 89 bears to the right. Take this road to return to Auxerre.

Points of Interest

① A busy and attractive town, Auxerre looks down on the River Yonne. Its skyline is pierced by the towers and spires of several churches, including the Gothic Cathédrale St-Etienne. Another of its famous sights is the colourful 15th-century Tour de l'Horloge, a clock tower which once formed part of the town's defences.

② World-renowned for its dry white wines, Chablis is a delightful little town on the banks of the River Serein. There is a lovely shaded walk beside the river along the Promenade du Pâtis, and there are plenty of opportunities to sample the wine.

③ Tonnerre, on the River Armançon and the Canal de Bourgogne, is a popular centre for boating holidays. Its greatest treasure is the Ancien Hôpital, similar to the more famous one at Beaune but built 150 years earlier, in 1293. It contains a highly detailed sculpture of the Entombment.

Joigny's church of St-Jean, seen through the porch of the belfry ▼

④ Ligny-le-Châtel has an unusual church built in two distinct styles, Romanesque and Renaissance. Parts of the interior were inspired by the nearby Abbaye de Pontigny. Among its treasures are a 16th-century painting of St Jerome and polychrome statues of the Virgin and St John.

⑤ Lying like an upturned boat in a field, the Abbaye de Pontigny is a superb example of austere

ARCHBISHOPS' REFUGE

Three Archbishops of Canterbury have taken refuge at the Abbaye de Pontigny. Thomas à Becket was the first, in 1164, spending several years there after quarrelling with the English king, Henry II, before being charged with treason. Living the austere life of a Cistercian monk, he wore sackcloth and worked in the vineyards. He also spent time at Sens and Vézelay, but despite being invited to stay by the French king, Louis VII, in 1170 he returned to England and to martyrdom in the cathedral at Canterbury in the same year.

Stephen Langton was exiled at Pontigny after a disagreement with King John in 1208, the year after he became Archbishop of Canterbury. While at the abbey he acted as a mediator between King John and the Pope, and after five years he was eventually able to return to England and resume his role until he died in 1228.

The third primate, Edmund Rich, argued frequently with Henry III, and after refusing to christen Prince Edward retired to Pontigny in 1240. He died later the same year and was buried at the abbey. Canonised a few years later, he is known in Burgundy as St Edmé. It is said that his veneration by the local population saved Pontigny from destruction in the Revolution.

Cistercian art. Built in the 12th century as the second 'daughter' of Cîteaux, it is the largest Cistercian church in France. In its time it has provided shelter for English archbishops and has been a literary centre.

⑥ Seignelay, overlooking the Serein valley, owes much of its present appearance to Colbert, Louis XIV's finance minister. The château was largely destroyed in the Revolution, but its grounds have left a fine park, and Place Colbert, with its town hall and covered market, has conserved its 17th-century character.

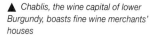

▲ *Chablis, the wine capital of lower Burgundy, boasts fine wine merchants' houses*

◄ *Chardonnay grapes near Chablis*

⑦ Known as the 'Key to Burgundy', Joigny lies mainly on the northern slopes of the River Yonne and has a number of fine 16th-century half-timbered houses. The best of these, at the corner of Rue Gabriel Cortel and Rue Montant-au-Palais, is known as the Tree of Jesse. Joigny also has a 12th-century gateway, the Porte du Bois, once part of the old castle.

⑧ Aillant-sur-Tholon, a small market town surrounded by fields of cereal crops, has a 19th-century church designed by Viollet-le-Duc, who was responsible for the restoration of the Basilique Ste-Madeleine at Vézelay. Inside is a tableau showing the town in its fortified days, under the protection of the Virgin.

The heights of Joigny

BURGUNDY

Joigny, built on the side of the Côte St-Jacques, is a town with history and well worth exploring. The countryside to the north offers some fine and mainly easy walking with the bonus of superb views over the town and the River Yonne.

Route Directions

Start from the Porte du Bois in Joigny, where you can park.

Walk along Avenue de la Forêt d'Othe opposite for a few metres and where the main road bears left carry straight on into Chemin de la Collinière. After about 100m the road becomes a track, and 150m further on turn right by an old shed ①.

After a little more than 500m, where the path meets a T-junction, turn left, climbing steeply between chalk embankments away from the town. After about 600m the climb eases off and after another 150m it reaches the edge of the forest. Several paths meet here, but take the main one, which bears slightly to the left. Through a gap in the trees the buildings of Beauregard Farm come into view and after about 300m the path reaches the D 20 ②.

Continue along the path for a few metres and just before it reaches the road turn left, still following red-and-white markers, and almost immediately bear left along the edge of a vineyard. The path stays at around the same level for about 600m and then begins to descend towards Joigny. Ignore tracks to left and right. As the track enters the outskirts of Joigny it becomes a surfaced road, Chemin de Voie Grasse, with houses each side. At the T-junction at the end of the road turn right into Chemin de la Collinière and return to the Porte du Bois ④.

Turn left and then follow the road for approximately 1.25km, going past Joigny aerodrome and through woods. Just after the point where the road emerges from the trees and where it curves slightly to the right take the track to the left. The track is clearly indicated by red-and-white markers. Follow the track for about 600m until you arrive at a belvedere looking out over Joigny ③.

Points of Interest

① There are good views of Joigny from this path, across the cemetery to the town's three churches, St-André, St-Thibault and especially St-Jean, standing out on the skyline.

② Opposite the point where the path meets the road in front of Beauregard Farm stands a tall stone cross called the Croix d'Arnault. It is inscribed with the date 1558.

③ Four rows of lime trees mark the belvedere. The view from here is superb and extends along the valley of the River Yonne.

④ The Porte du Bois, with its two massive round towers, is the only one of four 12th-century gateways to have avoided demolition. The best-preserved part of what were Joigny's fortifications, it leads to some of the town's half-timbered houses.

◀ A footpath leads into the pleasant countryside that surrounds Joigny

Joigny's Porte du Bois is one of the four original gateways to the castle. The other three, like the castle, have been destroyed ▼

Along the Canal de Bourgogne

No series of walks in Burgundy would be complete without a canalside stroll. This walk not only takes in a short stretch of the Canal de Bourgogne, but it also includes a fine example of another of Burgundy's major features, its châteaux.

Route Directions

Start from the bridge over the Canal de Bourgogne at Tanlay.

Walk away from the bridge along Rue du Port towards the village centre, then branch off to the left along the canal towpath, with the canal on the left ①.

At the first lock gate, cross the canal and continue along the towpath for 1km to the next road bridge. Cross the canal here and walk into the village of Commissey ②.

Go straight ahead at Place de la Mairie, along Rue Haute, and at the crossroads just outside the village carry straight on along a minor road signposted Quincy and Rugny. Walk uphill for 300m to a crossroads and turn right. Within 100m the surfaced road becomes a rough track ③.

Follow this track through open countryside for 400m, and about 100m before it enters a wood turn left on to a track between hedgeless fields. After 100m the track bears right over stony ground and then becomes a broad path going downhill through a lightly wooded area. Where the path forks near the edge of the wooded area, bear right and continue downhill with a wall to the right. After another 225m the path meets a road.

Turn right along the road and after 100m take the next road to the left, signposted St-Vinnemer and Lézinnes, and return to Tanlay. Opposite Rue du Port turn left into Grande Rue Basse, and after 250m reach the entrance to the Château de Tanlay ④.

▲ The château at Tanlay typifies the French Renaissance style of about 1550, which had begun to move away from the strong Italian influence

The peaceful Canal de Bourgogne is no longer a main trade route ▶

Turn right in front of the château, following signs to Auxerre and Tonnerre, and walk along an avenue of tall trees. Just past two football pitches turn right along the road towards Tonnerre to arrive back after 100m at the harbour.

Points of Interest

① The Canal de Bourgogne, which winds through Burgundy from the Yonne to the Saône and so provides the link between the Channel and the Mediterranean, was once a major highway for freight. Now it carries mainly holiday traffic.

② Commissey has a small church in Romanesque style (turn left at the crossroads in village) with an unusual stained-glass window in the dome above the altar. Notice also the wash-house on the left just after crossing the canal.

③ There are good unobstructed views from this path into the valley of the River Armançon and towards Tonnerre. The landscape is a mixture of cultivated fields and woods.

④ Built in the mid-16th century, the Château de Tanlay is an excellent example of French Renaissance architecture. Set in a beautiful park and surrounded by a moat, it was a Protestant stronghold in the Wars of Religion. Tours are available.

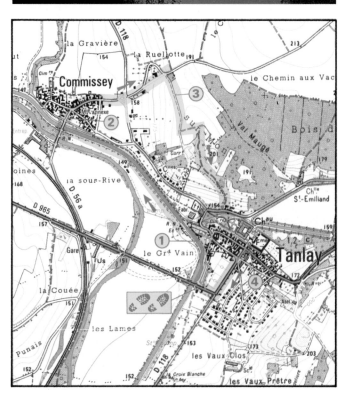

The Côte d'Or

BURGUNDY

Following little-used roads for the most part, this tour takes in a variety of scenery, beginning with forested hills around Plombières-lès-Dijon before passing through rolling farmland. Before and after Bouilland there are some outstanding limestone cliffs which rise high above the forest, then comes the last stretch between Beaune and Dijon, along the vineyard-covered slopes of the Côte d'Or, where some of Burgundy's most famous wines are produced.

Route Directions

The drive starts from Dijon ①.

Follow signs for the A38 motorway, signposted Paris, Auxerre and Nevers. Just after Lac Kir, where the A38 is signposted to the left, continue on the D 10 towards Sombernon. Soon after Plombières-lès-Dijon fork right under a railway viaduct towards Pasques and Prenois and then turn left on to the D 104, signposted Lantenay. At Lantenay bear left opposite a small château on to the D 104 and follow signs to Mâlain. At the D 33 turn right into Mâlain ②.

Follow signs through Mâlain for Savigny-sous-Mâlain and in Savigny turn right on to a road signposted 'Vers CD7' and Blaisy-Bas. At the D 16 turn left (no signs). Continue to Sombernon, following signs for the town centre. In Sombernon turn right at the D 905 towards Aubigny-lès-Sombernon and within 100m turn left along the D 977 bis. Pass through Montoillot to Commarin ③.

Continue to Vandenesse-en-Auxois, cross the Canal de Bourgogne and immediately turn left on to the D 18 to Châteauneuf ④.

Follow the D 18 through Crugey to le Pont d'Ouche, where the road continues, signposted Bécoup and

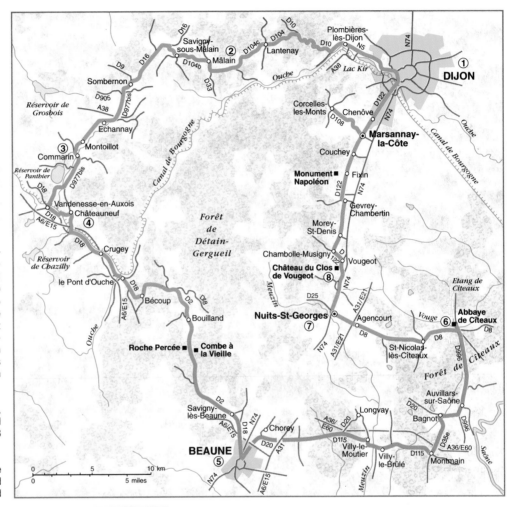

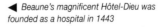

◄ Beaune's magnificent Hôtel-Dieu was founded as a hospital in 1443

Beaune. About 4km beyond Bécoup fork right on to the D 2 to Bouilland. The second walk starts from here.

Continue to Savigny-lès-Beaune and follow signs through village to Beaune. Cross the A6 motorway and at the junction with the N74 turn right and enter Beaune ⑤.

Leave Beaune by its ring road and take the last exit on the right before rejoining the N74 to Dijon, signposted Longvay and St-Jean-de-Losne. Immediately before passing over the A36 motorway fork right on to the D 115, signposted Villy-le-Moutier. About 6km after Villy turn left at the crossroads in Montmain on to the D 35e to

Bagnot. At the main road in Bagnot turn right and after a little more than 1km turn left at the Vieille Auberge on to the D 996 towards Dijon. Continue to Cîteaux ⑥.

From the Abbaye de Cîteaux turn right on to the D 996 and at the D 8 turn right to reach Nuits-St-Georges ⑦.

At Nuits-St-Georges turn right on the N74 towards Dijon and after 4km turn left to Vougeot. At the village centre turn left on to a road signposted Château du Clos de Vougeot ⑧.

Leave Vougeot on the D 122, signposted Chambolle-Musigny. At the T-junction in Chambolle turn right (no sign) and almost immediately right again. Go through the village and fork left on to the D 122 towards

Morey-St-Denis and Gevrey-Chambertin. Follow signs for Route des Grands Crus to Marsannay-la-Côte. Turn left in Marsannay on to the D 108 to Corcelles-les-Monts for the first walk. In Marsannay fork left on to a road signposted Dijon, and after Chenôve continue straight on until the D 122 joins the N74, which goes back to Dijon.

Points of Interest

① Dijon, the lively capital of Burgundy, is renowned for both its cuisine and its sights. Do not miss the Musée des Beaux-Arts, housed in the Palais des Ducs, the Cathédrale St-Bénigne, Notre-Dame with its medieval Jacquemart clock and extraordinary rows of gargoyles, and the many old houses, especially around Rue des Forges.

② Overlooked by the ruins of its fortress, Mâlain was once on a Roman road. A museum in the village contains several finds from excavations of Roman sites near by, including some bronze statues.

③ The little village of Commarin has one of the most beautiful châteaux in Burgundy. Surrounded by a moat and a large park, it has two round towers which were part of an earlier fortress, while the main building dates from the 17th and

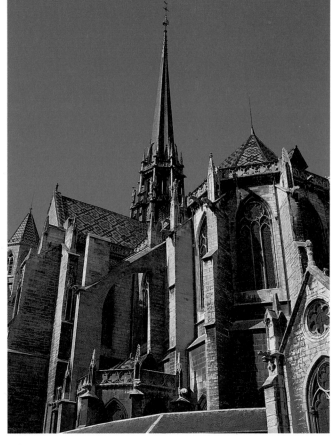

▲ Dijon's cathedral of St-Bénigne was built in the late 13th century in the Gothic style

18th centuries. Inside are some interesting tapestries.

④ Châteauneuf is a picturesque fortified village with a 12th-century fortress and many houses from the

15th and 16th centuries. There are extensive views from the village encompassing the Vandenesse valley and the Canal de Bourgogne.

⑤ A favourite town of the Dukes of

Burgundy in the 14th and 15th centuries, Beaune has inherited some beautiful buildings from the period. Best of all is the Hôtel-Dieu, with its Burgundian tiled roof, Grande 'Salle and museum housing the Roger van der Weyden polyptych of the Last Judgement. The dukes' former mansion now contains the Musée du Vin de Bourgogne.

⑥ The Abbaye de Cîteaux was founded in 1098 and espoused an austerity far removed from the richness of Cluny. Under the leadership of St Bernard the Cistercian order expanded widely, but it was abolished during the Revolution. Most of the abbey's present buildings date from the 19th century.

⑦ In the heart of the wine-producing area of the Côte d'Or, Nuits-St-Georges has been associated with wine for 1000 years. The Romanesque St-Symphorien is one of the most beautiful churches in the area.

⑧ Created by the monks of Cîteaux in the 12th century, the walled vineyard of the Clos de Vougeot is the most famous in the Côte d'Or. Its château dates from the 16th century, though its cellar is much older. It is now the headquarters of the Confrérie des Chevaliers du Tastevin.

COTE D'OR WINES

Many of the great wines of the Côte d'Or originate from tiny villages. Drive along the N74 to the south of Dijon and you will see signposts announcing one name after another – Fixin, Gevrey-Chambertin, Vougeot, Nuits-St-Georges, Beaune, Volnay, Montrachet, Meursault, Pommard. They read like labels on a wine merchant's shelves.

The natural conditions for producing these wines have been created by the ridge of hills running south from Dijon to Santenay, forming the Côte d'Or. This is divided into two further districts – the Côte de Nuits in the north and the Côte de Beaune in the south.

The area enjoys its own special microclimate, and because of its combination of

soil and weather conditions the best wines are generally produced from grapes grown halfway up the slopes. The best reds come almost exclusively from the Pinot

◀ Châteauneuf is a fortified village
Vougeot's château and famous vines ▼

Noir grape, while the best whites come from the Chardonnay.

Red wine from the region is often used to enrich local gastronomic specialities, such as *boeuf à la bourguignonne* and *coq au vin*.

Around Mont Afrique

Steep-sided Mont Afrique has played a defensive role for thousands of years, and a wander round its perimeter will show why. Though the climb from Corcelles-lès-Monts is hard going in places, most of the walk, which has an optional extension, is easy.

◀ A small wrought-iron calvary stands on the outskirts of Corcelles-lès-Monts

Route Directions

Start from the church in Corcelles-lès-Monts, in front of which you can park.

With the front of the church behind you, turn left and walk up Rue du Château. At the next crossroads turn left, still along the now very steep Rue du Château, and continue to Impasse du Réservoir on the right, at the edge of the residential area.

Take the path that forks right here, uphill through the trees. At the top of the climb and where two paths cross, turn right along a straight track between hedges and oaks. Follow the path for approximately 500m and then fork right to a ruin ①.

Retrace your steps to the main track, which climbs gradually for a while, occasionally giving views to the right through the trees. After about 1km there is a radio mast where the track becomes a surfaced road. After another 500m the road passes a huge radar station on the summit of Mont Afrique ②.

There are two options here. The first is to turn left immediately after the radar station and continue along the road for about 1km to a hairpin bend ③.

The second is to go straight ahead past the radar station along a track through the woods. This follows the edge of the escarpment and reaches the road at the hairpin bend after about 2.5km. Continue downhill along the road until you reach a second hairpin bend ④.

Follow the road down to a junction at the edge of Corcelles (note the small wrought-iron calvary), then walk along Rue du Camp de César back to Place de l'Eglise ⑤.

Points of Interest

① There are several ruins around the edge of Mont Afrique, all of them World War II defences. From this one there is a view over rolling forests and fields to the railway viaducts at Velars-sur-Ouche.

▲ Mont Afrique's height of 600m makes it good for aircraft navigation, for which purpose it has been used since 1925

② At 600m, Mont Afrique has had equipment for aircraft navigation on its summit since 1925, and the radio and radar station now on the site represents the latest in navigational aids. From in front of the tower there is a good view across the wooded combe to the isolated chapel of Notre-Dame d'Etang.

③ Dog kennels to the left of the road occupy what was a camp of Julius Caesar, who defended Mont Afrique against the Gauls.

④ There is a good view from the hairpin bend along the Combe de Beaune to Dijon in the distance.

⑤ The centre of Corcelles around the church is fairly old, but most of the village, which serves as a dormitory for Dijon, is modern.

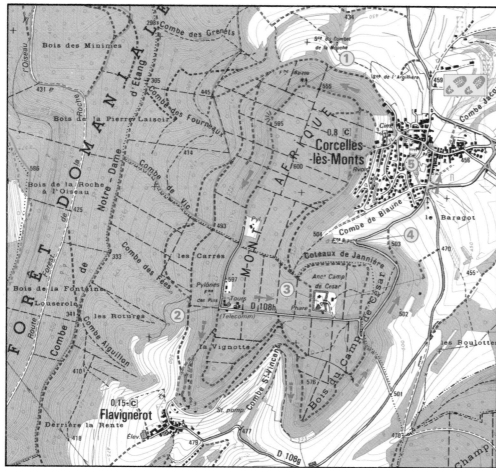

Bouilland

Taking in a little local history by way of an outstanding natural feature, this walk passes through some lovely scenery. A short section of the walk is very steep and stout walking boots are recommended.

▲ *The Abbaye de Ste-Marguerite, now in ruins, was founded by monks of the Antonine order in the 11th century. It stands in a secluded setting near Bouilland*

Route Directions

Start from the wash-house in the middle of Bouilland.

Walk along the road towards Beaune, with the stream on the right. After about 150m turn right over a bridge signposted Abbaye Ste-Marguerite. Continue along this road for 500m and where the abbey is signposted to the right, beside a cross, go straight on ①.

Pass through the hamlet of la Forge and at the T-junction, just after crossing a stream, turn right along the main road. After 750m turn right down a track with the sign 'Société de Pêche de Bouilland' at its entrance. Cross the stream again and continue straight on along a path going into the woods, following

yellow markers. The path becomes very steep as it climbs through a wooded gully between limestone cliffs and then passes under a natural arch ②.

Through the arch the path bears right and then continues on a more even level for about 250m before emerging from the wood in the corner of a narrow field. Continue along the left side of the field and at the road turn left. Walk along the road for about 200m, past a car park, and then turn right along a track that passes under the old gateway to the abbey ③.

Just past the gateway turn left on to a footpath marked by red-and-white markers, which climbs the wooded slope behind the abbey ruins and then follows the contours round the hillside. When the path joins another coming from the left, bear right downhill, still following the red-and-white markers, and carry on downhill until the path emerges from the woods ④.

Follow the track between fields for about 400m to the road and turn left. After about 200m the road reaches the T-junction at the cross passed earlier. Turn left and retrace your steps along the road for about 650m to the centre of Bouilland.

Points of Interest

① The cross on the outskirts of Bouilland was erected by the villagers in thanksgiving for the end of the 1848 revolution.

② The remarkable natural arch in the limestone cliff at the top of the Combe Portaut is known as the Roche Percée, the Pierced Rock. Although it is quite high, unfortunately the views from the rock are largely obscured by trees.

③ Founded in the 11th century by Antonine monks, the Abbaye Ste-Marguerite was affiliated to the abbey at Cluny, which was then Christendom's greatest centre. Visited by dukes, popes and kings in its heyday, it later fell into decline and after the Revolution of 1789 was sold and partially demolished.

④ From the path here there is a view over the fields to Bouilland and across the valley to magnificent limestone cliffs.

Affiliation to the powerful abbey at Cluny at one time lent prestige to the Abbaye de Ste-Marguerite, and it was patronised by royalty and popes before its decline ▶

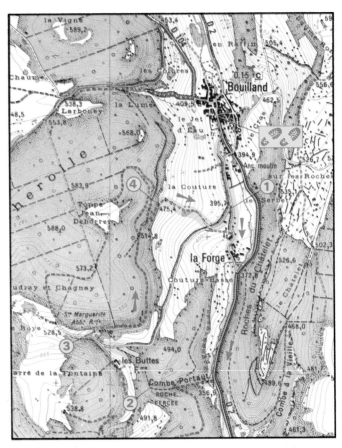

Pilgrimage to Cluny

Following a route through the Mâconnais between the valleys of the Saône and the Grosne, an area of great scenic variety and with extensive views in places, this tour takes in a number of important ecclesiastical sights. These include several Romanesque churches and culminate in the great former abbeys of Cluny and Tournus. None of the roads used in the tour carries much traffic, though at peak weekends parking in Cluny can be difficult.

Route Directions

The drive starts from Tournus ①.

Leave Tournus on the D 14, signposted Ozenay and Charolles, but on the outskirts, where the D 14 forks left, continue on the D 215 towards Mancey. Just before Mancey turn right on to the D 182, signposted Jugy and Sennecey-le-Grand. Pass through Jugy and continue on the same road until you reach Sennecey ②.

Leave Sennecey by Rue du Poirier-Chanin and at the T-junction with the D 18 turn left towards Laives and Buxy. Just after you have passed under the A6 motorway you will come to a rough track to the left which leads to the church of St-Martin-de-Laives ③.

Return to the D 18 and continue to Laives, and when almost through the village turn left on to the D 67, signposted Nanton and Cluny. Pass through Vincelle, Nanton, Sully and Tallant, and just after leaving Tallant fork left on to the D 159 towards Nogent and Brancion. At Nogent turn left on to the D 215, signposted Mancey, Tournus and Brancion, and after about 700m turn right at Collonge on to the D 159 towards Brancion. When the road reaches the D 14 at the Auberge du Col de Brancion, turn left and within a few metres turn left again into Brancion ④.

The first walk starts from here.

Leaving Brancion, turn right on to the D 14 towards Chapaize and Cormatin and where the main road bears right immediately before the Château de Nobles, carry straight on towards l'Echelette. At the T-junction beyond l'Echelette turn right (no signs) and at the next T-junction, at Fragnes, turn left (no signs). At Col de la Pistole turn right on to the D 487, signposted Blanot and St-Gengoux. Pass the Grottes de Blanot ⑤

Cluny, today with about 5000 inhabitants, had an abbey that was, in the 12th century, the greatest religious centre in Christendom. The abbey was ransacked in the Revolution, but what remains reveals its former magnificence ▶

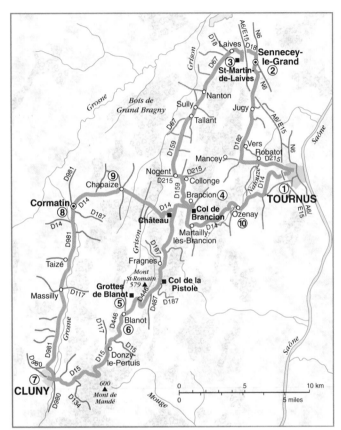

Continue on the D 446 to reach Blanot ⑥.

Leave Blanot on the D 146, signposted Cluny and Mâcon, and at the junction with the D 15 turn right towards Cluny. Skirt the village at Donzy-le-Pertuis and then cross the River Grosne and the D 980 to enter Cluny ⑦.

The second walk starts from the junction of the D 15 and the D 134, 2km from Cluny.

From Cluny's Rue de la Porte de Paris turn left on to the D 980, signposted Chalon-sur-Saône and Montceau-les-Mines, and after about 200m turn right on to the D 981 towards Taizé and Chalon. Pass Massilly and Taizé, then cross the Grosne to reach Cormatin ⑧.

At Cormatin take the D 14, the first turning to the right after the château, signposted Chapaize and Tournus, to arrive at Chapaize ⑨.

Continue on the D 14, passing past Brancion again, to Ozenay ⑩.

From here the D 14 winds down to Tournus.

it has a castle, a covered market hall, several medieval houses and a Romanesque church with 14th-century frescos.

⑤ The Grottes de Blanot, comprising 21 chambers, form the largest network of caves in Burgundy. Descending more than 80m, they have some impressive stalactites and stalagmites.

⑥ Built on the site of a Merovingian necropolis, Blanot is a charming village of balconied houses over-looked by its 11th-century church and 14th-century priory, formerly a dependent of Cluny.

⑦ Cluny was once the centre of the Christian world. Its abbey, founded in 910, was for a long time the largest church in the West, but after the Revolution much of it was destroyed. Its remains, however, which include the Clocher de l'Eau Bénite, Belfry of the Blessed Water, and a few towers, still give some idea of the immense size of the abbey.

⑧ Cormatin is famous for its 17th-century moated château with square towers and pepper-pot turrets. The sumptuous interior is one of the most richly decorated to have survived from the time of Louis XIII.

⑨ The Romanesque church at Chapaize, with its unusually high belfry, was once part of a Benedictine priory founded by monks from the Abbaye de St-Pierre at Chalon-sur-Saône.

⑩ A tiny village beside the River Natouze, Ozenay has a 12th-century church with a timber-framed porch roofed in limestone and a small château dating from the 13th century.

▲ Brancion is an attractive fortified village in the heart of the Mâconnais. It perches on a spur which overlooks two deep ravines

◄ Beautiful 14th-century frescos grace Brancion's 12th-century St-Pierre church

◄ Of Sennecey-le-Grand's castle, all that survives is the substantial building that is now the town hall. It stands at the edge of a square surrounded by a moat

Points of Interest

① An attractive town with tree-shaded quays along the River Saône, Tournus has a lovely old quarter with medieval houses and towers grouped around the beautiful former abbey of St-Philibert. Among these is the Musée Perrin-de-Puycousin, devoted to folklore. A lively market takes place in Rue de la République on Saturday mornings.

② Its position on the N6 helps to make Sennecey-le-Grand a busy little town. At its centre is a large square where what was once a moated castle now serves as the town hall. A large 19th-century church completes the picture.

③ The isolated 11th-century Romanesque church of St-Martin-de-Laives stands on a spur over-looking Sennecey. The views extend over the Saône valley and, on a clear day, as far as the Alps.

④ The picturesque fortified village of Brancion occupies a delightful spot, with extensive views, at the edge of a promontory. Though small,

ST HUGUES OF CLUNY

O f the seven great abbots of Cluny, only St Hugues was born in Burgundy. Hugues de Semur was born of a well-to-do family at the château of Semur-en-Brionnais in 1024. By the time he was 26 he was abbot of one of the greatest foundations in medieval Christendom.

Under his control Cluny flourished and through its portals thousands came to pray, study and teach, prompting Pope Urban II to describe St Hugues as 'the light of the world'.

Daughter abbeys were created, not just in Burgundy, but elsewhere in France and Europe, and Cluny itself continued to expand. In 1088 St Hugues laid the foundation stone for Cluny's third church, which until St Peter's was built in Rome was the largest in Christendom.

It was 177m long, had five aisles and four huge towers and was so richly decorated that it was described later as the Benedictine Versailles.

In later life St Hugues spent much time at the priory of Berzé-la-Ville in order to escape the pressures of Cluny. He died in 1109 after 60 years of rule and before his great church was completed, but leaving as his legacy a most prosperous abbey.

Below Brancion

BURGUNDY

▲ *Medieval Brancion retains its small but handsome 15th-century market hall, behind which can be seen the partly restored feudal castle*

Brancion, on its lofty perch, makes a good start and finish to a walk. On the whole the walking is easy, though the climb back to the village is quite steep and the forest section tends to become rather overgrown during the summer.

Route Directions

Start from the car park (small charge) at the entrance to Brancion.

Walk along the road to the village gateway and turn left on to a footpath, immediately turning left again downhill (in effect doubling back on the way you have come along the road). At the bottom of the slope cross the road on to a path which descends between hedges, and in 25m turn right on to another path, still descending.

Pass through a gate and narrow field (the path is not very clear), emerging at the far end on a more definite path which quickly peters out. Keep to the field's lower edge, then pass through a gap in the hedge on to a path and walk to the road ①.

The path continues across the road, first with a hedge on the left and then with one on the right, and after 250m bears right to a surfaced track. Turn left and in 600m the track becomes a rough path ②.

After 750m cross a small stream and bear right along a narrow path which passes through the edge of the forest. Follow this path for 750m and when it emerges from the trees carry straight on for 250m to a dirt track. Turn right and follow the track for just over 1km to a minor road. Turn right and after 800m reach a junction at the edge of la Chapelle-sous-Brancion ③.

Turn left and immediately right, walk round the church tower and take the road uphill past an ivy-covered house on the right. After about 100m, just before a large house surrounded by trees, turn left and follow a steep narrow path for 200m to the road. Ten metres to the right the path continues through a gap in the hedge across the road, climbing through woods, and after 400m arrives at the gate to Brancion ④.

Points of Interest

① From the path there are wonderful views to the north to la Chapelle-sous-Brancion and west to the Forêt de Chapaize.

② Ahead is the dark expanse of the Forêt de Chapaize, while the immediately surrounding countryside has few trees apart from the occasional tall poplar. This is a good area for spotting buzzards.

③ The little village of la Chapelle-sous-Brancion, a collection of small farms and houses, clusters around its Romanesque church amid fields at the foot of Brancion's hill.

④ The medieval walled village of Brancion is a delight to wander around and has an interesting church and castle. There is also an inn for accommodation and refreshment, and from the terrace in front of the church the fine view towards the Charollais and Morvan, encompasses the whole walk.

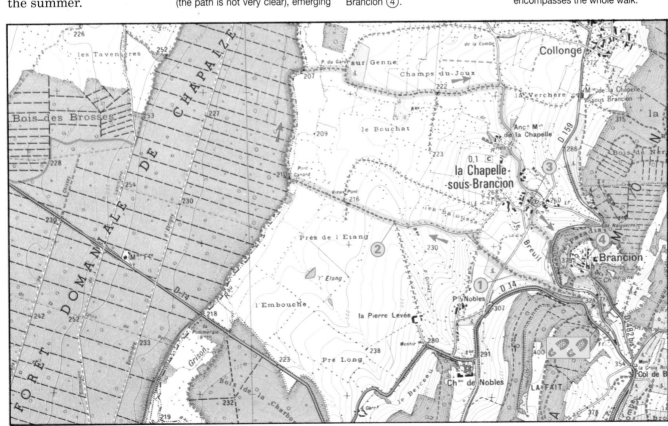

BURGUNDY

25B

Cluny woodland

This walk may spend much of its time wandering through woods, but it has a number of surprises in store, especially in terms of views. The going is generally easy except for a fairly steep climb on the GR 76A.

▲ A carving on a tree near the woodland source of the Croix

Route Directions

Start from the forester's house at the junction of the D 15 Azé road and the D 134 Berzé road, opposite which you can park.

Walk along the D 134 for 250m, then turn on to a path through the trees along the left of the road. Where the road bears right continue uphill into the forest along a wide track. After 600m, where the track climbs sharply left, go ahead along a path indicated by green markers ①.

After 500m the path bears left and after another 250m reaches a crossing of paths. Turn right and after 100m, where the main track

turns right, carry straight on along a narrow path indicated by red-and-white markers. The path climbs steeply through the forest, then at a small clearing descends gently for approximately 600m until it reaches the road at the Col de la Croix Montmain ②.

Cross the road and take the path with purple-and-yellow markers, which branches right downhill into forest. After about 250m the markers indicate a path to the left which leads in 100m from the main track to another, lower track ③.

Turn right and after almost 1km the path reaches the edge of the forest, with views to the left across a valley. Carry on for another 600m and then take the path to the right back into the forest, still following purple-and-yellow markers ④.

At a fork in the path bear right, still following the markers, but where a marker indicates a right turn uphill carry straight on. After a few metres leave the forest through a gate and walk 200m to a forester's house. Turn right past the house, and where the path enters the woods again turn left alongside a drystone wall. Descend to the road and turn right, walking for 500m to the junction with the D 134.

A gap in the Bois de Bourcier provides a fine view over the lush and fertile countryside of Burgundy ▼

▲ *East of Cluny lies the Bois de Bourcier, an area of dense deciduous woodland, where the traditional skills of the forester are in demand throughout the year. Paths are well maintained and signposted*

Points of Interest

① From the path there is a view through the trees beyond Cluny towards the hills of the Charollais region.

② Two roads meet at the Col de la Croix Montmain, the D 134 and the D 194. The clearing amid oak trees is a popular spot for picnickers, who can make use of a stone barbecue.

③ Where the path meets the lower track, an old tree-trunk supported by a latticework of branches marks the source of the Croix, a little stream that flows into the River Grosne near Cluny. Notice, at the foot of the trunk, a carving of a face with a finger cheekily touching its nose.

④ Through gaps in the trees there are views of Cluny with the Clocher de l'Eau Bénite at its centre, surrounded by the town's red roofs.

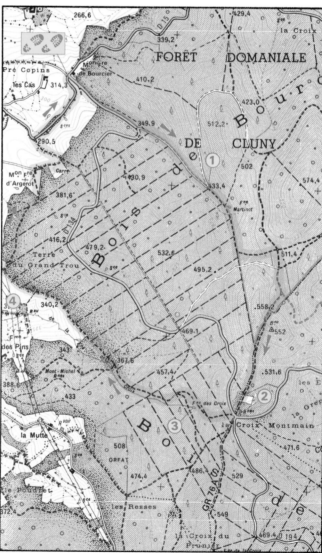

Around Lons-le-Saunier

T his tour provides the opportunity to sample the local wines and Comté cheese and to see the loveliest lake and waterfall in Franche-Comté. From Lons-le-Saunier the route runs near other salt centres such as Salins-les-Bains and Arc-et-Senans. Baume-les-Messieurs, a short drive from Lons-le-Saunier, should not be missed.

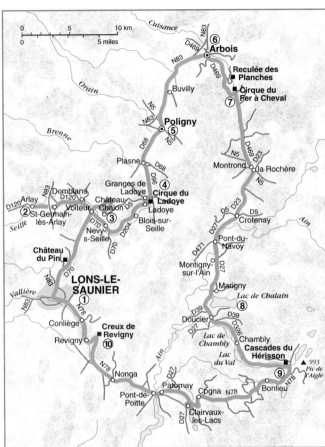

Mellow Arbois is the wine capital of Franche-Comté. The microbiologist Louis Pasteur spent much of his youth and all his holidays in the town ▶

Route Directions

The drive starts in Lons-le-Saunier ①.

Leave the town by the D 70, signposted Voiteur, which branches off the N83 to Poligny. To the left of the long, straight stretch of the D 70 is the Château du Pin. At Voiteur make a short detour along the D 120, through Domblans and St-Germain-lès-Arlay and under the N83 to Arlay ②.

Retrace your steps to the D 70 and carry on to Château-Chalon ③.

Continue on the D 70 through Nevy-sur-Seille. Soon after Nevy the road forks, the right-hand fork leading to Baume-les-Messieurs and the left-hand fork leading on the D 204 to

the Cirque de Ladoye, where there is a belvedere ④.

About 50m after the belvedere, at the crossroads turn left on to the D 96, signposted Poligny ⑤.

Leave Poligny by the N5 to Dole, then turn right on to the N 83, heading north towards Arbois ⑥.

Arbois guards the entrance to two of the best-known cirques, the Reculée des Planches and the Cirque du Fer à Cheval ⑦.

To reach them, leave Arbois on the D 469, signposted Champagnole via Montrond. Turn right on to the N5 shortly before Montrond, and from la Rochère, just after Montrond, take the D 23 to Crotenay. From here take the D 27, following signs to Doucier and Lac de Chalain ⑧.

From Doucier follow the D 39 east, signposted Cascades du Hérisson ⑨.

From the Cascades take the D 75 to join the N78, signposted Lons-le-Saunier. From Cogna to Clairvaux-les-Lacs this road runs along the top of a gorge, before crossing the River Ain at Patornay and going on to Pont-de-Poitte and the Creux de Revigny ⑩.

▲ *The Cascades du Hérisson, which lower the river by 300m in 3km, are the finest waterfalls in Franche-Comté. Popular spots are the Grand Saut and the Saut de la Forge*

Stay on the same road, passing through Conliège, to return to Lons-le-Saunier.

Points of Interest

① In Lons-le-Saunier the Puits Salé, a salt spring known to the Romans, supplies the municipal open-air swimming baths.

Rouget de Lisle, composer of *La Marseillaise,* was born, in 1760, at 24 Rue du Commerce, a pleasantly arcaded sidewalk with houses of pale local stone. The effect of the varied arches is pleasing and a peep into some of the courtyards will reveal elegant staircases. Lisle is also commemorated by a statue which stands in the Promenade de la Chevalerie. It is the work of Bartholdi, better known as the designer of the Statue of Liberty.

The Eglise des Cordeliers has magnificent carved woodwork in the choir. Nearby is the Promenade de la Chevalerie. Here Marshal Ney, commanded by Louis XVIII to stop Napoleon's progress towards Paris, changed his allegiance. Ney, whom Napoleon called 'the bravest of the brave', died in front of a firing squad after Waterloo.

② The château at Arlay was once a home of the Princes of Orange, and the village is a centre of production of the distinctive local wines. One family has been producing wine here since 1781. The present incumbent, bulky, bluff and leather-aproned, has a collection of wines some bottles of which date from before the Revolution. He currently offers for sale no wines earlier than 1928, the year of his birth.

③ Château-Chalon is a village of about 200 inhabitants, with a 12th-century church which, like many of the houses, is roofed with limestone slabs. Behind the church is a belvedere with a view over the vast plain, and to the left is the Cirque de Ladoye.

Château-Chalon is famous for its very special white wine, *vin jaune,* made from Savagnin grapes. It matures for six years in the barrel, and during this time 38 per cent of it will evaporate. The deep-yellow wine, with its most distinctive nose and flavour, is the only wine that the bureaucrats of Brussels allow to be sold in a 62-cl bottle rather than the EC standard of 75-cl.

④ The Cirque de Ladoye is 600m across and 200m deep, and the view from the belvedere is memorable.

⑤ For an unusual view over Poligny, climb up to the 'Trou de la Lune', a cavern beneath the Château de Grimont. Poligny is regarded as the home of Comté cheese. The huge copper cauldrons in which the milk for the cheese was heated can be seen used as flower containers in many villages in Franche-Comté.

Comté is made only from the milk of Montbéliard, or Pie Rouge, cows, fed on fresh grass. It is a tasty cheese, well suited to the local wines.

⑥ Grape varieties not encountered elsewhere in France are used for Arbois wines. They spend two or three years in the barrel, which accounts for their distinctive bouquet and flavour. Montigny uses Trousseau grapes, while Pupillin wine comes from Poulsard grapes. To ensure a more reliable harvest of grapes, the Pinot Noir has been introduced from Burgundy.

Louis Pasteur lived in Arbois as a child. His work on fermentation was of immense value to local wine-growers and subsequently those in other parts of France.

⑦ The Reculée des Planches leads into the cliffside for over 900m, and after rain the river tumbles down through a chain of pools. When it is dry there are fantastically shaped

▲ Lons-le-Saunier, which lies among vineyards scattered over the Jura foothills, and is perhaps best known as a spa town and a base for exploring the area's gorges and chasms, also has a fine theatre

and fancifully named features to be seen. A five-minute walk from a car park alongside the road leads to the belvedere overlooking the Cirque du Fer à Cheval.

⑧ Lac de Chalain is the second-largest natural lake in Franche-Comté, its clear blue water drawing many visitors to the camp site and marina at its eastern tip. The museum at nearby Marigny displays evidence of settlement here dating back 5000 years. Reconstructed lake dwellings are to be seen along the western shore.

⑨ A walk of 500m from the car park at the Cascades du Hérisson brings you to the bottom of the spectacular 65m drop of the Cascade de l'Eventail. A narrow path leads away from the water, crosses over a bridge and after 300m recrosses it. The best view of the Grand Saut, a sheer drop of 60m, is from the bottom, where you now stand. The river tumbles down a number of limestone lintels and steps as you continue upstream to the Saut de la Forge, a 12-m drop into a small, shallow basin. This is within sight of the car park at the top of the road which comes up from Bonlieu.

The uneven path can become very muddy and slippery, so wear shoes with rugged soles.

⑩ The Creux de Revigny is a cirque with intercommunicating caves in the cliffs. Here, during the Thirty Years War, the local inhabitants took refuge from Swedish marauders.

JEAN DE WATTEVILLE

In France in the second half of the 16th century monastic life was becoming less ascetic, and in time candidates were accepted only if they were from the nobility. In this way Baume-les-Moines became Baume-les-Messieurs.

Of the 'Messieurs', Jean de Watteville was undoubtedly the most notorious. As a soldier he had killed an opponent in a duel, and it is said that he became a monk in penance. Cloistered life did not entirely suit him, however. Discovered climbing over the wall by his Superior, Watteville shot him and fled to Spain, where he was made an officer in the armies of the Grand Turk and became a Muslim with his own harem. Later he was instrumental in saving Venice from capture by the Turks, by means of a little double-dealing involving the promise of Papal absolution and the position of Abbot at Baume-les-Messieurs. Here he spent the rest of his life, dying at 84. He drove his monks hard, if not along the straightest of paths.

◀ A statue in Arbois commemorates the achievements of Louis Pasteur

The Pasteur family home, in Arbois' Rue de Courcelles, is now a museum ▼

Lac de Chalain

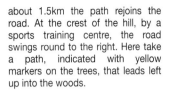

In the museum at Marigny are artefacts dating the earliest settlement on the shores of the lake to around 5000 years ago. Today fishermen, campers, scuba-divers and windsurfers enjoy this turquoise jewel, set in the limestone cliffs of a cirque now covered with beech trees. This walk near the lake is best done in the late morning, with the sun behind you.

Route Directions

Start from the car park at the Domaine de Chalain camp site, at the eastern end of Lac de Chalain.

Immediately outside the camp site gate is a little path down to the lake. There are yellow markers on the trees to the right of the path. After

Lac de Chalain lies at an altitude of nearly 500m and is considered the most beautiful of the many lakes in the heart of Franche-Comté. Neolithic people settled here 5,000 years ago and examples of their dwellings have been reconstructed on the lake shore ▼

about 1.5km the path rejoins the road. At the crest of the hill, by a sports training centre, the road swings round to the right. Here take a path, indicated with yellow markers on the trees, that leads left up into the woods.

A well-defined rocky narrow path now winds up through coppiced beech woods to the Belvédère sur la Roche ①.

The path continues along the top of a flat limestone area to the Belvédère de la Frate ②.

Continue on the same path to the Belvédère du Lac ③.

Instead of walking back down the road, go back along the path about 500m to a sign saying 'Sentier difficile et accidenté', indicating that the path is steep. Stout railings line a flight of metal steps down the first section, then a path leads along under the overhanging limestone cliff edge, well guarded to the right by strong rails. The steep twisting path has log-reinforced steps in places. Ten minutes' cautious walking leads you back down to lake level.

From the same starting point in the Domaine de Chalain camp site there is another walk, along the north clifftop path. It begins near the shower block, climbs up the Sentier

Neuf and then goes along the cliff towards Marigny. After about 1.8km you can walk down into Marigny (it is a 2km return trip) to visit the Maison des Lacs museum, or turn right, heading inland from the cliff edge and back to the Belvédère de Fontenu.

Points of Interest

① Strong railings line the edge of the steep cliff at the Belvédère sur la Roche. There is a bench from which to enjoy a magnificent view over the turquoise waters and across to the reconstructed prehistoric lake dwellings on the western shore.

② The Belvédère de la Frate gives views over the campers and fishermen enjoying the lake and the cliff walk along the opposite shore.

③ The Belvédère du Lac commands an excellent view across the whole length of the lake from behind the Domaine de Chalain camp site.

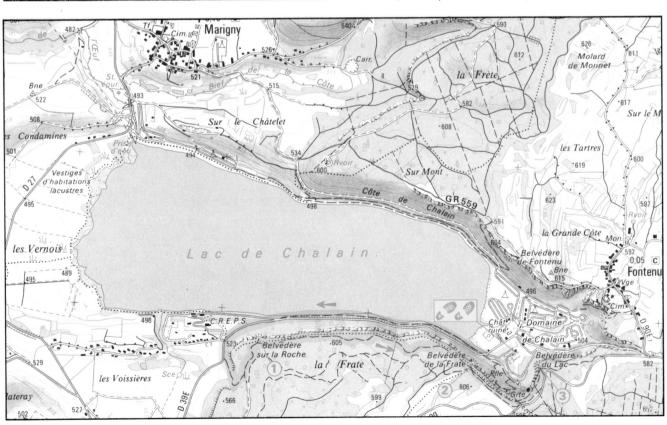

Around Château-Chalon

This lengthy ramble down country lanes and through vineyards ends with a stiff climb out of a limestone valley, after which a drink at Château-Chalon will have been well earned.

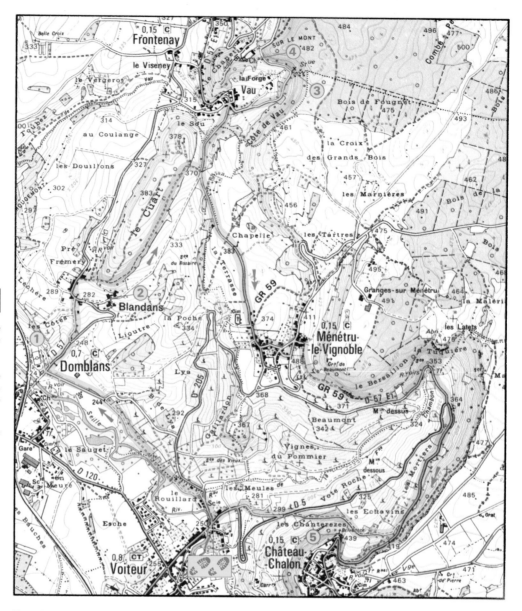

Route Directions

Start from the village side of the bridge at Voiteur, where you can park under plane trees.

Route de Ménétru leads along the bank of the River Seille, swinging to the left after about 200m. There are double yellow or orange bands on trees and telegraph poles. Soon the path leads into a thicket of poplars. Turn right at a T-junction with the D 57 from Domblans to Blandans ①.

After 200m a rough path leads off left to Blandans ②.

Follow this up the slope and at the T-junction turn right. Another rough, stony path leads left, marked with the double yellow bar sign. Climb gently up, between woods and pasture, and rejoin the road comes in from the right. From here there is a magnificent view back down a valley typical of Franche-Comté, with the Château du Pin in the distance.

Take the road down into Vau, turning right just as you enter the village. The road climbs up through woods and round the side of a steep limestone valley. As it bears left there is a grotto ③.

The road then leads up to the château ④.

Retrace your steps along the road into Vau and turn left on to the road to Ménétru-le-Vignoble. Turn left into the village, cross a minor road and pick up a footpath which leads through vineyard tracks and across the cirque, a steep-sided dead-end limestone valley, with Château-Chalon on the other side.

There is a concrete path through the vines at the bottom of the valley. This makes it unnecessary to walk all the way along the road, but take the D 205 into the village.

There is a stone cross and a belvedere at the entrance to Château-Chalon ⑤.

From here there is a splendid view over the valley and the vineyards. After exploring the village, leave by the same road and after 100m take a path to your left. This leads through woods, across the main road, on to a *chemin privé* which leads back to the bridge in Voiteur.

Points of Interest

① To the right of the road is a cross in memory of a local missionary nun, Marie Clavelin, martyred in Tientsin in 1870. *Clavelin* is also the name of the small bottle used for Château-Chalon wine.

② There are two imposing château-style country houses in Blandans.

③ The source of the Frontenay river flows into a mossy stone basin and the nearby shrine has Stations of the Cross climbing the slope behind it.

④ A fort was built at Frontenay in the 12th century to protect a salt road. In 1446 the local seigneur gave the château to his squire and it has remained in the same family ever since. Only the 14th-century keep and well remain of the original buildings. Visitors are welcome to use the terrace and courtyard, from where there are views over the surrounding countryside, and the picnic tables and benches.

⑤ The church of St-Pierre in Château-Chalon is early Gothic, probably on 10th-century foundations. Like many of the houses in the village, it is roofed with limestone slabs. Many small boutiques attract tourists and the tiny, cool cellar of the Taverne du Rocher is also inviting.

▼ One of Blandans' two châteaux

Baume-les-Dames, Belfort and Belvoir

FRANCHE-COMTÉ

This is a figure-of-eight circuit, centred on Isle-sur-le Doubs. It is a fairly long tour, but there is the possibility of splitting the route into stages and spending more time at Ronchamp or Belvoir, or in and around Belfort itself.

Leave Baume-les-Dames by crossing the distinctive concrete bridge over the Doubs, still on the D 492, signposted Ornans and Pont-les-Moulins. This road leads to the start of the first walk. At Pont-les-Moulins turn left on to the D 21, going along the wooded valley of the Cusançin, crossing the river several times. To the left of this road is the Source Bleue ⑤.

◄ *The little River Cusancin rises at the Source Bleue, so called because of the blue tint that characterises this horseshoe-shaped pool set in attractive woodland*

Continue on the D 21 to the crossroads with the D 119, turn right towards Vellevans, then take the D 464 to the left, signposted Sancey-le-Grand, Sancey-l'Eglise and Sancey-le-Long, and then turn left on to the D 31 towards Rahon and the D 21 to Belvoir ⑥.

Retrace your steps to the D 31, and go north over the Col de Ferrière, giving a vista of wooded valleys and little villages. From the crossroads at Glainans the road runs down through woodland and under the motorway to join the N83. Turn right here to return to Isle-sur-le Doubs.

Route Directions

The drive starts from Isle-sur-le Doubs.

Take the D 31 north, signposted Geney and Villersexel. Once in Haute-Saône, just after Geney, the road becomes the D 18. At Velle-chevreux-et-Courbenans turn right on to the D 9 towards Héricourt. After leaving the village of Saulnot, turn left at the top of a rise, on to the D 96, signposted Courmont and Ronchamp. This is a pleasant country road through beech woods, and after a short stretch along the D 438 (turn left then right), it leads into Frédéric-Fontaine ①.

Continue to Clairegoutte. After Clairegoutte take the D 4 to the right to Ronchamp. Turn right on to the D 464 to Notre-Dame-du-Haut ②.

Return to Ronchamp and take the N19/E54 east to Belfort ③.

Leave Belfort by the N83, signposted Héricourt. This is a 35km stretch along a main road, leading back, via the N463 after Médière, to Isle-sur-le Doubs.

Start the second stage of the circuit by leaving Isle-sur-le Doubs on the D 29, signposted Appenans. Stay on the D 29 and pass through Soye to Uzelle, turning left at Uzelle on to the D 114 and going through Fontenelle-Montby to join the D 492 at Vergranne, signposted Baume-les-Dames ④.

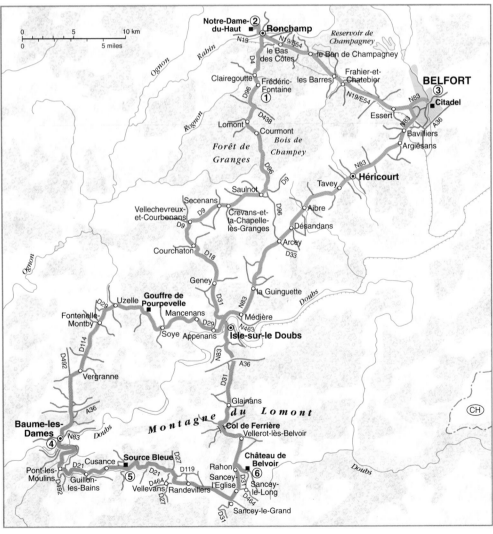

▲ The imposing church of St-Martin in Baume-les-Dames was rebuilt in the 17th century and has a chapel either side of the chancel

◄ In one of St-Martin's side chapels there is an 18th-century statue of St Vincent

④ Baume-les-Dames has many elegantly restored Renaissance houses and an abbey church. The tourist office is housed in the old wash-house and has much information, including several suggested walks, of which one is chosen here for its peace and quiet and views over the valley.

Baume is the old French word for a grotto, of which there are hundreds in the limestone countryside of Franche-Comté. The young Ste Odile, patron saint of Alsace, born blind, fled from her vindictive father to the Abbaye de Baume-les-Nonnes and was miraculously given her sight at her baptism. By the 18th century the abbey admitted only candidates from noble families and the name was changed from 'Nonnes' to 'Dames'.

⑤ The source of the 10km long River Cusancin is strikingly clear and blue in the dappled shade. The horseshoe-shaped pool is home to many large trout. A café nearby makes a pleasant spot for a short stop. On the other side of the road, in a grotto in a limestone cliff, is the Source Noire, a secondary source of the same river.

⑥ The Château de Belvoir dominates the surrounding villages. A long road trails up to the crest, the village clinging to both sides of the narrow ridge. The château is set at the road's end, with a portcullis gateway and a parking area for just two cars.

Belvoir is owned by an artist and his wife, who have furnished it beautifully. There are some works by Courbet – the artist lived at nearby Ornans – and a collection of toy cannon, given by Napoleon to his son, the little King of Rome. There are stupendous views from the tower rooms, but since it relies on the services of local guides, the château is open to visitors only on Sundays except in July and August.

The restored 12th-century château at Belvoir can be visited, and among its attractions is the kitchen with its copper utensils ▼

Points of Interest

① There is not much evidence today of the village of Frédéric-Fontaine, founded on 16 July 1588 by Protestant refugees who were given the land by Prince Frédéric and gratefully named their village after him.

② The unusual chapel of Notre-Dame-du-Haut at Ronchamp was designed by Le Corbusier in 1955. The building's contrasting features and jewel-like stained-glass windows soften the otherwise stark concrete of what seems more a piece of modern sculpture.

An Aztec-like sacrificial pyramid, built of the stones from the pre-war church, marks the front line where General de Lattre de Tassigny's First Army fought for two months to take the heights, in October 1944.

③ The massive citadel at Belfort is the work of Vauban, ordered by Louis XIV to 'make the city impregnable'. The city never passed into Prussian hands with the rest of Alsace and Lorraine. Between 1871 and World War I a chain of forts was built along the frontier, a defence policy leading in part to the belief in the impregnability of the later Maginot Line.

GROTTE DE LA GLACIERE

About 10km south of Baume-les-Dames is a relic of the last Ice Age. When the glaciers retreated from this part of France 10,000 years ago, in one cave, only 525m above sea level, with a northerly aspect and turbulence caused by the prevailing winds, the ice remained. Situated on the D 30, near Chaux-les-Passavant, this grotto – unique in France – retains ice all year round, even after several warm summers and dry winters.

The cave is over 60m deep and the denser cold air remains deep down in the cave, with ice stalactites and stalagmites forming between roof and floor. Because of the continual turbulence, some of these icy stalactites lean permanently out towards the mouth of the cave.

There is a café nearby and a large exhibition of mineral specimens from all around the world, collected by the present owner of the grotto when he was a merchant seaman.

Around Baume-les-Dames

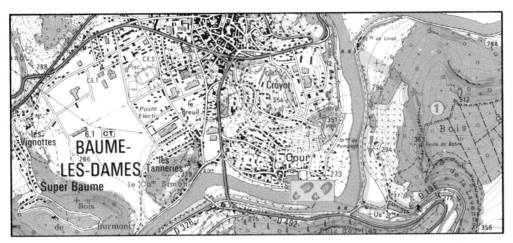

This short walk provides an introduction to some of the more strenuous routes along the limestone bluffs of Franche-Comté and the sandstone peaks of the Vosges.

Route Directions

Start from the River Cusancin not far from Baume-les-Dames. To reach the starting point leave Baume by the D 492 towards Ornans and go over the concrete Pont du Doubs. Continue towards Villers-St-Martin. A kilometre along this road turn left at a sign to the 'Usine des Pipes Ropp'. Cross the river and leave the car under the trees to the left of the road.

Five hundred metres up the road, a path marked with a red and white rectangle sign leads off to the left. It climbs up the limestone bluff and meets the road again at the top, on a bend marked to Villers-St-Martin. There is a statue of the Virgin here in a bright-blue robe. There is also a sign to 'Fente de Babre – 1200m'. It is marked red and white, part of another Grande Randonnée trail across France. The local colours, blue and yellow, are also visible on the trees. The track leads up through beech trees and climbs steadily to reach the impressive viewpoint at the Fente de Babre ①.

The track now leads down towards the Doubs, with the N 83 across the other side. Down almost at river level the track turns sharp left, and there is a gentle stroll back along the river bank to the car.

Points of Interest

① High above Baume, the Fente de Babre gives a splendid view over the valley, the town and the loop of the river on which it stands.

From the 1200m-high viewpoint of the Fente de Babre, there is an impressive view of the valley of the River Doubs and of Baume-les-Dames, named after a Benedictine abbey for noblewomen ▼

WALK 27B: 5KM/ALLOW 1½ HOURS

Vauban's forts around Belfort

There is a recently opened 65-km walk around all the Belfort forts, and this is an easy section of it. This walk includes Belfort's citadel, the Lion and two of the outlying forts.

Continue through a short tunnel in the rock, on to a path which zigzags down the hillside and is clearly marked with yellow rectangles. When you see a red disc sign, follow this, ignoring the yellow rectangles which indicate the start of the 65km walk. The red discs lead to the main road at the Carrefour des Fusillés ⑥.

Turn left here and enter Place de la République, then go left towards the church in Place d'Armes. The car park behind the town hall lies diagonally across the small square.

▲ The Porte de Brisach, the original gateway to Vauban's citadel in Belfort, survives intact. In front is a tank commemorating a Breton soldier who died here in 1944

Route Directions

Start from the bottom of the steps up to the citadel in Belfort ①.

Turn right and climb the flight of steps leading up to the platform below the Lion ②.

Go through a little tunnel, out into the daylight at the base of the citadel wall, and the whole town is spread out to your right. Small yellow rectangle signs mark the way. Carry on around a small outwork and along the dry moat to the Porte de Brisach ③.

Turn right along the walls, up an inclined plane to a pedestrian footbridge over the road. Pass through open grassland with newly planted trees to the Fort de la Justice ④.

Go through the gateway, turn right along a path outside the fort, then back to the left to steps to a footbridge over the N83 and across the valley. The citadel and its flag are visible to your left as you climb up to the Fort de la Miotte ⑤.

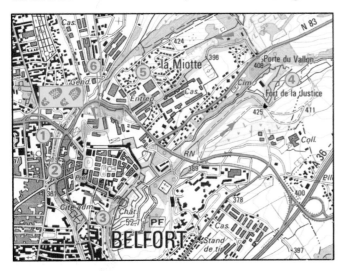

Points of Interest

① The Comte de Vauban finished Belfort's original citadel in 1705, and the outlying crests to the north were fortified as Fort de la Justice and Fort de la Miotte in 1794. The citadel in its present form dates from 1827, however.

Vauban's are classic designs, developments of fortifications built as far apart as Antwerp, Verona and Berwick-on-Tweed in the mid-16th century. Bastions hidden behind angles of the steeply sloping stone walls have direct sight-lines along the dry moats. Here is a chance to see at close quarters one of the greatest achievements of Louis XIV's military engineer.

② Bartholdi, the designer of the Statue of Liberty in New York, sculpted the massive Lion de Belfort, which measures 22m by 11m, in red Vosges sandstone. It symbolises Belfort's resistance in 1870, when Colonel Denfert-Rochereau and the 16,000-strong garrison defied a 40,000-strong Prussian army. A miniature of the Lion stands in the Place Denfert-Rochereau in Paris.

③ Under the symbol of the 'Sun King' on the original Vauban gateway, built in 1687, stands a tank. This is a memorial to a Breton, Lieutenant Martin, killed in action here on 21 November 1944.

④ From the Fort de la Justice there is a splendid view back towards the citadel.

⑤ The tall sandstone watch-tower of the Fort de la Miotte is in the neo-Gothic style with false *meurtrières*, murder-holes. The real counterparts of these were used for pouring boiling oil on assailants.

⑥ A striking statue to the memory of Resistance fighters stands under the walls at the Carrefour des Fusillés.

The vineyards of Bordeaux

Almost every village on this tour through what is France's greatest wine-producing region has a world-famous name. You will almost certainly want to linger in the beautiful old wine town of St-Emilion, perched on a hillside. The tour also crosses the River Garonne, which flows through Bordeaux, a thriving city and the wine capital of France.

◀ Medieval St-Emilion, famous all over the world for its wine, is blessed with a picturesque hilltop location

Route Directions

The drive starts from Langon ①.

Leave Langon on the N113, signposted Libourne. Just outside the town turn right towards St-Macaire ②.

Leave St-Macaire, cross over the N113 and on to the D 672 towards Sauveterre-de-Guyenne, passing through le Pian-sur-Garonne and St-André-du-Bois ③.

Continue to St-Laurent-du-Bois, and just after the village turn left on to an unclassified road, following signs to Sauveterre-de-Guyenne, St-Sulpice-de-Pommiers and la Réole. At the end of this small detour rejoin the D 672 and continue to Sauveterre-de-Guyenne ④.

Leave Sauveterre-de-Guyenne, following signs to Libourne on the D 670, passing the small town of le Puch. Continue on the same road and pass through St-Jean-de-Blaignac, cross the River Dordogne, and go through Lavagnac. Pass through a junction at Merlande, staying on the D 670 and following signs to Libourne and St-Emilion. Some 4km further on, take the right turn for St-Emilion ⑤.

Leave St-Emilion on the same road as you came in on. Cross straight over the D 670 on to the D 122, signposted Branne and Cadillac. (This is a very narrow and winding road.) After 3km turn left on to the D 19, signposted Branne. Continue and cross the bridge into Branne. Leave Branne on the D 936, signposted Cadillac and Bordeaux. Just under 1km later bear left towards Bordeaux, staying on the D 936. Turn left on to the D 11, for Targon and Cadillac. Pass through Grézillac and continue on the D 11. About 9km later, turn right on to the main road, the D 671, signposted Targon, and then immediately left back on to the D 11. Follow this into Targon.

Leave Targon on the D 11 towards Cadillac, following signs to Escoussans. After 6km bear right at the fork on the D 11 for Cadillac and

then pass through Escoussans. After 2km, at the T-junction, take a right turn for Cadillac and Bordeaux, staying on the D 11 into Cadillac ⑥.

As you come into the town go round the roundabout and follow the D 10 towards Bordeaux. Almost immediately after this turning, turn left on to the D 11, signposted A62 Cérons. Cross the River Garonne and enter Cérons ⑦.

Follow signs to Illats on the A62. One and a half kilometres beyond Cérons turn off the motorway on to the D 117e2, signposted Illats and St-Symphorien. Just after this turn left on to the D 11 to Illats. Pass through Illats and stay on the D 11, signposted Landiras and St-Symphorien. Go through Artigues and continue to Landiras, where you turn left on to the D 116, signposted Pujols-sur-Ciron and Langon.

After 3.5km turn right on to the D 118 towards Budos. After 6km turn left on to the D 125, towards Sauternes and Bommes, crossing the River Ciron. Continue to Sauternes ⑧.

In Sauternes follow signs for Roaillan and Langon. At the next junction turn left on to the D 8 to Langon. After 1km turn right, staying on the D 8, to return to Langon.

An intriguing water pump in St-Macaire ▼

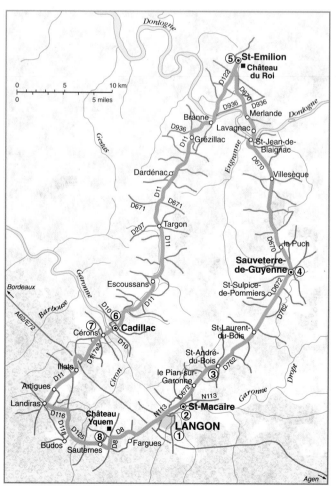

ARCACHON

The sheltered basin of Arcachon, where the Médoc meets the sea, has produced mussels and oysters for centuries. But its resorts are also very dependent on the wine trade, since for many years the rich of Bordeaux, whose wealth is largely based on wine, have regarded the area as their playground. Many have second homes in or around Arcachon.

Now one of France's most stylish seaside resorts, Arcachon started to develop when the railway line between the town and Bordeaux was opened in the mid-19th century. During Bordeaux's VinExpo exhibition, which takes place every June, it is almost impossible to rent a room or book a restaurant table in Arcachon, as the wine merchants of Bordeaux entertain buyers here.

Points of Interest

① Langon, on the banks of the Garonne, is an important wine centre known for its sweet dessert wines. Here you will find a partly Romanesque church with 12th-century frescos, and on the outskirts of town are 28 menhirs, said to be 28 girls turned to stone for missing evening Mass.

② St-Macaire, a medieval town built on limestone rock, is named after a 6th-century bishop. Visit the postal museum, which was a post house in the time of Henri IV, on the long Place du Mercadiou, and the impressive church of St-Sauveur.

③ In St-André-du-Bois is the Château de Malromé, the final home of Toulouse-Lautrec before he died at the age of 37. He is buried in Verdelais, just south-west of St-André. The château has a rare collection of the artist's drawings.

④ Sauveterre-de-Guyenne is an interesting small *bastide* (fortified town) with four large gateways and a castle built by Edward I of England.

⑤ St-Emilion perches in medieval splendour on a hilltop overlooking the Dordogne valley. Named after an 8th-century Breton monk who came to live here in a cave carved out of

the limestone rock, the village is famous throughout the world for its wine and locally for its macaroons. The quality of St-Emilion wines has been supervised for eight centuries by an elected council of peers, known as *Jurats*. Every spring they meet to attend Mass and then assess the wines from the previous year's harvest.

St-Emilion's other attractions include a 9th-12th-century monolithic church carved out of solid rock, the medieval Château du Roi and a small local museum.

⑥ Cadillac is a large fortified village on the banks of the River Garonne. It has an impressive 17th-century château, the vaulted basement rooms of which were at one time used by tapestry weavers. This very large and elaborate château was built by the Duc d'Epernon. Henri IV, realising how rich and ambitious the duke was, encouraged him in the project, hoping that the more time and money he spent the less dangerous he would be.

⑦ Cérons is an ancient port on the River Garonne with a Romanesque church which has interesting carvings on the doorway. This small village has its own *appellation* for dessert wines, as does its neighbour,

▲ *St-Macaire, which overlooks the River Garonne, is a charming little town, with its jumble of narrow streets, arcaded square and medieval houses*

It is said that St-Emilion's monolithic church was hewn out of the rock by disciples of St Emilion, who in the 8th century lived in the adjacent hermitage, also carved out of the rock ▼

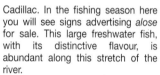

Cadillac. In the fishing season here you will see signs advertising *alose* for sale. This large freshwater fish, with its distinctive flavour, is abundant along this stretch of the river.

⑧ There is an information and wine tasting centre at the Maison du Vin in the square of the small, sleepy village of Sauternes. Just outside Sauternes, on a hilltop to the north, is the famous Château Yquem (though it is not clearly signposted). It is well worth making a detour to see this lovely château, which dates back to the 12th century and is famous for producing one of France's most prestigious white wines.

The vineyard of Château-Lamothe, among others, produces Sauternes, a sweet white wine which is exclusive to the Bordeaux region ▼

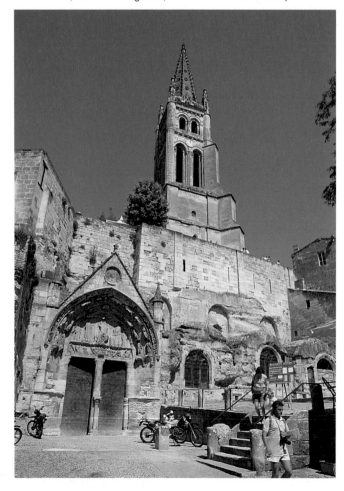

Sauveterre-de-Guyenne

THE ATLANTIC COAST

This walk takes you through the 13th-century *bastide* town of Sauveterre-de-Guyenne. It also explores the beautiful hills and countryside surrounding this fine example of the fortified towns which are scattered throughout this part of France.

A sturdy style of building characterises parts of Sauveterre-de-Guyenne, and recalls its role in centuries past as a bastide, or fortified town ▶

Points of Interest

① Sauveterre-de-Guyenne is a *bastide* town, built by Edward I of England in 1281, and it bears many of the hallmarks of the classic *bastide*, including a large arcaded square. *Bastides*, heavily fortified and usually built on a grid plan, are found in this region and Périgord and Quercy. They played an important part in the conflict between France and England.

② The church of Notre-Dame, which dates back to the 11th century, is just one of the town's many interesting historical landmarks.

③ This is one of the four large gateways built as entrances into the *bastide* town.

④ The Château de Madaillan is one of the many privately owned châteaux in the area.

⑤ From here there is a marvellous view over the area, including three large windmills.

⑥ Another privately owned château, the Château du Sandah, can be seen from the D 671.

Four substantial gateways, of which this is one, gave access to well-defended Sauveterre-de-Guyenne ▼

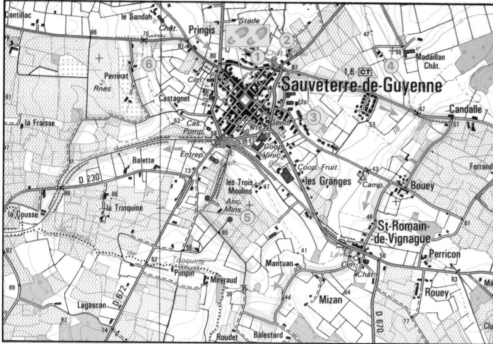

Route Directions

Start from Place de la République in Sauveterre-de-Guyenne ①.

Go down Rue du 8 Mai to the church of Notre-Dame ②.

Carry on down this road to the junction with Rue de Jourdan de Buch, where you turn right. Turn left off this road to pass through a 13th-century gateway ③.

Turn left and take the first road on the right, then the first on the left (passing some storage buildings), before taking the path on the right. From this path you will see the Château de Madaillan to the left ④.

Cross a little bridge before arriving at Candalle, where you turn right towards the little hamlet of Bouey. At Bouey turn right and then left to St-Romain-de-Vignague. Turn right on to the D 230, then take the first left (by the former wash-house) before continuing towards Mantuan.

Turn right at the top of the hill ⑤.

Follow the old railway track, which passes under a road and through cuttings before rejoining the D 230. Follow the footpath under the road, then turn right to double back to it. Turn right on to the road, then take a footpath on the left. This winds round to the right and the left before joining the D 671. Turn right to go back into the town ⑥.

The road then passes through another 13th-century gateway to return to Place de la République in Sauveterre.

St-Macaire

▲ Fortified gateway in St-Macaire

The medieval fortifications and narrow streets of St-Macaire make a fascinating start to this walk along the north bank of the River Garonne.

Route Directions

Start from the car park at the junction of Allées des Tilleuls and Allées Tourny, outside the medieval fortifications, and enter the old town through the Porte de Benauge ①.

Continue to the Maison du Pays, on the right at the corner of Rue de l'Eglise and Rue d'Aulède ②.

Turn left into Rue Carnot, then left again into Rue Yquem. Take the first road on the right, which leads to Place du Mercadiou ③.

At the end of the square turn right into Rue Carnot again and then first left. Carry straight over a crossroads and bear left and then right to reach the church of St-Sauveur and its priory ④.

Turn left out of the square in front of the church and carry on to a junction, where you bear left down Rue Amiral Courbet to reach the Porte Rendesse. Pass through the gateway and turn left on to a road which follows the River Garonne.

Carry on for 2km along a surfaced path which then becomes a dirt track. After passing a picnic area, turn left after les Pradiasses and then first left again to pass through the village of St-Pierre-d'Aurillac. At the junction where you rejoin the main road, the N113, turn right and follow the road to Mérigon. Pass under the old railway bridge and immediately turn left past the cemetery. Follow the road to the first junction, turn left and pass through Samaran to the crossroads at Bartouquey. Carry straight on and after nearly 1km take the footpath on the left. Where the path joins a minor road turn left and continue until you reach the D 672e4. Turn left, passing under the old railway, cross straight over the junction with the N113, and turn right to St-Macaire, avoiding the main road. Follow this road back to the car park.

Points of Interest

① In the 13th and 14th centuries St-Macaire was protected from incursions up the River Garonne by ramparts, a barbican and fortified gateways. The Porte de Benauge to the north, Porte Rendesse to the west and Porte du Thuron to the east all date from the 14th century.

② The Maison du Pays is a typical merchant's house of the 16th century. St-Macaire was, and still is, famous for its sweet white wines.

③ Place du Mercadiou is most attractive, lined by arcaded medieval houses with ribbed vaulting and mullioned windows.

④ The church of St-Sauveur dates back to the 11th century, though its bell tower was rebuilt in the 17th century. Inside are 13th-century murals depicting the life of St John. Of the 12th-century priory, originally a Benedictine foundation, only the south wing of the cloister remains. Restoration work was started in 1968. Beside the priory is the best-preserved section of St-Macaire's 13th- and 14th-century ramparts.

St-Macaire, which was built as a fortified town, retains much of its evocative medieval character ▼

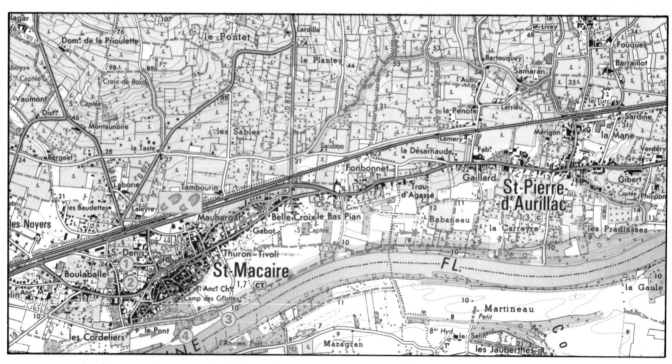

Inland from the Côte de Beauté

From the ancient Roman town of Saintes, through the cognac vineyards to the modern seaside resort of Royan, this tour combines the best of both the old and the new in the region. In the height of summer the roads into the resort towns can become busy, but most of the little towns along the way are pleasantly sleepy all year round.

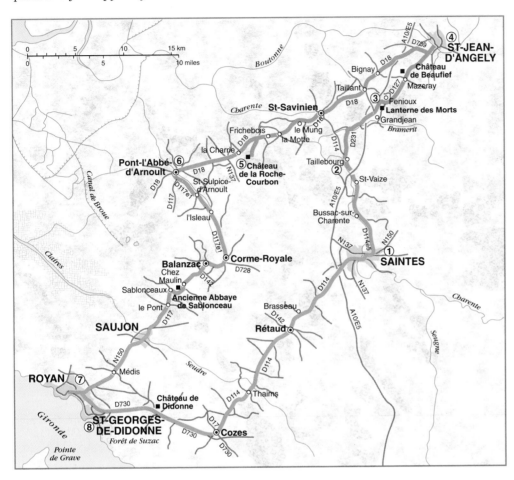

In Fenioux turn right past the Lanterne des Morts, follow this road and then turn left on to the D 127. Go straight through Mazeray, following signs to St-Jean-d'Angély. (On the way to St-Jean there is an interesting brief detour to the Château de Beaufief on your left.) About 2km from the turning to the Château de Beaufief you come to the D 739. Bear right here to go into St-Jean ④.

Leave St-Jean by the way you came in, turn right on to the D 739 and just outside the town look out for the left turn on to the D 18 towards St-Savinien. This road crosses over the motorway again and winds through corn fields and woods, passing through Bignay and Taillant to reach St-Savinien.

Leave St-Savinien on the D 18 towards Pont-l'Abbé-d'Arnoult, crossing the river by the swing-bridge. Pass through le Mung, la Motte and Frichebois. Just outside Frichebois turn left on to the D 122 to see the Château de la Roche-Courbon ⑤.

Rejoin the D 18 and pass through la Charrie. At the next crossroads go straight ahead to Pont-l'Abbé-d'Arnoult ⑥.

Leave Pont-l'Abbé on the D 117 towards Royan, on the opposite side of the town from where you came in. Just after passing the cross on the right-hand side of the road fork left on to the D 117e1, signposted St-Sulpice-d'Arnoult. Continue to St-Sulpice.

Leave St-Sulpice, staying on the D 117e1 and heading in the direction of Corme-Royale. Take the right fork at l'Isleau, and then drive through attractive wooded countryside to reach the village of Corme-Royale.

Leave Corme-Royale on the D 119 and turn right on to the D 728 to Balanzac. Turn left in Balanzac on to a minor road. Cross over the D 142 and continue to the village of Chez Maulin. Turn left at Chez Maulin to pay a visit to the Ancienne Abbaye de Sablonceaux. Go straight over another crossroads and take the right fork to Sablonceaux. Pass the turning for the abbey on your right.

Route Directions

The drive starts from Saintes ①.

Leave Saintes by crossing the River Charente eastwards on the N150 and turning left on to the D 114e5, which then becomes the D 114. Pass through Bussac-sur-Charente and St-Vaize to reach Taillebourg ②.

Stay on the D 114, pass the old railway station and just after the second level crossing turn right on to the D 231. This is a poor road and extremely narrow, so watch out for oncoming traffic. Just after crossing over the little River Bramerit turn right towards St-Hilaire-de-Ville-franche. Soon after, having crossed over the motorway, turn left down a very narrow farmyard track, following signs to Fenioux ③.

St-Jean-d'Angély's abbey was rebuilt in the 17th and 18th centuries ▶

At the next crossroads turn left on to the D 117 and continue into Saujon. Leave Saujon to join the N150, heading towards Royan ⑦.

Leave Royan on the D 730, following signs for Cozes towards the A10/ E5. The D 730 passes through the outskirts of St-Georges-de-Didonne ⑧.

Follow the D 730 to Cozes, looking out for the Château de Didonne on your left, about halfway.

Just as the dual carriageway starts, take the left turn into Cozes, a pretty town with Spanish-style houses. Leave Cozes on the D 114, signposted Rétaud and Saintes. As you approach Rétaud you can see the ancient church on your left. Staying on the D 114, pass through woodland to return to Saintes.

Points of Interest

① The marshes with their plentiful supply of salt, first attracted the Romans to the banks of the River Charente 2000 years ago, and as you walk round the busy town of

▲ *The well-maintained beaches of Royan, with their fine pale sand, combine with a lively atmosphere to make the town one of the most popular holiday resorts on the Côte de Beauté*

The old quarter of the market town of St-Jean-d'Angély, once a stronghold of Protestantism, still has some well-preserved half-timbered houses ▼

Saintes, with its southern French flavour, you can still see the monuments they left, including an impressively restored amphitheatre.

Saintes is also the birthplace of Dr J.I. Guillotin, the inventor of the device used to such deadly effect in the Revolution.

② It was at Taillebourg that St Louis vanquished the British in 1242. There are ruins of a 15th-century château on the right bank of the River Charente.

③ In Fenioux there is an interesting church, part of which dates back to the 9th century, with small windows and a 12th-century staircase to the top. But most fascinating is the church's Lanterne des Morts, Lantern of the Dead.

④ The River Boutonne flows through St-Jean-d'Angély, once an important stage on the pilgrim road to Santiago de Compostela. The abbey, where the pilgrims sometimes stopped, was destroyed and rebuilt several times over the centuries. The town has a museum and many 15th-century timber-framed houses.

▲ *The Romans, who built this arch in Saintes, were here 2000 years ago*

⑤ The mighty Château de la Roche-Courbon, surrounded by forest, was built by Jean de Latour at the end of the 15th century. Today there is a museum of prehistory in its keep.

⑥ Pont-l'Abbé-d'Arnoult grew up around an 11th-century priory and has an ornate church decorated with sculptures. In the museum is a craft centre, and many shops here still sell traditional hand-made rugs with *lirettes* (literally, strips).

⑦ Located at the mouth of the River Gironde, Royan is the main resort on the Côte de Beauté. During World War II the town was heavily bombed, and afterwards it was completely rebuilt. Its attractive sandy beaches have helped make it one of the most popular destinations for holiday-makers on the south-west Atlantic Coast.

⑧ St-Georges-de-Didonne is an unspoilt seaside resort with 2km of first-class beach, and the Suzac pine forest extending up to the Pointe de Suzac.

COGNAC

The world-famous brandy produced in the Charente was first made in the 17th century. The vineyards of Cognac had been cultivated since time immemorial, but in the 17th century Dutch merchants, who together with the English were big importers of the wine, discovered that 'burning' this wine – that is, distilling it – made it easier to transport. The process had the added advantage of making the wine even more agreeable, and thus *brandewijn*, or brandy, became an important export.

Cognac soon became the centre of the world brandy trade, and today its output is around 25 million bottles a year. The famous brandy is still aged traditionally, in oak barrels, and the *eaux de vie* from the different cognac-producing areas are mixed by the *maître de chai*. Brandy lovers say that cognac is best enjoyed on its own, preferably after a meal, from a tulip-shaped glass which enhances the spirit's aromas.

Most cognac houses organise guided tours of their *chais* or warehouses. The tourist office in Cognac also administers a museum with comprehensive displays on the subject.

A woodland walk near Royan

THE ATLANTIC COAST

This walk, which is pleasantly shaded on a hot day, follows well-maintained woodland footpaths and the going is easy. An interesting old chapel is encountered along the way.

Route Directions

Start from le Requin ①.

Follow the Chemin de la Chapelle footpath. After about 1.5km the path crosses a road that acts as a fire-break ②.

To the right is a sand-hill, around which are some old stones; this is the old chapel of Notre-Dame de Buze ③.

Just after this turn right at the next fork and when you meet the Chemin de Tournegrand footpath turn right. Follow this path back to the D 25, keeping right, and turn right along the road to the car park.

The Atlantic, often storm-tossed, lies just to the west of the 8000-hectare forest of la Coubre-la-Tremblade ▶

Points of Interest

① *Requin* means shark – a reminder that the Côte Sauvage is just to the west of this forest, which shelters the hinterland from the wild Atlantic weather.

② The 8000 hectares of the forest of la Coubre-la-Tremblade are, like many forests in France, crossed by a road serving as a fire-break. The footpaths themselves are regularly cleared of brushwood.

③ Notre-Dame de Buze is the subject of an interesting local legend. In the 12th century the strip of land that projects into the Atlantic above Royan, the Pointe de la Coubre, was virtually an island, covered in pines and oaks and sparsely populated. In the 13th century the monks of the Abbaye de Vaux cut down all the trees in order to cultivate the land. Sand gradually invaded the area, however, forming shifting dunes so high that it was said that you could tether a horse to the weather-vane on the chapel of Notre-Dame de Buze.

Attractive footpaths, kept clear of brushwood, wind through the forest ▼

Around St-Savinien

This riverside and woodland walk introduces you to the partly medieval town of St-Savinien, set on a bend in the River Charente, and the beautiful wooded countryside surrounding it.

Route Directions

Start from the far side of the bridge over the River Charente, on the Ile de la Grenouillette. Cross the River Charente ①.

Turn left and follow the river bank. After about 250m take a lane on the right and climb the stone steps leading up to reach the Abbaye des Augustins ②.

At the end of the square take the road on the right to the level crossing. After the railway take the first path on the right, the GR 360, and follow it to an old windmill ③.

Take the surfaced road down to a little stream to the right and follow the left bank, which leads to the Barbaras wash-house ④.

Continue on the GR 360. As it descends the path narrows before turning left along a surfaced road for a short while. Turn right almost immediately, still on the GR 360, to the village of Les Auzes. At the end of the village turn right, following yellow markers, on to a minor road. At the T-junction with the D 119 go straight over and take a footpath slightly to the left, still following the GR 360. This leads to a T-junction with a minor road where you turn left. Go straight over the crossroads some 500m further on, and 250m later you will see on the right a coach track. Follow this to join the D 18. Turn left along the D 18, then branch off to the right to reach les Bertons ⑤.

Leave the village by the GR 360 footpath, which turns off to the left before turning right and twisting and winding in the direction of the woods. After about 500m follow the GR 360 to the left. After another 500m this merges with a footpath coming in from the right. Branch off to the right almost immediately afterwards, and at the next crossroads turn right. This leads to a clearing before swinging to the right.

Almost as soon as you are out of the woods, turn left on to a footpath lined by hedges, which soon skirts the woods. Follow it round to the right after about 750m, through farmland to a minor road. Go straight over and carry on for about another 750m to the next road, ignoring a path going off to the left.

At this road, turn left, before turning right on to a stone path leading to the D 114. Turn left on to the road and follow it for a little way before turning right on to a footpath and then right again. Follow the footpath across a road and turn right to reach les Grelliers. Once past the houses, turn left on to a road that follows the old railway track. Turn left under the railway bridge and pass in front of the college buildings to reach the Charente. Turn right along the Quai des Fleurs and continue to the centre of St-Savinien. Turn left over the bridge and the Ile de la Grenouillette to return to the starting-point.

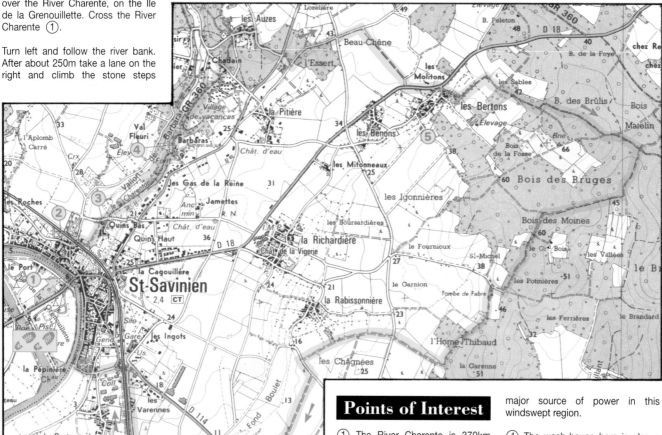

Points of Interest

① The River Charente is 370km long, and from the 11th century was an important trade route for salt and wine. You can take boat trips along the river from St-Savinien.

② The Abbaye des Augustins, constructed between the 12th and 15th centuries, is a major landmark.

③ The Quins windmill was built in 1681. Windmills were for centuries a major source of power in this windswept region.

④ The wash-house here is also a source of drinking water. Most villages had a *lavoir*, often in the centre, and many remained in regular use until the early part of this century.

⑤ Les Bertons is a charming hamlet of small stone houses, practically untouched by time. The houses were built originally for farmworkers and their families.

The Indre valley

S
tarting in the medieval heart of Châteauroux, this tour passes through the flat agricultural land of the Champagne-Berrichonne, visiting several fine châteaux and small towns, before crossing the River Indre into the Brenne. This, by contrast, is a beautiful remote area of lakes, marshes and hunting preserves. It is possible to shorten the route at Buzançais.

Route Directions

The drive starts from Châteauroux ①.

Leave Châteauroux on the D 956 towards Levroux. After 10km turn left on to the D 7 and follow signs to Villegongis. Turn right by the church for the Château de Villegongis ②.

Leaving the village, follow the D 7 round the left side of the church. After 1km turn right and follow the D 99 into Levroux ③.

From the centre of the town, turn left on to the D 926 towards Buzançais. After 10.5km turn right on to the D 63 and continue to the Château d'Argy ④.

Follow the D 11 south to Buzançais. (If you wish to shorten the route, take the N143 back to Châteauroux.) Continue south for 10km on the D 11 to the crossroads with the D 925. Turn right and 5km after Vendoeuvres take a small turning on the left to the Etang de Bellebouche ⑤.

Turn left from the car park to rejoin the D 925, and continue into Mézières-en-Brenne ⑥.

At the crossroads in the centre of Mézières, turn left on to the D 15, then fork right on to the D 17 towards le Bouchet. Go straight over

The château of Villegongis is among the finest Renaissance buildings in France. Its harmonious design is perfectly complemented by an elegant interior ▼

Grotesque carved heads adorn the corners of the Maison de Bois, built for Catherine de Medici, in Levroux ▶

the crossroads with the D 6a. Soon after, take a small turning on the right in to the Réserve Naturelle de Cherine ⑦.

Turn right on to the D 17. At the next crossroads turn right on to the D 44 towards St-Michel-en-Brenne. After 0.5km there is another entrance to the Réserve.

Back at the crossroads, turn right again on to the D 17. After 6km, past the bird sanctuary at the Etang de la Gabrière, the road forks on a corner. Take the left fork on to the D 32, and after 1.5km turn right to the Château du Bouchet ⑧.

Rejoin the D 32, turn right and keep going to Rosnay. In the centre of the village turn right on to the D 27. This is the main road to Châteauroux, which is clearly signposted from now on. Continue to Méobecq ⑨.

After Méobecq stay on the D 27, following signs for Châteauroux. After Neuillay-les-Bois, turn right at a major crossroads on to the D 925 to return to Châteauroux.

▲ *A statue graces the attractive market town of Mézières-en-Brenne*

THE BRENNE

Bleak yet at times very beautiful, the Brenne is a vast bowl of sand and clay at the southern edge of Champagne-Berrichonne. Lakes, marshy reed-beds and stretches of lightly wooded grassland break up the great tracts of heavy forest that cover some 800 square kilometres of eastern Berry, between the Indre and Creuse valleys.

Small villages dot the landscape, but the Brenne has never been heavily populated. Much of it is still given over to the hunting of deer, wild boar and a huge variety of water birds, and to fishing. This was once remote, malarial marshland, and it was the monks of the 11th and 12th centuries who first drained the marshes.

They created hundreds of dams and stocked the resulting ponds with fish.

Today the Brenne is one of the last great inland wetlands of Europe, a naturalist's paradise, with a number of sanctuaries preserving its flora and fauna.

It is also under threat. Water is drained off for use, and already many of the shallower ponds dry up in summer. In an attempt to preserve it, tourism has been promoted, with walking and riding trails, boating and fishing. Increasing numbers of tourists, however, have brought their own problems, for heavy use of the area threatens the fragile ecosystem of the marshes.

The remains of the chateau of Mézières-en-Brenne now house the museum. This market town has a 14th-century church with a handsomely sculptured porch ▼

Points of Interest

① At first glance, Châteauroux is a modern industrial city, but, hidden within the commercial district, is the old town, a charming maze of tiny alleys with ancient buildings and attractive shops. Also worth visiting is the ruined 10th-century Abbaye de Déols on the outskirts.

② Built between 1530 and 1570, the Château de Villegongis is similar in style to Chambord. An elegant building of white tufa stone, it has a highly decorated, asymmetrical façade, two fortified towers, and an elaborate roof and chimneys, all reflected in a moat. The park is open to the public and there are guided tours to the château on request.

③ Among the best of Levroux's many fine medieval buildings are the 16th-century Maison de Bois, built for Catherine de Medici, the ruins of the château and the town gatehouse. The 12th- and 13th-century St-Sylvain, a collegiate church dedicated to the patron saint of lepers who was also a local evangelist, houses one of only three Gothic organs in France.

④ The Château d'Argy consists of a 15th-century square keep, a 15th-century château with a delicately sculpted galleried courtyard, and fortified outbuildings which now house a museum of rural life. The château is used these days as a study centre for restoration techniques. There is also an animal park.

⑤ The Etang de Bellebouche is the largest of the Brenne's many lakes. Mainly used by local people, it has cafés, a swimming beach and boats for hire.

⑥ Mézières-en-Brenne is a pretty market town built over a number of small canals. The remains of the château house a small museum and there is a heavily restored 14th-century collegiate church. The town has a helpful tourist office and is a good base for walking, riding and fishing.

⑦ The 145-hectare Réserve Naturelle de Cherine has a variety of habitats, including lakes, reed-beds, marshes, meadows and woodland. Over 150 species of bird are found here, along with 40 species of amphibian and reptile, 21 species of mammal and around 350 different species of flora. There are also rare herds of Castor cows and Camargue horses.

⑧ The Château du Bouchet stands on a hill above the tiny village of le Bouchet, with superb views of the surrounding countryside. Dominated by a vast 14th-century keep, it also has 15th-, 17th- and 19th-century additions. Inside it is wonderfully atmospheric: dusty, crumbling and festooned with dead animals and birds.

⑨ Méobecq's abbey church of St-Pierre was built in the 11th century, burnt by the Huguenots in the 16th and repaired, with the addition of a classical façade, in the 17th. There are some fine capitals in the nave and 12th- and 15th-century frescos in the apse.

Châteauroux's old town

At the heart of the industrial and commercial city of Châteauroux is a small maze of enchanting streets and alleys that provide a pleasant stroll through 1000 years of history.

Route Directions

Start from the free car park beside the Couvent des Cordeliers ①.

Turn left up the hill towards Place Ste-Hélène, where there is a statue of Marshal Bertrand. From the square there are good views of the Couvent des Cordeliers, the Eglise St-Martial and the Jardin Public des Belles-Isles ②.

Turn first right into Rue St-Martial. After 200m you enter a small square, where on your right is the Eglise St-Martial and opposite it the Musée Bertrand ③.

Take the steps between the church and the museum and turn left into Rue des Pavillons. The road narrows and turns into Rue des Grands Moutons. Keep going until you meet Rue des Notaires on your left. Go left into Rue Dauphiné, then right into Rue Grande. Take the first turning on the right along Rue Traversier, then turn left into the large square beside the Eglise Notre-Dame ④.

▲ *Châteauroux may be the main industrial town of the Indre, but it has an interesting old quarter, and the ruined Abbaye de Déols is well worth a visit*

The lake, lawns and trees of Châteauroux's Jardin Public provide a welcome respite from the hustle and bustle of the town's commercial and industrial quarters ▼

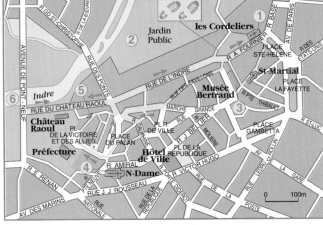

Go up the hill through the car parks into Place de la Victoire beside the Préfecture. Turn right along Rue Vieille Prison to the Porte St-Martin ⑤.

Turn right along Rue St-Martin and left along the city walls into Rue des Remparts. At the end, turn left and left again, into Rue de l'Indre, which leads down to the Pont-Neuf ⑥.

Go back to Rue de l'Indre and turn left to return to the car park.

Points of Interest

① The Franciscan Couvent des Cordeliers was founded in 1213 by Guillaume de Chauvigny. The church is now used as an art gallery and concert hall.

② The Jardin Public des Belles-Isles makes a huge, shady oasis, with lakes, a wide variety of mature trees, brightly coloured flowerbeds and lush green lawns.

③ The 18th-century Hôtel Bertrand was the home of Marshal Bertrand, an aide and close friend of Napoleon. It is now a major museum of fine art, Napoleonic history and Berry culture.

The 13th-century Eglise St-Martial opposite has a notable Renaissance belfry and porch.

④ The Eglise Notre-Dame, built in 1882, is chiefly remarkable for its florid confection of Gothic, Romanesque and Byzantine styles, all topped by a 6-m gilded statue of the Virgin.

⑤ The 15th-century Porte St-Martin was originally one of the main city gates but was later converted for use as a prison.

⑥ The Pont-Neuf, on the Indre, offers fine views over the 15th-century Château Raoul, which gave the city its name.

WALK 30B: 7KM/ALLOW 2 HOURS

The Etang de Bellebouche

This walk circles the largest and most developed of the many lakes scattered across the Brenne. It is easy going and the route is indicated by yellow bars painted on poles. However, these can be a little confusing and on occasion peter out, so proceed carefully.

Route Directions

Start from the car park, which is clearly signposted from the Mézières-Vendoeuvres road. Turn right along the lake shore ①.

Follow the path past the camping site under the pines and you will soon reach a wide, wooded path ②.

This follows the lake shore for some time, and has access paths at various points, giving views over the rushes and the lake. After about 1.5km the path winds away from the lake, across open grassland. After about another 1km turn left on to a road. Shortly before the crossroads the path branches off to the left, passing between pine forests on the left and deciduous woods to the right before heading back into open grassland.

After a few hundred metres a fork to the left leads towards marshy

▲ The Etang de Bellebouche

reedbeds. The correct route bends away from the lake again. Keep going, although it seems wrong, until you reach another road. Turn left on to this road and pass between the Etang de Bellebouche and the Etang du Grand Brun, then turn left back on to the path beside a ruined farmhouse. As you come back into the woods the path widens into a bridleway. The blue markers are for an obstacle course laid out on a smaller, winding path through the woods. Your instincts will tell you to turn towards the lake, but keep straight on and the lake will come to you. Soon the trees open out into a lawn with benches set out along the shore. From here it is an easy stroll back to the car park.

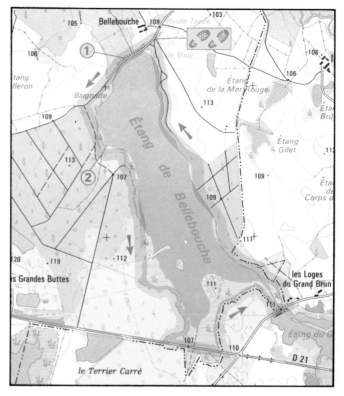

◄ The lake's sandy shoreline

Points of Interest

① On the lake shore near the start of the walk there are cafés and a small swimming beach. Boats and bicycles can be hired.

② The path is fringed by tree heather gorse, oak, chestnut and pine. Look out throughout the walk for a wide variety of wild flowers, dragonflies and butterflies to be seen here. You are also likely to see several species of birds, and reptiles such as emerald green sand lizards.

Around Aubusson

Perched on the edge of the Massif Central, this mountainous corner of the Limousin offers the sightseer a little bit of everything. It has spectacular scenery, the holiday playground of Lac de Vassivière, the ancient tapestry towns of Aubusson and Felletin and, here and there, faint echoes of the Crusades, in the form of churches of the Knights Templars and the Knights Hospitallers.

▲ *Like Aubusson, Felletin proclaims itself the birthplace of Limousin tapestry*

If you have time, it is worth driving right around the lake. The main tourist and hotel centre is at Aufelle at the west end, the château on the island is reached from Pierrefitte on the southern shore and the second walk starts from Masgrangeas on the northern shore. (From here it is possible to cut through to Royère and follow the route through the Rigole du Diable back to Aubusson.) Otherwise, follow the road round to Aufelle, turn right on to the D 222, then left on to the D 13, signposted Peyrat-le-Château. From here the D 940 offers a fast route to Bourganeuf, but the more scenic route is the smaller D 51a, signposted St-Martin-Château. About 7km on, just past St-Martin, are the Cascades des Jarreaux ⑥.

Stay on this road, which becomes the D 51 and is signposted all the way to Bourganeuf ⑦.

The fast route back to Aubusson is along the dual carriageway, the D 941. The rest of the route given here is across the mountains, and is slow but extremely beautiful. From Bourganeuf take the D 941 towards Guéret and then turn right on to the D 8, following it to Royère. In the centre of the town turn left on to the D 3. From here there are clear signs

all the way to Aubusson leading up through the Rigole du Diable ⑧.

Here the road becomes the D 7 before passing through Vallières and eventually meeting the D 941 at St-Michel-de-Veisse. Turn right to return to Aubusson.

The chapel, with its fine pilgrim cross, is all that survives of the commandery that the Knights Templars built in Paillier in the 12th century ▼

Route Directions

The drive starts in Aubusson ①.

Leave the town on the D 982 and continue south to Felletin ②.

There is a very complicated one-way system in Felletin. To leave the town, head down the hill on to the D 982 and take the second right, the D 992, towards Royère. Just after le Chiroux, turn left on to the D 26, then take the first right on to the D 35 to Paillier ③.

Stay on the D 35 and turn right at the T-junction with the D 8, signposted Royère. After about 2km you will arrive in Gentioux-Pigerolles ④.

Continue on the D 8, still signposted Royère, for 6km, until the crossroads at the hamlet of la Chaud Couraud. Here, turn left on to a minor road signposted Masgrangeas and Aufelle. This road joins the D 34, which follows the shore of Lac de Vassivière ⑤.

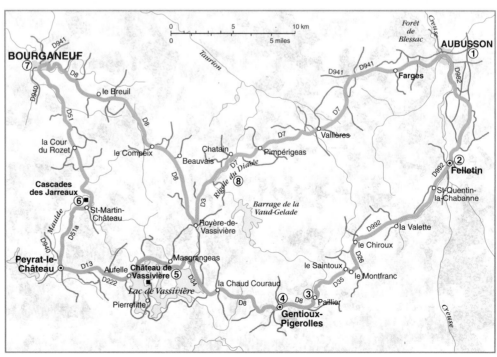

▲ *Aubusson's traditional style of tapestry originated in the 18th century*

AUBUSSON TAPESTRY

In the 14th century Marie de Hainault became Comtesse de la Marche and brought from her Flemish homeland the art of tapestry weaving. For the next three centuries the fame of Aubusson grew through such masterpieces as the series *La Dame à la Licorne*.

By the 17th century their reputation was so celebrated that the Corneille family of tapestry manufacturers was granted a royal warrant. Many of the weaving families were Huguenots, however, and when the Edict of Nantes was revoked in 1685 most of them fled the country. It took nearly a century for the trade to recover.

In the 18th century designs by famous painters of the time, such as Watteau, were used to make tapestries that featured the subtle blues and greens which have become Aubusson's hallmark.

After the Revolution there was another, even longer, decline, but in the 1930s a revival began, headed by Jean Lurçat, and based on designs by artists as eminent as Picasso and Dali.

Aubusson tapestries are produced using the *basse-lisse* technique, on a horizontal loom. The work is painstakingly slow, with the design being drawn on to a cartoon with tiny squares to indicate every individual knot. With a traditional design, it takes several hundred colours of wool and up to two months to produce one square metre. A weaver must train for three years.

Points of Interest

① Aubusson is famous the world over for its tapestries, but it is also an extremely pretty little old town, huddled under the cliffs of the Creuse valley.

② Felletin, like Aubusson, is famous for tapestry weaving, and rivalry between the two towns is intense. Felletin, however, claims to be the original home of the Limousin tapestries. The town also has two 15th-century churches and a lantern des motes. The mountains above Felletin are part of the Plateau de Millevaches, which forms the edge of the Massif Central. Views from the Crocq road are spectacular.

◀ *Lac de Vassivière is an artificially created lake with an area of 1000 hectares. It is an important tourist centre for the region and hosts sailing competitions every summer*

③ Only the 12th-century chapel now remains of the Templar Commandery at Paillier. This has a bell wall, and an interesting multi-faced pilgrim cross.

④ The mainly 15th-century church at Gentioux-Pigerolles has two magnificent examples of 16th-century Limousin primitive sculpture. On the hill above the town is a massive granite statue of the Virgin (accessible only on foot), erected by the Abbé Parinet as a monument to the medieval Limousin stonemasons. The views from the summit are superb.

⑤ The artificial Lac de Vassivière, formed in 1950, covers 1000 hectares. It is one of the area's main tourist centres, with camp sites, swimming beaches, boats for hire and cruises. The island château, reached by a bridge, houses a modern art gallery and a sculpture garden. The lake is beautiful from every angle and there is also plenty of good walking in the surrounding hills.

⑥ The Cascades des Jarreaux are pleasant little waterfalls on the River Maulde which tumble about 10m over rocks. They are about a 1-km walk from the car park.

⑦ The Knights Hospitallers founded their Commandery in Bourganeuf in 1195, and from 1427 to 1750 it was the regional headquarters. The Commandery buildings now house the town hall. The church was founded in the 12th century, but was heavily rebuilt three centuries later. The Tour Zizim was built in 1486 to house a Turkish prince, poet and musician, who was a political hostage here until 1489.

⑧ The Rigole du Diable is an 8-km stretch of winding mountain road bordered by vast granite balancing rocks. There are two observation points with excellent panoramic views.

Towards the end of the 15th century Bourganeuf's Tour Zizim served as a prison for a Muslim prince of that name. He had been transferred there from Rhodes by his captor, Pierre d'Aubusson, of the Knights of St John of Jerusalem ▼

A town walk in Aubusson

The centre of Aubusson is small, but an extraordinary amount of history is crammed into its narrow streets. This walk meanders through the prettiest areas, also passing the best of the town's museums and shops.

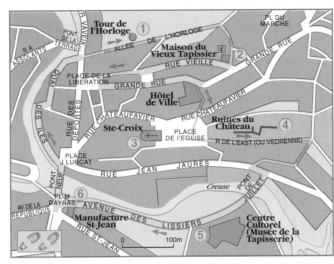

Route Directions

Start from the car park in Place Maurice Dayras.

Cross the Pont-Neuf, and turn left along the Quai des Iles to the Pont de la Terrade, then turn right into Rue des Déportés. Cross the road and enter the tiny Allée de l'Horloge, which climbs up several flights of narrow stone steps on to a path halfway up the cliff. After about 300m you will come to the Tour de l'Horloge ①.

Keep going until the path peters out, then turn right down Rue de la Roche. At the bottom is the Maison du Vieux Tapissier ②.

Turn right along Rue Vieille and follow it into Place de la Libération. Then take the first left along Grande Rue.

Turn right up the steps just after the art deco town hall into Place de l'Eglise, to find the Eglise Ste-Croix ③.

Rue de l'Est, opposite the church, leads to the château ④.

From here, turn right down the steps into Rue Jean Jaurès and then turn left to cross the river by the Pont de Juillet. Directly opposite is the Tapestry Museum ⑤.

Turn left on to Avenue des Lissiers and follow it until you come to the Manufacture St-Jean ⑥.

This is next to the starting-point.

Points of Interest

① The 16th-century Tour de l'Horloge is the only remaining watch-tower out of seven that once formed part of the city walls.

② The Maison du Vieux Tapissier was once the home of the Corneille family, powerful tapestry manufacturers. The 15th-century building now houses a fascinating museum and the tourist office.

③ The huge 13th-century Eglise Ste-Croix was modelled on the Holy Sepulchre in Jerusalem. It boasts a piece of the True Cross, some fine 19th-century windows and a massive organ with 1800 pipes.

④ Only a few ruins now remain of the château, begun in the 11th and 12th centuries and then one of the largest in France. It was destroyed in 1630 by Cardinal Richelieu.

⑤ Part of the Centre Culturel et Artistique Jean-Lurçat, the Tapestry Museum has a wonderful though small collection of tapestries, 18th-century and modern.

⑥ The Manufacture St-Jean is the only tapestry workshop in Aubusson offering guided tours which allow visitors to see restoration techniques as well as the manufacture of new designs.

The attractive little town of Aubusson, which lies on the River Creuse, first began producing tapestry in the 14th century. Its Musée de la Tapisserie traces the history of the craft and displays modern work ▼

Guided tours of the tapestry workshop of the Manufacture St-Jean in Aubusson offer visitors the fascinating sight of old tapestries being restored and new patterns being woven ▶

The shore of Lac de Vassivière

Lac de Vassivière was created in 1950 by damming the River Maulde. Benefitting from an attractive setting among gentle wooded hills, it is nowadays a busy holiday resort and an ideal location for water sports, notably sailing. A baroque castle graces the island ▼

Near Lac de Vassivière ▶

This gentle ramble through mature woods and along the lake shore is just one of many that criss-cross the hills on the edge of Lac de Vassivière. The route is marked with yellow bars (yellow crosses indicate wrong turnings) but some key markings are missing.

Route Directions

Start from the car park beside the holiday village about 2km east of Masgrangeas, on the north shore of Lac de Vassivière.

Turn right out of the car park and follow the road for about 1km as it crosses a small bridge then loops round a narrow bay. The turning off the road to the left is not easy to find: look out for a narrow path leading into the woods from the back of a large clearing. If you turn the corner and see the information point and crossroads ahead, you have gone too far.

The path widens into a good track and climbs slowly away from the lake, shaded all the way by huge beeches and other deciduous trees. Pass a ruined cottage and, as the landscape opens up into meadowland on your right, a turning that leads down to a farmhouse. Keep left and the main track slowly bends round behind the hill and plunges back into the woods, climbing all the way. As you reach the highest point there is a farm in the valley on your right, and a short path to your left leads up to the summit of the Puy de la Drouille ①.

Return to the main path and turn left. You will soon come to a T-junction. The right fork leads to Royère-de-Vassivière, 3km away. Turn left to complete this circuit.

The path now begins to descend, and on the right is a dyke ②.

After this you enter a mature pine plantation, where the path deteriorates for a short stretch, becoming rocky and muddy. As the path improves, it rises again briefly to the Croix Pradirot, a crossroads of five paths. Keep straight on down the hill towards the lake. As you come to the bottom there is a small sewage plant on the right. Turn left on to the road and follow it round the lake shore to return to the car park.

Points of Interest

① From here there is a good view over the 1000-hectare extent of the man-made Lac de Vassivière, formed in 1950 by damming the River Mauldre. The château and art gallery of Vassivière are now marooned on an island in the lake, and can only be reached from Pierrefitte, on the south side. The lake is popular with tourists and holidaymakers, and the prevailing westerly winds make it a good spot for sailors and windsurfers. Its principal purpose, however, is as part of a huge hydro electric power scheme.

② Dykes are an essential part of the complex systems of water management and irrigation in this area. This one, the Combe Noire, protects a small orchard.

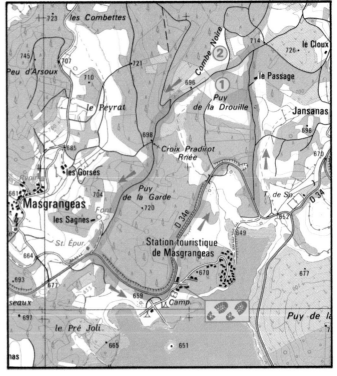

The Monts Dore

To the west of Clermont-Ferrand lies the Parc Naturel Régional des Volcans d'Auvergne, one of the most spectacular landscapes in France. The ancient volcanoes are laid out in a chain, with the Monts du Cantal to the south and the best-known peak, the Puy de Dôme, to the north. Between these are the Monts Dore, a superb stretch of country, with fine peaks towering above attractive villages. On this tour, which circles the Monts Dore, the roads are occasionally winding and cross several passes, but the way is straightforward and rarely crowded.

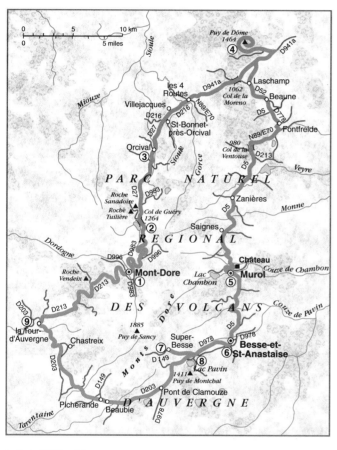

turn right on to a toll road that goes up the Puy de Dôme. Drive to the car park at the summit ④.

The second walk starts from here. Return to the main road beyond the zoo. Turn right back along the main road, signposted la Bourboule and Mont-Dore, and after 2.5km go left on a minor road signposted Laschamp. On reaching Laschamp turn right towards Col de la Moreno. Go through the village, passing the church on the left, and turn left at the next junction, signposted Beaune and St-Genès-Champanelle. In Beaune turn right on to the D 778, signposted Fontfreide. Go straight across at a junction with the D 5, following signs for Fontfreide and Theix. At the T-junction in Fontfreide take a right turn (not signposted), pass through the village and continue to the N89-E70. Turn right again (no sign). Follow the main road for 4km and then turn left on to the D 213, signposted Murol. After a few hundred metres take a right turn, signposted Murol and St-Nectaire, and follow the D 5 towards Murol. Go past the château and down to the main road. Turn left and then right into Murol ⑤.

There is good parking in Murol for those wishing to visit the town. To leave Murol turn right down the D 5,

signposted St-Victor-la-Rivière and Besse, and continue to Besse-et-St-Anastaise. Take a right turn on to the main road, the D 978, just before Besse, signposted Centre Ville, if you wish to visit the town ⑥.

From the centre of Besse the tour follows the D 978 again, now a long one-way street out of the town, signposted Super-Besse ⑦.

Pass signs to the left for Lac Pavin ⑧.

After 5km, having passed signs for Super-Besse, turn left on to the D 203, signposted Picherande and la Tour-d'Auvergne. Go through Picherande and bypass Chastreix, following signs for la Tour-d'Auvergne. The road climbs up into la Tour-d'Auvergne ⑨.

The road bears right and passes the main village square. Go straight on, on the D 213, signposted la Bourboule and Mont-Dore. The road twists up out of la Tour-d'Auvergne. After 1km fork right with the main road, signposted Mont-Dore. The road climbs to a col and then descends towards Mont-Dore, giving superb views of both the town and the mountains. Follow signs for Mont-Dore all the way back to the town.

Route Directions

The drive starts from the centre of Mont-Dore ①.

Cross the river bridge and go straight on, following signs for Clermont-Ferrand. Leave the town on the D 996, then take a left turn on to the Clermont-Ferrand road, the D 983, going uphill. After a climb of about 3km turn left on to a minor road signposted Rochefort-Montagne, Clermont-Ferrand and Col de Guéry ②.

Just over the top of the Col de Guéry there is a large car park on the left with exceptional views of the rocks of Roche Tuilière and Roche Sanadoire. Continue down the main road to reach a car park on the left called Roches Tuilière et Sanadoire. The first walk starts from here. Leave the car park and turn left on to the

D 27, signposted Orcival. The road drops into the valley to the east of the two Roches. Follow signs for Orcival all the way to the town, where a left turn, signposted Centre Ville, leads to a car park to the left of the church ③.

Leave Orcival along the D 27, signposted Clermont-Ferrand. The road climbs up to reach a junction with the D 216, where you go straight on. At the next left bend you will see the Puy de Dôme in front of you. Continue for 5km to reach a crossroads with the N89-E70. Go straight over on to the D 941a, signposted Clermont-Ferrand, Puy de Dôme and Col de la Moreno. Go over the Col de la Moreno (1062m) and continue for 5km. Turn left on to a road signposted Puy de Dôme and Ceyssat. Go past the zoo and then

The pleasant village of Orcival lies in the valley of the River Sioulet ▶

▲ Orcival's church of Notre-Dame is a fine example of Auvergne Romanesque

Set amid lush green hills, Orcival is a popular base for touring the area ▼

Points of Interest

① The hot-water springs in Mont-Dore persuaded the Romans to settle here, although today's town developed into a spa only two centuries ago. Visitors can take a guided tour of the thermal centre (daily, mid-May to September). Outdoor excursions include a walk along the Promenade des Artistes or a walk from the top of the cableway to the Salon du Capucin.

② From the Col de Guéry there is an impressive view of both Lac de Guéry and the twin rocks of Roche Tuilière and Roche Sanadoire.

③ The church of Notre-Dame d'Orcival is one of the finest examples of the Auvergne Romanesque style of architecture, a style that included a central bell tower and a circle of chapels beyond the choir. The church dominates the pretty village surrounding it.

④ See page 134.

⑤ Murol is a delightful spot, set among trees and with a château that seems out of all proportion to the village. The château is both picturesque and interesting: it was originally built in the 13th century on top of an old volcanic neck, a pillar of basalt, but there were additions over many years. The final touches were added by the d'Estaing family, one of the Auvergne's noblest.

⑥ The old and picturesque town of Besse-et-St-Anastaise was fortified in medieval times – though of the defences only the 16th-century Porte de Ville and Tour de la Prison remain – and retains an air of venerable sophistication. The best of the old town is seen in Rue de la Boucherie, where the houses, many from the 15th and 16th centuries, are built of black lava. The famous statue of Notre-Dame de Vassivière is to be found in the Eglise St-André. The town has a famous cheese market on Mondays.

⑦ Super-Besse is a new winter-sports resort, at an altitude of 1350m. It has good facilities for both downhill and cross-country skiing and is also a good centre for summer walking. A cable car links the resort with the summit of the Puy de Sancy.

⑧ Lac Pavin is claimed to be the most beautiful lake in Auvergne. Almost exactly circular and very deep – almost 100m – it is a near-perfect volcanic lake. The name derives from the Latin *pavens*, meaning frightening, as it was said that if a stone were thrown into the lake then violent local storms would

BLACK VIRGINS

Legend has it that the first of France's 'Black Virgins' was brought back from the Holy Land by Louis IX on his return from the Seventh Crusade. It was placed in the cathedral of le-Puy-en-Velay, though the one now to be seen in the cathedral is a copy, the original having been lost in a fire at the time of the Revolution. This first Black Virgin was very influential.

The Black Virgins were carved from walnut or cedar, both of them dark woods which age almost to jet-black. Originally they were in the Byzantine icon style, but later the Virgin's features came to be more individual, often being based on the faces of local girls.

The Black Virgin of Besse is one of the most famous of these statues. Each year on 2 July the statue is carried in procession 3km uphill to the Chapelle de Vassivière. The procession includes cattle and cowherds, and dancers in traditional costume, and there is a great deal of singing. At the chapel, built especially for the statue by Catherine de Medici, prayers are offered to the Virgin, asking her to keep an eye on the animals on the upland summer pastures. Then, with autumn approaching, on the Sunday after St Matthew's Day, the statue is carried back down to the church in Besse for the winter, the Virgin's journey mirroring that of the herds.

result. There is also a tale that the first village of Besse stood where the water now lies, but was drowned as punishment for the collective ungodliness of its inhabitants. Some say that on quiet days they have heard the bells of a submerged chapel ringing.

⑨ An example of volcanic architecture can be seen at la Tour-d'Auvergne, a village set high on a lava plateau. Beside the church look for the regular basaltic columns created as hot lava cooled on exposure to the air.

Roche Sanadoire

This walk offers fine views and gives some insight into the geology of the region. It starts with steps, and has quite steep descents and ascents, but the going is generally reasonable, and the walk is not long.

Route Directions

Start from the car park just below Roche Sanadoire ①.

From the car park go down steps to reach a viewing telescope ②.

Down to the right is a track in a gully. Take this and descend to a crossing of tracks at a col. Go straight over, and then climb up, still following a track, which soon forks. Take the right-hand, narrower fork, which soon joins a wider track on the right. This track rises, but it soon flattens out and where it does, go left up into the woods on a smaller track, to reach a clearing with tremendous views ③.

This is a convenient end point for the walk, but if you wish to continue, walk on, bearing a little to the right to reach the top of the rock. Return to the large track in the forest and go down the track you came up to reach the major crossing of tracks. Turn right and climb up to reach the gully running down from the viewing telescope. Turn left up the gully to return to the car park.

Points of Interest

① Roche Tuilière and Roche Sanadoire are volcanic necks or plugs. When a volcano erupts not all of the magma (the molten rock or

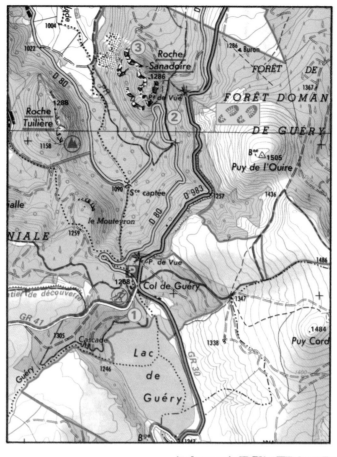

lava) is expelled from the crater, some being contained in the chimney within the mountain itself. When the lava flow slows, the cool, solidifying rock at the crater's top stops further flow and the chimney is left blocked with cooling rock. If the activity continues then this plug of solid rock is ejected at the next eruption, but if there is no further activity then the plug forms a hard rock mass. If the outer crater erodes away, this solid rock mass will be revealed as a neck or plug. Both the rocks here are such necks. Roche Tuilière shows the distinctive regular

basalt columns that are such a feature of lava flows. Roche Sanadoire is topped by the ruins of a castle built in the 15th-century, during the Hundred Years War.

② The valley that runs down from the Col de Guéry to Orcival, and that which carries the road between the two Roches towards Rochefort-Montagne, show evidence of later geological events, when the glaciers of the last Ice Age gouged out pathways between the old volcanic peaks.

③ Although Lac de Guéry itself is not visible from the route, lying just behind the Col de Guéry, the reason for its existence is all around. The lake is high, at almost 1244m, and large, around 25 hectares, but, surprisingly, it is little more than 15m deep. This is because it was not glacially formed, but created when a volcanic lava flow blocked the river valley. Lac de Guéry is the source of the River Dordogne.

▲ Roche Sanadoire is a twin to Roche Tuilière – two fine volcanic necks in the Monts Dore range. This is one of three ranges that divide the Parc Naturel Régional des Volcans d'Auvergne; the others are the Monts Dômes and the Monts du Cantal

◄ Woodland paths can be followed on the flanks of Roche Sanadoire

Puy de Dôme

Points of Interest

① The bust is of the flyer Eugène Renaux, who landed on the summit on 7 March 1911 in pursuit of the 100,000-franc Grand Prix Michelin. This was offered in 1908 by the Michelin brothers to the first flyer who left Paris with a passenger of at least 75kg and returned within six hours, having landed on the summit. Renaux's flight time was 5 hours 11 minutes. Closer to the summit is a plaque commemorating the flight.

② The Puy de Dôme has been an important pilgrimage site for thousands of years. It was a Gaulish

On the Puy de Dôme stands a monument to Eugène Renaux, a brave aviator whose flight in 1911 from Paris to the top of the peak and back took 5 hours and 11 minutes and won him 100,000 francs ▼

holy site before the Romans built a temple to Mercury, and in the 12th century a chapel was erected on the summit. The ruins of the Roman temple reveal it to have been about twice the size of the Maison Carrée in Nîmes and to have been built using at least 50 different types of stone. With its terraces and stairs it must have been one of the most beautiful buildings in Roman France.

③ From the summit over 100 old volcanoes can be seen, while further afield the Monts du Forez and the high Limousin plateau stand out. Because of the Puy de Dôme's central position on clear days about 10 per cent of France can be seen from here, the view extending over 11 *départements*.

④ The name of the peak derives from the Celtic *dumia*, meaning royal mountain, for the Celts believed it to be the home of gods. There may have been a Celtic temple here, a possibility that seems the more likely because the Romans decided to build their own. The Romans usually attempted to usurp 'pagan' sites from defeated tribes as it helped the process of assimilation to have their new subjects transfer their allegiance to the Roman gods. It is not clear why the Celts felt so deeply about the mountain, though the reason could have been in part climatic, since the Puy exhibits some curious atmospheric effects. It is recorded that one winter, when the temperature in Clermont-Ferrand was -16°C, the summit temperature was 4°C. These temperature inversions also sometimes create a clear, sunny world on the peak, apparently floating above a cloudscape stretching to infinity. On such occasions the Puy de Dôme can seem a magical place.

S ome idea of the way in which the Puy de Dôme has been taken over by the car-based walker can be gained from the fact that walkers on the GR 4, which traverses the top, are not allowed to walk on the road. However, no such difficulties will be experienced on this walk around the summit.

▲ *There are superb views from the summit of the Puy de Dôme, which lies at the heart of the Monts Dômes and, at 1465m, is the highest point in the range*

Route Directions

Start from the summit car park.

From the car park walk around the summit of the peak and up to the top. On the way, stop to see a commemorative bust ①; the ruins of the Temple de Mercure ②; two porcelain orientation tables ③; and the summit itself ④.

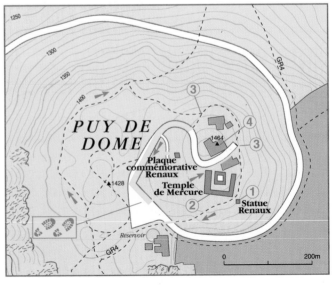

Monts du Cantal

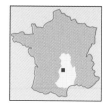

This tour follows the southern flank of the Monts du Cantal, the southern-most block of volcanic peaks within the Parc Naturel Régional des Volcans d'Auvergne. It goes over the Pas de Peyrol, a high Cantal pass which is reached by a road that is both steep and winding. But for the most part the tour passes through valleys where the going is a good deal easier. The Pas de Peyrol can be a little crowded in the height of the season, as can the delightfully atmospheric village of Salers.

Route Directions

The drive starts in Mauriac ①.

Leave the town centre, heading south-eastwards on the D 922, signposted Aurillac, St-Martin-Valmeroux and Salers. After leaving the town take the D 122, the first major turn on the left. There could be confusion here as the turn goes right off the main road before bearing left to cross it. Watch for the sign for Anglards-de-Salers, Salers, Puy Mary and Pas de Peyrol, and be sure to take that turn even if it looks wrong. Continue into Anglards-de-Salers ②.

Turn right on to the D 22, following signs for Salers ③.

In Salers turn left on to a road signposted 'Centre Ville' and 'Toutes Directions'. Turn right at the next junction to reach a car park on the left. The first walk starts from here. To leave Salers, go out of the car park, turn right and follow signs for the Pas de Peyrol. At the large hotel just outside the village follow the D 680 to the right, signposted Puy Mary. Drive up to the Col de Néronne, the top of which offers superb views, especially down the Vallée du Falgoux to the left and across the peaks of the Monts du

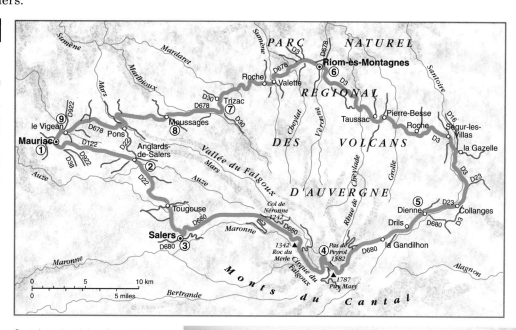

The peaceful village of le Vigean, near Mauriac, is typical of the quiet communities of the Cantal ▼

Cantal to the right. Go straight on from the Col, following signs for Puy Mary. Soon the steep, narrow road climbs again, offering a stunning view of the cliffs of the Cirque du Falgoux to the right as you near the Pas de Peyrol. Eventually you reach the top of the Pas de Peyrol (1582m) ④.

There are shops and a car park at the top, and the second walk starts from here. From the top of the Pas take the road to the left, signposted Murat, St-Flour and la Gandilhon. Descend from the pass and at the next junction go straight on (strictly speaking you are taking the right fork) on the D 680, signposted Dienne. The road drops down to and passes through Dienne ⑤.

Take the first left after the village, up a small lane signposted '3,8 Vers CD3'. This shortcut goes through Collanges and on to a junction with the D 3, where you turn left (no sign). The going is now very easy, the road passing through open countryside with fine views. At la Gazelle turn left over a bridge across a stream. Follow this road, the D 3 signposted Ségur-les-Villas and Riom-ès-Montagnes, to Riom ⑥.

As you reach Riom go left at a T-junction signposted Valette, Mauriac, Antignac and Bort-les-Orgues. Go into Riom, bearing right on to a road

signposted Mauriac. Soon you go left again, on to a road signposted Bort-les-Orgues and Mauriac, and on leaving Riom go left yet again, on a road signposted Bort-les-Orgues and Mauriac. Go left at the next fork on to the D 678, signposted Mauriac, which winds along hillsides and through the villages of Valette, Trizac and Moussages ⑦ and ⑧.

▲ *Le Vigean stands on the River Labiou, on the western edge of Auvergne. The church is unusual in holding a depiction of an English martyr*

The road is straightforward, but if in doubt follow the Mauriac signs. Pass through le Vigean ⑨.

Turn left at the junction with the D 922 to return to Mauriac.

VOLCANOES

About 60 million years ago, during the Tertiary Era, the Massif Central was formed by the pressure that created the Alps and the Jura to the east and the Pyrenees to the west. Faulting in the rocks allowed magma from the earth's core to vent to the surface, creating volcanoes. Three distinct periods of activity are recognised. During the earliest, from 13 million to 3 million years ago, the volcanoes of the Monts du Cantal – the area south of, but including, Puy Mary – were active; from 6 million to 250,000 years ago those of the Monts Dore, to the north, were erupting; while the youngest group, the volcanoes of the Monts Dômes, north of the Monts Dore, were probably still active when humans first arrived in Auvergne.

The Parc Naturel Régional des Volcans d'Auvergne, at 348,000 hectares, is the largest park created in France to protect natural scenery. This dramatic landscape contains volcanic craters, crater lakes (lakes formed inside old craters), hot-water springs and pillars of volcanic rock.

handsome 15th-century building. Inside there is a good collection of Aubusson tapestries, with some fine birds and animals, dating from the 16th century.

③ See page 137.

④ See 1 on page 138.

⑤ The small Auvergne Romanesque church at Dienne contains a 13th-century wooden statue of Christ and an equally good Louis XVI Nativity.

⑥ The name means 'Riom near the mountains'. The main industry is timber, and there are several sawmills. However, these are less picturesque then the Maison de la Gentiane, an exhibition centre for local plant life, where there is a display of medicinal plants and an audiovisual show. The root of the gentian is used in a distillery to produce a well-known local aperitif. Try some with some local cheese, of which Riom's dairies produce several varieties, including Bleu d'Auvergne.

⑦ The church at Trizac has a 12th-century statue of the Virgin and some good baroque work.

⑧ Moussages is a fine spot for a stroll, with its ancient fountain and an array of delightful old houses.

⑨ Unusually for France, the church at le Vigean has a representation of an English saint: a work depicting the martyrdom of St Thomas à Becket.

In the lower Lot valley, where the western Auvergne meets Quercy, many of the villages present an enchanting rustic scene, with their flower-filled tubs and window-boxes and their weathered half-timbered houses ▼

Points of Interest

① With its black lava houses and its setting on top of a broad basalt plateau, Mauriac is truly a volcanic town. The town's evident prosperity is built on being the local market town, and on glove making. The church is thought to be the finest example of Auvergne Romanesque in Haut-Auvergne. Dating from the 12th century, it is large, elegant and almost austere inside. Be sure to see the Black Virgin, one of Auvergne's most famous, and one to which there is still an annual pilgrimage, on the first Sunday after 9 May.

Elsewhere in the town, the Monastère St-Pierre has the remains of 14th-century cloisters and there is a local archaeology and history museum housed in the old prison in Rue Delalo.

② The tiny village of Anglards-de-Salers is worth a stop to admire the Château de la Trémolière, a

The Monts du Cantal, a range of peaks whose highest point is 1855m, are believed to be the product of the erosion of a much higher volcano ▼

Salers

Salers is a magical place: houses built of the local dark lava, with angled roofs set at all orientations, seemingly without any order; turrets, chimneys and gables; an elegant bell enclosed in its wrought cage; old lamps and signs. This easy walk visits the best sites in the village, and explores its narrow alleys.

Route Directions

Start from the car park near the church. Leave the car park and turn left on to the main road. Go left again past the front of the church ①.

Follow Rue du Beffroi, pass under the arch of the clock tower and turn left into Grande-Place ②.

A wood carving celebrates the Salers, a much-valued local breed of cattle ▶

Go across the square, past the fountain and along Rue de Templiers, passing the town hall and the Maison des Templiers ③.

Pass under the arch and go left at the T-junction. Cross the next square to reach the Esplanade de Barrouze ④.

Retrace your steps into the square and turn right to reach Rue des Nobles ⑤.

Follow this road back into Grande-Place. Cross the square and bear left, going past the post office on the right and the Hôtel Serre. At the T-junction at the bottom, go right, under the arch. Continue to where a track goes off right, and follow this, going up and down steps to reach a road. Turn right, back towards the town. At a fork continue right along Rue Notre-Dame to reach the church, and from there retrace your steps back to the car park.

built in the early 15th century, making it a little older than the beautiful Renaissance Bailliage, the Bailiff's House, which stands, complete with several towers, at the north-eastern corner. The bust is of Tyssandier d'Escous, the man responsible for obtaining country-wide recognition for the local breed of cattle, the Salers, which in France is now second in popularity only to the Charollais.

③ Beyond the wooden cow is the Maison des Templiers, the Templars' House, which houses a fine museum devoted to local folklore. It has been decorated in traditional Auvergnat style and includes a cheese-making room.

④ From the Esplanade de Barrouze there is a wonderful view, both of the local valleys and the aptly named volcanic peak of Puy Violent.

Points of Interest

① The first church on the site of St-Matthieu was probably built in the 12th century, though of this only the entrance porch now remains, the rest dating from the 15th century. Inside, be sure to see the remarkable *Mise au Tombeau*, a polychrome stone sculpture from the late 15th century, and the 17th-century tapestries.

② The town hall, on the south-western edge of Grande-Place, was

⑤ The earliest houses in Salers date from the time when the village was a refuge from bands of English soldiery and mercenaries, during the Hundred Years War. The later houses date from the brief period when it was a successful local market town. As a result there are virtually no buildings from before the 15th century or after the 16th century, which explains the architectural similarity discernible among the apparent chaos. The Maison de Flojeac, at the corner of Rue des Nobles and Grande-Place, is a particularly fine old house.

With its ornate 15th- and 16th-century houses, Salers has a magical atmosphere ▼

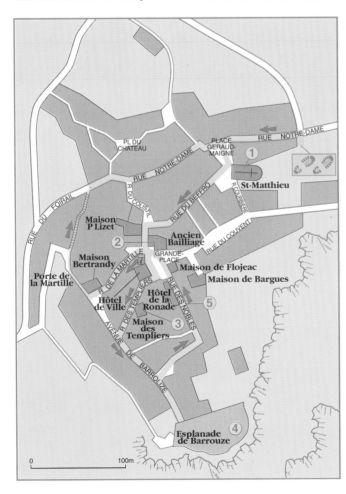

Puy Mary

Puy Mary is a distinctive peak and a fine viewpoint, but the walk to the top, though quite straightforward, is long and steep. Regular walkers will find no difficulties, but if you are new to high-level walking it would be advisable to take it easy, both going up and coming down.

Route Directions

Start from the car park at the Pas de Peyrol ①.

From the Pas de Peyrol the GR 400 footpath climbs up Puy Mary ②.

Follow this steep path right to the summit. From the summit the GR 400 heads south-eastwards (away from the line of ascent), then eastwards towards the distant Col de Cabre, about 5km away. For most walkers that will be too far. If so, content yourself with following the mule track to the top of the Brèche de Rolland, an awkward section of steep cliffs. Return towards the summit, but before starting the final climb take the GR 400 to the right, going downhill to reach the D 680. Turn right along the road, then left to pick up the footpath again, following it back to the Pas de Peyrol.

Head north from the Pas de Peyrol, going away from Puy Mary along the ridge of Puy de la Tourte. While the GR 400 takes a lower route, this walk stays on the ridge to gain the best of the view back towards Puy Mary and the pass. Return along the ridge and the D17 to the car park.

Points of Interest

① At 1588m, the Pas de Peyrol is the highest pass in the Massif Central. An inn at the col sells refreshments and souvenirs.

② Puy Mary is not named after the Virgin, nor even another woman, instead the name commemorates Marius, an early Christian missionary

▲ *The long, steep walk from the car park up to the viewpoint on Puy Mary, at nearly 2000m, is well worth the effort*

who arrived from Rome to evangelise the area. Marius is said to have set up his hermitage near Massiac, choosing a site close to a centre for the worship of Jupiter so that he could combat paganism at its source. It is said that he was buried at the site now occupied by the church of Notre-Dame des Miracles in Mauriac. Confusingly, Marius was frequently called St Mary, and in addition to the peak there are also two villages – St-Mary-le-Plain and St-Mary-le-Gros – named after him.

Puy Mary, at 1783m, is the second highest peak in the Monts du Cantal. Plomb du Cantal, a few kilometres to the south-east, is 70m higher. However, Puy Mary's position means it has a better panorama. The volcanic ruins of the Monts du Cantal are seen to perfection from the top, as are the results of later glaciation, with the 13 valleys that radiate from Puy Mary being laid out like the spokes of a wheel below. An orientation table at the summit helps pick out the higher crests, and identifies some of the valleys. Of these, the Cère valley is considered to be the most spectacular, though the Mandailles valley, leading off south-westwards towards Aurillac, is almost as fine. Of the peaks, to the north can be seen the Monts Dore, while to the far north-east can be seen the Livradois plateau and the Monts du Forez. Closer are volcanic Puy Griou and Plomb du Cantal.

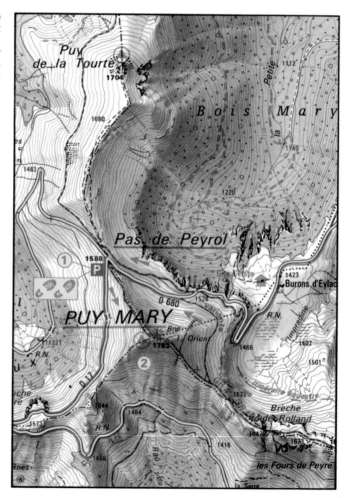

The Loire and the Ardèche

At the eastern edge of the Massif Central two of France's most distinctive rivers are born. The Loire needs little introduction; later in its journey to the sea it is famous for its landscapes and its châteaux. The Ardèche is a shorter river, but is well worth exploring, for its gorge is as fine a section of rugged river scenery as can be seen anywhere in Europe. This extensive tour follows the early stages of both rivers, passing through fine countryside along the way. Some of the roads are narrow and a little winding, and some are also steep.

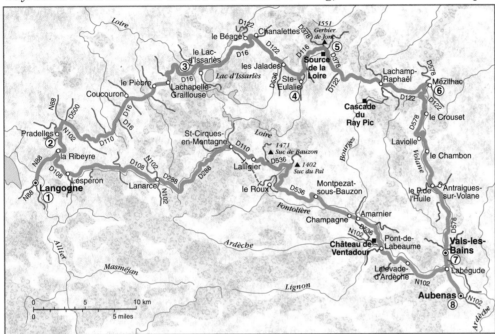

In Aubenas follow signs for 'Centre Ville' to reach a car park at the top of a hill. The second walk starts from here.

Retrace your route, signposted le-Puy-en-Velay, to the traffic lights at Labégude and turn left on to the main road, the N102, signposted Lalevade-d'Ardèche, Langogne, le-Puy-en-Velay and Mende. The road follows the Ardèche to a round-about. Take the right exit, signposted Mende. Bypass Lalevade, and at Pont-de-Labeaume cross the river and then turn right off the main road on to the D 536, signposted Montpezat-sous-Bauzon, Burzet and Chirols. Go through the narrow streets of Montpezat, and wind up the hillside to discover increasingly lovely views. Do not take a left turn signposted le Roux and tunnel, but continue on the main road towards the top of a col and turn left on to the D 110, signposted St-Cirgues-en-Montagne and Lalligier. Pass through Lalligier and continue to St-

Route Directions

The drive starts from Langogne ①.

Leave the town, heading north-eastwards along the N88, sign-posted le-Puy-en-Velay and Pradelles. The road climbs up to and passes through Pradelles ②.

At the junction at the top of the climb turn right on to the N102, signposted Aubenas, Lanarce and le Monastier-sur-Gazeille. Follow this road for 3km and then, at the end of a straight section and just after rounding a left-hand bend, turn left on to the D 110, signposted le Lac-d'Issarlès. Continue for 9km, then go left at the D 16, signposted Coucouron, le Béage and le Lac-d'Issarlès. At the roundabout at Coucouron take the exit signposted le Béage and le Lac-d'Issarlès. Follow this road and turn right off the main road by the village of le Lac-d'Issarlès ③.

Drive through the village to a car park at its far end. The first walk starts from here.

Return to the main road and turn right towards le Béage. The road

climbs, giving splendid views of le Béage. Turn right on to the D 122 at the junction in the village, on to a road signposted Lachamp-Raphaël and Aubenas. This road makes a hairpin bend to the right as it goes out of le Béage and climbs up still further. Just after les Jalades, follow the main road to the left, signposted Privas, Gerbier de Jonc and Lachamp-Raphaël. Turn off to the right to visit Ste-Eulalie ④.

Return to the main road and bear left at a junction where the main road, the D 122, turns right over a river, your fork being signposted Gerbier de Jonc ⑤.

At Gerbier de Jonc take a right turn, the D 378 signposted Lachamp-Raphaël and Privas, and drive past the source of the Loire. Continue down to a junction with the D 122 and turn left, following signs for Lachamp-Raphaël, Privas and Vals-les-Bains.

Pass through Lachamp-Raphaël and soon fork left, still on the D 122, now signposted Mézilhac and Privas. Drive into Mézilhac ⑥.

Go right, on to the D 578, sign-posted Vals-les-Bains, Antraigues-sur-Volane and Aubenas. At a

roundabout go straight over, following signs for Aubenas, until you reach Vals-les-Bains ⑦.

At Vals-les-Bains turn right, over a bridge, signposted 'Toutes Directions', and then left down the main road, signposted Labégude and Aubenas. Leave Vals-les-Bains by crossing the river and turn left at the traffic lights, following signs for Aubenas and the aerodrome. Continue to Aubenas ⑧.

▲ *A handsome war memorial can be seen in the village of le Lac-d'Issarlès*

Cirgues. Go through St-Cirgues, and turn left out of the village on to the D 288, signposted Lanarce. In Lanarce, at the junction with the N102, go left towards Aubenas. Go through the village on the N102, and turn right on to the D 108, signposted Lespéron. Pass through Lespéron and continue to a junction with the N88. Turn left to return to Langogne.

HUGUENOT MARTYRS

In France the earliest champion of the Protestant cause was Jean Calvin, who published a major reformist statement in 1536. Calvinism grew rapidly, becoming particularly strong in Auvergne, and by 1560 it looked as though the power of the Catholics in France would be broken. The French Protestants were called Huguenots. The origin of the name is buried in history, and no satisfactory meaning has yet been discovered.

The rise of Protestantism gave rise to numerous sectarian killings, culminating in the notorious St Bartholomew's Day massacre in Paris, in 1572, when as many as 4000 Huguenots were murdered by a Catholic mob. The root cause of the massacre was the marriage of Henri de Navarre, a Bourbon duke, to Charles IX's sister. Henri was a Huguenot, but quickly agreed to return to Catholicism. In the wake of the massacre there were battles all over France, but especially in the resolutely Protestant Massif Central. Issoire, in Auvergne, was captured and its Catholic population slaughtered. However, the victory was short-lived, for Issoire and around 400 villages in the region were retaken by the Catholics and burned to the ground. Eventually in 1598, the discord was brought to a halt by the Edict of Nantes, by which Henri IV gave the Huguenots equal rights of worship to those enjoyed by the Catholic majority.

The town hall in Aubenas occupies the château, parts of which date back to the 12th century, although much restoration and modification have taken place over the centuries. It played a leading role in a peasants' revolt of 1670 which was brutally suppressed. Aubenas enjoys an elevated position with fine views of the Ardèche valley ▶

Points of Interest

① Langogne is on neither the Loire nor the Ardèche, but in the valley of the Allier. It is a pleasant village set in a cattle-breeding area, and has a very good 15th-century church with fine sculpted capitals.

◀ *The characterful village of Pradelles lies on the River Allier, on the eastern edge of the Massif Central. Among its attractions are an ancient market-place, arcaded houses from the time of the Renaissance and the remains of the town's castle*

② Pradelles is a delightful old village. To get the best from a visit, make your way to Place de la Halle, where the remains of an old castle stand close to an ancient market-place with arcaded houses, some of which date from the time of the Renaissance.

③ See page 141.

④ The quiet, pleasant little village of Ste-Eulalie plays host to Europe's largest medicinal herb fair, the Foire-aux-Violettes, which takes place annually on or near 15 July. The local volcanic soil grows all manner of plants in profusion, and these are dried and sold, both to practitioners of homeopathy and for cooking. Violets are especially abundant close to the village, hence the fair's name.

⑤ The volcanic stump of Gerbier de Jonc, lying only a few hundred metres above the road, is famous as the source of the Loire, but where exactly does the river begin? The souvenir sellers have no doubt, but there are several springs on the hillside, each with as good a claim as the next.

⑥ Either Mézilhac, which is a minor winter-sports centre, or nearby Lachamp-Raphaël, can be used as the start of a trip to the Cascade du Ray Pic, where two streams tumble over a volcanic lip. As a visit requires a one-hour return walk, the falls are rarely crowded.

⑦ Stretching along the River Volane, Vals-les-Bains is famous for its mineral water, producing millions of bottles annually. The water springs from dozens of sources along the riverside, and is unusual in being cold (about 13°C), as spring water in this volcanic area is generally hot.

⑧ See page 142.

Lac d'Issarlès

Close to the source of the Loire at Gerbier de Jonc the countryside is a mixture of the striking volcanic scenery of Auvergne and the delights of the Parc National des Cévennes. The park is actually a little way to the south, but the scenic ingredients that make it so important are already noticeable. This walk follows the shore line of the beautiful Lac d'Issarlès.

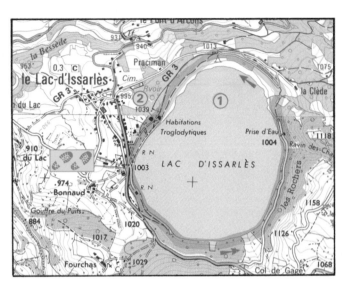

Route Directions

From the car park go to the lake and follow the shore anti-clockwise.

Just beyond the southern edge of the lake a path to the right reaches a good viewpoint to the right, where there are often surprising numbers of people. However, the reason is soon clear: the D 116 runs close by, allowing car-borne sightseers easy access. Continue around the lake, noticing both the striking clarity and the blueness of the water ①.

After 2km continue along the lakeside road to its end. Here the road becomes a track that climbs away from the lake to meet another road that leads to, and then passes through, a camp site. At the camp site entrance, to the left of the amenity building, follow a path that leads back to the lake, and continue along this path and the shore line back towards the car park. Before reaching it, however, take a rising path to the right. This goes through the pine trees to reach an old cave in a rock outcrop. Continue for a short distance to a second outcrop from where there is a superb view of the lake ②.

Retrace your steps back to the lake and continue along the shore back to the car park.

Points of Interest

① Lac d'Issarlès is a crater lake: a lake formed in the crater of an old volcano. Usually volcanic lakes are formed by lava flows damming valley exits, lakes being formed by a backing up of water in the stream bed behind the dam. Volcanic ash itself is permeable to water, so ash cones never form crater lakes, these only being produced when the original cone has been created in solid rock. Lac d'Issarlès was formed this way. It covers an area of 90 hectares, and at its centre is about 140m deep, an enormous depth for a relatively small lake.

Lac d'Issarlès, which formed in the crater of an extinct volcano, has an area of 90 hectares and a depth which is surprising for its size – some 140m ▶

The strikingly blue water, pleasant beaches and tree-shaded shoreline combine to make Lac d'Issarlès popular with holiday-makers and day trippers ▼

Lac d'Issarlès is breathtakingly beautiful with its extremely blue and clear water. In the early 1950s this clarity was threatened by the Montpezat hydroelectrical scheme, which took water from the bottom of the lake, replacing it by the diverting of streams. Following a national outcry it was agreed that all the inflowing water would be filtered to maintain water purity. As a result of this far-sighted decision the lake is as it was, though the water level does rise and fall a little. Even here, though, there has been a compromise, the hydroelectric scheme not using the lake water during the period from 15 June to 15 September, when the lake is popular with bathers and water-sports enthusiasts.

② The cave in the first rock outcrop is believed to have been inhabited by Stone Age man. Perhaps those early lakeside dwellers appreciated the lake's stunning beauty, which is seen to perfection from the second outcrop.

141

WALK 34B: 3KM/ALLOW 1½ HOURS

Aubenas

Set on a high ridge above the Ardèche, Aubenas gives excellent views of the fine countryside that lies to the west of the Rhône valley. This walk explores the town, whose former prosperity is seen in a collection of handsome medieval houses.

Route Directions

Start from the car park in Place O. de Serres in Aubenas ①.

Go out of the car park into Rue Lesin-Lacoste and turn right. Walk down to the crossroads and turn left into Rue Auguste Bouchet, following it past the fountain and then around to the left. This continuation of the same road is called Rue Jourdan. Follow it into Place Hôtel-de-Ville, where the château stands next to the town hall ②.

Walk along the front of the château and go left down its side, following Rue Henri Silhol to an excellent viewpoint ③.

From the viewpoint retrace your steps as far as the château, cross the square and go down Rue Delichères ④.

At the end of the street is the church of St-Laurent ⑤.

Turn right as you reach it and follow Rue 4 Septembre to a small square. Cross the square and follow the exiting street to a T-junction with Rue Auguste Bouchet. Turn left and retrace your steps to return to the car park.

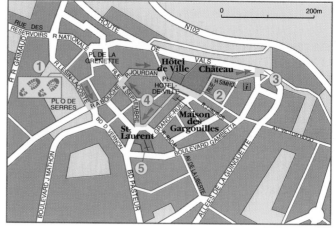

Points of Interest

① In medieval times the prosperity of Aubenas was based on the local olive trees, but a disastrous winter in 1669-70 killed most of them. Local people were appalled when the feudal lord decided to replant using different stock. A march on the estate office led to violence in which one of the estate clerks was killed. The assumed leader of the rioters was imprisoned, but freed by a mob who laid siege to the town. The governor of Languedoc sent out a force against the mob, but, fearing a bloodbath, tried to talk them out of the siege. However, Louis XIV chose to send soldiers to Aubenas. A short and bloody battle followed and the peasants' leaders were executed. Ironically, olives play no part in the town's current prosperity. Instead, Aubenas is one of the centres for the Auvergne chestnut industry, and for jam making.

② The oldest parts of the château in Aubenas date from the 12th century, though it has been extended, modified and rebuilt several times since then. Often such additions and 'restorations' do little to enhance the original building, but here the result is very attractive. The frontage of the castle is flanked by two round embattled towers, and is dominated by the keep, which has delightful lookouts. The château now houses the town hall and can be visited. An exquisite 18th-century stairway leads up from the inner courtyard, and inside there are excellent panelled rooms.

③ A panorama dial at the viewpoint indicates the best features of the view to the north, including the eye-catching Roc de Gourdon.

④ Rue Delichères, with its arch-ways, is the most picturesque street in Aubenas, but though many of its buildings are a delight, the town contains even finer architecture elsewhere. The best of its buildings is the Maison des Gargouilles, a superb 16th-century house across the main square from the château. The high tower with its gargoyles is excellent.

⑤ The church of St-Laurent is more interesting inside than it is for its external architecture. Look out for the fine altarpieces and the exquisite 17th-century carved pulpit.

Aubenas is an agreeable town with a number of fine buildings ▼

The Bourbonnais

The *département* of Allier, the most northerly in Auvergne, is more usually known as the Bourbonnais. This was the country of the Bourbons, a fertile land which allowed the family to become rich and influential, ultimately supplying France with eight kings, Spain and Belgium with royal lines and Luxembourg with its grand dukes. On this tour the high lands of the Massif Central give way to gentler landscape of fields and forests, with the occasional lake. The roads through this pastoral country are excellent, with few steep climbs and many straight stretches.

Route Directions

The drive starts from the centre of Moulins ①.

Follow signs for Clermont-Ferrand, cross the bridge over the Allier and at a roundabout go left on the N9 signposted Clermont-Ferrand, St-Pourçain and Vichy. Follow the N9 to St-Pourçain-sur-Sioule ②.

At the traffic lights in St-Pourçain go left, signposted Clermont-Ferrand and 'Centre Ville'. A few hundred metres further on there is a car park by the river for those wishing to explore the town. Return to the traffic lights and go left on to the D 46, signposted Montluçon, Montmarault and le Montet. After 2.5 km turn right on to the D 1, signposted le Montet, Caves de Saulcet, Saulcet and Bourbon-l'Archambault. This road goes through delightful open farmland and passes Saulcet ③.

Carry on through the village of la Roche and over a dual carriageway to reach le Montet ④.

In the village turn right on the D 945, signposted Tronget, Bourbon-l'Archambault, and later on Souvigny and Moulins. At a junction with the D 73 turn right (no sign) and then turn left on to a road signposted Marigny, St-Menoux and Bourbon-l'Archambault. Go through Souvigny ⑤.

Leave Souvigny on the D 253, signposted Bourbon l'Archambault and St-Menoux, then turn left on to

The former abbey church of Ste-Croix in St-Pourçain-sur-Sioule was built between the 11th and the 15th centuries ▶

the D 104, signposted Autry-Issards, and follow the road through this lovely village ⑥.

Carry straight on, following the D 134 towards Bourbon l'Archambault. At the junction with the D 953 go straight over into Bourbon, following 'Centre Ville' signs ⑦.

Leave Bourbon on the D 953, signposted Moulins and St-Menoux, which goes through the centre of St-Menoux ⑧.

On leaving the village continue on the D 953 which joins the D 945 on the outskirts of Moulins.

Moulins is situated on the right bank of the River Allier and is the capital of the Bourbonnais ▶

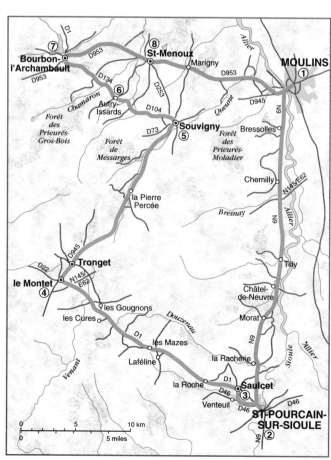

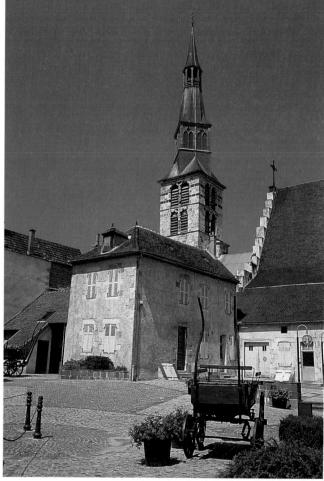

Points of Interest

① The former capital of the Duchy of Bourbon, and seat of the glittering Bourbon court in the 15th century, Moulins is the heart of the Bourbonnais. Though sizeable, with about 25,000 inhabitants, it is such a quiet old town that it seems smaller. The cathedral, the town's main attraction, is more distinguished for the works of art it contains than for its architecture. The building consists of two parts, the eastern half being 15th-century Flamboyant Gothic, while the western half is 19th-century. Inside, the 15th-16th century stained glass in the older section constitutes one of the finest collections in France. Equally fine is the late-15th-century Triptyque du Maître de Moulins. Housed in the Cathedral Treasury, this magnificent work shows Pierre II, Duke of Bourbon, and his wife Anne of France (daughter of Louis XI) flanking the Virgin and Child.

Moulins also has several fine museums. The Musée du Folklore et du Vieux Moulins, not far to the south of the cathedral, occupies a 15th-century house and deals with the late-medieval history of the town and its people. It also houses an important collection of antique dolls. Earlier items, mostly from the heyday of the Bourbons in the early Middle Ages, can be found in the Musée d'Art et d'Archéologie which occupies part of the former château of Anne of France to the north-west of the cathedral.

An attractive old quarter surrounds Moulins' Notre-Dame cathedral ▼

THE HOUSE OF BOURBON

In the 10th century an officer of the Duke of Aquitaine named Aylmard acquired lands near Souvigny. The land was very fertile, and he became a wealthy man. His descendants bought more land locally, so that as time went on the wealth of the family increased. By the 13th century the Bourbon family, as they had by then become known, were rich and powerful. The Dukes of Aquitaine and Auvergne, might have been richer and more powerful, but the Bourbons were shrewder, knowing when to confront the king of France and when to support him. In the main they took his side, and since the king was often at loggerheads with the dukes, the influence, and therefore the power and wealth, of the Bourbons increased.

By the 14th century the head of the Bourbon family had become a duke. Later, in 1400, the ruling duke married Marie de Berry, an heiress of the family which had given France several kings. Ultimately their line was to give France its last kings, starting in 1589 with Henry IV, the first king of the Bourbon dynasty, and ending when Louis XVI went to the guillotine. After the first attempt at Republicanism Louis XVI's brother became Louis XVIII, and was followed by two further kings (Charles X, another brother of Louis XVI and Louis-Philippe, a descendant of an earlier Bourbon king). By 1848 France was again in turmoil, however, and Louis-Philippe was forced to abdicate. The Second Republic had come, and though there was to be a brief flirtation with an emperor, there was no further return to monarchy. In 1850 Louis-Philippe died, and with him the Bourbon line.

Near the Musée du Folklore is the Jacquemart, a 17th-century bell tower in Place de l'Hôtel de Ville. The tower's upper section has twice been gutted by fire, each time being faithfully restored. Make sure your visit coincides with the hour, the half-hour or the quarter-hour, when chimes are struck by a mechanical soldier, his wife and their two children.

② Modern road building has not been kind to St-Pourçain-sur-Sioule, a distinguished and extremely pretty town. The Sioule is an attractive river, and the part of the old town which lies on an island in the river – and which has therefore been protected from major engineering works – is quaint and interesting. St-Pourçain can reasonably claim to be the oldest wine village in France, as there having been vineyards here since pre-Roman times. Its wine, red, white or rosé, can be tasted at the Maison de St-Pourçain.

③ Saulcet is an elegant village and has a fine church decorated with frescos from the 12th, 13th and 14th centuries.

④ A 12th-century church dominates the fine village of le Montet. The church is most remarkable for having been transformed into a fortress in the 14th century: evidence of the fortifications can still be seen on the north side.

⑤ Delightful though it is, Souvigny gives little indication now that it was the home of a family that was to become the most powerful in

▲ *Autry-Issards' old priory adds to the beauty of an already pretty village*

France, and one of the most influential in Europe. The celebrated priory, a wealthy daughter-house of Cluny, was founded before the rise of the Bourbons, having been endowed by a Duke of Aquitaine in the earth 10th century. The priory church of St-Pierre is 11th/12th century, though much restored and added to – the façade, for instance, is 15th-century. Inside is the carved, time-worn tomb of St Mayeul, a 10th-century abbot of Cluny, along with the ornate marble tombs of several Bourbon dukes.

The church also houses a Musée Lapidaire, which contains a beautiful 12th-century octagonal stone pillar, 1.8m high and almost a ton in weight, exquisitely carved as a calendar of canonical activities. The Souvigny monks are shown at the labours of the months – treading grapes for instance – while other faces are carved with motifs including the signs of the zodiac.

⑥ With its old priory, its spired church, and its spacious layout, Autry-Issards is a strong contender for the title of prettiest village in Auvergne.

⑦ The view to the ruined Bourbon castle from across the lake at Bourbon l'Archambault is excellent. Of the castle itself only three towers remain, the destruction at the time of the Revolution having been very thorough. The Tour Quinquengrogne stands as part of the original fortified walls. An old spa building – Bourbon once having been the height of fashion as a spa – now houses a Musée d'Archéologie, d'Histoire et d'Ethnographie, and is decorated in traditional Bourbonnais style, complete with costumes. The 15th- and 19th-century church is also of interest.

⑧ The 12th-century church at St-Menoux is interesting not only for its architecture but also for the sarcophagus of St Menoux himself. The saint was reputed to be able to cure stutterers: sufferers would come to the church (some say they still do) and put their heads through the hole in the side of the tomb in the hope of being cured.

The Gorges du Tarn

In addition to the volcanoes of Auvergne, the Massif Central also possesses another unusual geological feature to delight the visitor: the Causses, a chiselled limestone plateau, about 1000 metres high. The climate of the plateau is harsh, with hot, dry summers followed by cold winters, during which the area is scoured by high winds. The Causses are divided into four blocks of steep valleys. Of these blocks the highest and harshest is the Causse Méjean, lying between the gorges of the Tarn and the Jonte. The Gorges du Tarn are one of the most beautiful areas of France, and this tour explores both them and the Gorges de la Jonte. The route is an arduous one, with narrow, winding roads, the occasional steep section and, in the Gorges du Tarn, too much traffic if you are there on the wrong day. But it is also a rewarding route, with magnificent natural scenery.

▲ Cobbled lanes and old stone houses lend charm to Ste-Enimie, which lies below cliffs on a bend in the River Tarn

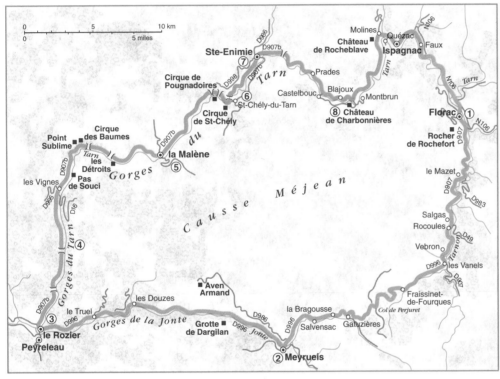

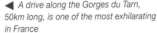

◄ A drive along the Gorges du Tarn, 50km long, is one of the most exhilarating in France

Route Directions

The drive starts from the centre of Florac ①.

Leave Florac heading southwards, but do not take the main road, the N106, that crosses the river. At a roundabout, go straight over to take the D 907, signposted Meyrueis, Barre des Cévennes and St-Jean-du-Gard. After 5km take a right fork signposted Vebron, Meyrueis, St-André-de-Vigne and Mont Aigoual, and drive for 10km through a lovely valley to reach les Vanels. Take the D 996 to the right, signposted Fraissinet-de-Fourques, Meyrueis, Mont Aigoual and Grotte de Dargilan, which follows a long and splendid climb to the Col de Perjuret. At the

top go straight on, following signs to Meyrueis, to descend from the col into Meyrueis ②.

To stop in the village go over the bridge, bear right and take the main street to the left to reach a car park. The first walk starts from here.

Leave Meyrueis down the main street, and rejoin the D 996 to the left, signposted Millau and Gorges de la Jonte. Follow this narrow road out of town, following the road to right and left into the gorge. The gorge itself is very attractive and easy to follow, with signs for the Gorges du Tarn. At the western end is the tiny village of le Rozier ③.

Leave le Rozier over the bridge and then turn right on to the D 907b, signposted les Vignes, Florac, Gorges du Tarn and Point Sublime. Follow the road through the Gorges du Tarn ④.

From les Vignes the road becomes even more beautiful as it leads to la Malène ⑤.

There then follows a series of tunnels set close together, a 1.5-km stretch of open road and one final tunnel. Take the next turning to the right after this tunnel, a very sharp turn, signposted St-Chély-du-Tarn. The road passes over a bridge and then bears right into St-Chély ⑥.

The second walk starts from here.

Retrace the route to the gorge road and turn right (no sign). Follow signs to Ispagnac and Florac to Ste-Enimie ⑦.

Beyond Ste-Enimie the gorge opens up a bit, but it still has surprises in store, especially the stunning châteaux on either side of the route as it approaches Ispagnac ⑧.

Continue through Ispagnac and turn right at the N106, signposted Alès and Florac. This road takes you straight back to Florac.

▲ *Florac is a delightful little town built around the Source du Pêcher, a stream that runs into the River Tarnon, a tributary of the Tarn. The cliffs of the Rocher de Rochefort tower above Florac, while just north of the town are the spectacular Gorges du Tarn*

CAVES

The limestone of the Causses is a basic calcium carbonate rock, soluble in rainwater – rain being a mild acid as a result of dissolved carbon dioxide. Owing to the action of rainwater over millions of years much of the water of the Causses flows underground, the underground streams producing the caves that are such a feature of the area. Eventually the underground streams reach a layer of impervious rock – under the Causses it is a bed of marl – and run along it before reaching the surface again at a point where the limestone cap has been eroded or at a geological fault. The point of re-emergence is known as a resurgence.

The effect of rain on the rock surface is gradual. At first the rainwater erodes the rock into a shallow depression known in the Massif Central as a *cloup*. As the depression deepens it becomes a *sotch*, more of a pit than a hollow, and further erosion creates an *aven* or *igue*. *Avens* are steep-sided chimneys and are at their most spectacular where they link into underground chambers.

Two of the finest caves in France lie close to our route, near the village of Meyrueis. The Grotte de Dargilan has a main chamber 140m long and 35m high, though the smaller 'Mosque' chamber is much prettier. Best of all is the Chambre Rose, with wonderful pink formations. The cave also has a petrified waterfall 100m wide and 40m high. Aven Armand is even more spectacular: its size, and the quality of its rock formations and the purity of their colours are breathtaking.

Points of Interest

① The picturesque tranquillity of Florac today belies its violent history. Because it occupied a strategic position on the edge of the Causse Méjean the village became a local capital and was constantly fought over and in. The castle was destroyed and rebuilt several times. The present 17th-century building is the administrative centre of the Parc National des Cévennes, and houses displays on the park and its wildlife. Florac stands at the foot of the impressive Rocher de Rochefort, and a fine walk follows the tumbling Source du Pêcher stream back up to its source below the cliffs. The walk starts close to the castle, on its southern side.

② See page 147.

③ Le Rozier sits at the point where the Jonte reaches the Tarn, and it makes the most of this enviable position. The Hôtel de la Muse, for instance, a strange but interesting building, stands right beside the river. Close to le Rozier but separated from it by the width of the Jonte is Peyreleau, a prettier village grouped around a modern church and an old tower, the last remnant of a medieval castle.

④ The beautiful gorge of the Tarn is 50km long and can be followed not only by car (the easiest way) but also by boat (the most exciting way) or on foot (hard work but rewarding). The Tarn receives no tributary streams in the gorge other than one or two very minor ones, but is fed instead by the water of over 40 resurgences – much of the water flowing in as waterfalls – which gives some idea of the extent to which the Causse Méjean is penetrated by rainwater. The gorge is tight, never more than 500m wide and occasionally narrowing to just 30m,

with sides that are always steep, sometimes vertical and occasionally overhanging.

⑤ Beyond les Vignes the gorge enters its tightest and for many most spectacular section. Here are the Pas de Souci, where the Tarn flows over and under huge blocks created by the collapse of part of the gorge walls, and les Détroits, 400m-high sheer cliffs. Both of these features are best viewed from a boat which can be boarded at la Malène.

⑥ See page 148.

⑦ St Enimie was a 7th-century princess ordered to marry by her father, the king, when she wished to be allowed to become a nun. At the news of her intended marriage she contracted leprosy, which not surprisingly drove her suitor away. After his departure an angel told her where to go for a cure, but although the cure worked, when she returned to the Tarn gorge her leprosy also returned. On the angel's advice she bathed in the waters of the Fontaine de Burle and was cured again. She then stayed here as a hermit. Outside the village that now bears her name the persistent visitor can find a grotto said to have been lived in by the princess, but it cannot be entered; within the village the fountain can be seen. For the rest, the village is pure delight – old paved or cobbled lanes and superb stone houses. Place au Beurre is a delightful old square.

⑧ As the route nears the end of the gorges look out for the fine 16th-century Château de Charbonnières to the right of the road near Montbrun, and Quézac, a tiny village with a Gothic bridge over the Tarn, Ispagnac is the last village in the gorge, a delightful spot with an interesting 12th-century church.

Boat trips can be taken from la Malène along the River Tarn, to see the Gorges ▼

Meyrueis

Meyrueis has one of the most enviable positions of any Massif Central village, close to Mont Aigoual, the Parc National des Cévennes and the Gorges du Tarn. This walk explores the village, then takes a short climb to a chapel viewpoint. The climb involves a short series of steps.

◀ *Wood is an important commodity in Meyrueis, where sawmills serve both the building and the paper industries*

Lying between the Causse Noir and the Causse Méjean, Meyrueis has long been a market town for the scattered local communities, yet it remains peaceful ▼

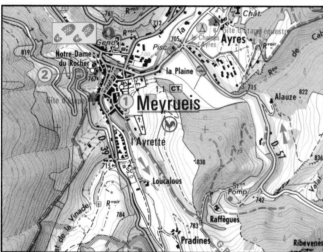

Route Directions

Start from the car park in Meyrueis. Take the tiny street to the left of the Grand Hôtel de France as you face the hotel. This street, Rue de Roch, is typical of the tangle of old streets that make up Meyrueis ①.

The narrow street soon narrows even more and eventually becomes a grassy track. Follow the track uphill to the bottom of a series of steps. Climb these to a road, the D 39. Turn right and after 20m right again up a track to the chapel of Notre-Dame du Rocher, a lovely chapel with splendid views ②.

Retrace your steps to Meyrueis and cross over the stream to the square in the old part of the village. Turn right and then left towards the cemetery. Go to the right of the cemetery to reach the GR 6A footpath which climbs steadily south-eastwards up the flank of the Béthuzon valley. After 1km turn left on to the track that leads past Raffègues and a pumping station to reach the D 57 in the Brèze valley.

Turn left and follow the road to a T-junction by a bridge. Turn left back to Meyrueis.

Points of Interest

① Meyrueis grew up at the confluence of two small streams, the Béthuzon and the Brèze, with the River Jonte, at the start of the Jonte gorge. As it also stands at the meeting point of the Causse Noir and the Causse Méjean it has long been an important village, if a small one. As it lies at a height of 700m it is a cool spot even in the heat of summer, which makes it a popular tourist centre. Despite this it is a quiet place, as a stroll under the fine old plane trees on Quai Sully or around the narrow streets will show. Look out for Maison Belon, with its elegant Renaissance windows, and the clock tower, a last vestige of the ancient fortifications. Only close to the sawmills is the idyllic atmosphere troubled.

Just south of the village, reached by a small road off the D 986, is the Château de Roquedols, a vast 15th-16th century quadrilateral castle with

two round towers, beautifully set in the lush green Béthuzon valley. The château houses an information centre for the Parc National des Cévennes.

② The chapel of Notre-Dame was built in 1876 and would be improved if the ugly blue statue of the Virgin were removed from the top. The interior of the chapel, by contrast, is simple and quiet. From here the views to the village and up the Béthuzon valley towards the Parc National des Cévennes are splendid. It is thought that the slopes of Mont Aigoual were once clothed with

forests which were largely destroyed by Bronze Age farmers and their sheep. The naturalist Georges Fabre realised the importance of the forests to the hydrology of the area, and early in this century encouraged the government to start replanting the peak. Today there are almost 20,000 hectares of new forest containing a good mixture of deciduous and coniferous trees. It is carefully managed, certain sections being strictly protected while others are exploited for timber: the sawmills at Meyrueis produce wood for both the construction and the paper industries.

St-Chély-du-Tarn

In addition to the nearby cirque, the attractions of St-Chély-du-Tarn include a Romanesque church with an external stairway, a fine bridge and old stone houses such as this one with a tower ▼

▲ *Chapel in the rock at St-Chély-du-Tarn*

▲ *Less well known than many Tarn villages, St-Chély-du-Tarn is well worth a visit*

Walking is quite restricted in the Gorges du Tarn, with their high, steep cliffs. Close to the top of the gorge, however, it is possible to get a little closer to the scenery. This walk starts in St-Chély-du-Tarn, one of the smaller and lesser-known Tarn villages which is nevertheless very pretty, and from which a reasonable walk visits several sites that display the remarkable geology of the Tarn.

Route Directions

Start from the centre of St-Chély-du-Tarn. Walk back towards the road bridge with the church on your right. Just before the road bridge turn off the road, going down to the right to reach the river bank – almost a beach at this point. There is a charming view of the village ①.

Walk back up towards the road, but take the small path that goes under the road at the beginning of the bridge. This very pretty path leads back to the village square with its bread oven ②.

Turn to the right as you enter the square, crossing a stream and following signs for the *chapelle*. The path winds up past a tourist shop that is built into the rock and has internal streams ③.

Eventually you reach the chapel ④.

From here you can either retrace your steps to the village or add about 30 minutes to the walk by continuing along the path to the cliffs of the Cirque de St-Chély ⑤.

It is best to return along the same path, as the alternative path at a higher level involves a steep climb and is quite rugged.

Points of Interest

① St-Chély is a pretty little village set on the left bank of the Tarn. It is positioned very dramatically at the point where the Causse Méjean ends suddenly in the superb cliffs of the cirque named after the village (see 5 below). The bridge over the Tarn is believed to date from Roman times, and this walk passes under one of its elegant arches. The church passed on the walk is unusual for having an external stairway to its attractive square bell tower. Equally pretty are the old village houses with their Renaissance chimneys and doorways.

② This well-preserved old bread oven has a beautifully tiled roof. Communal ovens of the Massif Central are of standard design, only the size changing with the size of the village: wood was stored to dry in a small outer chamber, behind which lay the hemispherical brick-lined oven itself.

③ At several places in the village, some of them extremely unlikely, there are resurgent streams that fall into the Tarn. The limestone of the Causses is permeable to water, so that most of the rain that falls on the high plateau disappears to form underground rivers that run along the top of an impervious rock layer. Where this layer reaches the surface again, as here where the Tarn has cut deep into the limestone, the streams suddenly reappear from caves or fissures.

④ The tiny chapel was built into the rock of the Tarn gorge walls in the 12th century. It shares its cave-like site with another resurgent stream, and offers eye-catching views towards the lower gorge and the village.

⑤ In river plains and on more impermeable soils rivers sometimes form ox-bow lakes by cutting a straight path across the neck of a particularly deeply incised meander. In the Causses these cut-off bends empty of water to become dry gorges known as cirques. In the upper reaches of the Tarn gorge there are two cirques, one here at St-Chély-du-Tarn, and the other a few kilometres downstream at Pougnadoires. In each case the old gorge cliffs are superb.

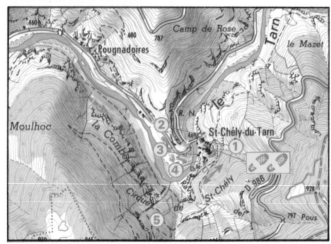

The southern Massif

At the southern extremity of the Massif Central is the last of the four limestone Causses, the Causse du Larzac. This tour explores both the high Causse and the valleys, visiting one of the finest of the limestone features and one of the prettiest villages in the whole Massif. The roads are surprisingly good for such a plateau-and-valley tour, with few winding or steep sections.

Route Directions

The drive starts from Ganges ①.

Take the D 986, signposted Montpellier, and at the first round-about take the first exit, signposted le Vigan. Continue straight over at the next roundabout, again following a sign for le Vigan, and then turn left on to a road signposted Lodève, Cazilhac and Clermont-l'Hérault. Go over a bridge and turn right on to the D 25, signposted St-Laurent-le-Minier, Madières, Lodève, Millau and Cirque de Navacelles. Continue through the Gorges de la Vis ②.

Continue to Madières, and there take the left fork, still on the D 25, for St-Maurice-Navacelles, Lodève, and Cirque de Navacelles. Cross the River Vis and follow the road to the right, climbing up and up to reach St-Maurice-Navacelles. Here turn right on to a road signposted Cirque de Navacelles for a 'there-and-back' visit to one of the finest features of the Causses ③.

Returning to St-Maurice, turn right and through the village on the D 25. The road is on the plateau now, which makes the going easier. At the

end of a stretch of straight road 8km out of St-Maurice, turn left on to the D 152, signposted la Vacquerie-et-St-Martin-de-Castries. Go through this narrow village, whose name is almost as long as itself, and continue on the level, joining the D 9. Watch out for a right-hand bend about 8km from la Vacquerie: near here is a sign on the right for the Forêt Domaniale du N-D de Parlatges, and some 20m further on is a parking place on the left, just before the road goes through a rock cutting. The first walk starts from here.

The road stays on the plateau for a while before winding down steeply into Arboras. Go straight through the village and over the viaduct-like bridge. At Montpeyroux, the next village, take the left fork to reach the village centre. Turn left in the centre on to a road signposted St-Jean-de-Fos, Gignac and Montpellier. Follow this road out of the village, and bear left at a fork on to a road signposted St-Jean-de-Fos ④.

From St-Jean turn left, following the signs for St-Guilhem-le-Désert and Ganges. Just outside St-Jean the road, the D 4, bears left to reach the Grotte de Clamouse ⑤ .

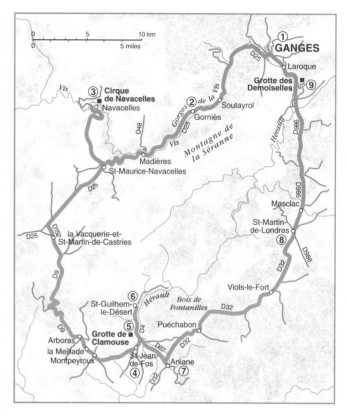

Go on to St-Guilhem-le-Désert ⑥.

The second walk starts here. Return on the D 4 to the fork outside St-Jean and turn left on the D 27, crossing a bridge over the splendid gorge of the Hérault and following signs for Aniane and Montpellier. Fork right on to the D 32 to reach Aniane ⑦.

Return to the fork with the D 27 and follow the D 32 to the right, signposted Puéchabon, Viols-le-Fort and St-Martin-de-Londres. Go through Puéchabon, bypass Viols-le-Fort to the left and continue to a junction at St-Martin-de-Londres ⑧.

From St-Martin-de-Londres take the D 986, signposted Ganges, to the Grotte des Demoiselles ⑨.

Return to Ganges on the D 986.

◀ *The narrow streets of St-Guilhem-le-Désert play their part in making this village, built around a former abbey, one of the most enchanting in France*

Points of Interest

① Set at the confluence of the Rieutord stream and the Hérault, Ganges was famous in Louis XIV's time for the manufacture of silk stockings. The vagaries of fashion and the development of nylon caused the trade to decline, but recently there has been a revival in stocking making in Ganges, as one of several small, light industries that now support the town.

② The name Vis means 'screw', and apt name for this river which corkscrews its way through the landscape, especially as it nears the Cirque de Navacelles.

③ The best of the cirques on the Causses is that at Navacelles. The tiny village of Navacelles, reached by following the Vis valley, is a good starting point for a trip to the local viewpoints. To the south is la Baume-Auriol, while to the north is the aptly named Belvédère Nord. Both offer fine views of the bleached, bare sides of the cirque.

④ The route from St-Jean to St-Guilhem crosses the River Hérault over the Pont du Diable, an 11th-century bridge built by St Guilhem's monks. The more modern bridge that takes the route over the river towards Aniane offers a tremendous view of the Hérault gorge, and of the aqueduct that carries water to the local vineyards, St-Jean being a wine village, as is nearby Montpeyroux.

⑤ The Grotte de Clamouse is another of the fine caves that abound in this area, and can be explored for over 1km from the resurgence of the river that created it. Clamouse has more mineral deposits than most of the caves, but is renowned chiefly for its pure white formations and for the filigree delicacy of its stalactites.

⑥ See page 152.

⑦ The centre of Aniane offers a welcome refuge for the driver, as it is mostly too narrow for cars. Aniane is one of the oldest villages in the area, having been founded with the Abbaye de St-Sauveur in the 8th century by a Christian Visigoth, attracted by its abundant water supply, a rarity in these arid parts. The springs still supply water to the village houses. The centre, the oldest part of the village, has a good number of houses dating from the 16th century.

⑧ Many a Londoner has arrived here intrigued by the prospect of a link between this village and the metropolis. The name has an entirely different etymology, however, though opinion is mixed. Some detect a derivation from the Celtic *lund*, a swamp, while others believe the Provençal *loundres*, an otter, to be the root. St-Martin is a delightful village, with arcaded houses set around a three-sided main square. It also has remains of fortified walls dating from the 12th century, and a pleasant church built in the 11th century by monks from nearby St-Guilhem, though much restored in the late 19th century.

⑨ The Grotte des Demoiselles is named after the fairies whom local people believed to inhabit it, a vestige of the time when all such holes in the ground were thought to have supernatural properties. The cave was first explored in the 1880s and 1890s by Edouard-Alfred Martel, the father of French cave explorers and a world pioneer in the science of speleology. He was also captivated by the beauty of cave formations and in this respect Demoiselles must have delighted him. The formations are magnificent, and the sheer size of the cave – the main cavern is 120m long and almost 50m high – is awesome. To add to its delights, the visitor is carried in on a funicular railway.

▲ *During the reign of Louis XIV Ganges was famous for the manufacture of silk stockings, which was its main industry. The advent of nylon damaged the industry but recently there has been a revival in silk stocking making in the town*

SHEEP AND THE TRANSHUMANCE

Visitors to the area in the autumn, around All Saints' Day (1 November), may be fortunate enough to witness the transhumance. On that day the shepherds and goatherds, and even the cowherds who are lucky enough to have high land capable of sustaining cattle, gather their animals together and drive them to lower pastures for winter. The animals are 'dressed' for the journey with flags, flowers or pompoms on their heads, and are driven along special ancient paths known as *drailles*. For those animals whose journey does not end at the abattoirs on the plains of Bas-Languedoc, there is a return journey in spring. The transhumance is a great sight, but motor transport may soon make it a thing of the past.

The Cirque de Navacelles, in the valley of the River Vis, between the Causse de Blandas and the Causse du Larzac, is the most dramatic of the cirques in the area ▼

The flank of Mont St-Baudille

AUVERGNE
AND LANGUEDOC

The Causse du Larzac is the largest of the Causses, covering nearly 1000 square km and rising to nearly 1000 metres. It is subdivided into five separate blocks, so that it appears less a single large plateau than a succession of smaller, dry plateaux divided by green valleys.

Route Directions

Start from the lay-by off the D 9, as described in the tour route directions. The lay-by lies almost opposite a very derelict house, from which two paths fan out: take the uphill one that passes to the right of a 'Feux Interdits' sign. The clearly defined path climbs into some lovely woodland to reach a fork under a large tree. The right fork leads quickly to a dead end from where there is a fine view of the rock outcrops on the other side of the road from the lay-by. Take the left fork, which soon climbs again. Soon afterwards the path flattens out and offers a view across the valley towards Mont St-Baudille ①.

Beyond is the high Larzac plateau ②.

The path now descends to a small and none too obvious T-junction. Go

left here on a narrow path that drops down and becomes more overgrown and meandering as it does so, passing huge boulders, one of which has an oddly artificial-looking hole in it. Eventually, just as you have become convinced that you are heading the wrong way, the path emerges into a clearing. Go left here, confirmed by a yellow paint way-marker, dropping down into woodland again. The path zigzags through the woods to reach a T-junction. Go left here to reach another T-junction, where a turn to the left offers a direct route back to the lay-by.

A longer walk turns right and eventually loops up to the D 9 road. Now turn left and follow the road back to the lay-by.

Points of Interest

① Mont St-Baudille, at 848m, is one of the higher peaks on the Causse du Larzac. Though undistinguished in itself, it makes a good viewpoint. Those who prefer to drive to the top can take a small road off the D 9.

▲ *Footpaths wind through attractive woodland on the flanks of Mont St-Baudille. The summit, at 847m, gives fine views over the surrounding area*

② The high plateau of the Causse du Larzac supports a thin grass and little else. This would make it ideal sheep farming country, were it not for the local rainfall's frustrating habit of disappearing below ground before forming streams or pools. To overcome this the local sheep farmers have had to create special clay-lined pools, or *lavognes*, where their animals can drink.

WALK 37B: 1KM/ALLOW 2 HOURS

St-Guilhem-le-Désert

Set in the gorge of the River Herault, just north of the Pont du Diable, is St-Guilhem-le-Désert, one of the loveliest villages in France. This walk explores its delightful streets and historic buildings.

Route Directions

Start from the car park in St-Guilhem-le-Désert.

From the car park go up the road towards the village, taking the first turn to the left, the Grand Chemin du Val de Gellone, which offers superb views of the village ①.

At the top car park in the village bear right with the road into Place de la Liberté, the centre of St-Guilhem. To the right here are the abbey church, the monastery cloister and the village museum ②, ③ and ④.

Go through the square, passing the abbey to reach the main street through the village. Turn right down the street, passing the Tour des Prisons, said to date from Roman times but apparently medieval, and

with no pedigree to support the name, and continue to St-Laurent, a fine Romanesque church dating from the 11th-12th centuries. Turn right here to return to the car park.

Points of Interest

① The village is named after William (Guilhem), a grandson of Charles Martel on his mother's side, who was born in 755 and became a great friend and trusted lieutenant of

The nameplate of the Abbaye de Gellone ▶

Of the once-powerful abbey in St-Guilhem-le-Désert, only the church, consecrated in 1076, has survived ▼

Charlemagne. A brave soldier and skilful general, he took Aquitaine for Charlemagne and was made its governor as a reward. Later he led an army to repulse a Saracen invasion of Provence, winning battles at Nîmes, Orange and Narbonne and being rewarded with the title of Prince d'Orange. He was still fighting at the age of 48, but when his beloved wife died he decided that he wished to retire peacefully. He therefore handed on the title and duties of Prince d'Orange to his son, and travelled to Paris to see Charlemagne for the last time. The meeting between the two men was tearful, Charlemagne not wishing to lose William's services. Finally he agreed, and gave William a piece of the True Cross which he had been given in Rome. William left Paris and came here, founding a monastery in this remote valley, and labouring to build the church and to make the valley habitable. He created a water supply by diverting streams and made gardens to grow food. In 812 he died, and was buried in the church he had raised.

② Of the monastery founded by William only the crypt of the old church remains, the present abbey church dating from the 11th-century church. Inside, this fine building is understated, with a good vaulted roof. The shrine of St Guilhem and the relic of the Cross made the church a stopping place for pilgrims on their way to Santiago de Compostela.

③ The cloister is reached from the church. By the 13th century there were over 100 monks at the monastery, though numbers declined sharply over the next 200 years. Today the abbey has just six monks. Of the original two-level cloister that was, and still is, a place of silent contemplation for the monks, only two sides now remain. One section of the cloister is now in the Cloisters Museum in New York.

④ The village museum, housed in the old monastery refectory, contains archives and photographs of the abbey as well as some sculpture. It also has a sarcophagus that is known as that of St Guilhem, though it almost certainly pre-dates him by at least four centuries.

◀ *The village of St-Guilhem-le-Désert grew up around the Benedictine Abbaye de Gellone, which from the 9th century was an important place of pilgrimage*

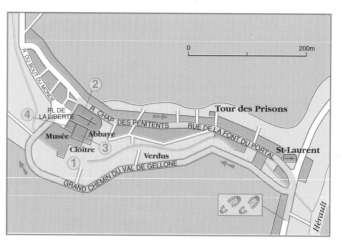

The Causse du Larzac

The Causse du Larzac is the largest of the four blocks that make up the Massif Central limestone plateau, covering over 1000 square km. Larzac is a high, dry Causse, cut by occasional green valleys. Here feed the sheep that produce the milk for Roquefort cheese, and here also the visitor is most likely to see a *lavogne*, a clay-lined pool for holding drinking water for the sheep, natural pools being virtually non-existent. This tour takes in both high plateau and river valley, dipping down to the Tarn twice and following the fine Dourbie valley for a short distance. These rises and falls are on narrow, winding roads, but none of them is particularly steep.

Route Directions

The drive starts from the centre of Millau ①.

Take the D 911, signposted Rodez, Cahors and Clermont-Ferrand. Go over a level crossing, and at the next roundabout go straight over, still on the D 911, signposted Cahors, St-Germain and Pont-de-Salars. Follow this road for 9.5km, and then turn left on to the D 30, signposted Azinières and St-Beauzély. Drop down and through St-Beauzély, then fork left, still on the D 30, signposted Bouloc and Villefranche-de-Panat, and follow the road round to the right and uphill, passing a right turn to the village of Comberoumal ②.

Continue up and through Estalane to reach a col, where there is a car park. The first walk starts from here. The tour continues along the road into Bouloc. Turn left here on to the D 993, signposted Montjaux, St-Rome-de-Tarn and Vallée-du-Tarn.

Follow further signs for St-Rome-de-Tarn as you pass through the outskirts of Montjaux. Drop down into the Tarn valley, still on the D 993, cross a bridge over the river and go up into St-Rome-de-Tarn. In the centre of the village follow the D 993 to the left, signposted St-Rome-de-Cernon, St-Affrique, Roquefort-sur-Soulzon and Millau, and follow further signs for Roquefort on the road ahead. Go through Tiergue, and take the second turn to the left after leaving the village, the D 23, signposted Lauras and Roquefort. Go left at the junction with the D 999, then almost immediately right on a road signposted Roquefort. There will be no doubting your arrival at Roquefort ③.

Continue out of the village on the same road, the D 23, and take a left fork, signposted Tournemire. Go through Tournemire, following a sign for Viala-du-Pas-de-Jaux. The road now climbs up to a large white cross that overlooks the village of Tournemire. By the cross the road goes around to the right. Continue

▲ *The Gorges de la Dourbie tower above the river, in places reaching 300m in height*

along the same road, going through Viala-du-Pas-de-Jaux. Beyond the village the road bears left and climbs towards the Pic de Cougouille. Before reaching the peak, turn left on a minor road signposted Ste-Eulalie-de-Cernon ④.

As the road drops down towards the village there are magnificent views of it. Go through Ste-Eulalie, and after a 3km climb through lovely meadowland turn left on to the D 277, signposted la Cavalerie ⑤.

At la Cavalerie follow the road round to the right into the main square, and leave the square from the far left corner. Turn right at the next road to leave the village, and pass through a military camp and across the Causse. Eventually the road drops down into Nant ⑥.

On entering Nant turn left and then left again at the main road, the D 991, signposted la Roque-Ste-Marguerite and Millau, and go down the beautiful Gorges de la Dourbie ⑦.

Continue on the same road to la Roque-Ste-Marguerite. In the village take the tiny road, leading right and up, signposted Peyreleau and Montpellier-le-Vieux. The road is narrow and steep. At a junction turn left, following signs to Millau, Longuiers and Montpellier-le-Vieux. At the next junction go left, signposted Montpellier-le-Vieux ⑧.

The second walk starts from here. Go back to the last junction and turn left on to the D 110, signposted Millau, following the road back into Millau.

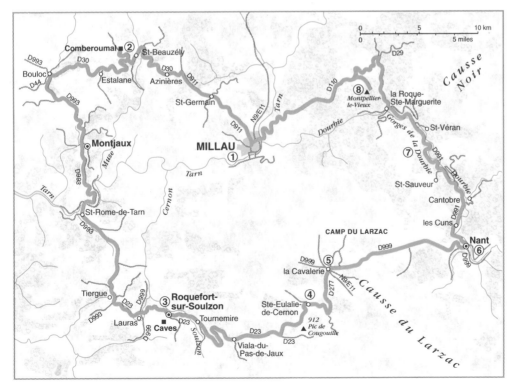

▲ *The Knights Templars of nearby la Couvertoirade had a commandery at Ste-Eulalie-de-Cernon, where the fortifications are still largely intact*

▲ *Ste-Eulalie-de-Cernon*

Points of Interest

① Millau is a pleasant town set on the right bank of the Tarn which has known fame twice in its history. Under the Romans it produced the best-known pottery in Europe. The site of the pottery, Graufesenque, is about 1km to the south, and its products can be seen in many museums including Millau's Musée Archéologique in Place du Maréchal-Foch, the best square in the town. A Roman column in the square's arcading is inscribed *Gara que faras*. The significance of this remains cryptic, though it can be very roughly translated as 'Watch your step'.

Millau's second claim to fame was its glove-making trade, which is still practised in the town.

② Although a little off the route, the priory at Comberoumal is worth a visit. Founded at the end of the 11th century, it is very well preserved.

③ As the smell that intensifies as you approach implies, Roquefort-sur-Soulzon is a cheese town. The cheese caves can be visited. The local museum has a good collection of local Bronze Age finds, and the Rocher St-Pierre can be climbed – about 150 steps – for a view of the Soulzon valley. But it is the cheese that makes Roquefort famous.

④ Once a local headquarters of the Knights Templars, Ste-Eulalie-de-Cernon still has the larger part of its old fortifications intact, with walls, towers, gates (the eastern gate is splendid) and arches. During the summer months there are guided tours of the old Templar building, with an audiovisual presentation.

⑤ La Cavalerie was the secondary headquarters of the Knights Templars and later the headquarters of the Knights Hospitallers. When the present military camp nearby suddenly grew in size, without any consultation, local protests were long and loud, and ultimately the camp expansion was reversed.

⑥ Formerly the site of a Benedictine monastery, of which only the abbey church survives, Nant is a large village built around a central square in which stands an arcaded market hall dating from the 14th century. The River Dourbie, on a bank of which the village sits, is crossed by a fine bridge, also dating from the 14th century.

⑦ The beautiful Gorges de la Dourbie are entered near les Cuns, a tiny village with a 12th-century church. The next village, Cantobre, is an architectural marvel, the natural rock overhang having been built on to create a terrace of cantilevered houses. The final village, la Roque-Ste-Marguerite, is overlooked by a 17th-century tower. The village is quite beautiful, both in situation and in appearance.

⑧ See page 156.

An ancient gateway in Roquefort-sur-Soulzon, a town renowned for its cheese ▼

ROQUEFORT AND ITS CHEESE

Many thousands of years before the village of Roquefort existed, the edge of the Cambalou plateau collapsed into the valley of the Soulzon, creating a jumble of huge rocks seated on the impervious marl of the valley floor. In the caves formed by the stabilised blocks a specific form of penicillin, *Penicillium glaucum roquefortii*, formed. Today the cheese created with the help of this penicillin is big business, and only those visitors to Roquefort who have lost their sense of smell can remain unaware of its existence.

The basic ingredient of the cheese is sheep's milk, the efforts of half a million sheep on the Causses now being supplemented by imports.

The milk, obtained in dairy parlours by milking machines, just as for cattle, is not pasteurised or altered in any other way before 'standard' cheeses are made from it. After the round cheeses have been formed – by about ten cheesemakers – they are taken to the caves formed by the ancient rockfall and stored on oak tables for three months. In the cool (about 10°C), humid air the penicillin grows in the cheese, producing the famous blue marbled appearance.

Today about 17,000 tons of cheese is produced annually, the majority for home consumption and only some 15% being exported. Exports go chiefly to the countries of the EEC and the USA.

Plateau du Lévézou

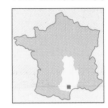
This short walk explores the high plateau that lies to the west of the Causse du Larzac, an interesting and rarely visited upland area. For the walker it offers fine, open walking with superb views, and for the naturalist a chance to see one of Europe's most magnificent birds of prey.

into blocks, the easternmost of which is the Plateau du Lévézou. Lévézou is a hard rock area stretching from Rodez to Millau and supporting a plant life that is quite different from that of the limestone Causse. The plateau falls towards Rodez, being at its best, both scenically and from the point of view of wildlife and plantlife, near the route of this tour. Here the plateau rises to over 1000 metres and offers

superb views westwards towards the huge Lac de Pareloup, named after the wolves that once roamed here, and northwards towards the plateau's highest part.

② Among and around the pine woods there are carpets of flowers in spring and summer. These are mainly wild pansies, kingcups and daffodils, but also include both yellow and purple orchids. The flowers attract

As well as horses, the Plateau du Lévézou has abundant wildlife and flowers ▼

masses of butterflies. There are also many birds, including woodpeckers, tree creepers, cuckoos, falcons and buzzards. Until the 1920s the *vautour fauve*, the griffon vulture, was widespread, if not common, in the south of France from the Pyrenees to the Italian border. Gradually, however, the bird population declined, and by the 1970s there were none left on the Massif Central. It was then decided to re-introduce the birds into the area, and old nest sites were prepared. Over the next 10 years about 60 aviary-reared birds were released. Today perhaps 20 pairs of birds are breeding regularly, and rearing 8-10 chicks annually. There are those who see no beauty in vultures, but in flight they really are magnificent birds. This walk is within their territory, and anyone lucky enough to see one soaring overhead will be an instant convert.

▲ *Wild orchids adorn Lévézou*

Route Directions

Start from the car park situated at the col beyond Estalane on the tour route. From the car park take the path to the right of the road over rough moorland towards the forest. Soon the main plateau is reached ①.

The track now levels out and open fields drop away to the left. When the track enters the forest there is a junction of tracks: go ahead on a straight track which eventually leaves the forest at a fork. Fork left here, and follow the new track on the edge of the plateau, with fine views to the right ②.

When this track reaches another fork, after some 1.5km, bear left and soon left again, continuing to the junction at the edge of the forest. Turn right to return to the car park.

Points of Interest

① To the east of the Causse du Larzac lies an area known as the Ségala after the rye (*seigle*) that used to be grown on the poor soil. Like the Causses the Ségala is divided

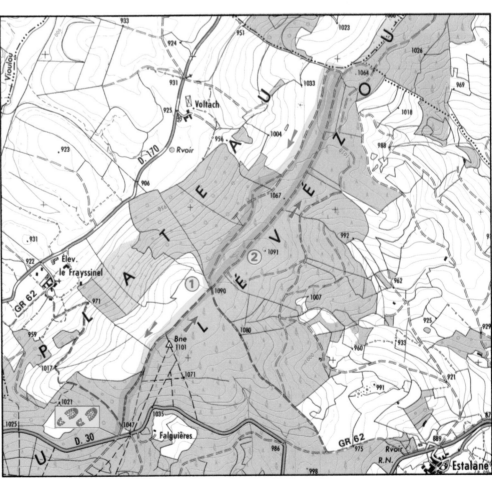

WALK 38B: 2KM/ALLOW 2 HOURS

Montpellier-le-Vieux

The 'ruined town' of Montpellier-le-Vieux is an extraordinary natural phenomenon: a landscape of weirdly twisted and contorted rocks that tempt the imagination to wild flights of fancy. Access to the site is regulated and an entrance fee is payable.

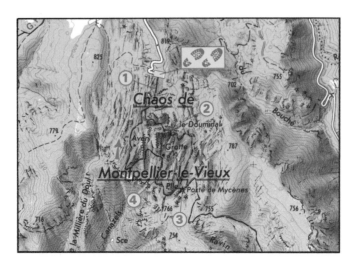

and from a distance, tend to look like the ruins of an old city.

Montpellier-le-Vieux was given its 'old town' name by local shepherds. They feared the site: an impenetrable surrounding forest kept people away and tales grew that it was the remains of an old town that had been cursed for the ungodliness of its inhabitants and was now the home of demons. Occasionally a sheep or goat that wandered into the forest would be lost forever, yet more proof of there being something in the city. In reality the sheep were probably eaten by wolves living among the rocks and trees.

② The first viewpoint offers a wonderful view of the site, with the feature called the Cross (la Croix) to the left, and also of the Causse du Larzac and the Dourbie valley to the south and the Causse Méjean and the Tarn valley to the north.

③ The Porte de Mycènes was so named by Edouard-Alfred Martel – the father of the science of speleology and the first man to map the *chaos* – after the famous Lion Gate at Mycenae. One of the site's best features, it is a 12-m natural arch.

④ Beyond the Porte de Mycènes is a rock with the self-explanatory name of Cyrano's Nose, and a cave, the Grotte de Baume Obscure – *baume* being a local word for cave – in which Martel found the remains of cave bears. On again is another superb viewpoint (*belvédère*) and an aven, formed by the collapse of a cave roof into the cavern below, leaving a huge hole in the ground. In this case the aven is 53m deep.

Next you will reach Porte de Mycènes, one of the most famous features ③.

Turn right, close to the Porte, and then right again to reach the train. Alternatively follow the path back to the car park, passing several other fine features ④.

Points of Interest

① Interspersed among the calcium-based limestone matrix of the Causses are nodules of the magnesium-based rock, dolomite, which is more resistant to water and the wind. Where it outcrops it therefore tends to be left behind as the softer, calcium-based limestone dissolves or erodes away. Where this happens the lumps of dolomite that remain form a *chaos*, an aptly named heap of boulders. Such sites are also known as *rochers ruiniformes*,

▲ Rochers ruiniformes *such as those of Montpellier-le-Vieux are a fascinating sight. From a distance the contorted rocks resemble a ruined city*

Route Directions

Start from the car park at the end of the access road to the site. Instructions are almost superfluous on this route as there are both abundant waymarks and adequate plans. From the car park follow the path towards the site. Immediately you gain some idea of why it has been given its strange name ①.

At the first path junction, after about 200m, you can go right or left. The main paths have been laid out to form a figure-of-eight, and several hours would be required for a full exploration. This walk visits the best sites and offers the option of a return by train. Turn right at this first path junction, and left at the next. Soon you will pass the first viewpoint ②.

The shepherds who tended their flocks near the bizarre rock formations of Montpellier-le-Vieux feared the place, believing it to be the remains of a city cursed for its sins ▶

The Beaujolais

There is more to the Beaujolais region than vine-covered hills. As this tour heads westwards from Villefranche-sur-Saône, vineyards are soon left behind for a wilder landscape. The route winds through wooded valleys and over high passes where viewpoints are frequent and the vistas far-reaching. The traffic is never heavy but progress can be slow at times along winding roads.

▲ *Fleurie produces good, light Beaujolais wines that are best drunk young*

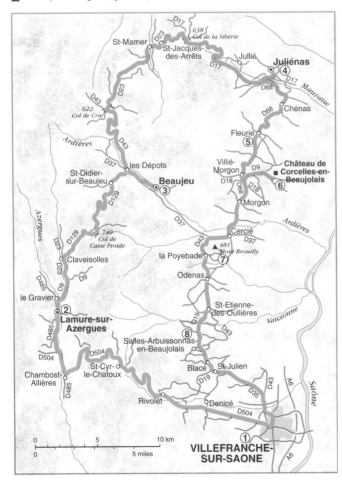

Route Directions

The drive starts from Villefranche-sur-Saône ①.

Leave Villefranche on the D 504, signposted Gleizé and Lacenas. After Denicé and Rivolet the road winds through wooded hills down to Chambost-Allières. Turn right here on to the D 485 to Lamure-sur-Azergues ②.

Pass through Lamure and after 1.5km, at le Gravier, turn right on to the D 9, signposted Claveisolles and Marchampt. After 2km turn left at Pont Gaillard on to the D 23 towards Claveisolles, Chenelette and Monsols. At Claveisolles turn right on to the D 129 towards the Col de Casse Froide, St-Didier-sur-Beaujeu, Valtorte and Soubrant. The road reaches an altitude of 740m at the Col de Casse Froide and then descends into a deep valley, eventually reaching les Dépots. Turn right on to the D 37 and continue to Beaujeu ③.

Return to les Dépots and turn right on to the D 43 towards the Col de Crie and Monsols. After 7.5km reach the Col de Crie (622m) and at the crossroads bear right on to the D 23, signposted St-Mamert and St-Jacques-des-Arrêts. Turn left at le Razay on to the D 18 towards St-Mamert and Tramayes. In St-Mamert fork right on to the D 23 towards St-Jacques-des-Arrêts and Cenves. The road winds uphill to St-Jacques. The first walk starts from here. After about 3km fork right where the D 23 meets the D 17 towards Jullié and Pontanevaux. At the Col de la

Sibérie (638m) continue in the direction of Pontanevaux. About 3km past the vineyards of Château de la Roche a detour to the left on the D 17e leads to Juliénas ④.

Return to the D 68 and pass through les Deschamps and Chénas to reach Fleurie ⑤.

Leave Fleurie, following signs for Villié-Morgon and Cercié. In the centre of Villié-Morgon turn left and follow the D 18 towards Pizay and Belleville. As you leave Villié-Morgon, turn left on to the D 9 to visit the Château de Corcelles-en-Beaujolais ⑥.

Return to the D 18 and just outside Villié-Morgon branch right on to the D 68 to Morgon and Cercié. At the traffic lights in Cercié go straight on to St-Lager for the second walk, which goes around Mont Brouilly ⑦.

To continue the drive turn right on to the D 37 at Cercié towards Beaujeu and after 2km turn left on to the D 43, signposted la Poyebade and Villefranche-sur-Saône. Pass through Odenas to St-Etienne-des-Oullières and at the crossroads in the middle of the town turn right on to the D 19 to le Perréon and Salles-Arbuissonnas-en-Beaujolais ⑧.

From Salles-Arbuissonnas continue on the D 19 through Blacé and then pass through St-Julien on the D 35 towards Villefranche. On the outskirts of Villefranche turn right at the junction with the D 43 and continue to return to the town centre.

A mural at Juliénas, depicting Bacchus ▼

BEAUJOLAIS WINE

The east- and south-facing slopes of the Beaujolais, which in places rise to more than 1000m, are covered in vines, and in the valleys tiny villages quietly produce large quantities of very agreeable wine. The character of village life here was superbly captured by Gabriel

Beaujolais grapes near Juliénas ▼

Chevallier in his novel *Clochemerle,* inspired by Vaux-en-Beaujolais.

The Beaujolais region extends from south of Mâcon to the outskirts of Lyon, but it is the area north of Villefranche-sur-Saône that produces the best wine. Best of all is Beaujolais-Villages, comprising 10 *crus*: Moulin-à-Vent, Juliénas, St-Amour, Chénas, Chiroubles, Fleurie, Côte de Brouilly, Brouilly, Morgon and Régnié. Some white wine and a small amount of rosé are also produced.

Red Beaujolais is best drunk cool and young, which is why Beaujolais nouveau has become so successful in recent years. Released by the vineyards at midnight on the third Wednesday in November, it is rushed at breakneck speed to bars and restaurants all over Europe.

Points of Interest

① A busy commercial town with wine as its most important trade, Villefranche-sur-Saône is the capital of the Beaujolais. Along the N6, which passes through the town, there are many houses dating from the 14th century to the 16th.

② Nestling among wooded hills in the lovely Azergues valley, Lamure-sur-Azergues makes a good base for exploring the surrounding area. Notice the old mill in the valley to the right of the D 485.

③ The small town of Beaujeu, squeezed between vine-covered slopes, gives its name to the Beaujolais region. Among its sights is the Musée des Traditions Populaires Marius-Audin, which has an interesting collection of 19th-century dolls and a section on local folklore, including a reconstructed domestic interior.

④ Juliénas is one of the better-known wine-producing villages of the Beaujolais. An unusual place to taste the local wine is the former church at the centre, which has been decorated inside with colourful scenes of Bacchanalian revelry.

⑤ Fleurie produces the most popular of the Beaujolais *crus*. The village itself, at the foot of slopes which offer extensive views over the Saône plain and beyond, has some lively and welcoming restaurants.

⑥ The Château de Corcelles-en-Beaujolais was built in the 15th century as a fortress to defend the border between the Beaujolais and Burgundy. Later alterations, including the addition of Renaissance galleries around the courtyard, have given it a more domestic appearance.

⑦ Mont Brouilly, with its chapel at the summit and its slopes covered with the vines of the Côte de Brouilly, is a place of pilgrimage for wine producers in early September.

⑧ Salles-Arbuissonnas-en-Beaujolais is the site of a priory founded in the 10th century by monks from Cluny. Among the surviving buildings are the church and adjoining cloisters, and a vaulted chamber containing frescos, unfortunately in poor condition.

Like many châteaux built for defensive purposes – this fortress protected the border between the Beaujolais and Burgundy – the 15th-century Château de Corcelles-en-Beaujolais was later made into a comfortable home ▼

Pastoral Beaujolais

There is no need to venture far from the vineyards of the Beaujolais to find a very different landscape. This walk is easy going but has some wonderful views and an interesting variety of places to see.

gradually for about 1km along the valley side to the small farming community of Chagny ⑥.

Pass through Chagny and turn right on to the main road, the D 23, and after 500m take a right fork into St-Jacques-des-Arrêts. Follow signs to the car park where the walk began.

Charollais cows, the most popular breed in France, abound in the Beaujolais ▶

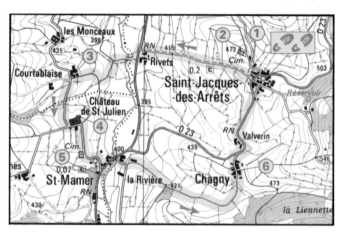

② In gaps in the hedge to the left of the lane there are lovely views along the Grosne valley to St-Mamert and across to the wooded slopes above the hamlet.

③ Courtablaise is a charming farm with a rustic courtyard where *gîte* accommodation is available.

④ Situated on a corner site beside the road is the private Château de St-Julien, which, despite its pepper-pot turrets, is more of a fortified farm than a château. Charollais cattle graze many of the fields around here.

⑤ St-Mamert may be tiny but it still has a church, modern but built in the Romanesque style, looking down on it from a promontory at the side of the valley. Its attractive stained-glass windows date from 1898.

▲ *An ornate wrought-iron cross adorns the village of St-Jacques-des-Arrêts*

⑥ A number of closely built farm buildings give Chagny the air of an isolated mountain village, even though St-Jacques-des-Arrêts is not far away.

Route Directions

Start from the car park behind the church in Place des Anciens Combattants in St-Jacques-des-Arrêts.

Walk to the church, turn left in front of it and turn left again on to the main road through the village ①.

After about 75m turn right into a narrow, hedged lane signposted Rivets ②.

Go down the hill, turn left at the main road and after 50m turn right on to a track. Cross a small stone bridge over the River Grosne and after about 100m fork left along a path that in summer is usually a little overgrown. The path climbs gradually and at the next junction in the path, after about 200m, turn right to Courtablaise farm ③.

Turn left on to a narrow lane and after 350m reach a T-junction beside the Château de St-Julien ④.

Turn left, follow the road round to the right for another 400m and descend to the hamlet of St-Mamert ⑤.

Turn left at the junction with the main road and at the edge of the hamlet, immediately after crossing a stream, turn right along a narrow lane signposted la Rivière and la Tonne. After about 100m bear left on to a surfaced track which climbs

Points of Interest

① Just after the bend below the church, notice between the houses to the right a beehive-shaped covered well built of stone and topped by a metal cross.

Away from the vineyards for which the Beaujolais is best known, quiet farming villages such as St-Jacques-des-Arrêts lie among wooded hills ▼

Over Mont Brouilly

This hill, which is situated at the edge of the Saône plain, is the source of what is considered to be the best Beaujolais wine produced under the Brouilly name. Though steep in places, it provides some outstanding views.

The chapel on the summit of Mont Brouilly offers a fine prospect of the Saône plain and the Dombes to the east ▼

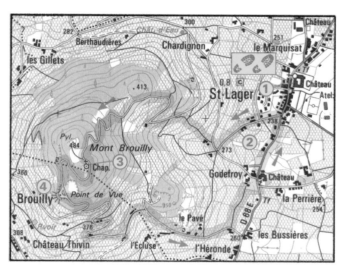

Descend to the next hairpin bend and then after about 100m turn left on to a rough track winding downhill through vineyards. At the fifth hairpin bend on the track, opposite a house, turn left on to a rough track following the contours of the hillside. After about 225m the track reaches a surfaced road. Turn right here and follow the road downhill for about 650m. About 100m before reaching a T-junction with the D 68e turn left opposite a large house on to a track leading through the vineyards. Just before reaching the hamlet of Godefroy turn right on to another track that leads to the road close to the small Château de la Perrière. Turn left on to the road and return after 600m to the château at St-Lager.

Points of Interest

① The château at St-Lager is owned by the Institut Pasteur, which carries out biological research there. Little can be seen of the château from St-Lager – the best views are from the slopes of Mont Brouilly.

② The road heads directly towards the vine-covered slopes of Mont Brouilly. Notice on the left of the road a hedge shaped like a cross.

③ The vineyards of Mont Brouilly are owned by the southernmost producers of Beaujolais wine. The chapel at the summit stands at an altitude of 484m and gives far-reaching views eastwards over the Saône plain and the Dombes region.

④ This viewpoint, a wide terrace facing west, offers an entirely different panorama from that seen from the chapel. Here the view looks down on the village of Brouilly and across to the vine-clad mountains of the Beaujolais.

Route Directions

Start from the small square in front of the château in St-Lager ①.

From the square turn left into the road that passes through St-Lager, and after about 200m turn right along a minor road signposted Domaine des Fournelles ②.

Walk to the T-junction at the end of the road, turn right opposite a group of four houses, then take the rough path to the left just after the last house to climb steeply through the vineyard. After about 250m the path joins a better one which climbs more gently up to a road.

Turn left on to the road, which winds uphill, first through vineyards and then through woods. Soon after entering the woods turn right on to a narrow footpath indicated by blue-and-white markers. This cuts off two bends in the road, and after crossing the road once, continue on the path until it meets the road again and then turn left. Follow the road to the chapel at the summit of Mont Brouilly ③.

Continue along the road and descend for 500m to reach a viewpoint ④.

A good view of St-Lager and its château can be gained from the top of Mont Brouilly, which reaches 484m ▶

The Vivarais

Along and winding route through the Vivarais mountains, this figure-of-eight tour visits engaging places and offers some of the most spectacular views in the Rhône valley. Although the route is slow going, it is possible to complete it in a day. However, if you would like to spend a little longer on the tour, there are plenty of hotels. Snow could be a problem in the higher areas in winter.

▲ St-Romain-de-Lerps enjoys a commanding position overlooking the Rhône plain. From the chapel of le Pic a panorama of 13 départements can be seen

Route Directions

The drive starts from Valence ①.

Leave Valence on the N532, signposted le-Puy-en-Velay and St-Péray. Just after joining the N86 follow the 'Toutes Directions' signs into St-Péray ②.

Take the D 533 through St-Péray towards le Puy and Lamastre, then, after passing through the town centre, turn right on to the D 287 towards St-Sylvestre. Continue to St-Romain-de-Lerps ③.

Continue on the D 287 towards St-Sylvestre and after about 1.5km turn right on to a minor road signposted Plats. At the T-junction in Plats turn right (no sign) and after about 800m, where the main road is signposted N86, Mauves and Tournon, take the unsigned turning to the left. At Suzeux bear right along a road that doubles as the GR 42A footpath (note red-and-white markers). At a fork with three unsigned routes take the middle route past a cross and continue to Tournon ④.

The first walk starts here. Drive through Tournon, turn left on to the N86 towards Annonay and Condrieu and on the outskirts of Tournon turn left on to the D 532 towards Lamastre. After about 3.5km turn right to follow the D 532 towards St-Félicien and Lalouvesc. Drive through Crémolière and la Croix du Fraysse, and at the crossroads outside les Clots turn right on to the D 578, signposted St-Jeure-d'Ay. Continue through St-Jeure on the D 578 towards Quintenas and Annonay and after 3.5km turn left on to the D 6 towards St-Romain-d'Ay and Satillieu. At the D 578a bear left to Satillieu ⑤.

Continue through Satillieu and then for 11km along the winding, climbing D 578a to arrive in Lalouvesc ⑥.

The second walk starts here. In Lalouvesc turn left on to the D 532, signposted St-Félicien and Tournon, and after 3km fork right towards Lamastre on the D 236. Continue to the Col du Buisson ⑦.

Stay on the D 236 towards Nozières and Lamastre and after about 3km a cross on a bend marks the turning right to the Château de Rochebloine ⑧.

Return to the main road, pass through Nozières and continue to Lamastre ⑨.

Drive through Place des Frères Montgolfier and turn left on to the D 533, signposted Valence. After 50m turn left again, still on the D 533, towards Tournon and Valence. Just after the Hôtel des Négociants turn left on to the D 534, signposted le Crestet and Tournon, and drive along the Gorges du Doux ⑩.

Continue for 32km on the D 534, which joins the D 532, and at the junction with the N86 turn right and drive through Tournon towards Valence. Pass through Châteaubourg and Cornas to St-Péray, then bear left on to the N532 to return to Valence.

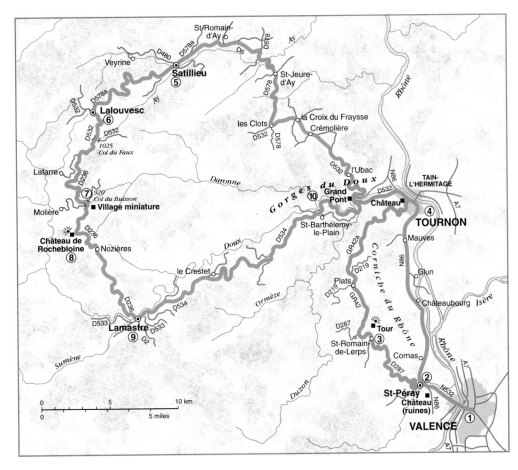

▲ *Tournon-sur-Rhône is a pleasantly situated little town. Among its attractions are a 15th-century castle and a tree-shaded riverside promenade. It faces Tain-l'Hermitage, with its vineyards, across a broad stretch of the river*

Points of Interest

① Ancient Valence is a lively and attractive town, although little remains of its Roman origins. Occupying a terrace on the eastern bank of the Rhône, it offers fine views of the Ardèche mountains from the Parc Jouvet and the Champ de Mars.

② The busy, wine-producing village of St-Péray is best known for the ruined 12th-century Château de Crussol, which looks down from its lofty perch 200m above the Rhône. A road leads part of the way from St-Péray, and the last section has to be completed on foot.

③ St-Romain-de-Lerps is on the Corniche du Rhône, a spectacular road that looks down from high above the Rhône plain. The best views are from the chapel of le Pic (signposted from the village centre) which looks out over 13 *départements*.

④ Facing the famous vineyards of Tain-l'Hermitage across the Rhône, Tournon occupies a delightful spot beside the river. Overlooking quays shaded by huge plane trees, the 15th-century castle has an attractive terraced hanging garden and a museum.

⑤ The mountain resort of Satillieu in the Ay valley has a former château, now serving as the town hall, where one of the rooms is decorated with 18th-century murals. Worth a diversion is the tiny village of Veyrine with its 11th-century Romanesque church.

⑥ Lalouvesc, clinging to the side of a hill at a height of 1050m, has fabulous views down the Ay valley. A pilgrim centre with a basilica, it is famous for its two saints, Thérèse Couderc and Jean-François Régis.

⑦ As well as widespread views, the Col du Buisson has a miniature village built of granite.

In summer passenger steam trains of the Chemin de Fer du Vivarais wind their way through the Gorges du Doux between Tournon-sur-Rhône and Lamastre ▼

MARC SEGUIN

On the Quai Farconnet in Tournon stands a statue of Marc Seguin, who was born in nearby Annonay in 1786, one of the greatest French engineers of the 19th century.

Seguin built the first railway in France, between Lyon and St-Etienne, and developed a new type of boiler which enabled steam engines to travel faster.

His boilers were also used in steam boats since they provided more power than their predecessors to battle against the strong river currents.

One of the greatest transport problems of the time was crossing the Rhône. There were few bridges, partly because of the expense of spanning such a wide river and partly because the Rhône

was often extremely turbulent.

Seguin's solution was to develop a suspension bridge which exploited the massive strength of tensioned steel cables, and in 1825 the first such bridge across the Rhône was opened between Tournon and Tain-l'Hermitage. Within 25 years there were more than 20 bridges of this type over the river.

⑧ Hardly anything remains of the *château-fort* of Rochebloine, but from its promontory superb views of the Doux basin show what an excellent vantage point it was.

⑨ A colourful resort on the River Doux, Lamastre is known as the gastronomic capital of the Vivarais and has some excellent restaurants.

⑩ The road winds high above the Gorges du Doux and there are frequent viewpoints and paths leading down to the river. In summer a passenger steam train runs along the gorge between Tournon and Lamastre.

Above Tournon

This walk on the hillside behind Tournon takes full advantage of the town's position on the Rhône, with views extending over red roofs and in both directions along the river. The first part of the walk is quite steep.

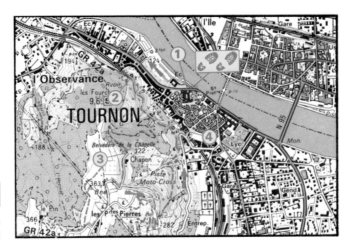

Route Directions

Start from in front of Tournon's château on the Quai Farconnet ①.

With the river on the right, walk along the Quai Farconnet to the municipal camp site and then, 200m along Avenue Maréchal Foch, turn left into Rue Cettier. After about 100m turn right under a low railway bridge and immediately turn left up a steep path which in a few metres becomes stepped. This is the GR 42A long-distance footpath, indicated by red-and-white markers. Climb to the top of the steps to reach the Tour de Pierregourde ②.

The path continues past the tower, winding up the side of the hill. After about 350m turn right on to a track signposted Belvédère de la Chapelle. After another 20m turn left up some steps and follow the narrow path winding uphill through woods for a further 850m to the belvedere ③.

Follow the road, Route de Pierre, from the belvedere and after about 250m, just before the road bends sharply right, turn left down a rough track next to a motocross circuit. At the point where the track starts to climb again, join a footpath descending to the left, and just before this path meets the motocross circuit turn left on to another path going steeply downhill. Follow this path downhill for about 600m to a surfaced track and turn left. In about 150m reach the Tour de l'Hôpital ④.

The Tour de Pierregourde, above Tournon ▼

Retrace your steps then continue down the track and turn left into a road winding down into Tournon. Just past the hospital turn left down a flight of steps, the Montée Ste-Marthe, and continue into Rue Gabriel Fauré. Take the second turning left into Grande Rue, go through Place St-Julien and turn right to return to the Quai Farconnet.

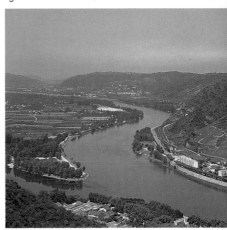

▲ *The Rhône flows between Tournon and vine-covered Tain-l'Hermitage*

Points of Interest

① The Rhône was once notorious for flooding, and high on the wall of the Hôtel La Chaumière on the Quai Farconnet are marks indicating the level reached by disastrous floods in 1840 and 1856.

② Offering superb views along the Rhône from its lofty position, the Tour de Pierregourde was built as a watch-tower in the 16th century by Claude de la Tour de Turenne, Comtesse de Tournon.

③ Standing 322m above the Rhône, the Belvédère de la Chapelle gives marvellous views to both north and south along the valley, and eastwards to the mountains of the Vercors. The ruined chapel lies a few metres below the belvedere.

④ The Tour de l'Hôpital was built as part of the same defences as the Tour de Pierregourde, but on top of this tower stands a huge figure of Notre Dame looking out over Tournon.

40B

Around Lalouvesc

This is a walk through and around an attractive mountain village that has strong religious connections and a number of interesting sights. If you prefer to do the walk without crowds avoid pilgrimage days.

Route Directions

Start from the basilica in Lalouvesc ①.

With the basilica entrance behind you, turn left and walk a few metres to the crossroads at the village centre. Go straight along the narrow Rue de la Fontaine, signposted Chapelle Ste-Thérèse Couderc and Fontaine St-Régis. Pass the chapel on the right ②.

Continue another 600m to the Fontaine St-Régis ③.

Go on for 100m and take the left fork, indicated by a green-and-white marker. Continue to the edge of a pine forest and then follow a rocky footpath straight ahead, still following the green-and-white markers. After another 250m reach a crossing of paths in a clearing and turn left, following a white marker downhill. At a house called Bellevue the track becomes surfaced. Follow this track for about 500m to the

▲ Lalouvesc's Basilique Notre-Dame was built in the 19th century on the burial place of St Régis. A fine view can be enjoyed from in front of the basilica

road, then turn left and walk for 100m to a bend in the road where two paths lead away to the right. Take the one that forks uphill through open fields, and on entering the forest take the less obvious path, which bears left and goes gently downhill. Carry on for 500m to a narrow path to the left that descends a steep gully for 200m to the road.

Near Lalouvesc ▼

Across the road take a wider track opposite that descends to the left, and after about 400m bear right and cross a small stream ④.

Cross the bridge, bear right again and climb up to the road. Turn left, follow the narrow road for 750m and at the edge of Lalouvesc fork right to return to the basilica.

Points of Interest

① Constructed in the last century at the spot where St Régis was buried, Lalouvesc's gaudy basilica was designed by the architect who built the Basilique Notre-Dame at Fourvière in Lyon. Annual pilgrimages take place on 16 June and the following Sunday, 15 August and the second Sunday in September.

② The chapel is at the former home of St Thérèse Couderc, who founded the Convent of the Cenacle in the 19th century. She was canonised in 1970.

③ The Fontaine St-Régis is a natural spring where in 1640 Jean-François Régis, a priest on his way to preach a Christmas sermon in the village, is said to have taken refreshment, having walked 70km in a blizzard from le Puy-en-Velay. He died of pleurisy a few days later and was canonised in 1737.

④ The track is part of a 'parcours botanique', botany trail, through an arboretum. A guide to the trees is available from the tourist office in Lalouvesc. Note the little statue of St Régis on the bridge over the stream.

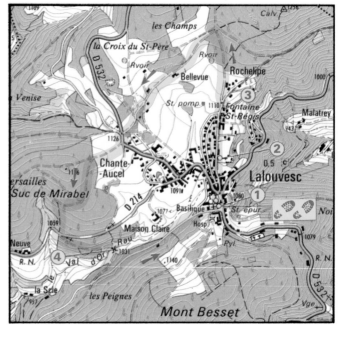

Taninges to Lac Léman

THE ALPS

T his gentle Alpine route of great contrasts traverses the western edge of the huge Portes du Soleil ski area, descends to the shores of Lac Léman, and returns southwards via the rolling hills surrounding the Vallée Verte. There are no particular problems for the motorist other than the often congested roads between Evian and Thonon, though snow could be a consideration late or early in the season.

Route Directions

The drive starts from Taninges ①.

Follow the D 902 to les Gets and Morzine, climbing into a gorge via a huge zig-zag. After 12km the road brings you to les Gets ②.

After taking a short detour through the village centre, following signs for 'Centre Station', continue along the D 902 and turn off on to the D 28 for Morzine ③.

Rejoin the D 902, signposted Thonon, and continue for 15km to le Jotty and the Gorges du Pont du Diable ④.

Four kilometres further on turn right on to the D 22, signposted Abondance ⑤.

Retrace your steps to join the D 152, signposted Bernex, then take the D 52 and D 21, following signs to Evian-les-Bains ⑥.

Take the N5 along the lake shore to Thonon-les-Bains ⑦.

Leave Thonon by following signs for 'Toutes Directions', Genève and Annemasse. Immediately after the village signpost for Marclaz turn left on to the D 33, signposted Allinges. At the next junction cross the D 903, still following signs for Allinges, and at the next T-junction turn left for Noyer, where you turn right on to the D 12, signposted Bonneville. Two

Thonon-les-Bains is a spa town renowned for the efficacy of its mineral waters. The former capital of the Chablais district, and nowadays a town of some 30,000 inhabitants, it is attractively situated on the southern shore of Lac Léman ▶

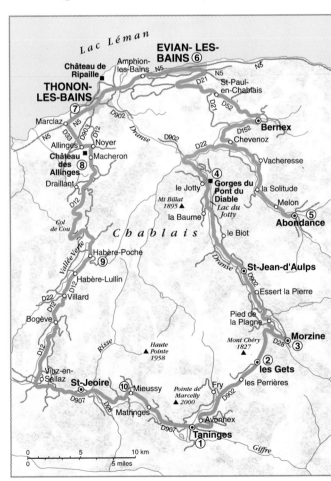

kilometres further on is Macheron, and signs for the Château des Allinges ⑧.

Return to Macheron and turn right onto the D 12 again, passing over the Col de Cou before descending to the Vallée Verte ⑨.

9km from the col, at Villard, take a left turn, still on the D 12, following signs for Bogève and Viuz-en-Sallaz. At Viuz follow 'Toutes Directions' signs, then signs back to Taninges along the D 907, after 12km passing through Mieussy ⑩.

Points of Interest

① Taninges is a sprawling summer and winter resort with excellent walking and ski touring areas near by. It is also situated at the junction of several important tourist routes, The Pointe de Marcelly, a few kilometres north-west of the town, is a superb viewpoint.

② Les Gets is a ski centre at the edge of the Portes du Soleil which possesses a unique museum, the Musée de la Musique Mechanique, housing a varied and fascinating display of musical boxes, mechanical

organs and the like. Above the town, Mont Chéry is a classic viewpoint which can only be reached on foot, though the ski lift reduces the walking time to around 1 hour.

③ A thriving, bustling winter resort, Morzine is the main tourist centre for the area, and also the geographical meeting point of several important valleys which descend from the frontier ridge.

④ Just after the Lac du Jotty, which resembles a green/grey mushy soup, is the village of le Jotty. It is worth walking down to the dam, where the overflow falls 50m, like a mini-Niagara. Even better is the descent into the apparently bottomless gorges of the Pont du Diable, a dark and mysterious place which is now easily accessible on newly constructed paths.

⑤ An attractive high-altitude town, Abondance is well known as a winter-sports centre, as well as for its high-quality dairy produce, clean air and superb abbey. The latter has long been an important focal point and its frescos and cloister would alone make a visit virtually mandatory. Also worth visiting is the Musée d'Art Religieux.

SPAS

The Haute-Savoie region has three famous spas, two of them on the shores of Lac Léman – Thonon-les-Bains and Evian-les-Bains. Waters in these two resorts come from the rain and snows of the Chablais mountains. Research has shown that it takes 15 years for the Evian mineral water to filter through the glacial deposits. This results in a very slow purification process, and the water is said to have a very stable composition and to be completely free from any form of pollution.

The range of illnesses that the waters are said to treat are varied indeed. They include ailments of the urinary tract and kidney disorders; metabolic disorders, gout, prevention of heart disease and high blood pressure; digestive disorders and irritation of the colon; and rheumatism and after-effects of joint and bone injuries.

A variety of therapies is also available, including baths, showers, 'taking the waters' and boiling-water baths.

All this has now been elevated to a fine art, and the quality of service and back-up is very high. Couple this with the magnificent settings, clean air and relaxing surroundings, and the reason for the spas' popularity is clear.

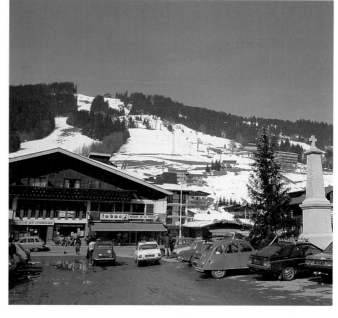

▲ *The skiing centre of les Gets*

(6) Poetically christened 'the pearl of Léman', Evian-les-Bains possesses an air of quality and well-being, and occupies an enviable position between the shores of Lac Léman and the Chablais hills. Its famous waters were ignored by the Romans and 'discovered' in 1798. Now they form the basis for thriving thermal baths, and 55 million bottles of it are sold each year. The old baths and the Casino are remarkable examples of the architectural styles found hereabouts at the turn of the century.

(7) The largest centre on this part of Lac Léman, Thonon-les-Bains lies above a shallow, curved bay and enjoys wonderful views across the lake. A tiny funicular links the port area with the newer town above, and though the busy modern town has its attractions, the cobbled streets, shutters and wrought iron trellis-work of the 19th-century houses in the old quarter will live longer in the memory. Close by is the Domaine de Ripaille, with its superb château and arboretum which can be visited.

(8) Château des Allinges, now a marvellous viewpoint, has been inhabited since the 5th century and has strong connections with St François de Sales.

(9) Driving south from Thonon, the increasingly serpentine road climbs to the Col de Cou. Beyond here, the landscape suddenly opens out into an enormous high-level valley, the Vallée Verte, studded with villages, surrounded by rolling hills and streaked with tree-lined ski runs. The villages tend to be working places that also happen to be linked with winter and summer sports, and there is plenty to do here throughout the year. Both the villages and the landscape are well worth exploring.

(10) Known locally as the paragliding capital of the world, the small but exciting activity centre of Mieussy is impressively situated at the end of the Giffre valley. For the armchair sportsperson this is a great place to watch everyone else take the risks!

The valley of Abondance is well known for its reddish dairy cows and the cheese they produce – Tomme ▼

Maxilly and the Bois de la Dame

The walk passes a stone trough and follows a tumbling stream ▼

The final descent from the Chablais hills to Lac Léman takes the form of a steep, forested escarpment, which becomes increasingly gentle as it descends to the lake's shore. This walk traverses the forest in a leisurely manner.

Route Directions

Start from the square near the church in the centre of Maxilly-sur-Léman ①.

Walk directly uphill, past a small park and a stone water trough, and then past the cemetery, from where there are good views to the hills above. Continue uphill past Rue de Curtenay and head up a steep path through the woods. Pass a caravan site on your left and continue up another smaller road, lined with sweet chestnut trees, to meet the D 24. Turn left and follow the road past a left-hand bend followed by a sweeping right-hand bend over a bridge. Take a track that leads off to the right 50m past this, then continue straight on at a crossing of paths ②.

Continue on the same path to rejoin the D 24, and cross this on to a surfaced road signposted 'Colonie de Vacances'. Follow this, then walk straight through the holiday village ③.

Continue on a rough track for a short distance, then turn left at a junction and go into an orchard ④.

Carry on straight down through another squeeze stile into the woods beyond. The path then sweeps down to the right, away from the stream, and leads to a series of steep, rounded zigzags which descend through the forests.

A rough stream bed now cuts across the path at an angle, looking deceptively like another path when dry. Cross it diagonally and descend, bearing right over a fast-flowing stream. Keep left at the next two path junctions, then turn left almost immediately, descending past some chalets to a road. Cross the road and follow a little track alongside the stream, then pass through a smallholding, Chez Busset ⑤.

Turn left at the road, pass les Nives, and continue along the road through Vieille Eglise. Turn left on to the D 21 and continue for just over 1 km to return to the starting-point in Maxilly.

Points of Interest

① A pleasant suburb of Evian, Maxilly has an interesting church and, on the other side of the crossroads, a huge stone water trough hewn out of rough granite.

② This section of woodland is thick with sweet chestnuts, easily recognisable by the characteristic spiral pattern of the bark and their large, pointed leaves with heavily serrated edges. In autumn the floor of the forest is carpeted with the soft-spiked husks of the chestnuts.

③ Small holiday villages are common in many parts of the Alps. Busy in summer and winter, they are often deserted at other times of the year, and sadly many have been built with little regard for the traditional forms of architecture.

④ A row of eight large apple trees plus a selection of other fruit trees provide a fine display of spring blossom. The lovely spring colours and the russets, reds and bronzes of autumn make these seasons ideal times for visiting this area.

⑤ The narrow stream flows beside the path and beneath these lovely old buildings in a scene which could be centuries old.

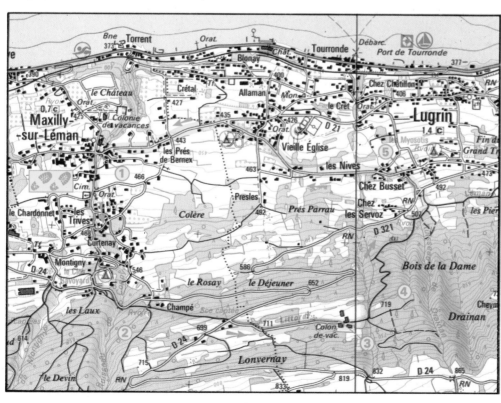

Lac de Montriond

Bounded by steep forests and a precipitous barrier of high cliffs, the walks around Lac de Montriond are surprisingly relaxing and gentle, with only a few short ascents. Though the area is likely to be busy during the summer and the winter, it is considerably quieter out of season.

Route Directions

Start from the car park at the western end of the lake ①.

Leave the car park on a track which leads away from the road, and almost immediately take a small track leading up to the right. The rear of the sign says 'Les Albertans 1hr par Balcon Nord du Lac'. Steep zigzags then lead to a rising traverse through the woodland ②.

The path zigzags sharply to meet a path which comes in from Montriond. Turn left here, and the path soon becomes easier. Continue along the gentle traverse, descending slightly to a stream which is fed by an impressive waterfall slicing a line through the cliffs of les Echertons ③.

Continue along the traverse to a path junction. The left branch drops down to the lake and an easy waterside path which leads back to the walk's starting-point. Alternatively, continue traversing to reach les Albertans ④.

Beyond les Albertans is Ardent, where there is a waterfall ⑤.

Although the road offers the easiest return route, it is also possible to climb a path which leaves the road a few hundred metres west of Ardent, passing through le Choseau on to a traverse line which leads left and back to the road at les Albertans, or further on past la Maison Neuve, descending to les Gaillardets and back to the car park.

A waterfall plunges down the cliffs above Lac de Montriond (below) ▶

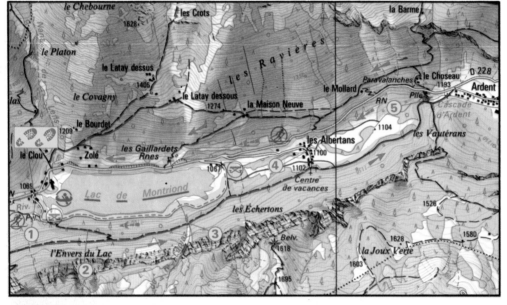

Points of Interest

① Lac de Montriond is a relatively high-level lake at over 1000m, with waters that are often pea-green, reflecting the stands of fir and beech which surround it. This quiet and somewhat sombre site is popular for cross-country skiing and walking, and ice-skating in winter.

② Mixed Alpine forests offer a rich and well-proportioned scenery, and the lack of grazing stock in areas like this allows regeneration and the growth of ground-cover plants. As a result wildlife is more prolific than in the uniformly coniferous plantations. This site has a wide selection of plants associated with traditional woodland habitats, and there are some magnificent specimen trees.

③ The cliffs above the forest are steep, sometimes loose, covered with vegetation and unattractive to climbers. They make remarkable vertical habitats for birds and plants, however, and it is miraculous how so many trees have found a home on the seemingly steepest and most barren sections of crag. It is possible to scramble up to the foot of the huge falls which have gouged out a rift in the cliffs, but only with care, as this too is loose in places.

④ Les Albertans is a popular holiday centre in summer and winter, though it is likely to be almost deserted out of season.

⑤ A few minutes' walk from Ardent and just below the road is the Cascade d'Ardent, a spectacular waterfall after heavy rain and at times of heavy snow melt.

The two sides of Mont-Blanc

This circumnavigation of the loftiest peak in the Alps takes in some superb high-level driving, including the Col du Petit St-Bernard (normally closed between November and May). Other roads could also be difficult from time to time because of snow. Impervious to weather is the Mont-Blanc tunnel, one of the longest in Europe, which burrows its way beneath the famous Vallée Blanche to exit on the Italian side of the Mont-Blanc massif. This route of great character also takes in busy Alpine towns such as Chamonix-Mont-Blanc.

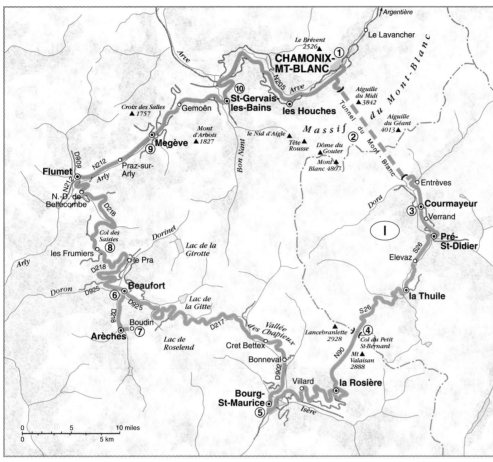

▲ Chamonix is widely recognised as the world's foremost Alpine sports centre. But above all the bustle the trees display their quiet autumnal beauty while the Aiguilles de Chamonix rise majestically

Continue on the N212 to St-Gervais-les-Bains ⑩.

Return on the D 902 and the N205 to Chamonix.

Route Directions

The drive starts from Chamonix-Mont-Blanc ①.

Leave town on the N506, signposted Argentière, to make a detour for 24km over the Swiss frontier to Col de la Forclaz. Retrace the route to Chamonix, then follow the signs for the Tunnel du Mont-Blanc ②.

On the Italian side, follow the S26 past Courmayeur ③.

Carry on for about 10km, then take a right turn near Pré-St-Didier, signposted la Thuile and Col du Petit St-Bernard ④.

The long climb to the col leads over and into France again, and the road now becomes the N90. A long descent then leads into Bourg-St-Maurice ⑤.

Take the D 902 to the right, signposted Beaufort and Vallée des Chapieux. This road later becomes the D 217 and the D 925. After 40km of narrow mountain road you reach Beaufort ⑥.

A left turn here gives a short but worthwhile detour on to the D 218 to Boudin ⑦.

Return to Beaufort and continue westwards. Turn right after 3km on to the D 218, signposted Flumet and Col des Saisies ⑧.

Descend the valley of the Nant Rouge to Flumet. Turn right onto the N212, signposted Megève ⑨.

The Aiguille du Midi, which reaches 3842m, looks down on Chamonix ▶

▲ *At 1252m, Argentière is the highest of the Alpine centres in the Chamonix valley. Behind the village can be seen the Aiguille du Charbonnet (3824m)*

Points of Interest

① Lying at the foot of Mont-Blanc, Chamonix is one of the greatest mountaineering centres in the world. Ski lifts give tourists and mountaineers alike access to some of the most respected and admired peaks in Europe – the Aiguille du Midi and le Brévent *téléphériques* being an essential part of anyone's visit. North of the town are several other villages worth a visit, for example Argentière and le Lavancher (the name means a place exposed to avalanches), but no matter how enchanting the old chalets and how peaceful the forests, the valley remains dominated by its magnificent mountains.

② One of the most important trans-Alpine routes, the 12-km Tunnel du Mont-Blanc, which provides the easiest crossing of the Alps for a large area, was completed in 1965. It now carries a huge amount of freight 2480m beneath the Aiguille du Midi and the Glacier du Géant.

③ At the upper end of the vast, traffic-congested Aosta valley, Courmayeur is a colourful and well-placed winter resort. A ski lift near the tunnel entrance gives access to the huge snowfields of the Glacier du Géant, the start of the Vallée Blanche, the most famous off-piste ski-run in Europe.

④ Although the strategic importance of Col du Petit St-Bernard has now diminished, it still remains an important route, though prone to closure by snow. There are ample reminders of its military significance, and a statue of St Bernard de Menthon, who died in 1008. Sandwiched in a col between the Lancebranlette (a fine viewpoint but a rough walk away) and Mont Valaisan, it provides the only feasible crossing of the frontier ridge for many miles in either direction.

⑤ Bourg-St-Maurice, though relatively small, is an important town, the major centre for the Haute Tarentaise. In July the famous Fête des Edelweiss takes place here, an international festival of folklore where the traditional Tarentaise costumes can be seen in profusion. Worth visiting for its superb crystals is the Musée des Mineraux et de la Faune des Alps.

⑥ As well as giving its name to a tasty cheese, Beaufort has a traditional old quarter whose church contains a superbly carved pulpit.

Beaufort lies where the Arèches and Rose-lend valleys meet. The town has given its name to the surrounding district and to a strong-tasting gruyère-style cheese ▼

OFF-PISTE SKIING

As a ski resort Chamonix has few equals, its combination of magnificent scenery and high-quality runs being the envy of many other areas. Particularly note-worthy is the quality of the off-piste skiing – that is, skiing which takes place away from the pisted and patrolled conventional ski runs.

Taking pride of place in off-piste ski runs is the descent from the Aiguille du Midi to Chamonix via the Vallée Blanche. Advisable only to good skiers with a guide, or to those with extensive mountaineering skills, the route descends 2800m in about 17km, making it the longest frequented ski run in the Alps.

The route starts by taking the two-stage *téléphérique* to the summit of the Aiguille du Midi. From here an ice cave gives access to a steep ridge, guarded in winter with fixed ropes, which gives a route down on to the easier terrain below. Once under way, the route descends the Glacier du Géant to the Mer de Glace, but the going is not easy. The risk of avalanches and the dangers posed by crevasses have to be continually assessed, but the rewards are huge – a breathtaking descent through some of the finest mountain scenery in Europe.

Téléphériques like the one which serves the Aiguille du Midi provide views of some of Europe's finest peaks ▼

⑦ Boudin is a classic example of a traditional mountain hamlet, with large, ancient wooden chalets.

⑧ Col des Saisies is more of a plateau than a defined pass, stretching for about 3km and providing summer pastures and a first-class *ski de fond* area in winter.

⑨ The famous ski resort of Megève is the home of Emile Allais, the inventor of the 'French method' of learning to ski, in which the beginners start on short skis and progress rapidly to longer ones. Megève is one of the region's very best year-round tourist centres, providing excellent facilities for children and a wide variety of activities. Mont d'Arbois and the Croix des Salles are outstanding local viewpoints, accessible via *télécabines* and short walks.

⑩ The starting-point for the traditional route up Mont-Blanc via le Nid d'Aigle, Tête Rousse and Dôme du Gouter, St-Gervais is a perfect base for exploring this part of the Alps, suitable for both the adventurous and the sedate.

Le Chapeau

Though predominantly a woodland walk, this route embraces sufficient grand views of famous peaks and enough climbing to give it a strong mountain flavour. The walking is always easy and exceptionally well marked.

Route Directions

Start from the railway station car park in the suburb of les Praz de Chamonix ①.

Follow signposts for les Bois, Mer de Glace and le Chapeau along a road which runs close to the station. After crossing the railway line the road bends round to the left and forms a prominent divide between the chalets and the open forest. The signs for le Chapeau and le Lavancher continue, and the route climbs for a short section, crosses a wide forest track and then continues straight ahead on a narrower path. Cross the forest track again and bear left to join another path marked by paint flashes. Climb a short crest, then descend to another forest track. Continue along the crest of a moraine ②.

Carry on, still following signs for le Chapeau ③.

At a major path junction turn right, signposted le Chapeau. Continue climbing past the Dôme du Chapeau climbing area ④.

A final series of zigzags then gives access, at 1576m, to the hut at le Chapeau Chalet ⑤.

▲ *Chamonix is surrounded by impressive peaks, including the Aiguilles and Mont-Blanc*

Descend the same way, this time watching for signs for the Source de l'Arveyron ⑥.

This path will bring you out on to the river's edge. The path downstream then leads back to les Bois.

Points of Interest

① Les Praz de Chamonix is a pleasant part of Chamonix which is convenient for many walks, as well as the Flégère/Index *téléphérique*. There are excellent views up to the Aiguilles des Drus to the east.

② Much of the lower section of the walk traces a line along a spine of moraine left by ancient glacial activity. Normally moraine on existing glaciers can easily be spotted on the banks. Often dirty and mixed with old, hard ice, it can also take the form of a continuous knife-edge ridge which may form a convenient route into the mountains. On this route, the forest has had time to grow, binding the poor soil and preventing erosion.

③ This part of the route gives dramatic views up to the massive spire of the Aiguille Verte, which is a very impressive mountain and one of the most respected peaks in the area. To its right is the spiky ridge of les Flammes de Pierre, which makes a striking silhouette against the rising sun.

④ Between the path and the river is a sizeable, smooth sweep of slabs of polished granite – the Dôme du Chapeau. Climbers can often be seen in action here, where balance and technique rather than brute strength are required to overcome the smoothness of the slabs.

⑤ A welcome refreshment point, le Chapeau Chalet also has one of the finest views of the Chamonix valley.

⑥ The everlasting snow and ice of the Mer de Glace give birth to the Arveyron, the cold, grey river which flows down the huge gorge and is clearly visible from the path. Its icy, vapour-shrouded waters flow right through Chamonix.

The route near le Chapeau ▼

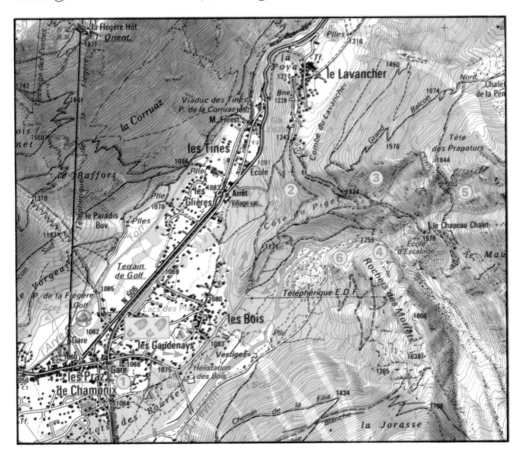

La Flégère and Lac Blanc

◀ Extensive *téléphérique* systems around Chamonix serve attractions such as Mont-Blanc to the south and the Gorges de la Diosaz to the west

Made more accessible by the Flégère *téléphérique*, this walk now enjoys classic status and should not be missed. Snow patches could well be found early in the season, so walkers without appropriate experience should wait until the way is clear – normally late July.

Route Directions

The walk starts by taking the *téléphérique* from les Praz de Chamonix to the first station, la Flégère ①.

The path can be located by walking up to the right of the station, following signposts for Lac Blanc. A slight descent leads under the la Trappe ski lift, after which the route turns left ②.

Some steep zigzags lead up to the left of and then across the line of a ski lift. (Route changes are possible in this area as a result of the ski-run development.) An easier section follows as the path wanders past Lac de la Flégère ③.

It then passes a large cairn to enter the Aiguilles Rouges nature reserve ④.

Continue along the general traverse line for 300m or so, then climb some rocky terrain, past a tiny lake on the left, to some steeper zigzags which lead to a path junction. Continue left to another path junction, from where a short climb leads to Lac Blanc and its refuge ⑤.

The return to la Flégère is a straight reversal of the ascent.

Points of Interest

① At 1877m, la Flégère is a fine viewpoint and very popular. The privately owned refuge is open from June to September and refreshments are also available in the cablecar station. It is possible to take the next stage to the Index station, a good place to watch paragliders, and superbly positioned at the foot of the Aiguilles Rouges.

② Just past the ski lift is the chalet of la Chavanne, an old shepherds' refuge which is currently used by the French Army's mountaineering school.

③ Lac de la Flégère is a tiny lake set at over 2000m which is likely to remain frozen well into the summer. Below here a traversing footpath can clearly be seen. This is the Grand Balcon Sud, part of the famous Tour du Mont-Blanc walk.

④ Conservation in the French Alps, though sometimes pushed to one side because of the vast size of the area, is now rightly seen as a high priority. Even the mighty Alps can only take so much. The Aiguilles Rouges nature reserve was founded in 1974 and is the most important in the area. Just north of Argentière is the Col des Montets information centre, which houses a considerable variety of displays, literature and other information on the reserve.

⑤ Lac Blanc and its refuge are at a height of 2352m, in a marvellous location under the crags, scree and snowfields of the Aiguille du Belvédère. With refreshments at the hut available from June to September, and one of the finest views in the Alps available relatively easily yet without the intrusion of a *télécabine*, it is no wonder that you are unlikely to find yourself alone on this walk.

Montenvers to Plan de l'Aiguille

42C

THE ALPS

This traverse follows the famous Grand Balcon Nord, a line sandwiched between the glaciers and scree of the Aiguilles and the forests which drop steeply into the main valley. Ice axes are essential before late July.

Route Directions

Start from the railway station car park in Chamonix. Next to the main SNCF station is the Chemin de Fer du Montenvers ①.

This railway provides the easiest access to Montenvers. Take the train (late morning is best as much of the walk will then be in the sun) as far as Montenvers ②.

Above the hotel and museum a good path rises above the Mer de Glace ③.

This makes a pleasantly tiring zig-zag walk to a small plateau on the blunt ridge which descends from the Fretes des Charmoz, known as Signal Forbes ④.

Now established on the Balcon, the route descends, gently at first, then steeply down some zigzags before levelling off ⑤.

It then rises steadily towards Plan de l'Aiguille. There are several glacial streams to cross which may be snowbound (and best avoided by the inexperienced) early in the season, but which present no real problems later on. A short ascent at the end of the traverse leads to the Plan de l'Aiguille refuge (open June onwards), and a short way above this is the *téléphérique* station, halfway up the ascent to the Aiguille du Midi. Take the *téléphérique* (check the time of the last departure before setting out) back to Chamonix.

Points of Interest

① The small rack-and-pinion railway running from Chamonix to the banks of the Mer de Glace was once the principal route for Alpinists heading for the main peaks, and even now it gives access to many of the faces and ridges which tower above the ice. It is also a popular tourist attraction, and justifiably so.

② Discovered and first recorded by the Englishmen Windham and Pocock in 1741, Montenvers quickly became a place of interest. The view is simply stunning. In addition the hotel provides refreshments, and there is a museum, a zoo (in one of the world's most cruelly ironic settings), and a cablecar which gives access to the ice caves on the glacier.

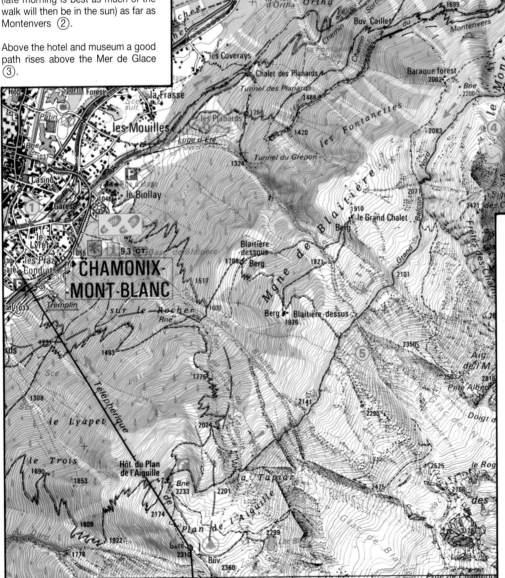

③ The second largest glacier in Europe – at one time it stretched right down the Arve valley towards Chamonix – the Mer de Glace is now shrinking at the rate of about 7m a year. It is nonetheless very impressive, and its name is wholly justified by its scale.

④ The Scottish geologist James Forbes gave his name to this wonderful viewpoint, the vista back to the Aiguille Verte being especially fine.

⑤ Above the traverse, the famous Chamonix Aiguilles etch distinctive shapes against the skyline. The curiously-named Aiguille de l'M is small but shapely, and backed by the Petits and Grands Charmoz. Above the Nantillons glacier is le Grépon, and then the Aiguille de Blaitière can be recognised by the light-grey streak up the centre of its north face.

A fine way to end the walk is to take the *téléphérique* to the summit of the Aiguille du Midi, admire the situation and descend the full distance to the valley bottom.

WALK 42D: 8KM/ALLOW 2½ HOURS

Les Chavants and Charousse

The Chamonix valley swings round a right angle to the north-west, close to the village of les Houches. This walk through woodlands high above the valley floor gives dramatic views to Mont-Blanc and the Aiguilles. The going is easy and the path is well marked.

Route Directions

Start from the car park situated near the small lake at the foot of les Chavants ①.

Return to the les Houches road, turn right for about 500m, then turn left up a series of long hairpins. Some 250m after the third one a small path leads off to the left, signposted Col de la Forclaz. Follow this, crossing a road, to join a road coming in from the right. The going is steep for a few minutes until the road bears left, where the path continues straight on, signposted Forclaz. There follows a steep climb, traversing the hillside to reach some chalets ②.

The view to Col de la Forclaz ▶
Chalets at Chaumont, with the Aiguilles de Chamonix behind ▼

Continue up the main track to the left to reach the Granges des Chavants ③.

Retrace your steps to the first chalets and take a small path which leads off to the left. Cross a stream and continue along a stony path ④.

Pass under some pylons and climb gently to a fork. Take the right fork, signposted Vaudagne. After a big hairpin to the right the route descends steadily ⑤.

The path soon starts to bear left. At this point, follow a small path which leads down through the trees, past a stream, to join a major track. Turn

right, climbing steeply at first, to a level area and a delightful cluster of chalets at Charousse ⑥.

Continue straight ahead, through the chalets, until you arrive at another track and then turn left, following a pleasant descent through woodland to join a surfaced road which leads back down the hairpins to the starting-point.

Points of Interest

① Perched above the main valley, and away from its traffic and noise, les Chavants is an attractive resort and a popular starting-point for the ascent of Mont-Blanc.

② It is very pleasing to note that in most cases newer buildings (even small ones such as these) have adopted traditional styles, ensuring a continuity of appearance. This section of the walk is particularly lovely in autumn, the golds and yellows of the birch and larch contrasting vividly with the dark greens of the conifers.

③ This attractive group of chalets enjoys the definitive view over the Chamonix Aiguilles from the Drus to the Goûter, the whole ridge stretched out like the spiny back of some gigantic prehistoric monster.

④ This part of the walk has yet more superb views, both back to the main peaks and also across to the massive forests which stretch from Servoz to Chamonix. In autumn and spring they provide a colossal bank of colour, highlighted by the contrasting snow and limestone. This section of the route is also part of the Tour du Pays du Mont-Blanc, which in this area weaves its way around the classic Tour du Mont-Blanc walk.

⑤ Forestry work seems to be more evident here than in many other parts of the valley, no doubt partly because of the slightly easier access which the terrain affords. There may well be damage or alterations to routes hereabouts as a result of extraction work.

⑥ The delightful cluster of chalets at Charousse is typical of the ancient summer farmsteads found at altitude throughout Haute Savoie. This relaxing and spectacular spot is an ideal place to linger, have lunch and admire the view. Many of the main peaks are identifiable and the proximity of the huge glaciers which fall chaotically from the Goûter add a certain savage splendour.

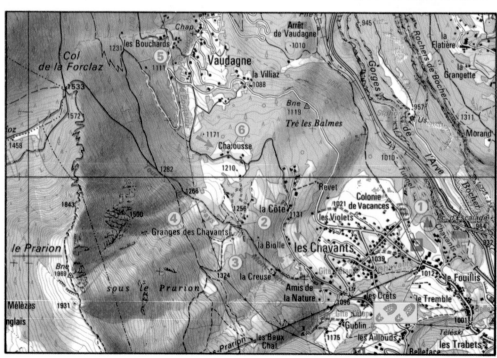

Chambéry and Lac du Bourget

Quite different from the severe landscapes of the main Alps to the east, this region is one of quiet contrasts. Huge forests topped with dazzling white limestone pinnacles sweep down to the lake, whose delicate hues alter with the subtle shifts in light. The drive itself, although on narrow roads in places, presents no real problems and should be enjoyed at a relaxed pace, allowing time to enjoy the superb scenery and fascinating places.

Route Directions

The drive starts from Chambéry ①.

Follow the N6 towards Voiron until you reach Cognin on the outskirts of town. Turn right here on to the D 916, signposted St-Sulpice and Col de l'Epine. Continue over the col and descend into Novalaise. A short detour to the left here leads to Lac d'Aiguebelette ②.

The right turn leads along the D 921 towards Marcieux and Yenne ③.

A detour can be made from Yenne, via the villages of St-Paul and Trouet, to Mont du Chat ④.

The second walk starts from here. The detour can be continued by descending towards the lake to le Bourget-du-Lac ⑤.

From here retrace the route to Yenne. The D 921 bisects Yenne, then continues northwards along the Rhône towards Lucey and Chanaz. Turn right here on the D 18 and turn right on to the D 914, following signs to Abbaye de Hautecombe ⑥.

At the northern end of Aix-les-Bains, best known for its curative hot springs, is the Grand Port, with its tree-lined promenades and flotilla of boats ▼

Return to the D 921 at Chanaz and turn right. At the junction with the D 904 turn right for Ruffieux. From here turn right on to the D 991, following signs for Aix-les-Bains ⑦.

The road follows the lake shore. Leave Aix on the N201 towards Annecy, then after 2km turn right on to the D 911. This leads in 15km to the Pont de l'Abîme ⑧.

Continue on the D 911 to Lescheraines ⑨.

From the village centre follow the D 912, signposted le Noyer and Chambéry. After 13km cross the Col de Plainpalais and descend to la Féclaz. A right turn on to the D 913 as you enter the village leads to Mont Revard ⑩.

Retrace your steps to the D 912 and turn right to descend to Chambéry.

▲ *Among Chambéry's many attractions is the 19th-century Fontaine des Eléphants*

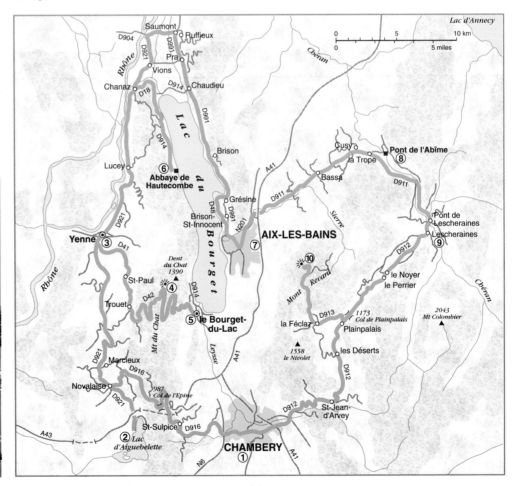

▲ *Lac du Bourget*

Points of Interest

① Chambéry's historical, cultural and commercial vitality vie with the wonderful surrounding scenery for attention. The Vieille Ville is full of character and curiosities, with arched alleyways and tiny courtyards leading to long avenues lined with chic shops, bars and cafés. Cultural and commercial events, both local and national, abound. Places worth visiting include the Fontaine des Elephants, the Château des Ducs de Savoie and the Cathédrale de St-François-de-Sales.

② Although Lac d'Aiguebelette is the smallest of the Savoyard waters it boasts the richest variety of fauna and flora, its two islands supporting a delicately balanced ecology. The area is well managed, with conservation interests co-existing with recreational demand. Summer bathers will be able to enjoy surface temperatures of up to 28°C.

The 1452-m peak of the Dent du Chat – seen here in the distance – thrusts up between le Bourget-du-Lac and Yenne ▼

③ Yenne is a most attractive small town retaining a gentle, rustic charm and some particularly attractive weathered limestone houses. These give the place a mellow, warm feel, very different from the austere granite villages of the eastern Alps.

④ Yenne and le Bourget-du-Lac are separated by a predominantly wooded limestone ridge, topped with two obvious peaks, the Molard Noir and the Dent du Chat. A simple drive over the serpentine road that links the two towns is pleasant enough, reaching a high point on the Mont du Chat near the radio and television mast at 1504m.

⑤ Le Bourget-du-Lac, a thriving town at the southern end of the lake, used to be a busy port providing a link with the Rhône. As well as its delightful setting, le Bourget also has an ancient priory with attractive formal gardens lined with dark spruce, firs, cedars and cypresses.

⑥ Magnificent in both structure and setting, the Abbaye de Hautecombe overlooks the shores of Lac du Bourget and is backed by huge forests. A superb old barn houses a display depicting the daily life of the monks, and the site can be viewed from boats which sail regularly from the adjacent jetties. There are regular guided tours to the abbey's fine works of art, such as the frescos which adorn many of the arches of the church. The abbey also makes its own wine.

⑦ Although a Celtic tribe, the Allobroges, took advantage of the hot springs at Aix-les-Bains in about 400 BC, it was the development of the baths in the 13th century and the rapid expansion of the town in the 19th century that created present-day Aix, an affluent and open town which attracts visitors from all over the world. There are many attractions here, including the thermal baths, the Musée Faure with its sculpture and impressionist paintings, and the Grand Port, an area of open spaces and elegant, tree-lined lakeshore.

⑧ Pont de l'Abîme enjoys an absolutely splendid setting, spanning the Gorges de la Chéran and suspended defiantly 94m above the floor of the gorge.

⑨ Lescheraines is a pretty, small village with an old-fashioned feel in a pleasant low-Alp setting. On the outskirts of the town is a busy camping and holiday centre, but this is well hidden and unobtrusive. The town forms a perfect base for touring and exploring the surrounding areas, the villages between here and the ridges of the Charbon peaks being most attractive. Good walking can be found on the grassy slopes of the nearby Grand Colombier.

⑩ Mont Revard is a high but easily accessible plateau and viewpoint which affords a magnificent panorama taking in the Mont-Blanc massif to the east.

ALPINE GEOLOGY

The Alps possess a varied, interesting and very distinctive array of geological features. The eastern Alps exhibit a mixture of schists, granites and other metamorphic rock: the wonderful crystalline granite of the Chamonix area, for example, or the friable schists of the Queyras region near the Italian border. Moving west, the granites become mixed with sedimentary rocks, notably in the Ecrins, the Grandes Rousses and the Belledonne Massif. Then, to the west of a line which curves from Gap to Grenoble, and right up the Combe du Savoie to the Rhône, is a huge barrier of cretaceous limestone, with its north-western limits around Lac du Bourget.

The lake is surrounded by forested hillsides, typically capped with gleaming white limestone, such as at the Dent du Chat and the Molard Noir. This gives rise to a scenery characteristic of many parts of the western Alps – the Vercors and the Chartreuse being good examples.

The limestone has many advantages. It makes a good building material and it generally supports a prolific and varied selection of Alpine plants. It also provides a natural playground for climbers, its steep and dramatic nature making it particularly attractive to the new breed of gymnastic rock-athletes. It also produces excellent conditions for hang-gliding and paragliding, as it stores and releases heat in the form of thermals.

La Chambotte and Mont de Corsuet

THE ALPS

The north-eastern side of Lac du Bourget is bounded by an increasingly steep, wooded and rocky mountainside which culminates in a long line of white crags. This walk, which is one of the easiest in this section, traverses the lip of this escarpment and gives exceptional views.

③ This superlative viewpoint is high enough to make the lake and its environs look like a map laid out below. Beyond the lake the views include the Abbaye de Hautecombe, the Allevard massif, the Grande Chartreuse and the grassy pyramid of the Grand Colombier.

④ Another superb vantage point, this spot looks down over the spreading forests and is a sunny and first-class picnic site.

⑤ The descent through the forest back into open countryside presents several points of interest. Coppiced areas can be seen beside the path, the evidence of coppicing being the growth of multi-stemmed hazel from a common base. It is also possible in some places to find circular level platforms where wood used to be allowed to smoulder to make charcoal. The woodland fringe area is also home to buzzards, graceful birds of prey which can be identified by their large, almost eagle-like appearance, their gentle, soaring flight and their clearly audible, repetitive mewing.

With an area of 4500 hectares, Lac du Bourget is the largest natural lake in France ▼

Route Directions

Start from the car park just outside la Chambotte ①.

Turn right and right again, and walk up the winding road to the Belvédère de la Chambotte ②.

Then descend slightly, and take a path which leads off to the right from the first hairpin as you go down. This leads into open meadows. Walk through these to the very end, where they taper to join another path. Turn right and after 50m follow the path as it bears left on to a short uphill stage. When this climb eases off, a narrow path leads off to the right. This leads down to a clearing and a viewpoint ③.

Return to the main path and carry on for 200m to another deviation to the right on to a wider track, which again leads to an open viewpoint ④.

Return to the main path, turn right and walk to a fork. Bear left here and descend into open countryside ⑤.

This track leads back to the road just above la Chambotte.

Points of Interest

① La Chambotte is a small village with a tiny chapel and some interesting old buildings. It is well worth walking back down the road and through the tunnel to the hairpin bend at the foot of the crags. Rock climbers can be seen in action here, working a complex and often gymnastic route up the steep limestone.

② The restaurant-bar here commands a first-rate view over the northern end of the lake.

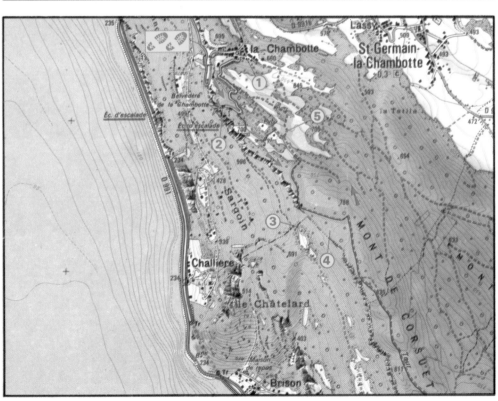

43B

THE ALPS

The Dent du Chat and the Molard Noir

Though these truly magnificent viewpoints are easy enough to reach, the ascent of the Dent du Chat is a scramble suitable only for experienced walkers with a head for heights. More sedate pedestrians will find the ascent of the Molard Noir adequate compensation.

Route Directions

Start from the car parking area on the D 42 from le Bourget-du-Lac, 2km below the second hairpin from the summit. Immediately opposite the car park, take a track that leads into the forest, initially zigzagging,

then following a long traverse. Carry on to a junction and a welcome drink at the Fontaine des Côtes ①.

Here the route goes straight on, signposted Dent du Chat. The path takes a rising traverse across very steep ground and is narrow in places, demanding care when wet or snowy. At a point where the path suddenly descends in front, revealing the limestone cliffs ahead, turn left up a series of ten zigzags ②.

This leads to a col and signposts. Only experienced walkers should attempt the next part of the walk. Turn right and follow a rocky traverse marked by red paint spots into a gully. Climb this, then follow waymarks and polished rock to the summit of the Dent du Chat ③.

Retrace your steps to the col and follow the signed path to the Molard Noir ④.

From the summit a signposted path follows the crest of the ridge towards the Relais television mast.

About 500m from the summit turn left, signposted 'Bourget-du-Lac par Sentier Côte', and take this to reach a road. Turn left, and descend 400m to a sign for the Fontaine des Côtes. Follow this zigzag descent to the Fontaine. Regain the original traverse and turn right to reach the starting-point.

Points of Interest

① A wooden trough at the Fontaine des Côtes makes a useful early refreshment point on the walk. In front is a 330-m climb to the summit, much of it through fine woodland, with cover just thick enough to make the views out across the lake elusively vague, ensuring the impetus to attain the summit with its stupendous views is not lost.

② This series of zigzags covers exceptionally steep ground at a gradient which is kind to legs and lungs. These paths should be adhered to, as any short-cutting, particularly in descent, can lead to serious erosion problems.

③ The Dent du Chat is a graceful spire of limestone, but not attained easily. The intrepid have to scramble up a loose gully, in which any permanent stone is polished to a high gloss, then continue scrambling to an airy summit which has a huge drop to the west and produces what climbers call exposure – an awareness of the size of the drop. There is a viewing terrace at an altitude of 1470m which gives an attractive vista over Lac du Bourget and Aix-les-Bains.

④ The Molard Noir is an easier summit to attain, and offers equally fine views. An orientation table shows the full 360-degree panorama, picking out Mont-Blanc and the Chamonix Aiguilles, the Jura, the Vanoise and the Maurienne peaks. Closer at hand, the Dent du Chat and the long, curving ridge to the north are most impressive, while Lac du Bourget and its surroundings are clearly etched, map-like, below.

The Dent du Chat is the highest of the range of limestone peaks that lie to the west of le Bourget-du-Lac ▼

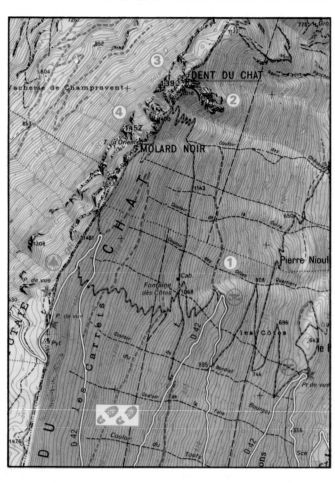

Grenoble and the Chartreuse

THE ALPS

The mountains north of Grenoble, the Massif de la Chartreuse, present a bold and proud profile, overlooking the Isère, which has flowed from its source near the distant Col d'Iseran. The mountains are a mixture of limestone cliffs, deep gorges and seemingly endless mixed forest whose colours in autumn are rich and varied. The route is easy to follow and involves a picturesque tour around the main peaks of the Chartreuse.

▲ *St-Pierre-de-Chartreuse is a medium-altitude Alpine centre with fine views*

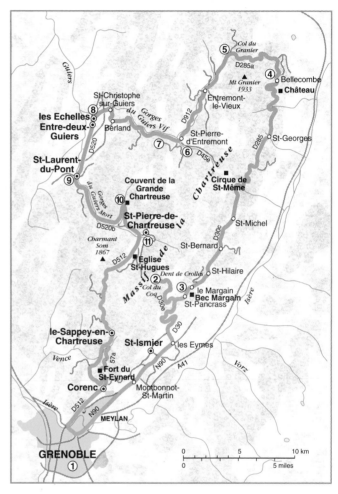

Grenoble lies on the River Isère, with the peaks of the Chartreuse to the north ▼

Route Directions

The drive starts from the magnificent city of Grenoble ①.

Take the N90 towards Chambéry, passing through Montbonnot-St-Martin to reach les Eymes. Here turn left on to the D 30, signposted St-Pancrass and St-Hilaire, though the slopes above are so steep that it is difficult to imagine where a road might go. After 6km take a turning on the left, the D 30e, to Col du Coq. The second walk starts from here. Just past this junction are some automatic avalanche detectors ②.

Return to St-Pancrass and go through the village, and continue to the fine viewpoint of Bec Margain ③.

Pass through St-Hilaire and on to St-Bernard. Turn left here on to the D 30c, following a rising series of bends with excellent views. After the Col de Marcieu the road narrows and crosses great forests before joining the bigger D 285 towards the St-Marcels. Pass through St-Georges, Grand St-Marcel and Petit St-Marcel to reach Bellecombe ④.

At a T-junction after the village turn left, to arrive soon at another T-junction. Turn left again on to the D 912 to the Col du Granier ⑤.

Continue through Entremont-le-Vieux to St-Pierre-d'Entremont ⑥.

From here take the D 520c towards Entre-deux-Guiers, passing through the Gorges du Guiers Vif ⑦.

At the foot of the gorge turn right to St-Christophe and les Echelles ⑧.

From here the D 520 leads to St-Laurent-du-Pont ⑨.

Turn left here, on to the D 520b, signposted St-Pierre-de-Chartreuse, and follow the Gorges du Guiers Mort for 7.5km to reach a turning to the left to the Couvent de la Grande Chartreuse ⑩.

Rejoin the D 520b and continue to St-Pierre-de-Chartreuse ⑪.

Turn right on to the D 512 towards Grenoble and follow this road for 14km, when a turning on the left, the D 57a, leads to the viewpoint of the Fort du St-Eynard. Rejoin the D 512 to make the exciting descent into Grenoble.

LA GRANDE CHARTREUSE

The first Couvent de la Grande Chartreuse was started in 1084, the same year as the Carthusian Order was founded by St Bruno. The monks became farmers and foresters, and at some point during those first few hundred years some imaginative and patient individual combined no fewer than 130 plants, to create an 'elixir'.

The manuscript listing the names of the plants were then donated to the Carthusian monks living in the monastery of Vauvert, near Paris, later finding its way to la Grande Chartreuse. Here, after many efforts, Brother Jerôme Maubec managed to perfect the techniques required for the manufacture of the 'herbal elixir of la Grande Chartreuse'.

Following this work, Brother Antoine produced the elixir and the health liqueur, the present-day green Chartreuse. A milder and sweeter liqueur, yellow Chartreuse, was then created by Brother Bruno Jacquet. The three together went to form the liqueurs which are now manufactured in Voiron.

The mystery surrounding the ingredients still persists, with only three brothers knowing the formula required for the successful distilling of these fine liqueurs.

The cellars in Voiron are open to the public throughout the year, free of charge.

Points of Interest

① The magnificently situated city of Grenoble amply justifies its accolade of capital of the French Alps. It has a very old (1339) and well respected university and is a great cultural centre, with a long history and strong sense of tradition. Several major industries are based here, including the manufacture of ski lifts. There are too many worthwhile attractions to list them all, but the Fort de la Bastille and its *téléphérique,* the Musée de la Peinture et de la Sculpture, and the old town are particularly good. A visit to the large modern tourist information centre in the town centre would be a useful start to a visit to the city.

② Avalanches are a major problem in many Alpine areas, and although different 'management techniques' have reduced the risks, there are still places where avalanches are regular occurrences. Such a place can be seen here, where a long couloir descends from the Dent de Crolles. Sensors placed in the track of the avalanche relay to lights on the roadside, providing an early warning system.

③ In le Margain a good track leads off just past the sports ground to the edge of the escarpment and the remarkable viewpoint of Bec du Margain. An orientation table assists in identifying the myriad of dazzling peaks visible across the flat-bottomed valley below.

④ Winding around the contours of the couloirs which descend from Mont Granier, this section of the road is a real delight. Many of the buildings in the small villages are old and weather-worn, the timber gnarled and bleached. In Bellecombe are the ruins of an old château, perched on the rim of the escarpment.

⑤ Towering above the pleasant forest drive which leads to Col du Granier is Mont Granier, which exhibits an unusual geological feature. The limestone crags so typical of this area are in this case supported on a massive base of darker sedimentary rock. At the col itself are the usual restaurant, bar and shop facilities found on most of the high passes.

⑥ The river which runs through the small town of St-Pierre-d'Entremont now divides the Isère region from Savoie, and was formerly the boundary between the old states of France and Savoie. The D 45 leads out of the village to the Cirque de St-Même, with its fantastic backdrop of crags and waterfalls.

⑦ Between St-Pierre-d'Entremont and les Echelles the road follows the side of the Gorges du Guiers Vif. The road clings to the cliff sides like a smugglers' path, sometimes tunnelling, sometimes creeping between hacked-out overhangs. Towards the foot of the gorge a small parking area on the right allows a dramatic look back to appreciate the scale of the setting.

⑧ Les Echelles and its environs on the west side of the Chartreuse massif exhibit a different, almost lowland character by comparison to the villages on the plateau. The corn-coloured, stone-built houses have pantiled roofs and shuttered windows, many with elaborate balustrades and balconies.

⑨ At the foot of the exciting Gorges du Guiers Mort, St-Laurent-du-Pont is a busy holiday centre and an ideal base for touring the western side of the Chartreuse.

⑩ The famous and beautiful Couvent de la Grande Chartreuse lies in a magnificent setting. The monastery itself is never open to the public in order to protect the tranquil and isolated life of its occupants. It is possible, however, to visit la Correrie, approximately 2km from la Grande Chartreuse. This annexe houses the Musée de la Correrie, where excellent displays depict the history of the monastery and life within its walls.

⑪ St-Pierre-de-Chartreuse, in the heart of the Chartreuse, offers a wide variety of sporting and cultural activities throughout the year. Well worth visiting some 4km to the south is the Eglise St-Hugues, which contains an astonishing array of modern works of religious art.

The Couvent de la Grande Chartreuse epitomises religious seclusion ▼

The Route Sarde and the Gorges de l'Echaillon

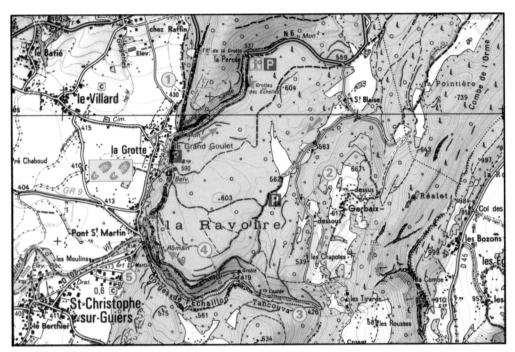

This fascinating route follows the line of a Roman road down a hidden gorge, before gaining and traversing the lip of the awesome Gorges de l'Echaillon. It offers a combination of historical interest and spectacular scenery.

Route Directions

Start from the car park off the Route Sarde just south of la Grotte. Follow the Route Sarde to the north-east, heading towards the Grottes des Echelles through a gorge ①.

Walk northwards through the gorge to its end where it meets the N6. Turn right here, taking great care because the road is narrow for the first 100m, after which it opens out to allow safe walking. After a few hundred metres turn right on to a minor road signposted Gerbaix. Walk past a large barn to a fork and bear right to another junction where the road turns left, rising slightly at first. Pass some old farmsteads and orchards ②.

The road descends here, and after passing a house on the right takes a sharp turn to the left. On the apex of

the bend a little path leads off to the right. Follow this (it soon improves) through woodland until an obvious path junction is reached. From here another path, recommended only to fit and experienced walkers, descends right to the bottom of the gorge ③.

Continue straight on at this junction, soon joining a major track at which the path turns left. Keep to this route as it follows the gorge rim to the Belvédère ④.

At the end of the gorge the path goes down some steps and then through woodland to regain the road. Just left from here is the Pont Romain ⑤.

Turn right to return to the starting-point.

Points of Interest

① Though the band of high cliffs seems impenetrable, this old Roman road known as the Route Sarde, re-opened by Charles Emmanuel II and then Bonaparte, follows a giant cleft which provides a superb natural route. At the gorge entrance is a fine viewpoint, and nearby is an enormous stone monument, 9m high and 7.5m wide, commemorating the creation of the route. There are also caves here which can be visited on tours advertised locally.

② This part of the route passes some quaint traditional farmsteads and has excellent views across the main valley to a huge arch-shaped fold of limestone undercut by steep

woodland. There is also a prehistoric site near by which can be visited with a guide during the summer months. The woodland is carpeted with fungi in the autumn.

③ This steep descent rewards experienced walkers with a close encounter with the torrent which has eroded the gorge. There are deep, green-blue pools, rushing falls and a sense of isolation that makes the steep walk back up seem well worthwhile.

④ The Belvédère is a well-marked viewpoint on the top of the gorge, though vertigo-sufferers would be well advised to keep away from the edge.

⑤ In times gone by serving as the boundary dividing France and Savoy, the river, which is crossed here by a Roman bridge, is particularly beautiful at this point.

The Pont Romain spans the river which at one time divided France and Savoy ▼

44B

Col du Coq and the Dent de Crolles

The south-eastern corner of the Chartreuse massif is dominated by the great limestone prow of the Dent de Crolles. From Col des Ayes an ascent is possible (although some experience is strongly recommended). Alternatively, take the easier but still worthwhile route back via grassy Alpine pastures.

Route Directions

Start from the car park at Col du Coq ①.

Walk back down towards St-Pancrass, and at the hairpin turn off to the left along a good track signposted 'Alpage'. Follow the path round to the right, then left, then directly uphill towards Col des Ayes ②.

Here a huge limestone boulder marks the routes. For the ascent of the Dent de Crolles, which should be attempted only by experienced walkers wearing good boots, turn right at the col and follow a long series of zigzags up steep pastures which lead to tree-dotted pastures beneath the giant west face. The path then makes a long ascent to the right before a steep, narrow scrambling path leads up the easiest line on to the plateau, and the summit which overlooks the south-east face ③.

Retrace the line of ascent to Col des Ayes and continue up another steep zigzag which passes below the peak (1760m) ④.

Follow the grassy ridge to the right (looking up the ascent) for a short way, then take a path which cuts off left towards Habert de Pravouta. A good path is then reached in the valley, leading to the left and up, with forests to the right. This will eventually bear left into the forest, bringing you out a little way above Col du Coq.

The Dent de Crolles ▶

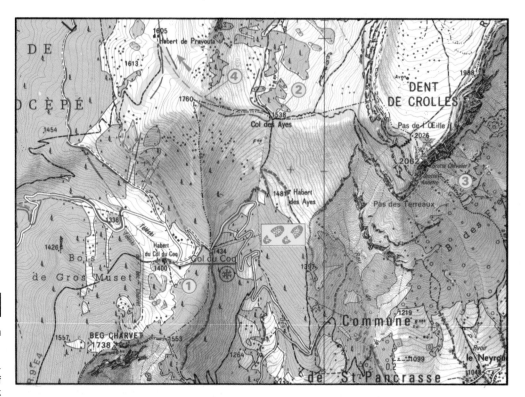

Points of Interest

① Col du Coq is a very popular walking area which also boasts a small ski development. There is also a splendid view of the vast slopes of the Dent de Crolles.

② A col is a gap or pass, and can range from this grassy low point among Alpine meadows to the snow-bound South Col on Everest.

Col des Ayes is a true junction with paths radiating in four distinct directions. It is also in the centre of an area of *alpage*, the grazing land so valued by local herdsmen.

③ The squat, fortress-like peak of the Dent de Crolles is actually a large plateau almost entirely protected by bulging limestone cliffs. It is a popular peak, with views that are a match for virtually any in the Alps. To the south is Grenoble, to the east the enormous Isère valley, with the main Alps strung out in a formidable barrier beyond. The closer peaks of the Chartreuse to the west and north complete a stunning panorama.

④ Alpine pastures are well known for their flowers, and this area, with its nutrient-rich though thin soil, provides plenty of botanical interest. A pocket-sized book on Alpine flowers is well worth carrying.

The southern Vercors

T his drive takes in the sun-drenched southernmost escarpments of the Vercors massif, several impressive passes and some magnificent mountain scenery in between. Though the peaks are low in comparison with those in the northern Alps, the scale of the sheer calcareous cliffs and the long sweeps of woodland which cling tenaciously to the vertiginous slopes give the area a powerful sense of drama.

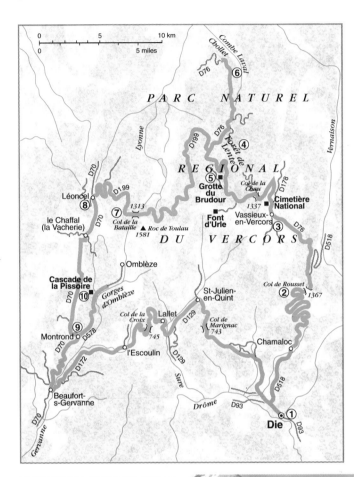

▲ The Vercors presents an enchanting blend of densely wooded hills, waterfalls and gorges, and steep limestone cliffs. In addition, this magnificent landscape is dotted with welcoming villages

Lying at an altitude of just over 1400m, the Col du Rousset divides the northern from the southern Alps ▼

Route Directions

The drive starts from Die ①.

Leave Die on the D 93 towards Crest, soon turning right on to the D 518, signposted Col de Rousset. After 6km pass through Chamaloc, then follow some big hairpins with superb views to the tunnel which leads to the Col de Rousset ②.

Once through the tunnel, turn left after 1km to reach another junction, where you turn left on to the D 76. This leads down to the broad, high-level valley which holds Vassieux-en-Vercors ③.

Leave Vassieux on the same road, signposted la Chapelle-en-Vercors, then turn left just after the Cimetière National du Vercors, signposted St-Jean and Lente. This section leads over the Col de la Chau and through the Forêt de Lente ④.

Continue past the Grotte du Brudour ⑤.

At another junction turn right to St-Jean-en-Royans and Combe Laval ⑥.

Retrace your steps and turn right on to the D 199 towards the Col de la Bataille ⑦.

Cross this col (closed in winter) and descend to Léoncel ⑧.

Join the D 70 just by the abbey. The first walk starts from here. From Léoncel continue southwards along the D 70, through la Chaffal (la Vacherie) towards Beaufort-sur-Gervanne and Crest, until you come to a small left turn to the Croix du Vellan ⑨.

Return to the D 70 and turn left to Montrond. There take a left turn, the D 578 signposted Gorges d'Omblèze ⑩.

From Montrond, follow the D 70 to Beaufort, then return to Die along the sunny southern edge of the Vercors. First take the D 172, passing through l'Escoulin and over the Col de la Croix, then turn left on to the D 129, signposted St-Julien-en-Quint. This leads over the Col de Marignac to Die.

The bracing air of the Col du Rousset is popular with both walkers and skiers

⑤ About 3km past the turning for the Font d'Urle are two hairpin bends. The Pont du Brudoir is at the apex of the second of these. A delightful walk up from here leads to the cave, which is in fact a resurgence, indicative of the vast subterranean cave systems beneath the Vercors. This area is well known as one of Europe's best for caving.

⑥ This road to Combe Laval is probably one of the most spectacular in Europe. Hugging a most improbable route along a line of huge limestone cliffs, alternately tunnelling through it and clinging doggedly to its edge, the drive provides excitement and surprises to the end. The route can be very congested during peak periods.

⑦ The Col de la Bataille is closed during the winter but well worth a visit at any other time. The narrow summit pass is overlooked by the Roc de Toulau, and forests extend in virtually all directions. The views are extensive and there is excellent walking.

Vassieux-en-Vercors was a major centre of the Resistance and a museum commemorates its members' bravery ▼

⑧ See 1 on page 185.

Points of Interest

① Die is an attractive town, once an important Roman stronghold and now more reminiscent of Provence than the Alps. On a narrow main street lined with shops and bars stands the squat limestone church, with bells housed in a cage-like iron dome. Also of interest are the old city walls and ramparts, the 12th-century mosaics in the Chapelle St-Nicolas and the museum. Die makes a good base for touring the southern Vercors and Drôme region.

② The Col de Rousset is a popular starting-point for walkers and skiers. It is reached from the south by a serpentine road overlooked by a stand of towering limestone pinnacles. The col forms a distinct boundary between the warmer climate to the south and the cooler conditions found on the plateau itself.

③ Well known as a centre of the Resistance movement during World War II, Vassieux-en-Vercors was virtually destroyed by the Germans in July 1944. In the village, near the church, is the Musée de la Résistance, and on the road towards Chapelle is the Cimetière National du Vercors. Together they serve as a powerful and disturbing reminder of those dark times.

④ The Forêt de Lente is a popular and extensive woodland walking and ski-touring area set on a high plateau. The Font d'Urle near by provides a strong contrast with its open, flower-strewn pastures.

THE RESISTANCE

A great centre of the Resistance movement between 1942 and 1944, the Vercors is in a fact a natural fortress well suited to the purpose. The tough Resistance fighters, known as Maquisards, were a constant irritant to the Germans and inspiration to the French. Nowadays their brave exploits are commemorated by monuments, cemeteries and museums throughout the region, which is widely known as the 'citadel of the Resistance'.

The area's main battle occurred in July 1944, when three German divisions, including SS and troops specially trained in mountain combat, parachuted on to the high plain at Vassieux. Two days later the heavily outnumbered Maquis were forced to retreat into the mountains, taking shelter in forests and caves as best they could. In the course of these battles 700 Maquisards and local people were killed, and St-Nizier, Vassieux and la Chapelle were completely destroyed.

Wounded Resistance fighters sheltered in a giant cave, the Grotte de la Luire, reached by following the D 518 road towards la Chapelle from Col de Rousset for 8km. They were eventually located by Austrian troops and many were executed. Today the caves are open to the public, and at the entrance a shrine is dedicated to those who lost their lives.

⑨ The southern end of the Vercors has a very different feel from the central area, the stunted pine and scrubby vegetation appearing more Mediterranean than Alpine. The view south from the Croix du Vellan, a huge iron cross on the rim of the plateau, confirms this, as the landscape drifts away, gentler and more mellow, into the Drôme region.

⑩ The superb Gorges d'Omblèze are dominated by massive overhanging calcareous crags, stained into zebra-like stripes of black, creamy whites and ochre. The road and river wind up the gorge, passing the Chute du Pissoir, a vegetation-cloaked waterchute, and continuing through some very fine scenery to the small village of Omblèze.

Léoncel and le Grand Echaillon

THE ALPS

This pleasant walk has only one steep section, at the end of the climb on to the summit plateau. Attractive woodland, fine views and the nearby abbey make for an enjoyable excursion.

Route Directions

Start from the car park beside the Abbaye de Léoncel ①.

Turn on to the D 199 towards Col de la Bataille and round a sweeping left-hand bend, then turn right on to a path just after some buildings. This is the GR 93 footpath, signposted le Grand Echaillon and Font d'Urle. Follow this steadily up through the woods to a junction with another footpath. Continue straight on uphill, following red-and-white paint flashes. Cross several forestry tracks which traverse the ever-steepening ground, and climb some obvious zig-zags which suddenly give way to the summit plateau. Having joined the better track on the plateau, turn left to find a fenced area reached through a stile. Go through this and make your way to the cross on the cliff edge ②.

Return to the stile and turn left to the Grand Echaillon hut ③.

The path runs past a small stone construction which is an ancient well ④.

From the hut return to the edge of the plateau, and instead of turning down into the forest on the route of ascent, go past this and follow a wide track which descends gently across the face of the forest. At the foot of the main hill turn back right towards the abbey ⑤.

From here follow a good path which leads to the rear of the abbey.

Points of Interest

① The Abbaye de Léoncel was a fine old Cistercian abbey but it now no longer exists and all that remains is a 12th-century church and monastic buildings that were altered in the 17th century and which now accomodate a gite.

② This marvellous viewpoint is perched on top of the limestone crags which line the rim of the plateau. The panorama extends beyond the abbey to the Montagne de l'Epenet.

③ One of a whole network of plateau-level huts, le Grand Echaillon is in the heart of a major ski-touring and walking area and is a popular base for those activities.

④ This centuries-old well, now flashed with waymark paint, was used for centuries by the monks.

⑤ The pasture land at the foot of the forest eventually declines into marshland, but before that there are numerous delightful picnic sites.

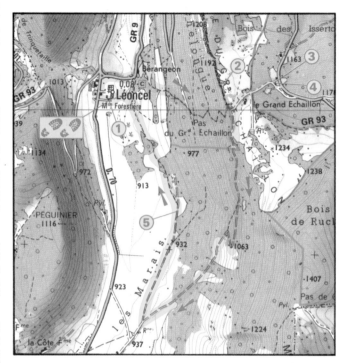

The Apollo butterfly, although fairly common in the mountainous regions of Europe, is protected by law in many areas. Another familiar sight in alpine meadowland between March and August is the deep blue of spring gentian ▼

The heart of the Vercors

A bove 1000 metres for the whole of its length, this walk follows a circuit on the shallow valley containing Vassieux-en-Vercors. The route combines an appreciation of the area's natural history with a glance at the role it played in World War II.

Route Directions

Start from the car park attached to the Cimetière National du Vercors ①.

Cross the road to join a track which leads off immediately opposite the junction with the D 76. Carry on for about 500m to a junction ②.

Turn left here and continue on a good track through an area of exposed limestone. This path eventually bears round to the right to reach le Château ③.

Go through the tiny village centre and bear right, then take another right turn about 200m out of the village. Several hundred metres beyond this point is a well-marked junction, where the route turns left to lead to a group of cross-country-skiing waymark signs ④.

Continue straight on here, and up a gentle incline to a rounded hollow on the left which contains the entrance to a cave ⑤.

From the edge of the hollow, look across to the small hill on the right, from which a good path leads back towards Vassieux ⑥.

From the town follow signposts for la Chapelle-en-Vercors along the Avenue du Mémorial, making a detour to the Musée de la Résistance beside the church. On leaving the town take a track to the right which leads behind the football pitch before curving back to reach the starting-point.

Rose-hips (above right) and juniper (right) are well suited to the soil of the Vercors. Also commonly seen in the area are blackthorn and viburnum ▶

Points of Interest

① At the Cimetière National there are regular slide/tape presentations telling the story of the Maquisards.

② The initial section of the walk enters an undulating area of rocky pastures and scrubby woodland. Many rock cairns can be seen – evidence of clearance of the meadows for agriculture. The outcrops of limestone also make natural rock gardens, backed by stunted pines and firs.

③ A huge stone water trough marks the centre of the tiny village of le Château, many of whose buildings had to be rebuilt following the German onslaught in July 1944.

④ The return footpath passes a great variety of plant life. Lichens, the abundance of which bears testimony to the purity of the air, cover the exposed limestone, which also houses a variety of Alpine plants such as stonecrop and saxifrage. The shrubby growth consists largely of pine, juniper, blackthorn and viburnum, creating a mixture of textures and colours.

⑤ This hollow is a good example of the many cave entrances found throughout the Vercors, giving access to some of the best caving in Europe.

⑥ Destroyed by the Germans in 1944, Vassieux has been rebuilt, though it still bears its scars. The Musée de la Résistance is a privately run museum which traces the story of the Resistance movement and the deportation, thus providing a fascinating and disturbing insight into those dark times.

Around Périgueux

Périgord Vert, Green Périgord, is well named. On this tour you will enjoy beautiful views of rivers, mountains and woods and sample the produce of the region in its market towns. Some of the roads are winding and steep, making progress slow at times, and in the autumn early-morning mists rise from the river, so you may suddenly find yourself driving through dense fog.

▲ *Périgueux's St-Front cathedral is largely the result of extensive restoration work carried out in the 19th century*

towards Mussidan, and pass through St-Vincent-de-Connezac and Beauronne, following signs to Mussidan ⑧.

Join the N89 – E70 at Mussidan and drive through Gâbillou and continue to Sourzac. In Sourzac take a left turn, signposted St-Louis-en-Isle, and cross the bridge. At the junction take a right turn, on to the D 3, signposted Neuvic and St-Astier. At the next junction continue on the D 3 until you reach St-Astier ⑨.

Leave St-Astier on the D 3, signposted Gravelle and Périgueux, and pass through Gravelle. After about 8km turn right on to the D 710 to return to Périgueux ⑩.

Route Directions

The drive starts from Périgueux. Leave Périgueux on the D 939, then turn left on to the D 710 towards Chancelade. Take the first right, signposted Chancelade, and look out for a small turning on the right, signposted Abbaye de Chancelade ①.

After viewing the abbey rejoin the road and very soon after look out for a left turn, signposted Lisle and la Chapelle-Gonaguet. After 5km, at a crossroads, turn right for the Ancien Prieuré de Merlande ②.

At the next crossroads turn right and look out for the abbey on your left (it is not clearly signposted). Continue to a T-junction, then turn right towards Périgueux.

At the next junction turn left on to the D 2 (no signs). Turn right and right again, following signs for Château-l'Evêque ③.

Follow the road to Château-l'Evêque. At the T-junction turn sharp left by the water pump, then bear right on to the D 3e, signposted Agonac. After 500m turn left, and

after another 8km turn left at the crossroads. After 250m turn left (no signs) and almost immediately take a right turn, signposted Lasserre and la Besse. Continue for 6km and turn right on to the D 939, staying on it until you reach a large roundabout. The first exit takes you to the centre of Brantôme ④.

Leave Brantôme by the D 939, going back to the roundabout. Take the left exit, signposted Nontron, Angoulême and Mareuil. Shortly afterwards turn on to the D 78, following signs for St-Julien-de-Bourdeilles, Bourdeilles, Valeuil, Lisle and Ribérac. Continue on the D 78 to Bourdeilles ⑤.

After entering the village, continue on the D 78, signposted Ribérac and Lisle. Pass through Lisle and after 3.5km turn right on to the D 710, signposted Tocane-St-Apre and Ribérac. Almost immediately after entering Tocane look out for a right turn by the church, signposted Montagrier ⑥.

Return to Tocane. From Tocane pass through St-Méard-de-Drône and St-Martial to reach Ribérac ⑦.

Leave Ribérac on the D 709

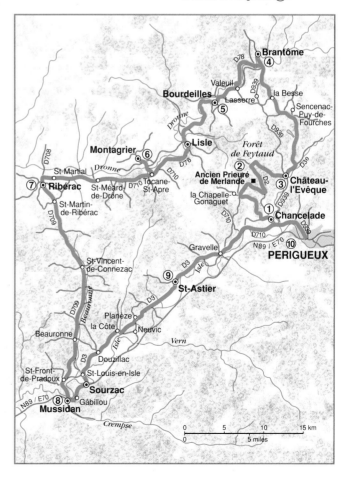

▲ *A picturesque water-mill recalls Brantôme's past*

Points of Interest

① The Augustinian Abbaye de Chancelade, founded in the 12th century, was destroyed and rebuilt during the 17th century. It occupies a beautiful spot, overlooking the River Beauronne. One of its most interesting attractions is its museum of religious art, including vestments.

② In the 12th century the monks of Chancelade also founded the Prieuré de Merlande, in the middle of the Forêt de Feytaud. All that remains is a small fortified chapel and the prior's house.

▲ *The Tour de Vésone, in Périgueux, is all that remains of a Roman temple built in the 2nd century AD*

③ Well worth seeing in Château-l'Evêque is the 14th-century château, formerly the residence of the Bishops of Périgueux.

④ Brantôme is one of the finest towns in Périgord. It has a wealth of attractions, including a Benedictine abbey founded by Charlemagne, and near by are many archaeological and prehistoric sites.

⑤ Bourdeilles has a 13th- and 16th-century castle with a fine collection of furniture. Prettily located overlooking the valley of the River Dronne, the village also has a picturesque fortified water-mill in the shape of a boat.

⑥ From the terrace of Montagrier, next to the small Romanesque church, you can see the valley of the River Dronne. The surrounding hills are dotted with historic attractions such as churches, towers and former cliff dwellings.

⑦ Ribérac is one of the most important markets for farmers in the Périgord region, and one of the main centres for the production of foie gras. Tuesdays and Thursdays are the best days to visit. In October and November there is also a nut market.

⑧ Just on the edge of Périgord Blanc, Mussidan is the administrative centre for several surrounding villages. It is a good place to get touring information and, though small, it has parking for 500 cars. Do not miss the interesting museum of local crafts and traditions.

⑨ St-Astier is best known for its Romanesque church, St-Martin d'Astier, with its magnificent bell tower. The town is a good base for exploring the mysterious Forêt de la Double.

⑩ Périgueux is the capital of the *département* of Dordogne, and is attractively situated on the River Isle. It has many historic and artistic features, including a museum of prehistory with one of the largest and most important collections in France, a fine cathedral and many old houses. There are several good restaurants where you can sample the best of Périgord cookery.

Onions and garlic sell well in Ribérac's popular market ▼

BASTIDES

A feature of the countryside of south-west France is its *bastides,* or fortified towns, constructed in medieval times for purposes of defence. During that period life in the country was seldom peaceful. Marauding bands combed the land, and the nobles had to protect their peasants if they wanted to keep them working in the area. Later, when the region was repeatedly fought over by the English and French, further *bastides* were built as protection.

Bastides are recognisable from their layout, characterised by three long straight roads criss-crossed by shorter, narrower ones. The market-place is usually in the centre of the town and is walled around. Churches in *bastides* are also usually very heavily fortified, and often look more like castles.

Monpazier, south-east of Bergerac, is regarded as the perfect example of a surviving *bastide* built on the classic pattern. Others are more irregular, having been adapted to take advantage of the lie of the land.

Looking over Brantôme

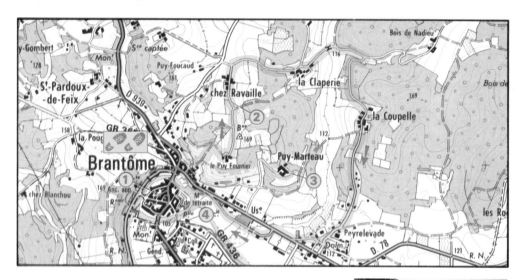

② Depending on the time of year you pass through the farm, you may see tobacco drying in the roofs of the barns. It is still an important local crop. In summer you will see wood being stockpiled for the winter.

③ An imposing golden-stone building, the Château Puy-Marteau dominates the landscape.

④ The Château de la Hierce, unfortunately not open to the public, dates back to the 17th century.

◀ *Brantôme enjoys an attractive situation on the River Dronne*

An elegant riverside pavilion, built around 1530, stands near Brantôme's Porte St-Roch ▼

The first part of this walk is quite steep, so on a hot day take it slowly. In addition to giving fabulous views of the town, known as the 'Venice of Périgord' because of its riverside situation, the walk brings you close to the farms that are so important to the local economy.

Route Directions

Start from the station car park in Brantôme. Leave the car park and walk away from the river to the cross-roads. At the side of the Hôtel Fernandel, take the steep path that climbs upwards through woods and fields, giving fine views of Brantôme ①.

The path passes through the farm of chez Ravaille ②.

Just after the farm the road forks to the right and starts to go downhill. On your right you will see a little stone *borie*, a type of hut typical of the area. Follow the road through la Claperie, another farm; soon afterwards it forks to the right. This part of the walk is lined by trees, which give welcome shade from the

heat in summer. Continue on through la Coupelle.

From la Coupelle there is a distant but good view of the Château Puy-Marteau ③.

On the descent, just before you reach the main road, there is a dolmen on the left. Just before you reach the main road the road forks right. Cross the main road and follow the path, by the tennis courts and football stadium. At the football stadium turn off the main road and take the path to the right, which runs parallel to the main road.

Passing a farm with an old cast-iron well-head in the garden, the path affords a view, just opposite an old ironmonger's, of the beautiful Château de la Hierce ④.

Stay on this path for the station.

Points of Interest

① Brantôme is dominated by its Benedictine abbey, the belfry of which can be seen clearly from the walk and is thought to be the oldest in France. The town is also famous for its museum of prehistory, the Musée Fernand-Desmoulin, and its cave dwellings.

Brantôme's 16th-century bridge is unusual in having not only unequal arches but also an elbow built into its design ▼

PÉRIGORD AND QUERCY

A woodland walk near St-Astier

As well as giving wonderful views of the town of St-Astier and the surrounding countryside, this walk takes you through the atmospheric Forêt de la Double.

Route Directions

Start from the market square in St-Astier ①.

Follow the road along the river until you come to a crossroads. At the crossroads turn left on to the D 43 towards St-Aquilin. Soon the D 43 meets a path leading off to the right, marked in yellow. It is important to keep to the path, which bears round to the left and after about 1.5km rejoins the D 43. Keep to the left and follow the D 43 for 100m before returning to the path marked in yellow. Follow the path for about 500m, then turn left to the Chapelle des Bois ②.

▲ The Chapelle des Bois commemorates the hermit St-Astier

Carry on for a further 100m, then turn right to reach a birdwatchers' post. After 250m turn left and follow a little path to les Chapelles. Just before you reach les Chapelles leave the little path and follow the footpath to the left for about 100m. On leaving the woods you will have a good view of the village of Davalant on your right.

At the edge of the woods you will see the Château de Puy Ferrat. From here take the path to the left, and

▲ St-Astier

you will come to a crossroads by an equestrian centre.

Continue on the road until you reach the Rigole estate. Take the Eugène Le Roy road and stay on it until the ring road. Take the street opposite you to return to St-Astier.

Points of Interest

① St-Astier, situated on the banks of the River Isle, is dominated by its 12th-century church. There is a lively market every Thursday and the town is a good base for exploring the area. St-Astier is also known for its cement works, which takes away a little of its charm but has contributed greatly to local prosperity.

② St Astier was a hermit who lived in a grotto in the woods in the 6th century, and the tiny Chapelle des Bois was built to commemorate him. It is not locked, though there is nothing much to see inside. The chapel's charm lies in its setting.

Riding is very popular in the region, and is a good way to explore the countryside.

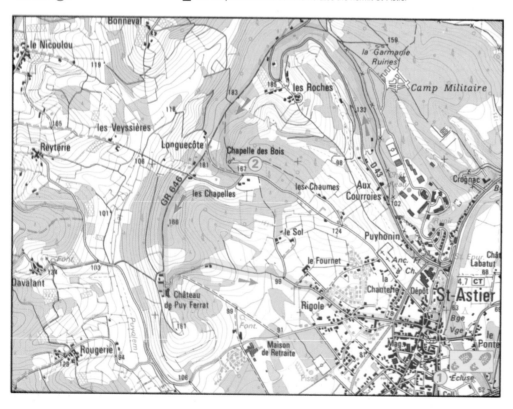

The heart of Périgord Noir

This tour takes you to some of the most popular sights in Périgord, so you may want to stop and explore. If you are travelling at the height of the season you may be forced to linger, particularly if you are still on the roads in the late afternoon, when the towns become very congested. The route makes up for this by revealing some of the most beautiful scenery in the region: rolling green hills, dramatic rock faces and lovely river valleys.

Route Directions

The drive starts from Sarlat-la-Canéda ①.

Leave Sarlat on the D 704, signposted Salignac-Eyrigues. After 5km take a left turn, signposted St-Quentin, Etang de Tamniès and Marcillac-St-Quentin. About 1km later, bear right at a fork signposted Marcillac. Follow this winding, uneven road until you reach Marcillac. About 1.5km outside Marcillac, where the road forks (no signs), bear left, and pass a trout farm. Go straight over the crossroads, following signs for la Chapelle-Aubareil. After about 3km you come to a fork (no signs), where you bear left. Drive through la Chapelle-Aubareil, following signs for Montignac. The caves at Lascaux II are reached by turning sharp right off this road ②.

Return to Thonac and stay on the D 706 for la Roque St-Christophe ⑥.

Not far away, at Tursac, is Préhistoparc ⑦.

Continue on the D 706, signposted Tursac and les Eyzies-de-Tayac-Sireuil. Pass through Tursac and carry on up the winding road for a further 5km until you reach les Eyzies-de-Tayac-Sireuil ⑧.

After crossing the bridge that leads into the town, take the first right, signposted Centre Ville, Vallée de la Vézère and Périgueux.

From les Eyzies, continue on the D 706, following signs to le Bugue and Campagne. After Campagne, take a left turn on to the D 35 at the junction, signposted St-Cyprien ⑨.

After 6km turn right on to the D 49, signposted St-Cyprien. Just after entering the town, take a left turn, signposted Centre Ville, Sarlat and Souillac. Follow signs for the D 703 to Beynac-et-Cazenac ⑩.

Pass through Beynac-et-Cazenac and 1.5km outside the town take a left turn, on to the D 57, signposted Vézac and Sarlat. Continue through Vézac and after 8km you will arrive

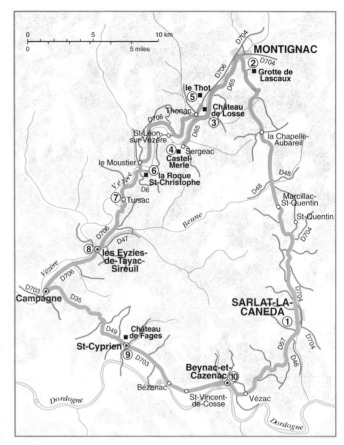

One of the most atmospheric towns in the region, Sarlat-la-Canéda is full of medieval and Renaissance buildings in narrow, winding streets ▼

Just after the junction signposted D 704 Castel-Merle and before the bridge, turn left on to the D 65, signposted Sergeac. Some 5km from Montignac, you will pass, on your right, the Château de Losse ③.

Just under 1km from the château, go straight over the crossroads, still on the D 65, towards Sergeac. Go through Sergeac and follow signs for Castel-Merle ④.

After Castel-Merle, go back through Sergeac and turn left over the bridge at the crossroads, signposted Thonac. After crossing a narrow bridge over the River Vézère, turn right on to the D 706 to pay a visit to the prehistory museum at le Thot ⑤.

PREHISTORY

Although the Vézère valley cannot really justify its claim to be the 'cradle of humanity', as evidence of life here dates back only 40,000 years whereas sites in Africa are believed to have been inhabited for much longer, it can certainly claim to be the world's foremost centre for prehistoric art. It is also an important centre for the study of prehistory, and the museums at les Eyzies-de-Tayac-Sireuil (right) and Périgueux are among the richest in the world. The region as a whole has hundreds of sites, rock shelters, caves and much other evidence of early man, including many cave paintings (above).

The Vézère valley was an obvious site for early man to settle in, as the limestone cliffs provided shelter and the reindeer and other animals which roamed the area provided meat. The area around les Eyzies has the biggest concentration of prehistoric sites in France but there are reminders of man's early history all over the Dordogne and Lot region. The Grotte de Pech-Merle, near Cabrerets, is one of the most spectacular examples.

Scientists have for a long time tried to decipher the meaning of the cave paintings. Because so many of the paintings are of animals, some experts believe that they were created as part of a religious ritual that preceded the hunt.

⑤ The prehistory museum at le Thot is an extremely informative introduction to sightseeing in the Vézère valley, the cradle of early man in France. It includes enlightening audiovisual displays.

⑥ La Roque St-Christophe is one of the oldest and most important cliff fortresses in the world. Some 900m long and 60m high, overlooking the River Vézère, it was occupied first by Neanderthal man.

⑦ Préhisto-parc at Tursac is a reconstruction of scenes from the life of early man. It is one of the best introductions to the prehistory of the region.

⑧ Les Eyzies-de-Tayac-Sireuil is known as the capital of prehistory and is surrounded by important sites. Its museum of prehistory is in an old fortress on a cliff overlooking the village. A massive statue of prehistoric man marks the entrance to the site.

⑨ St-Cyprien is a picturesque town built on the banks of the River Dordogne. It is dominated by a huge church, built in the 12th century and restored during the Gothic era.

⑩ The imposing feudal stronghold of Beynac stands on a cliff overlooking the River Dordogne and gives wonderful views of the now peaceful valley right along the Domme. The village of Beynac-et-Cazenac huddles below the fortress.

◀ *Beynac lies below cliffs flanking the River Dordogne*

Sarlat has a famous market where you can sample truffles. You can also buy examples of a wide range of local artefacts.

② The caves at Lascaux are among France's most famous tourist attractions, for they contain spectacular prehistoric paintings, discovered in 1940. The original caves are closed to the public, because pollution from human breath and other sources began to damage the paintings. Fortunately, they have been meticulously re-created at Lascaux II.

③ The 16th-century Château de Losse is a country house famous for its echo. Standing on the bank of River Vézère, it has beautiful French and Italian 16th- and 17th-century furnishings and tapestries.

④ The ancient shelters of Castel-Merle are carved out of the rock, and on the site there is a small museum of prehistory.

Sarlat's narrow streets are best explored on foot

Points of Interest

① Sarlat-la-Canéda is an enchanting medieval and Renaissance town, with narrow streets and turreted and gabled buildings. Wonderfully preserved, it is full of interesting historical buildings, such as the 16th-century Maison de la Boétie, the Lanterne des Morts, the Chapelle des Pénitents Blancs and the former bishopric.

Above la Roque-Gageac

This walk above a riverside village widely renowned for its beauty takes you through wooded hills that offer fine views over lush countryside. It is very steep in parts, but since there is shade it should not be too difficult in hot weather.

◀ *Cliffs overlooking the River Dordogne provide an impressive setting for la Roque-Gageac, whose houses are mainly of the honey-coloured local stone*

Route Directions

Start from the car park facing the river at la Roque-Gageac ①.

Walk back along the main road to the east, along the bank of the River Dordogne ②.

Walk past the tennis courts and the maize fields, and you will come to a left turn on to a footpath. Follow this to the large cross that you will see facing you ③.

When you reach the cross fork right. You will come to another, smaller cross, where the path forks left, signposted Gageac, by the side of a house. At this point, the path becomes a very steep dirt track offering excellent views. As you walk uphill through the trees on the left, you will see a *borie*, an old stone hut ④.

Stay on this steep path until you reach a fork, when you will see a large shed used for drying tobacco.

Turn left on to a path which is fairly stony and takes you through woods. Through the trees you can catch glimpses of the Château de la Malartrie ⑤.

The route takes you past some ruins, just after which you take the path on the left back into the woods, passing another stone hut on your right.

The path leads back to la Roque-Gageac, giving spectacular views of the village and the River Dordogne. Follow the stone path through the village until you come to steep steps which lead down into the car park.

▼ *La Roque-Gageac is considered to be one of the prettiest towns in the Dordogne valley and indeed the whole of France*

Points of Interest

① La Roque-Gageac, with its honey-coloured houses in a huddle on the cliffs overlooking the river, has been called the prettiest village in France.

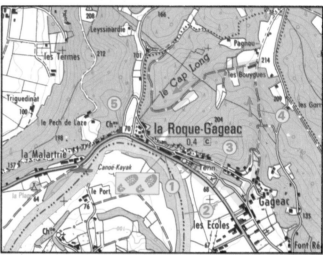

② Since it is no longer an important freight route and tourism is becoming more important, the River Dordogne is increasingly used for water sports, of which canoeing is among the most popular. However, at one time the river trade included boats carrying salt and wood with which to make wine stakes and barrels.

③ Throughout this area crosses and statues are a frequent sight on corners of roads. Here, perhaps, pilgrims used to stop and pray.

④ *Bories* were used to store food for animals, though some people have more fanciful explanations, perhaps because their curved construction resembles primitive human dwellings in other parts of the world.

⑤ The village is very old, but the Château de la Malartrie, at its western end, is not as old as it looks. It was built in the 19th century to resemble a 15th-century château.

47B

PÉRIGORD AND QUERCY

Brénac and Lascaux

The rural part of this walk gives you a sense of how this area might have looked to early man, and reveals its simple attractions: rich land, abundant water, and fine views.

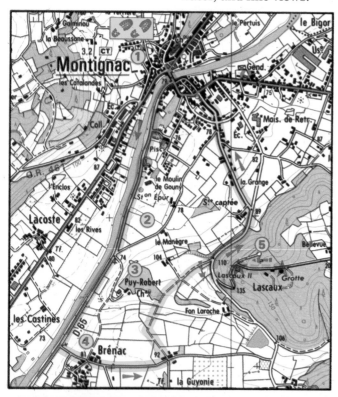

▲ Peaceful woodland paths can be found near busy Montignac

Route Directions

Start from Montignac ①.

At the bridge over the Vézère, take the road that follows the left bank to the south (the D 65) ②.

Pass the swimming pool on the left. Stay on this road and pass the entrance to the Château Puy-Robert ③.

Continue on the same road until you reach a left turn towards Brénac ④.

Take this road into Brénac and in the village stay on it (do not take the right fork to le Truffet) until you come to a footpath at the left of some houses. Follow this footpath and you will be rewarded with some superb views of Montignac. The footpath passes through fields and goes behind the Château Puy-Robert, eventually reaching the main road. Here you can make a detour to see the caves of Lascaux II ⑤.

Otherwise, follow the road down the hill to return to Montignac.

Points of Interest

① Montignac is a small town which, with its population of 3000 plus tourists, gets very busy during the summer. Well worth visiting is the Musée Eugène-Le-Roy, named after the 19th-century French author famous for his descriptions of the poverty of the rural community. No doubt he would be pleased with its current prosperity.

② This stretch of the River Vézère shows what must have attracted early man to the area. It is green, fertile country, very beautiful and peaceful.

③ The Château Puy-Robert, an imposing 19th-century country house, is now a luxurious hotel and restaurant. It is very popular with American cycle tourists.

④ The hamlet of Brénac had a certain importance in the 13th century, because of its connections with the powerful Abbaye de St-Amand-de-Coly. In the village today is a cemetery with a little chapel and a lovely house with an old tower – all that remains of the former monastery.

⑤ The caves of Lascaux II, where the cave paintings discovered at Lascaux have been re-created, are among the region's most famous prehistoric sites.

◄ The Château Puy-Robert
The stone-built village of Brénac ▼

Upper Quercy

This tour takes you through some of the most dramatic scenery in Périgord and Quercy, a landscape of limestone cliffs and steep-sided river valleys. It also takes in some of the area's most popular attractions, such as the spectacularly situated village of Rocamadour and the Gouffre de Padirac, so do not expect to be able to rush around.

Route Directions

The drive starts from Souillac ①.

Leave Souillac on the N20, signposted Cahors, Payrac, Gourdon, Grottes de Lacave and

Rocamadour is famed for its spectacular setting on a steep, 150m-high rock face above the River Alzou ▼

Rocamadour. About 1km from Souillac, just before the bridge over the River Dordogne, take a left turn on to the D 43, signposted Pinsac, Rocamadour and Grottes de Lacave. Follow the winding D 43 down the hillside and over another bridge to reach Lacave. (Bear left to see the Grottes de Lacave. A small train leads into the caves, where you can take a half-hour tour.) Head back up to a turning signposted Rocamadour. Take a sharp right turn, signposted Rocamadour. Carry on up the hill on this road, passing the Auberge de la Garenne on your right. After 10km you will reach Rocamadour ②.

Turn left at the T-junction on to the D 673, signposted Autres Directions, la Cité, Sanctuaires and l'Hospitalet.

Leave Rocamadour on the D 673, signposted Martel, Brive and St-Céré. About 3km from Rocamadour, at a crossroads, go straight on towards Alvignac. Just after this cross over the N140, still following signs for Alvignac. Drive straight through Alvignac, following the D 673, signposted Padirac and St-Céré. At Padirac take a left turn, signposted Gouffre de Padirac ③.

After 2km you will reach the Gouffre de Padirac and the zoo. Return to

Padirac and then turn left on to the D 673. Soon, turn left on to the D 38, signposted Autoire ④.

Carry on down the road into the pretty village and then return along the D 38 to the D 673 where you turned off and turn left, signposted St-Céré. Soon after, at the next crossroads, take another left turn, signposted St-Céré, Château de Montal and Grotte de Presque. About 3km down the hill you will pass the Grotte de Presque ⑤.

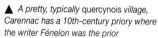

▲ *A pretty, typically quercynois village, Carennac has a 10th-century priory where the writer Fénelon was the prior*

Descend for another 2.5km, passing through St-Jean-Lespinasse. At the next junction take a right turn on to the D 673, signposted St-Céré. Shortly after look out for the sign on your right for the turning to the Château de Montal ⑥.

Continue on the D 673 to St-Céré ⑦.

To leave St-Céré, go back to the D 673, signposted Rocamadour, Gramat and Padirac. About 2.5km from St-Céré follow signs for Gintrac and Carennac. (About 6km further on there is a worthwhile detour. A turning to the right is signposted Bretenoux, Prudhomat and Château de Castelnau ⑧.)

Continue on the D 30, signposted Gintrac and Carennac. Drive through the outskirts of Gintrac, staying on the D 30, and after about 4km you will reach Carennac ⑨.

Immediately after entering Carennac bear right, following signs for Mezels. Shortly after Mezels, turn right on to the D 80 over a single-span bridge. After passing under a railway bridge turn left on to the D 703 and continue to Martel ⑩.

Stay on this road and pass under an impressive viaduct on the way back to Souillac.

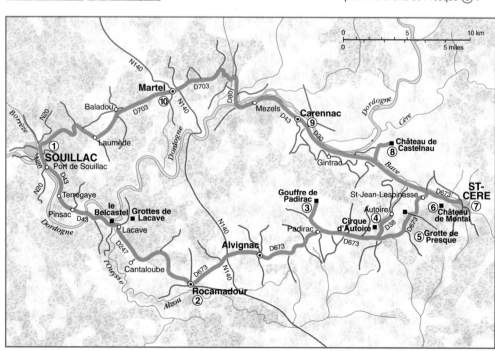

Points of Interest

① Souillac is a busy little town on the banks of the River Dordogne at the confluence with the Borrèze. Its attractions include a 12th-century abbey church in the local style and a 15th-century tower.

② Rocamadour is a deservedly renowned medieval village and important pilgrimage town. It is dramatically sited on a steep rock face in the gorge of the River Alzou and dominated by a 14th-century castle. The single street, with 216 steps up to the Chapelle Notre-Dame, used to be packed with penitents on their hands and knees. Today it is filled with camera-laden tourists. There are seven churches in the town square.

③ The Gouffre de Padirac, a massive underground cave, is one of the best-known sites in the area. A lift takes you the 75m down into the cave and you cross a subterranean lake by boat.

④ Autoire is officially described as one of the prettiest villages in France. Its old stone houses are dominated by a château, and above the village is a series of attractive waterfalls.

⑤ The Grotte de Presque is a huge series of caves stretching 380m into the rock, with dramatic stalagmites. Each cave is named evocatively – for example, the Salle des Merveilles and the Salle de Marbre Rouge.

⑥ The imposing Château de Montal, restored at the beginning of this century, has a sad but romantic history: built in 1523 by a widow for her son, it was never destined to receive him, for he failed to return from the wars.

⑦ St-Céré, an attractive little town, nestling in the Bave valley, has many houses which date back to the 15th, 16th and 17th centuries. It is a good base for touring in Haut Quercy.

⑧ The Château de Castelnau was once the stronghold of the

Autoire's half-timbered houses give the village great charm ▼

TRUFFLES

The 'black diamonds' of Périgord, truffles are indeed the most expensive vegetable in the world. That is why, although they feature in many traditional regional menus, they are served in minute quantities: usually little shavings of truffle are used as a garnish. They have a strong, earthy taste, which most people love or hate, so fortunately a little goes a long way.

Truffles are edible fungi which grow underground close to the roots of certain trees, particularly oaks. Traditionally they are harvested between December and February with the help of pigs or specially trained dogs. A 'ripe' truffle weighs about 100g. As they cannot be cultivated commercially, rarity adds to their attraction. During the truffle season hordes of chefs and food enthusiasts from all over the world descend on Périgord to join in the fun.

The strong flavour of truffles marries well with eggs, fish and meat, and pâté is frequently made *'aux truffes'*. So, if you see any little black specks in your food when eating in Périgord, do not be alarmed – be grateful.

▲ *The Grotte de Presque*

The fine medieval fortress of Castelnau dominates the town ▼

Castelnau family, who were among the most important families in Quercy in the 11th century. Much fought over for centuries, it eventually fell into decline. Restored at the beginning of this century, it can now be visited all year round.

⑨ Carennac is romantically sited on the River Dordogne, opposite the little island nicknamed Calypso. It has a Romanesque priory and a 15th-century château overlooking the river, as well as many charming old houses.

⑩ Martel is known locally as the 'town of the seven towers'. It was founded by Charles Martel, who built a church there to celebrate his defeat of the Saracens in the 8th century. The fortified church of St-Maur is still an impressive sight today.

Around Souillac

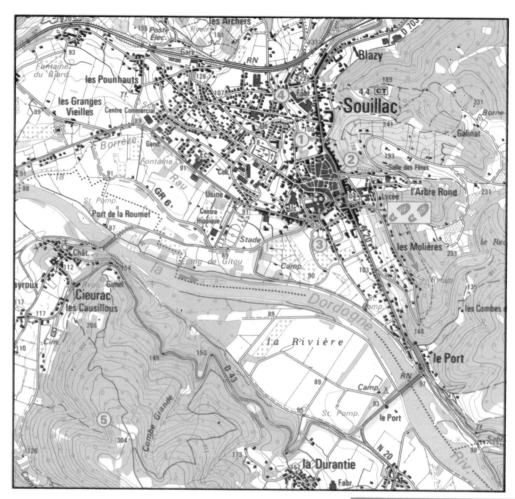

② The abbey church of Ste-Marie, which many historians of the region rate as second in importance and interest only to the cathedral of Cahors, was attacked by the English in the Hundred Years War and then by the Huguenots during the Wars of Religion, but has been restored.

③ The belfry dates back to the 12th century and is all that remains of the old parish church, destroyed in the Wars of Religion.

④ It was the Romans who first established Souillac as an important staging post and on the hillsides above the town, near the viaduct they built, evidence of Bronze Age and Iron Age settlements has been found.

⑤ If you are feeling energetic you may want to walk through the woods up to this landmark. The views across the valley from here are spectacular.

Now a market town, Souillac was once an important port of call for Dordogne shipping ▼

This is a gentle walk through the green countryside surrounding Souillac. Along the way there are some lovely views, including one that takes in a Roman viaduct. There is also an optional challenge for the fit walker.

Route Directions

Start from the centre of Souillac, in front of the abbey church ① and ②.

Bear left, cross the N20 and follow signs for the town's swimming pool. The road bears right. Follow this road, Boulevard des Molières, which is lined with substantial and attractive modern houses. Looking down you will see some fine views of Souillac, including the church and the belfry ③.

You will also see, on the hills above the town, a huge viaduct ④.

When you reach the viewpoint the road forks down to the right and rejoins the N20. Go under the railway bridge and then cross the river. Pass the camp site and you will come to the D 43 on the right, following the edge of the woods. (The more adventurous and athletic can climb higher to the television transmission mast ⑤.)

Follow the D 43 and fork to the right to the Château de Cieurac. Turn right again to the Dordogne and follow the path along the river, to return to Souillac, passing a riding club and a football stadium.

Points of Interest

① Bustling Souillac, on the banks of the Dordogne at its confluence with the Borrèze, is a popular tourist town. This is an extremely fertile area, so it is not surprising to discover that its history can be traced back some 40,000 years. Nowadays Souillac is a popular crossroads town. It takes its name from the Celtic word *souilh*, which means 'boar's lair'. The animal features on Souillac's coat of arms.

St-Céré

This walk around St-Céré is a long one and is very steep in places. It is not suitable for those who are not fit or for the very young. However, older children will enjoy it.

Route Directions

Start from Quai des Récollets on the left bank of the River Bave in St-Céré ①.

Going in the direction of Gramat on the D 673, pass the bridge. There are several bridges in the town, but this one has a war memorial ②.

Keep left until you reach a junction of three roads beside a large factory. Turn right so that you are in front of the factory. You are now on the road that leads to the Château de Montal ③.

Continue on this road for 0.5km to reach a footpath on the left (marked by a little man carrying a rucksack). At the next fork turn to the left and follow a path that climbs steeply up the Causse de Lauriol. This takes you up the side of a vineyard. The route is marked with footpath signs that are rather hard to see, and the path becomes very steep and narrow at this point. However, you eventually reach a superb viewpoint from where you can see the Tours de St-Laurent ④.

From here you can also see the châteaux of Montal and Castelnau-Bretenoux. Take the track in the middle of the plateau and walk down until you join a path. Turn right and after 200m turn left. At the next fork bear left and continue until you come to a path on the left which follows a little stream. Follow this until it joins a road and you have passed the buildings of le Moulin Haut.

Take the left-hand footpath by the side of the stream and you will come to a very attractive shaded country road. Bear left to return to St-Céré.

Points of Interest

① St-Céré, perched on the River Bave, is very picturesque, with its medieval market square and half-timbered houses. In the centre of the square is an old fountain with the statue of a young girl. In recent years St-Céré's Jean Lurçat tapestry museum and its collection of old cars have become some of the town's main attractions.

② However small the village, there is always a monument to its dead in both World Wars. St-Céré also has a number of monuments to members of the Resistance who were killed there.

③ The Château de Montal, 3km west of St-Céré, has one of the most romantic histories of all the châteaux in the region. Jeanne de Balsac d'Entraygues, widow of Amaury de Montal, had it built by the finest craftsmen for her son Robert, who was away fighting for the French in Italy. Sadly he never returned.

④ The medieval Tours de St-Laurent, perched on a hill above the village, are a well-known local landmark.

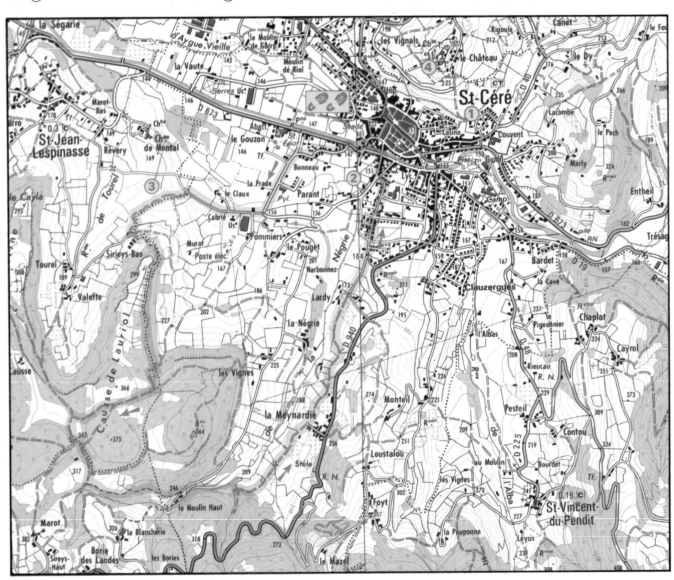

Châteaux and villages of the Lot

PÉRIGORD AND QUERCY

Following roads that are in many cases steep and winding, this tour visits some of the most beautiful villages and towns of the Lot. Spectacular limestone cliffs provide a stark contrast to the lush river valley, and you can also explore one of France's best prehistoric sites, the Grotte de Pech-Merle.

Route Directions

The drive starts from Cahors.

Leave Cahors on the D 653 towards Figeac, with the River Lot on your right. After 12km you reach the pretty flower-decked village of Vers. Turn right and cross the bridge, and then turn on to the D 662 towards St-Géry. Pass through St-Géry. After 8km take a right turn, signposted St-Cirq-Lapopie, on to the D 40, crossing the River Lot to pass through Bouziès. This is a very steep road with fine views. Continue to St-Cirq-Lapopie ①.

Drive through St-Cirq-Lapopie, following signs for Cahors, towards Figeac, cross over the bridge and turn right on to the D 662. Continue for 4km until you reach St-Martin-Labouval, and then Cénevières. Just after Cénevières bear left at the fork. Follow the narrow road straight up the hill to see the château ②.

Return to the same road to continue to the ancient hilltop village of Calvignac, where there are some lovely views. Pass through Calvignac and after about 7km turn left on to the D 19, signposted Cajarc and Figeac. Cross the bridge and stay on the D 662. Carry on through Montbrun and after 7km turn left to the Château de Larroque-Toirac ③.

You can park by the church and walk up to the castle.

Carry on along the D 662 to St-Pierre-Toirac. Take a left turn on to the D 18, signposted St-Pierre-Toirac Eglise, park and follow a footpath to the fortified church ④.

Continue through the village until you regain the D 662 (the road is very winding) and carry on to Figeac ⑤.

Leave Figeac on the D 662 and the D 19 and turn right to join the D 41 for Boussac. Pass through Boussac on the D 41 and at Corn continue on the same road, signposted Brengues, 6km from which is St-Sulpice. Be careful not to turn up the hill here, but carry straight on to Marcilhac-sur-Célé ⑥.

The Grotte de Bellevue is signposted to the right here ⑦.

Continue on the D 41, signposted Cabrerets and Sauliac-sur-Célé. About 4km after Sauliac is a church built into the cliff, just after which there is a turning on the right to the open-air museum of Cuzals ⑧.

Go back down the hill, following signs to Cahors, and after 7km you reach Cabrerets, a pretty village

A mill on the River Célé at Cabrerets ▼

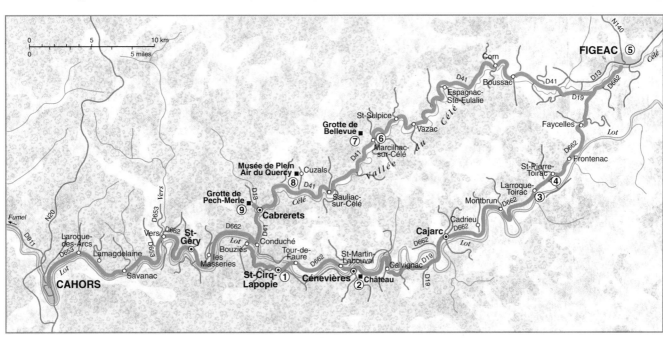

▲ *St-Cirq-Lapopie, with its dramatic setting above the River Lot, is justly popular*

FOOD IN THE LOT

There are many traditional dishes to enjoy in Quercy. The food tends to be on the rich side: although fish from the river are always a feature, truffles and goose take pride of place on most menus. Also popular is lamb, served as *l'agneau fermier du Quercy*.

Nuts are used frequently, made into oils to dress salads, baked in bread, or baked in a *pastis quercynois,* a rich flaky pastry containing apples, strawberries and walnuts.

Every meal includes *cabécous*, little goat cheeses from the Causse de Gramat. Duck and goose *confits* are a traditional local delicacy. The birds are cooked and preserved in their own fat, and most local shops sell jars of *confit*. Foie gras is another local tradition and is often served with a *salade aux gésiers* (gizzards). Meals frequently begin with a *tourin*, or soup. Local people pour some of their wine into the dregs of the soup and drink the mixture straight from the bowl.

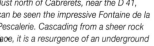

Just north of Cabrerets, near the D 41, can be seen the impressive Fontaine de la Pescalerie. Cascading from a sheer rock face, it is a resurgence of an underground river ▼

dominated by the Château de Gontaut-Biron on the right. Take the D 13 to see the Grotte de Pech-Merle ⑨.

Go back down the hill and follow the D 41 to Conduché, the D 662 to St-Géry and Vers, and finally the D 653 to return to Cahors.

Points of Interest

① The medieval village of St-Cirq-Lapopie, clinging to the cliffs overlooking the Lot, was among the first to be judged officially one of the most beautiful in France. With its towers, turrets and higgledy-piggledy houses, now occupied by craftsmen and artists, it looks like an illustration from a fairy story.

② The Château de Cénevières is a 13th-century castle 7km from St-Cirq-Lapopie. Perched on a cliff overlooking the Lot, it has fabulous views from its terrace. The interior is also impressive with much of interest, including Flemish tapestries from the 15th and 16th centuries.

③ The Château de Larroque-Toirac clings to the rocks overlooking the River Lot. First built in the 12th century, it has been destroyed and rebuilt several times since. A spiral staircase in a Romanesque tower serves the different storeys.

④ The fortified Norman church in St-Pierre-Toirac was built in the 11th

and 14th centuries, but recent work suggests there was probably an earlier church on the same site. For the agile, an awkward outside staircase leads to a watch-tower with commanding views of the Lot and nearby villages.

⑤ The ancient town of Figeac, on the River Célé, has some fine old buildings. The Hôtel de la Monnaie, the former Mint, houses the town museum, whose exhibits include a cast of the Rosetta Stone.

⑥ The tiny village of Marcilhac-sur-Célé nestles beneath the limestone cliffs lining the River Célé, and is also in the shadow of the ruins of a former Benedictine abbey.

⑦ The Grotte de Bellevue, 1.5km north of Marcilhac, is a series of caves discovered in 1964. Among the impressive stalagmites and stalactites is the massive Colonne d'Hercule, a 4-m high stalagmite

with a circumference of 3.5m which extends from floor to ceiling.

⑧ The Musée de Plein Air du Quercy at Cuzals is a 'living museum' set in 50 hectares of countryside. It includes two farms re-created from the times of pre-Revolutionary France, and displays of traditional crafts such as pottery and leatherwork.

⑨ The Grotte de Pech-Merle, near Cabrerets, should not be missed. The cave paintings, discovered as late as 1922, are rated by many as the most impressive in the area. The grotto, 1200m long, contains about 600 prehistoric paintings and engravings.

The fine village of Cabrerets lies at the confluence of the Rivers Célé and Sagne ▼

Around Cajarc

This walk around Cajarc takes a look at the limestone cliffs, or *causses*, that are characteristic of this region and lend drama to the landscape. It also goes through a peaceful hamlet and offers fine views of Calvignac and Cajarc itself.

Further on, as it turns to the right, the path briefly rejoins the D 662. At the crossroads you will see a beautiful stone cross. Turn right and after about 20m turn right again, on to a footpath. This twists and turns along the cliff before you come to a turning on the left leading to Prajoux. Just after passing a spring on the left the path turns sharp right to leave Prajoux behind, sweeping north and east and passing on the

② The *causses*, or limestone cliffs, which make this landscape so spectacular, have until recent times also rendered the area inaccessible. The *causses* above Cajarc are dotted with old phosphate mines.

③ Calvignac is one of the old fortress towns of the Lot, perched dramatically on a cliff, with some of its houses cut out of the cliff face. It is not as well preserved as its more famous neighbour downriver,

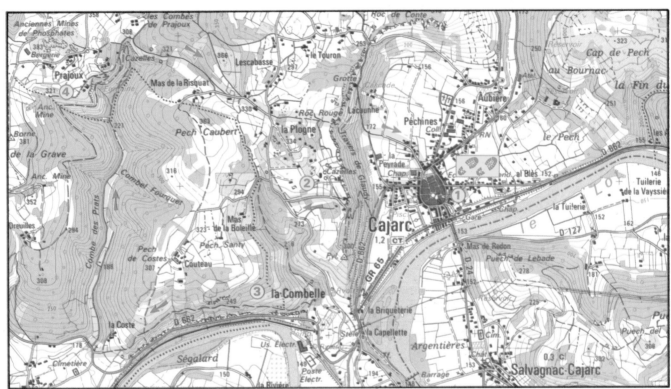

Route Directions

Start from Cajarc ①.

Walk along the D 662 towards Limogne and Cahors. Take the first turning on the right, a surfaced road, and, 30m further on, take a footpath leading to limestone cliffs ②.

Follow the path until you come to a track. Continue along the track for about 250m until you come to a junction, then turn right, then left 150m further on. At the first turning on the left follow a footpath which leads down into the woods. After about 500m this reaches a junction with a surfaced road. Turn right and follow the road for about 250m. Then turn left and take a left-hand fork shortly afterwards to follow the path leading to the cliffs, from where there is a splendid view of the Lot valley and the town of Calvignac ③.

right some circular stone huts known as *cazelles* ④.

Bear right and the path widens and rejoins a surfaced road, which you take, keeping left. At the next crossroads take the footpath opposite. At the first fork follow a path which leads down beneath the cliffs, where there are some lovely views of Cajarc. The path joins the GR 65 long-distance footpath. Turn right and continue back down into Cajarc.

Points of Interest

① The old town of Cajarc, almost circular in form, is beautifully situated in a valley between cliffs and the River Lot. There are a few shops and restaurants and it is a pleasant place to watch the world go by. It has a very efficient tourist office, which may be housed either in an old church near the market square or in the town hall.

St-Cirq-Lapopie, but some may feel it is the better for it.

The peaceful town of Cajarc ▼

④ *Cazelles*, or stone circular huts, were used to store food for animals.

St-Géry

▲ St-Géry's memorial to children killed in two World Wars

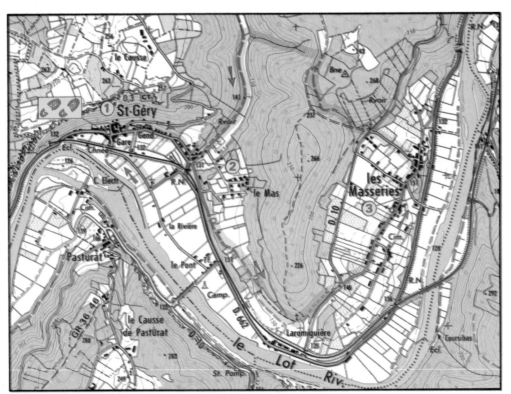

Although it may seem steeper than it really is on a hot day, this walk is worth the effort, for it serves as a lovely introduction to the charm of the Lot, with its unspoilt countryside and tiny hamlets.

Route Directions

Start from St-Géry ①.

Facing the church, turn right and pass the police station. At a fork, take the little road leading uphill on the left. At the next crossroads take the road going down to the right. On the left you will see a *lavoir* ②.

Leave the road and follow the railway line to the right. Follow this path for nearly 2km until it rejoins the road at a fork. Take the right fork and follow signs for les Masseries ③.

Cross the village, passing beside a large parasol pine, and at the crossroads go to the left of the cross. Higher up, fork left and then almost

◄ Pleasant paths run through the woodland around St-Géry

immediately left again, on to a little path. Pass a ruined wall and then follow the little path which runs beside it. Leave the old footpath and take the path down the *causse* that descends to the reservoir. Skirt the reservoir and then turn left down the hillside to reach the broad path which runs along the valley floor. Turn left to follow this path back to the crossroads on the outskirts of St-Géry. Rejoin the road to cross the railway line at the level crossing. Turn right immediately afterwards and then left. After about 250m turn right along a road that follows the river bank to return to St-Géry.

Points of Interest

① St-Géry is a sleepy little village of pale-coloured stone, nestling between limestone cliffs and the River Lot. It has a boat stopping place, used today by pleasure craft.

② The *lavoir*, or wash-house, may date back to Roman times. Nearby Vers has a Roman aqueduct.

③ Les Masseries is a tiny hamlet which, with its stone houses, church and cemetery surrounded by vineyards, typifies the appeal of the Lot.

◄ St-Géry lies on the River Lot

Wine and history from Cahors

This tour passes through the vineyards of the Lot before providing a glimpse of the region's history by visiting *bastide* towns and châteaux among the nearby mountains. Since some of the roads are winding and steep, progress can be much slower than you would expect. Luckily, the attractive countryside provides ample consolation for any delays.

Route Directions

The drive starts from Cahors ①.

Leave Cahors on the D 8, signposted Luzech and Pradines, and pass through Douelle to arrive at Luzech ②.

Leave Luzech on the D 8 by crossing the bridge and following signs for Albas. Continue on the D 8, signposted Lagardelle and Puy l'Evêque, through Anglars-Juillac to Lagardelle. Just after Lagardelle and before Grézels, look out for a turning on the left signposted to the château ③.

After leaving Grézels the D 8 joins the D 44, and 4km further on is Puy l'Evêque ④.

Follow signs for Centre Ville and cross the bridge. The best view of the town is from the bridge as you enter it. Leave Puy l'Evêque and go back over the bridge and on to the

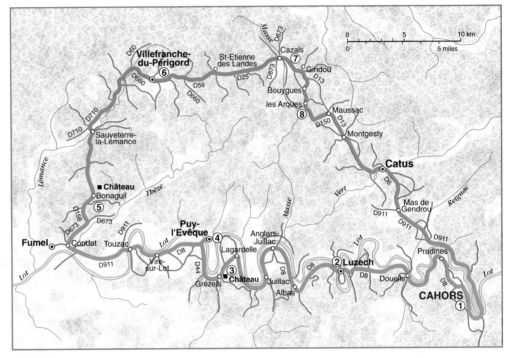

D 8 again. Pass through Vire-sur-Lot to Touzac. Cross the River Lot. Continue to Condat. Turn right on to the D 673 and first left on to the D 158, signposted Bonaguil. At a junction turn right for Bonaguil ⑤ .

After the château at Bonaguil, follow signs for St-Front and Sauveterre-la-Lémance. Beware of humps just outside Sauveterre. Turn right on to the D 710 and at the roundabout about 6km from Sauveterre, take the second exit, on to the D 660, signposted Cahors, Sarlat and Villefranche-du-Périgord ⑥.

About 3km after Villefranche turn left on to the D 59 to Marminiac, and pass through St Etienne des Landes. At the next crossroads go straight on along a windy road, the D 25, through woods, signposted Cazals ⑦.

Leave Cazals on the D 13, following signs for Cahors and Luzech. About

0.5km after Gindou, take a right turn (easily missed), signposted les Arques. Pass through Bouygues and follow the left fork up the hill to les Arques ⑧.

Leave les Arques on the D 150. After 4km turn right on to the D 13 to Montgesty, and another 4km further on turn left to Catus. From Catus, follow the D 6 towards Cahors, then turn left on to the D 911, signposted Cahors, to return to the starting-point.

Bonaguil was one of the first châteaux to withstand cannon fire. It is among the finest examples of military architecture of the 15th and 16th centuries ▼

◄ *Villefranche-du-Périgord, like its traditional rival Monpazier, is well known throughout the region for its mushroom market. Also like Monpazier, it is a former bastide, a fortified town built on a grid plan*

⑤ The Château de Bonaguil, just north of Fumel, is an excellent example of late-medieval military architecture, built in the 15th and 16th centuries and extremely well preserved. Built to withstand an onslaught by 10,000 men, ironically it did not face a siege until the time of the Revolution.

⑥ Villefranche-du-Périgord, a former *bastide* town, still has its ancient covered market and arcaded main square, surrounded by 12th- and 13th-century houses. Today the old-fashioned market, which is still held, is augmented by some rather stylish shops.

⑦ Peaceful Cazals, like Villefranche-du-Périgord a former *bastide* town, is built around a central square on the banks of the River Masse.

⑧ The hamlet of les Arques boasts two interesting old churches, St-Laurent and St-André-des-Arques, both of which have been lovingly restored. The latter has some impressive 15th-century frescos.

▲ *Among the sights of Cahors is the Pont Valentré, a fine example of 14th-century engineering with its three 40-m towers and six arches. The bridge took over half a century to build*

Bonaguil, a robust late-medieval château set where Périgord Noir meets Quercy, hosts musical evenings in summer ▼

CAHORS WINE

In the 17th century Cahors wine was considered to be better than the wines of Bordeaux, and was used as the altar wine of the Russian Orthodox Church. The stony soil of the Quercy Blanc region and the long hours of sunshine helped the vineyards flourish, and created the wealth of many of the towns in the area. The wine all but disappeared in the 19th century, however, as a result of the phylloxera epidemic. Many of the vineyard owners had to turn to other crops to make a living, and the plums and walnuts which today alternate with the vineyards would not have been so intensively cultivated had it not been for the devastating epidemic.

Local people also make delicious, if rather strong, spirits, flavoured with plums or walnuts, known as *eau de prune* and *eau de noix* respectively. Gradually, the vineyards were replanted and now they cover some 4000 hectares. Almost a century after its disappearance, the local wine, so deep red it is almost black, is today once again receiving acclaim. In 1971 it gained an AOC *(appellation d'origine contrôlée)* classification.

Points of Interest

① The Roman and medieval town of Cahors is attractively situated on a bend in the River Lot. It has a lively shopping centre and open-air market in the square around the Cathédrale St-Etienne. As well as some fine old buildings, it has a superb early-14th-century fortified bridge, the Pont Valentré.

② The market town of Luzech stands on a natural peninsula in the river, shrouded by steep, wooded banks. The village still has some medieval houses and there is a museum. About 4km north of the village, and reached by a steep path,

is the Colline de l'Impernal, a hill that was once a Roman city. On it stands a medieval keep.

③ The Château de la Coste, overlooking the village of Grézels, has been restored several times over the centuries and now houses a Musée Terroir et Vin, devoted to the food and wine of Quercy. It is open every day from 1 July to 30 September. There are daily guided tours of the château at 5pm.

④ The attractive town of Puy l'Evêque, with its honey-coloured houses perched on a rocky promontory overlooking the Lot, stands in the midst of vineyards, and is on the Cahors wine route.

Puy l'Evêque

T his walk in the attractive wooded countryside around Puy l'Evêque and along the River Lot has some wonderful views.

However, in order to enjoy them you have to climb for quite a way up a steep hill, so it is not recommended in high summer.

▲ *Puy l'Evêque*

Route Directions

Start from the car park by the town hall in Puy l'Evêque ①.

From the town hall, carry on up the D 28, from where you will see, on your left, rolling hills covered with vines ②.

You will eventually pass signs indicating that you are leaving the town. Continue uphill on the D 28 (now Avenue de Martignac). Take a left turn signposted 'Evasion', and after about 200m, having passed a stone wall on your left, turn left through chestnut woods ③.

(This turning is easy to miss as it is not marked.) Continue through the woods, taking the path that goes uphill and to the right. When you reach a signpost, turn left on the road to Roubert, passing through a wooded area which provides welcome shade in summer. Bear left and continue to Sicard. Turn left when you reach a crossroads, following the GR 36 footpath, then turn left on to the main road, the D 911, which leads back to Puy l'Evêque. This lovely road following the Lot can be busy, so proceed with care ④.

Points of Interest

① Puy l'Evêque, with its golden-coloured houses running up the banks of the river, and its church and castle, is one of the most attractive towns on the Lot. To get the best view or photograph, cross the bridge and view the town from the other side of the river.

② Cahors wine was once more popular in England than the wines of Bordeaux. Now the deep red, almost black, wines are enjoying renewed popularity. Puy l'Evêque is on the official Cahors wine route, which takes you to Fumel and back to Cahors along the other side of the river.

③ After grapes for wine, nuts are the most popular crop in the Lot valley. Walnuts are the most common, but many other sorts of nuts are cultivated too.

④ The Lot valley is heavily wooded, one of the reasons why the area is so attractive, particularly in summer. The green of the trees contrasts with the white limestone cliffs, reflected in the river's sparkling waters.

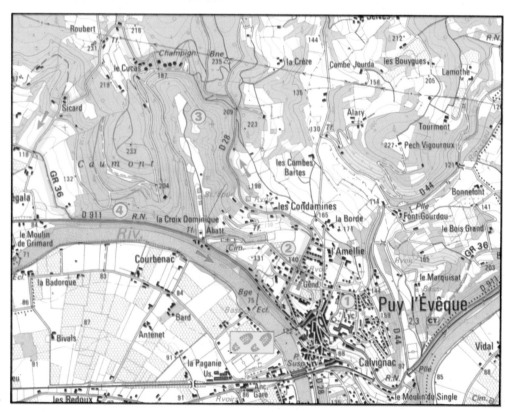

WALK 50B: 4.5KM/ALLOW 1¼ HOURS

Mercuès

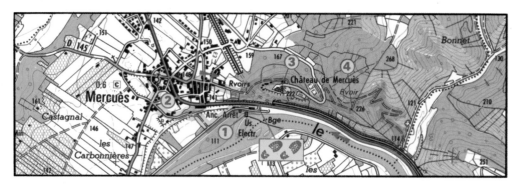

This walk up to the Château de Mercuès involves a fair amount of uphill walking, but there is also a lot of shade, so it is not too difficult in hot weather. A statue of the Blessed Virgin is an added attraction along the way.

Route Directions

Start from the footpath which leads to the river from the D 911 in Mercuès. Turn right and follow the river past the electricity works ①.

Continue uphill to rejoin the road at an electricity pylon. Keep climbing until you reach a crossroads of five roads, where you take the road opposite and to the right. Keep to the left, passing the church, and then turn right to reach the town hall in Mercuès ②.

Pass the town hall to the right, and continue on this road for some 500m, until it peters out as it passes between two reservoirs.

Where the road ends, there is a lovely view of the Lot. Follow the footpath which leads on from the road. At a fork take the right-hand path and go on to the entrance to the château ③.

Follow the path down from the château until you reach a little turning on to a footpath on the right. The path along the cliffs winds round steeply, to reach a statue of the Blessed Virgin ④.

The views from here are breathtaking. From the statue, take a footpath leading downhill. This eventually winds down to a railway bridge ⑤.

Pass under the bridge and follow the footpath along the river to the right, which leads back to the main road.

Points of Interest

① Although the Lot has now been developed for leisure use, fishing and boating, it is still an important source of hydroelectric power.

The Château de Mercuès has its origins in the 13th century ▼

② The little village of Mercuès is divided into two. One part is grouped round a Romanesque church, believed to date from the 12th century and altered during the 17th century, and the rest around the château.

③ The Château de Mercuès, which towers fortress-like above the village, was during the 15th century the country residence of the Bishops of Cahors. At this time, it is believed, its beautiful terraces and gardens were created. There was a castle on the site as long ago as the 12th century, but this was virtually destroyed during the Hundred Years War. Today the original cellars are used to mature wine, and you can taste, and buy, from a vast selection of local wines. The castle itself is now a luxurious hotel.

④ The statue of the Blessed Virgin dates back to when the Bishops of Cahors inhabited the château. She may have been given her commanding position overlooking the Lot for the benefit of boats on the river, along which Cahors wine used to be shipped.

⑤ The building of the railways along the river during the 19th century caused the navigation system of the Lot to fall into disuse. However, in recent years the locks have been restored in keeping with their original style. Many date back to the 17th century.

The Blessed Virgin, Mercuès ▼

The Basque hill country

Waves of forest and pasture-clad hills paint the Basque country in vivid shades of green. This tour explores some of the best of its scenic delights, with broad vistas and a preview of the frontier peaks. Several cols are crossed, mostly by narrow but good-quality roads, and with gradients that are generally not excessive. Lingering patches of snow, however, can make driving conditions difficult in springtime.

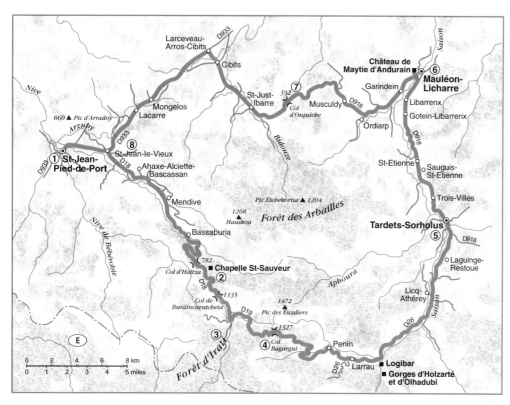

Climb down the eastern side, with some tight hairpin bends, to Larrau (13km) and 2.5km further on cross a bridge and pass the buildings of Logibar standing on the right of the road beside the river. A track here leads to the start of the first walk. In a little under 15km from Logibar the D 26 joins the D 918 to reach Tardets-Sorholus ⑤.

Continue on the D 918 for 13km to the edge of Mauléon-Licharre ⑥.

Just after passing the entrance sign to Mauléon turn sharp left (with care), still on the D 918, signposted Col d'Osquiche and St-Jean-Pied-de-Port. At a T-junction 500m later turn left again and begin a gentle ascent for some 18km to Col d'Osquiche ⑦.

Cross the col (392m) and descend through St-Just-Ibarre and Cibits to reach Larceveau-Arros-Cibits, 10km from the col, where the second walk begins. Turn left at the major T-junction and follow the D 933 for 11.5km to St-Jean-le-Vieux ⑧.

Continue for another 4.5km to return to St-Jean-Pied-de-Port.

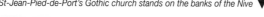

St-Jean-Pied-de-Port's Gothic church stands on the banks of the Nive ▼

Route Directions

The drive starts from St-Jean-Pied-de-Port ①.

Leave St-Jean-Pied-de-Port following directions for St-Palais and Mauléon. After 4.5km turn right in St-Jean-le-Vieux on to the D 18, signposted Ahaxe-Alciette-Bascassan and Mendive. Follow the D 18 to begin the long climb to a series of cols. After Bassaburia, on a green crest about 1km beyond Col d'Haltza, just out of sight on the left of the road, stands the Chapelle St-Sauveur ②.

Continue to climb among beech woods until you reach Col de Burdincurutcheta (1135m), which is 13km from Mendive. Descend for 2.5km to a pastureland basin and a small tarn where the road forks. Bear left and shortly afterwards enter the Forêt d'Irati ③.

Rising once again through forest, continue for 7km, through les Chalets d'Irati, until you arrive at Col Bagargui (1327m) ④.

Points of Interest

① An attractive small town on the River Nive, St-Jean-Pied-de-Port was formerly the capital of Basse Navarre and a meeting point for thousands of pilgrims making their way to the shrine of Santiago de Compostela in Spain. The town has many interesting features; not least is the pretty bridge over the Nive which makes a focal point for picturesque views along the river. The old part of St-Jean is contained within 15th-century fortified walls, while the Citadelle owes its sturdiness to Vauban's 17th-century design. A walk along the ramparts affords views over the town's narrow streets and alleyways.

② The Chapelle St-Sauveur, the setting for an annual Corpus Christi pilgrimage, is barn-like in size and appearance and at first glance would seem to belong to a local hill farm. But surrounding it are 13 small crosses, with a larger stone pedestal bearing a crude but powerful crucifix near by. A plaque fixed to one wall remembers with gratitude the help given by the Basques of Irati to

country, to the conflicting delight of ornithologists and pigeon hunters. In October Col Bagargui is a fine vantage point from which to view the flight of birds such as honey buzzards, storks, cranes, kites and, of course, thousands of wild pigeons. But to Basques pigeon hunting with nets and guns, or *la chasse à la palombe,* is virtually an institution.

⑤ Tardets-Sorholus is a centre of Basque folklore. A small town enjoying fine long views to the frontier mountains, it has a charming arcaded square. The Chapelle de la Madeleine stands on a peak high above the valley to the north. A centre of pilgrimage twice a year, it also gives magnificent views over the high Pyrenees.

⑥ Mauléon and Licharre stand on opposite banks of the River Saison 13km downstream from Tardets. Capital of the Soule district, Mauléon is an old feudal town clustered beneath the ruins of its 15th-century castle. A Renaissance château with a splendid roof stands on the corner of Rue de la Navarre on the left bank of the river. The town is now noted

▲ *A shopping street in the old quarter of St-Jean-Pied-de-Port*

for the manufacture of Basque berets and espadrilles.

⑦ Another site for the *chasse à la palombe,* Col d'Osquiche marks the border between Basse Navarre and the Soule district. Despite its modest altitude (392m) it affords extensive panoramas over the surrounding area. The approach from the east is especially fine.

⑧ In the Middle Ages St-Jean-le-Vieux stood on the Chemin de St-Jacques, and beside the road in nearby Aphat-d'Ospital can be seen the near-derelict 12th-century Chapelle St-Blaise, a tiny place of worship used by the pilgrims.

Mauléon has a church and cemetery in the Basque style ▼

▲ *The Chapelle St-Sauveur*

Belgian forces 'on the long march to freedom' in World War II. The chapel is normally kept locked when not in use.

③ Sprawling across both sides of the frontier, the Forêt d'Irati is one of the great forests of the Pyrenees, predominantly of beech and yew but with some pine. In past centuries large quantities of Irati timber were used for ship-building. Today the forest has leafy trails winding through it, and picnic areas alongside the Burdincurutcheta-Bagargui road. Cross-country skiing is encouraged in winter.

④ During the autumn migrations millions of birds cross the Basque

LIMESTONE RAVINES

South-east of Larrau dramatic limestone clefts slice the green hills that swell towards the frontier ridge. Scoured out over the millennia by mountain streams, these great chasms are distinctive features of the Basque country. The Gorges d'Holzarté, d'Olhadubi, de Kakouéta and d'Ehujarré are linked by the long-distance footpath GR 10, which allows their tentative exploration,

sometimes from above, sometimes in their very depths. The Kakouéta gorge, accessible from the lovely valley of St-Engrâce, is by far the best of the managed ravines of the Pyrenees. A catwalk and handrails have been provided to safeguard walkers on sections requiring particular care as they pick their way alongside the rushing stream, brushing against the dripping, overhanging rock walls that

rise some 300m above the stream bed, and which in places are less than 5m apart. The neighbouring Gorges d'Ehujarré, cutting south of St-Engrâce village, are less often visited by the public, though they have been used by generations of shepherds to transfer sheep from the valley to the high pastures of Pic Lakhoura (1877m). The gorges of Olhadubi and Holzarté are briefly explored on the first walk.

The Gorges d'Holzarté

THE PYRENEES

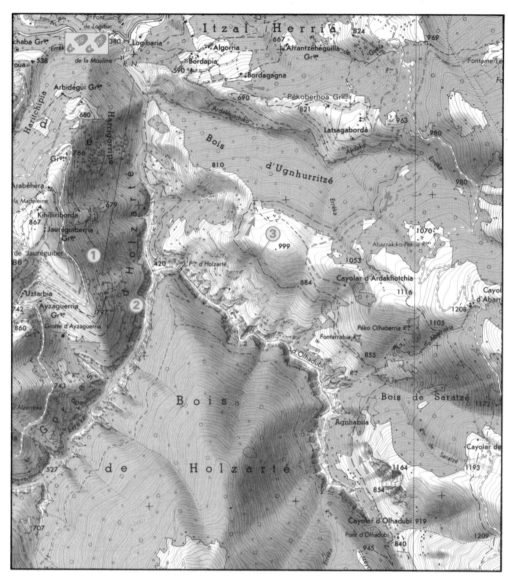

Points of Interest

① The stupendous Gorges d'Holzarté slice a 3-km cleft in the limestone hills that line the frontier. Steep grey walls tower 200m above the stream, each band and layer of rock revealing chapters in the geological history of these ancient Basque hills.

② Built in 1920, the footbridge suspended across the mouth of the Gorges d'Olhadubi is of a type found in other mountain ranges, including the Himalaya. Although it tends to bounce and swing from side to side as walkers cross, it is well protected and considered safe.

③ From the belvedere path above the Gorges d'Olhadubi there are splendid views not only of the depths of Olhadubi, but also to Pic d'Orhy (2017m) to the west, and north-west towards Col Bagargui. The hillside meadows are starred with gentians, orchids and other alpine flowers in late spring.

This strenuous walk crosses a foot-bridge suspended 200m above the river and descends a steep hillside. Though safe, the bridge may be difficult for vertigo sufferers, in which case return by the upward path to give a walk of about 1¼ hours.

Route Directions

Start from the parking area, reached by a track heading south 100m before the auberge at Logibaria. Leave the parking area by the GR 10 long-distance footpath, heading south beside the stream. In 10 minutes it climbs quite steeply and goes through beech woods. Out of the woods continue ahead to gain views into the Gorges d'Holzarté ①.

The path curves round the hillside and comes to the suspension bridge hanging across the entrance to the Gorges d'Olhadubi ②.

Go over the bridge and resume climbing through beech woods. On reaching a broad track crossing the path at right-angles, turn left. This track may be muddy in places. It leads above the unseen lip of the Olhadubi gorge and reaches a wooden footbridge at its head. Over the bridge a narrow path swings north-west among trees, then traverses an open hillside. Enter woods again, cross two minor streams and a few paces beyond the second stream, on the woodland edge, the path forks. Take the left-hand, lower, path which gives superb views over the gorges ③.

After passing high above the suspension bridge the path rounds a mountain spur, enters more beech woods and joins a broad forest track. Bear left. Ignore a second track which breaks away to the left a few paces after, and continue ahead. Pass above a few farm buildings and almost immediately afterwards take a path heading left. This enters some woods, then follows a fence on the left, crosses a stile by a barn and descends a steep grassy spur to the left of woodland. On reaching a crossing path bear right on to a level stretch that enters woods, then descends to return to the parking area.

Huge gorges cut through the limestone hills south-east of Larrau. Among these are the Gorges d'Olhadubi, which are crossed by a wooden footbridge that was erected in the 1920s ▶

209

Basque farms

This gentle walk makes an ideal family outing, following a series of farm tracks, minor roads and footpaths from one farm to another. After rain it may be a little muddy in places. There is a small stream to cross.

A well-maintained farmhouse and an old stone barn testify to the prosperity of the Basque farming area ▶

the valley behind it. The way becomes a tree-lined lane leading to the hamlet of Chahara ②.

Down the slope out of Chahara the lane bends sharply to the left. Leave it to head right, then go left again on a track heading towards a large farmhouse. Pass along the right-hand side of the house and continue ahead along the farm track, cross a small stream on stepping stones, and continue straight ahead between fields.

Pleasant rounded hills rise on the right. Pass a barn on the left and at a crossing of tracks by a house bear left, and 30m later go sharp right along a hedge-lined track. This leads through a small patch of woodland and soon comes to yet another house and a lane. Go left, then leave the lane a few paces later and head to the right towards a farmhouse.

Bear left in front of this and walk along a farm track extending from it. This leads to yet another farm with an old barn nearby. Just beyond the farm leave the track and bear left on a rough track which crosses a stream and veers left as if to follow it. Dog-roses and arum lilies grow alongside the stream. The way now traces the lower edge of an oak wood and comes to the main road near a house opposite the farming hamlet of Utxiat.

With care, cross the road to Utxiat. Follow the farm drive for about 50m and fork left between fields. Continue along the farm track for about 3km to reach the small village of Cibits ③.

Turn left at the crossroads and walk down the road to Larceveau.

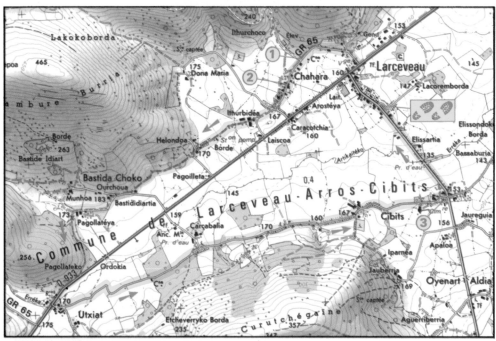

Route Directions

Start from the car park next to the church in the village of Larceveau. From the church walk along the road a short distance to join the main road, the D 933, and turn right. After 100m turn left up a narrow road, following red-and-white waymarks. This is the GR 65 long-distance footpath ①.

The path veers to the left to give views looking over Larceveau and

◀ *Dairy farming underpins the economy of Basque villages such as Utxiat*

Points of Interest

① The footpath here follows the Chemin de St-Jacques pilgrim route, which covers more than 1000km on its journey from Le Puy in Auvergne to St-Jean-Pied-de-Port.

② In Chahara, note the inscription and date (1793) carved on the lintel of a doorway of a house on the right. Such inscriptions are typical of Basque houses, many bearing a short homily or the name of the builder.

③ Cibits is a neat, well-cared-for village with attractive farms and whitewashed houses. Next to the church stands the *fronton* or wall against which *pelota*, the Basque national game, is played.

High peaks of Béarn

Two cols with contrasting features highlight this tour: Col de Marie Blanque, embraced by forest and soft green pastures, and Col d'Aubisque, a land of rocky peaks emerging from deep shadowed valleys. These mark the start of the High Pyrenees: lofty mountains, squat grey houses and flower-studded meadows. Col d'Aubisque is regularly blocked by snow from November to June, and the route round to Col de Soulor demands care.

▲ *Oloron-Ste-Marie's fine church, formerly a cathedral, dates from the 12th century, but the choir was rebuilt after a fire two centuries later*

Route Directions

The drive starts from Oloron-Ste-Marie ①.

Head southwards out of town on the N134-E7 along the Gave d'Aspe, following signs for Sarrance and Col du Somport. After 13km take a feeder road on the right, signposted Escot, which then swings left to cross the main road (take care here) on to a narrow unclassified road leading into Escot. In the heart of the village turn sharp right near the church on to a road signposted Col de Marie Blanque, enter the Barescou valley and climb steadily for 10km through beech woods to Col de Marie Blanque (1035m). Beware of slow-moving timber lorries on this road. Descend the eastern side to emerge from the forest into the open grassland of the Benou pastures. The first walk starts from here ②.

Follow the road down to the Vallée d'Ossau, turning right on to the D 934 ③.

Continue on the main road for another 7.5km to reach Laruns ④.

Drive through Laruns, following signs for Spain and Col d'Aubisque. South

of town the road forks. Bear left on the D 918, signposted Col d'Aubisque, and begin the ascent to the pass. After Eaux-Bonnes the road becomes more demanding, with frequent hairpin bends. Continue through the ski resort of Gourette, with more tight bends, and over the Crêtes Blanches, to reach Col d'Aubisque (1709m) ⑤.

The road now winds for 10km along the exposed corniche of the Cirque du Litor to reach Col de Soulor (1474m) ⑥.

Immediately before the summit of the pass turn left on to the D 126, signposted Pau. The descent is lovely: first through pastures, then into a large basin dotted with barns and farms. After 8.5km the road passes the village of Arbéost, the start of the second walk. Below Arbéost the valley narrows and is densely wooded. The road now follows the River Ouzon through tiny hamlets and villages for 18km before

reaching Asson. At a crossroads in Asson turn left on to the D 35 for Bruges-Capbis-Mifaget and Louvie-Juzon. After 1km turn left again at a T-junction to stay on the D 35. Follow the D 35, parallel to the main range of the Pyrenees, to reach Bruges ⑦.

From Bruges continue on the D 35 for almost 12km, rising steadily through woodland before descending into Louvie-Juzon. Turn left at a T-junction on to the D 934, cross the river and turn right at the next junction on to a minor road signposted Buzy and Oloron. After 3km this road passes Arudy ⑧.

After Arudy continue on the D 920 for 11km to a major T-junction. Turn left on to the N134-E7 to return to Oloron-Ste-Marie.

Ornamentation such as this sculpted window surround can be seen on Bielle's 15th- and 16th-century houses, many of which have slate roofs ▶

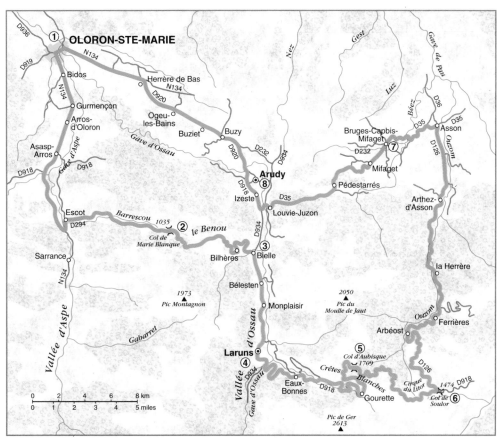

THE BROWN BEAR

The Ossau valley is one of the last remaining haunts in the Pyrenees of the European brown bear (*Ursus arctos*). Virtually hunted out of existence (though now protected), this usually timid creature has become something of a *cause célèbre* among conservationists who are fighting to save the last few survivors.

For generations the brown bear faced great hostility among mountain shepherds, who blamed it for attacks on their flocks. Hunters sought it as the ultimate prize, while others sold bear fat as a cure for baldness. Elsewhere individual cubs were captured and taught to dance, and

until World War I could be seen travelling with their keepers throughout the range. Even after a hunting ban had been imposed in 1962 (when there were only about 50 left), bears were still being shot.

Despite claims to the contrary, brown bears are not normally dangerous and could never rival the ferocious reputation of the grizzly. These shy, peaceful creatures inhabit lonely forests, where they live on a largely herbivorous diet. In recognition of the plight that faces them the commune of Laruns has made an effort to protect any bears that might still exist in local forests by controlling timber extraction.

▲ *Pony-carts are an additional hazard on Col d'Aubisque*

Points of Interest

① Oloron-Ste-Marie stands at the confluence of two rivers, the Gave d'Aspe and the Gave d'Ossau. The Romans had an encampment on the hill occupied today by the interesting Ste-Croix quarter, from whose Promenade Bellevue a fine view overlooks the town. On the other side of the Gave d'Aspe rises the 12th-century Eglise Ste-Marie, once a cathedral, with an ornately carved marble doorway of magnificent proportions.

② On the eastern side of Col de Marie Blanque the Benou pastureland is a delightfully tranquil spot with a superb panorama of distant high mountains. It is a popular place for picnics and a base for numerous walks. A little below the pastures a grassy basin holds a small tarn from which there are yet more fine views.

③ Seen from the pass road the grey slate roofs of Bielle blend together in attractive patterns. The village, formerly the capital of the Vallée d'Ossau, has a number of houses of the 15th and 16th centuries, a church with a sculpted doorway, and a touching war memorial in the main street.

④ Laruns, a small, neat town occupying a pleasant open valley site, makes a good base for walking and mountaineering holidays. On 15 August each year the inhabitants, wearing colourful Ossau costumes,

gather to dance *en fête* to a one-man band.

⑤ One of the Pyrenean passes often included in the three-week-long Tour de France, Col d'Aubisque offers a remarkable panorama. To enjoy it to the full, climb the grass-covered hillside to the south of the road. The stark limestone rock faces of Pic de Ger (2613m) dominate the Cirque de Gourette in the south, and from it a vast array of peaks spread out to both east and west. North of the col, from the mound which rises above the hotel, you peer down into a maze of low green valleys.

⑥ Separated from the Aubisque by the Cirque du Litor, Col de Soulor (1474m) also offers a fine panorama: perhaps not so extensive, but interesting nevertheless for the striking contrast between the impressive mountain peaks and the pastoral hillsides.

⑦ Bruges is an attractive village set in the midst of agricultural countryside below the Pyrenean foothills. It has a wide village square bordered by an arcaded town hall. Pride of place is taken by a war memorial.

⑧ South-east of Oloron, Arudy stands on a curious loop of the Gave d'Ossau, caused by a bank of moraine from one of the great Pyrenean glaciers which scoured out the Ossau valley. The village church houses an exhibition depicting the prehistory of the range, as well as displays of local flora and fauna.

▲ *Bielle is divided in two by a stream that flows from the Gave d'Ossau. A plain church stands in the village centre*

The Benou pastures

THE PYRENEES

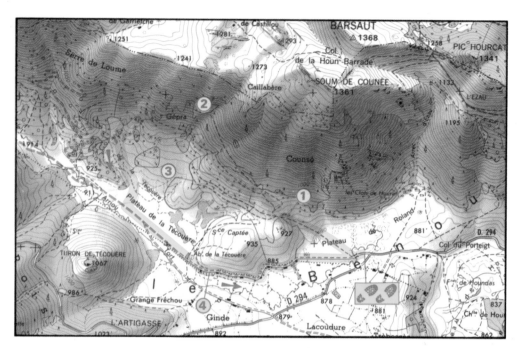

The rich pastures of Benou ▼

This short, easy walk makes a circuit of gentle pastureland with delightful views. Footpaths are not always clearly marked, but no difficulties should be encountered. Large herds of dairy cattle and horses graze unattended.

Route Directions

Start from the D 294 on the Plateau de Benou, beyond a cattle grid and where the fences end, where you can pull off the road. To the north of the road a gravel farm track heads west towards farm buildings. Follow it for 100m, cross a bridge over a stream and then leave the track to head across pastures, bearing right on a path rising towards a grassy saddle ①.

Continue straight ahead, skirting the right-hand side of the next level of pasture. The path is faint at first, but soon becomes clearer and leads to a second partial saddle marked by holly trees. Pass this to come into a higher section of pastureland, and keep to the right-hand side. The hillsides above are clothed with beech and yew ②.

Tracks passing through meadows make for gentle walking ▼

The path apparently disappears here, but keep straight on towards a grassy bluff with more holly trees. From it there is a view into a pastureland basin divided by a spur clad with beech woods. Go down into the basin and veer left to the southern section, beyond the spur. On the far side the narrow Arriou stream flows down from the hills to make a popular picnic site. All this pastureland is heavily grazed in summer ③.

Just before the stream bear left and walk down the pasture to regain the farm track by a cattle trough. (Do not stray too far to the left as the ground is marshy.) Continue along the track, passing a barn on the right and a low bluff on the left ④.

The track leads back to the D 294 and the parking area.

Points of Interest

① Pic de Ger (2613m) dominates the view to the south-east. This conspicuous rocky peak, rising above Gourette on the Aubisque road, somehow appears more formidable than the loftier peaks behind it.

② The Bois du Bergoueits, on the east flank of Col de Marie Blanque, is mainly beech trees. Footpaths lead into the woods: some are overgrown but towards the col they are well-trodden and clear.

③ Cattle and horses are brought to the pastures from Ossau valley farms for summer grazing. Foals are

born here and cattle milked for cheese; the straps of their cowbells are inscribed with the name of the owner's farm or commune.

④ Before the cattle arrive in late spring the pastures are rich in wild flowers, gentians and orchids being especially abundant. On a low bluff beside the track innumerable alpine plants cushion exposed rocks.

To the Pas de Tartas

Scenically enchanting, with a mixture of high mountain views and pastoral tranquillity, this walk has sections that are steep and a little strenuous, but nothing too severe. After wet weather boots should be worn; otherwise, trainers should be adequate.

▲ A track in high pastureland

Route Directions

Start by the church in Arbéost ①.

Head south-west along a minor road, signposted as a dead-end, and soon descend to les Bourinquets, a hamlet of barns and cottages ②.

The road now becomes a track. At

Peaks above the Pas de Tartas ▼

the foot of the slope veer to the left, through trees and then steeply uphill. Go through a small meadow, with a ruined barn on the left. The way divides. Continue ahead on a narrow path that slants to the left. Pass under an avalanche chute and carry on along a hillside shelf leading to another meadow and a broad track. After 100m the track swings left and climbs steeply.

At the top of the slope turn right on to a crossing track. Follow this beyond the cliff face of the Pas de Tartas to a short grass slope offering views of the valley head ③.

Retrace the upward path to the top of the steep track. Continue ahead, soon among trees, and come to a level terrace lined with beech trees. At a water trough bear left along a stony path between low walls. Beyond a group of barns and cattle byres enter some beech and box woods. Follow waymarks to reach another barn. Bear right and follow a wall. Go through more beech woods to come to a farm track, where you bear left ④.

The track is now surfaced and winds downhill. Bear left when it forks, and take a footpath on the left to continue downhill among hazel thickets. Cross a road and continue straight ahead to reach the D 126. Bear right and follow the road back to Arbéost.

Points of Interest

① In splendid walking country, Arbéost lines the Soulor road. Architecturally typical of Béarn, it is unpretentious, with a church and small café/bar facing each other across the road.

② The hamlet of les Bourinquets, a collection of low farming cottages and barns, is rather dilapidated yet has great charm in its half-hidden situation.

③ From the slope above the Pas de Tartas an uninterrupted view looks south into the Cirque du Litor.

◄ *Les Bourinquets is a pleasant farming hamlet below Arbéost*

High overhead Pic du Petit Gabizos and Pic du Grand Gabizos are linked by the cliffs of the Crêtes des Tailladés Blanques.

④ Between Arbéost and Col du Soulor to the south a beautiful basin of pasture hangs as a great green shelf below the road. Dotted with barns, small farms and drystone walls forming low boundaries, it is one of the walk's best features.

Across Col du Tourmalet

South of Lourdes foothills rise to the high peaks and wild contortions of the Néouvielle massif. Col du Tourmalet nudges this untamed land and its crossing makes a demanding drive on a road that is busy in summer. (It is closed in winter.) Before tackling this, however, the route from Lourdes to Bagnères-de-Bigorre explores a little-known landscape of narrow lanes and sudden green hills.

Route Directions

The drive starts from Lourdes ①.

From the centre of town follow signs for the N21 to Argelès-Gazost and the Pyrenees. In 3km the road veers to the right to cross the Gave de Pau at Pont Neuf. Immediately before this, turn left on to a minor road signposted Lugagnan and Ger, and left again at a T-junction on to the D 26 for Juncalas and Pouzac. The road goes through wooded country to Juncalas; and 2.5km later, turn right on to a narrow road signposted Pouzac and winding into hill country.

Below Arrodets-ez-Angles there are fine views to the north. As you descend, go straight ahead at an unmarked crossroads to reach the hamlet of Neuilh, 7.5km from the turn-off near Juncalas. Pass a large convalescent home, and 2.5km from Neuilh take a tricky sharp right turn into the lovely Oussouet valley, signposted Fontaine de Labassère. Follow the Oussouet stream for 6km until the road forks. Bear left and, climbing steeply, pass beneath the church at Soulagnets and continue ahead at a junction soon after to reach Labassère ②.

Immediately past the village church turn right and descend on the D 88 to Bagnères-de-Bigorre ③.

Bear right at a T-junction by the Casino; pass the Musée Salies and the Grands Thermes and turn left at another junction, signposted Route des Cols, then right on the D 935 for la Mongie. After 5.5km this brings you to Campan ④.

The ski resort of la Mongie ▼

Continue up the valley for 6.5km and in Ste-Marie-de-Campan turn right on to the D 918, the approach to the Col du Tourmalet. Climbing easily at first, the road then negotiates hairpin bends to reach la Mongie ⑤.

After la Mongie the climb continues for another 4km to gain the Col du Tourmalet ⑥.

Descend through more hairpins, one of which cuts back to the left (south) to a café/bar at Pont de la Gaubie. The first walk starts here. Continue through the valley to reach Barèges ⑦.

Continue on the D 918 to reach Luz-St-Sauveur ⑧.

Bear right at a junction signposted Lourdes, cross the river and turn left at the next junction on to the D 921. The road leads through the Gorge de Luz and Pierrefitte-Nestalas to arrive at Argelès-Gazost. The second walk starts above Argelès-Gazost ⑨.

▲ *Luz has a church that was fortified in the 14th century*

Continue down the valley on the N21 to return to Lourdes.

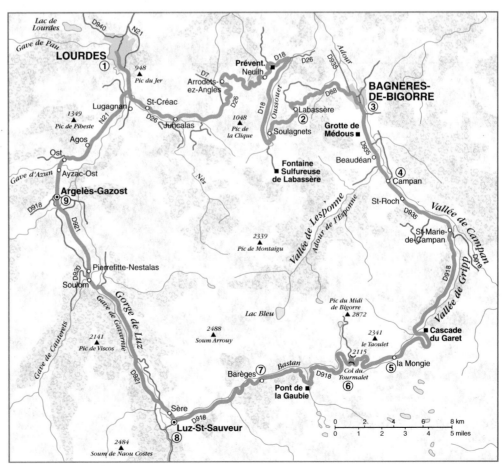

Points of Interest

① Until the peasant girl Bernadette Soubirous saw visions of the Virgin Mary in 1858, Lourdes was simply a small foothill town overlooked by a medieval castle. It has since become a world-famous pilgrimage centre for Catholics, with four million annual visitors. The Grotte de Massabielle is the focus for pilgrims, while the massive underground Basilique St-Pie X is capable of holding 20,000 people. Apart from its religious significance, Lourdes also has the fascinating Musée Pyrénéen housed in the castle.

② The crest-top village of Labassère has the singular remains of a one-time castle keep, the Donjon de Labassère, perched on a rocky knoll above the church. A bust of the *curé* Jacques Pédefer (1756-1854), who discovered the Fontaine de Labassère, adorns the village square.

③ Bagnères-de-Bigorre is a fashionable resort and thermal spa which was known to the Romans. The nearby Grottes de Médous, where the underground course of the Adour flows beneath lovely limestone formations, may be explored by boat.

④ A 16th-century covered market occupies a corner of the main street of Campan, a village with some interesting buildings. The church has an unusual belfry and an ornate retable. In the churchyard a porch contains a wooden crucifix, and there is a touching war memorial near by.

⑤ La Mongie, on the Tourmalet road, is an ugly modern ski resort, the highest and biggest in the Pyrenees: with Barèges on the far side of the col it has 69 pistes. The top lift reaches 2440m and there are many exhilarating runs.

⑥ At 2115m Col du Tourmalet is the highest road col in the Pyrenees. From the pass a toll road followed by an hour's walk will lead to the summit of Pic du Midi de Bigorre (2872m), bristling with antennae and the site of a famous observatory founded in 1878. Needless to say, the summit is a noted viewpoint.

⑦ Barèges makes an excellent base for walking tours in the neighbouring Néouvielle mountains, and enjoys a good reputation for its skiing facilities. Originally the village prospered as a spa under the patronage of Napoleon III.

⑧ Luz and St-Sauveur are separated by the defile of the Gave de Pau. St-Sauveur is an old thermal spa, while Luz is the main town, a small resort with a fortified 12th-century so-called Templars' church (in fact built by the Knights Hospitallers), and a Parc National information centre with displays of the region's fauna and flora.

⑨ Situated in a sunny protected corner at the mouth of the Val d'Azun, Argelès-Gazost is a neat resort and thermal spa. The picturesque village of St-Savin lies to the south, while across the valley flight displays of birds of prey are given in the ruined Donjon des Aigles.

▲ The Basilique du Rosaire in the pilgrimage centre of Lourdes

THE TOUR DE FRANCE

Although the first Tour de France took place in 1903, it was another seven years before the race visited the Pyrenees. In mid-July this classic marathon now punishes cyclists with stages that climb the highest Pyrenean passes, including Col du Tourmalet.

Since it was first included in 1927, the col has formed a crucial part of more than thirty Tours, a gruelling challenge that is often the crux of a stage which crosses other cols such as the Peyresourde and Aspin.

The Tourmalet is a natural favourite, with spectators gathering in huge crowds to see who will win the coveted polka-dot jersey of the King of the Mountains – a prestigious award considered second only to that of overall race winner. To win such an award requires not only strength and tenacity, but considerable daring, and those who wear the *maillot à pois du meilleur grimpeur* thereby gain for themselves a heroic reputation.

To stand any possibility of finishing the Tour in Paris as overall victor, cyclists must score well in the mountains. Here the gap between first and second place may be measured in minutes rather than fractions of seconds, as elsewhere.

▲ A TV mast and an observatory stand on the top of Pic du Midi de Bigorre

At nearly 3000m, Pic du Midi offers far-reaching views ▼

To the edge of the Néouvielle massif

THE PYRENEES

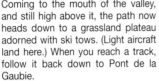

This moderately taxing circular walk gives a brief introduction to the Néouvielle massif by visiting some of its northern tarns. Paths are good for most of the way and few difficulties should be encountered.

Coming to the mouth of the valley, and still high above it, the path now heads down to a grassland plateau adorned with ski tows. (Light aircraft land here.) When you reach a track, follow it back down to Pont de la Gaubie.

Points of Interest

① The GR 10 is a classic, 700km-long walk which crosses the Pyrenees from the Atlantic to the Mediterranean.

② The dammed Lac d'Escoubous gives a preview of the Néouvielle mountains. A simple unmanned refuge nearby provides basic accommodation for walkers.

③ Pic du Midi de Bigorre dominates the view north. A popular climb for 200 years, the summit has now been disfigured by a TV mast, antennae and a famous observatory.

④ The fast-growing sport of *parapente* is taught on slopes overlooking Pont de la Gaubie. The gaily-coloured parachutes can often be seen floating overhead.

Route Directions

Start from the parking area at Pont de la Gaubie, which is on the D 918 about 7km below Col du Tourmalet.

Walk up the road a short distance to a path heading into the valley on the right, signposted Etangs d'Escoubous. This leads to a major track to be seen a little higher up the left-hand slope, beginning 150m from the restaurant. The track is part of the GR 10 long-distance footpath ①.

Ahead is a small rocky peak with an obvious saddle on its right. This is the saddle to make for. Follow the track heading south. It eases to the left, crosses a stream emerging from a side glen and reaches a junction of paths. Ignore the one which heads left and continue straight ahead, soon rising in zigzags over increasingly stony terrain, to reach the Coubous tarn ②.

Beyond, unseen from here, lie several more small tarns. It is worth making an hour-long detour to skirt the left-hand side of the lake and follow the path for grand views.

Retrace the path for a short distance, but instead of taking the zigzag route down, continue ahead along a narrow, minor trail which leaves the main path to traverse the hillside. Soon there are views to Pic du Midi de Bigorre, ahead to the north-east ③.

Cross below a marshy bowl sliced with streams. Cairns guide the way where the path is otherwise ill-defined. Then the trail becomes clearer and crosses a few stone chutes and narrow scree slopes (caution is needed here). Continue along the hillside, looking out for wild flowers and marmots. Ahead it is possible to see *parapentes* in flight ④.

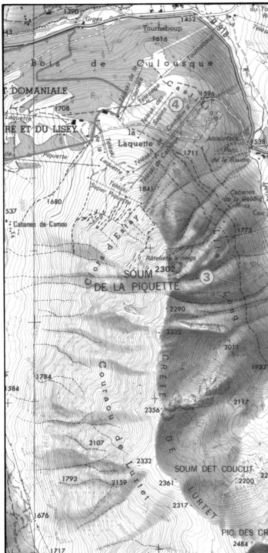

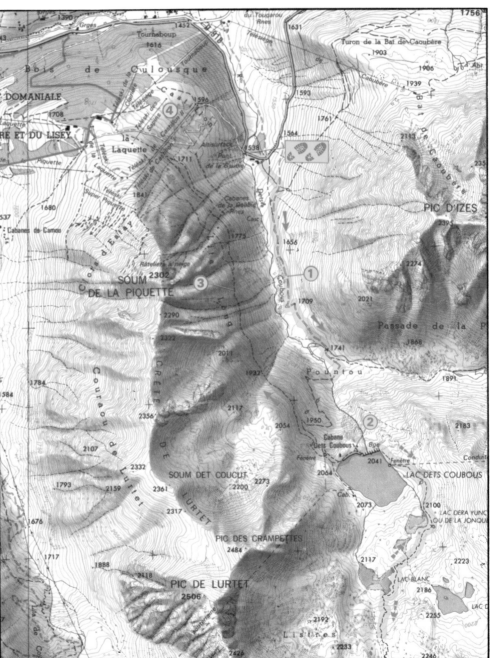

217

Around Mont de Gez

Mont de Gez guards the entrance to Val d'Azun above Argelès-Gazost, and this tour around it makes a pleasant outing among woods, pastures and farms. There is some climbing and descending, but none of it severe.

Route Directions

Start from the centre of Gez, reached by taking the second turning right from the D 918 above Argelès-Gazost ①.

Leave Gez heading west (up the valley). On the outskirts of the village, where the road forks, bear left, signposted Haugarou Chalet-Refuge. When the road veers to the left, go straight ahead along a track towards a farm. Continue on a paved path between stone walls to a road. Cross this to go straight ahead ②.

Pass a water trough stained with orange lichen and continue among trees to reach a track among silver birches. Keep straight on to pass a second water trough. Continue to reach a junction of tracks with a third water trough, with a barn on the left and another ahead on the right. Turn left on a stony track which then bears right alongside a wood.

The track veers to the right again towards some buildings, but a footpath continues straight ahead. Follow this to a crossing of paths and turn hard left, almost parallel with the former path. This new trail soon veers almost due east through the woods. Passing a meadow on the right, the trail reaches a track. Bear right along this to pass between Mont de Gez and Pic d'Arragnat ③.

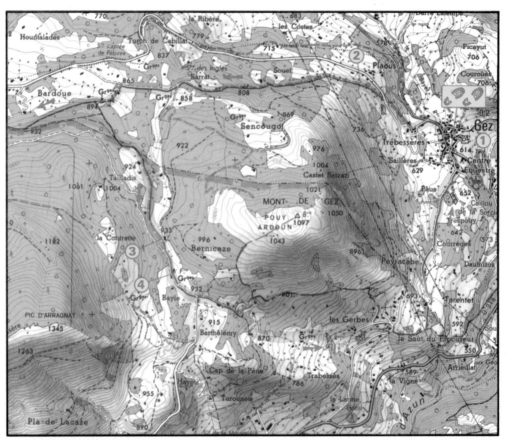

▲ A stone water trough stained with lichen is passed on the walk

Losing height, join another track and continue straight ahead, now with views across Val d'Azun ④.

The track turns hard right here. Leave it to walk briefly downhill, then turn left on to a path marked Gez/Mont de Gez. (There is a barn in the next meadow.) Climb uphill among trees to a path junction with a marker stone. Turn right and descend through woods. At a junction of trails on the edge of meadowland bear left. Below and to the right is the tarn of Arcizans-Avant. After a level section the path, marked by yellow waymarks, zig-zags down through trees, beneath

power lines and on to a narrow road. Turn left to return to Gez.

Points of Interest

① The small farming community of Gez overlooks Argelès-Gazost from a natural hillside terrace. Every road entrance is marked by a large stone cross.

② The drystone walls that run alongside the paved mule-path are hung with wall pennywort, or navelwort (*Umbilicus rupestris*), which bears flowers on long spikes between May and July.

▲ A triangular hay store (top)
Cattle byres in Gez-Argelès (above)

③ Mont de Gez and Pic d'Arragnat are the eastern outliers of a gently ascending ridge of hills that form the north wall of Val d'Azun. Clear trails wind along it.

④ Open meadows and trim villages characterise Val d'Azun. Its western end climbs to Col du Soulor, while to the south lie the narrow valleys of Estaing and Arrens and the raw heights of Balaitous.

Painted caves of the Ariège

Prehistory haunts the Ariège, a land of grotto-riddled hills and dolmen-topped crags. Crossing Col de Port, Port de Lers and Col d'Agnès, this route explores that history in the valleys of the Arac, Ariège, Vicdessos and Garbet, among hills that are either lush with forest, broom and heather, or outlined by stark walls of rock. Roads are narrow, with the added potential hazard of straying sheep or cattle. Sections will be closed by snow in winter.

▲ *Aulus-les-Bains and its valley*

Route Directions

The drive starts from St-Girons ①.

Leave town heading south on the D 618, following signs for Col de Port and Aulus-les-Bains. About 13km from St-Girons the road forks. Take the left fork, staying on the D 618 in the direction of Massat and Col de Port, and enter the Gorges de Ker ②.

After Biert the valley broadens, and 3km later the road reaches Massat. The first walk starts from here ③.

Bear left by Massat church, descend

to the river and then begin the easy 12-km climb, still on the D 618 to Col de Port. The way twists over Col des Caougnous (947m) before passing a few remote hamlets and going on to reach Col de Port itself ④.

The road descends via hairpin bends to Saurat, and on towards a pair of conical hills, with historic Bédeilhac-et-Aynat between them ⑤.

Continue for 7km towards Tarascon-sur-Ariège, following signs for Ax and Vicdessos. Keeping Tarascon on the left, cross the River Vicdessos and turn right on to the D 8, signposted Vicdessos. After 5km the road reaches the village of Niaux ⑥.

The road continues along the valley, passing the Château de Miglos on its crown of rock on the left and with Pic de Montcalm ahead. About 14km beyond Niaux, bear right over a bridge to enter Vicdessos ⑦.

Turn sharp right in the village on to the D 18 for Port de Lers (or de Massat) and Aulus-les-Bains. The road climbs steeply at first, then settles to a comfortable gradient through verdant countryside, before climbing again in a series of twists

▲ *Massat is a small mountain town overlooking the Arac*

towards the pass. Then it skirts a waterfall cascading from the Etang d'Arbu, and soon after gains Port de Lers (1517m). At the road junction on the pass where the D 18 turns sharp right, carry on straight ahead, passing the Etang de Lers and climbing again for another 5km to reach Col d'Agnès (1570m).

Descending by way of hairpins at first, the final run into Aulus-les-Bains is easy. On the edge of the village the road forks; bear right and go through the very narrow streets in the centre of Aulus. The second walk starts from here ⑧.

At a junction near the river in Aulus, turn right on to the D 32 to Ercé, Oust and St-Girons. The road goes along the flat-bottomed Vallée du Garbet past several hamlets, then through Ercé and to the outskirts of Oust, where it bypasses the village to arrive at Vic d'Oust ⑨.

Stay on the D 32 until it reaches a T-junction with the D 618. Turn left on to the D 618 and continue for 13km through the Gorges de Ribaouto and on to St-Girons.

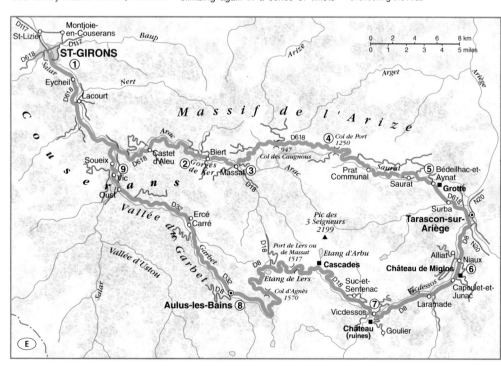

Points of Interest

▲ St-Girons lies on a locally important crossroads

① A bustling town on two rivers, St-Girons has an attractive centre and makes a convenient base from which to explore the Ariège. Near by, St-Lizier and Montjoie-en-Couserans are also worth visiting.

② The Gorges de Ker leading to Massat have been carved by the River Arac. Heavily wooded at their western end, they become more rocky as the road snakes eastwards. Cascades of broom soften the otherwise stark appearance of the rock.

③ See 1 on page 221.

Col de Port, east of Massat, has a high point of 1249m▼

④ Col de Port (1249m) boasts a lovely panorama, both from the pass itself and from the road leading to it. Not only does the col form an obvious passage between the districts of Couserans and Foix, it also marks the boundary between Gascony and Languedoc. On the eastern side the influence of the Mediterranean begins to make itself felt.

⑤ The Grotte de Bédeilhac, which was discovered in 1906, is enormous; its entrance is more than 35m wide and 20m high and it contains a wide variety of well-preserved prehistoric paintings and engravings from the Magdalenian period, some 10,000 years ago. In addition there is a huge stalagmite, more than 100m in circumference. During World War II the Germans used the cave as an aircraft hangar.

⑥ The village of Niaux is best known for its painted cave with drawings of bison, horses, ibex and deer, also dating from the Magdalenian period. There is another grotto at nearby Alliat (Grotte de la Vache) with a display of flint tools discovered there, and

between Tarascon and Niaux the interesting little Musée Paysan repays a visit.

⑦ In itself Vicdessos has little of interest, but the nearby ruined Château de Montreál, built by the Templars, is worth a visit for the view it affords. Also near by, and reached by a winding road from the southern outskirts of the village, is the Dolmen de Sem, in a dramatic position high above the valley.

⑧ The site of Aulus-les-Bains was known by the Romans for its spa qualities. It occupies a position near the head of the Vallée du Garbet in the heart of popular walking country. The narrow streets and tall houses have about them a slight air of decay, while its riverside buildings present a more cheerful face.

⑨ North of Oust, the small village of Vic d'Oust is remarkable for its 11th-century Romanesque church. Inside is a 12th-century wooden Christ and a ceiling of painted panels dating from the 16th century. On the opposite side of the road stands the Manoir de Roquemaurel, with its château-like tower.

PREHISTORIC CAVE ART

Discoveries made in numerous Pyrenean caves have shed light on the activities of the prehistoric inhabitants of the region, and of the great animals that once roamed here, many of which have long since become extinct. At the forefront of cave exploration were E.-A. Martel and Norbert Casteret (1897-1987), the latter a professional speleologist who lived near St-Gaudens and who devoted his life to unravelling the secrets of this underground world.

In 1922 Casteret explored the Grotte de Montespan, where he penetrated an ancient sanctuary and there set eyes upon the statue of a bear carved in clay. This was subsequently recognised as the oldest statue in the world. In addition he found many carvings of horses and lions, and more than 50 animal pictures engraved in the rock. On the clay floor were imprints of naked feet, unseen for several thousand years.

▲ The Grotte de Niaux

Other Pyrenean caves reveal wonders from the Magdalenian era too. The vast caverns of Bédeilhac and Niaux are especially well known; the latter, discovered by Molard in 1906, contains some of the most beautiful and best-preserved cave art of all. At Gargas, near St-Bertrand-de-Comminges, the speciality is outlines of hands, some with mutilated fingers.

While the significance of this art is still a matter of conjecture, the amount of prehistoric waste that litters the floor of many of these grottos suggests that these Pyrenean cave communities enjoyed a fair degree of stability.

A figure-of-eight from Massat

THE PYRENEES

PROMENADE DE SOUEGNES
Massat - Souègnes
Durée: 1ʰ30

An easy double loop, this walk falls into two distinct stages. The first forms part of the waymarked Promenade de Souègnes north-east of Massat; the second follows the River Arac downstream, linking one or two remote farms with the hamlet of Lirbat.

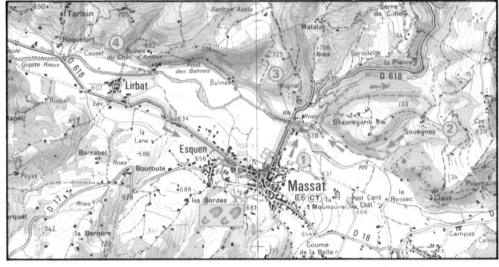

Route Directions

Start from the square in front of the church in Massat ①.

Leave the village on the Col de Port road. Cross the River Arac and turn right on to a lane signposted Promenade de Souègnes. Passing some houses, bear left uphill and leave the lane before a second hairpin bend. Take a footpath climbing to the right, cross the lane and continue towards woodlands. The path now becomes a track in the woods.

After the woods the path reaches a saddle of open meadowland between two hills, where it forks. Bear right towards a farm (Souègnes), and right again at a junction on to a lane. Across the valley Pic des 3 Seigneurs rises from forested hills ②.

Walk along the lane among broom-covered hillsides before descending – here there are good views ahead to Massat and the Gorges de Ker – to reach the bridge that crosses the River Arac ③.

Cross the road and follow a narrow farm drive, at first alongside the river, then easing away and rising a little to reach an isolated farm. Carry straight on between farm buildings on a footpath tracing the lower edge of woodlands. Where the path forks keep to the lower path, undulating above the river. Before long this passes behind a solitary house with yellow shutters ④.

▲ Massat was formerly the capital of the Couserans

The path leads down to a track. Bear left, pass in front of the house and cross a bridge on the right. Follow the track into the hamlet of Lirbat. Go up to the D 618, the Biert-Massat road, bear left and walk along it to Massat.

Points of Interest

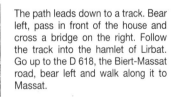

① Perched on a slope above the River Arac, Massat was once the capital of the Couserans. The church, with its 15th-century tower, stands at a crossroads: two roads cross the mountains to south and east via Port de Lers and Col de Port, and another minor road crosses Col de Saraillé to Oust in the Vallée du Garbet.

◀ The yellow-shuttered house

② The view from Souègnes includes Pic des 3 Seigneurs, whose ragged summit peers above its ·neighbours, looking grand not only from Souègnes but also from Col de Caougnous. Small tarns lie in corries on the upper slopes, and the River Arac rises on its western flank.

③ A feature of the second loop of the walk, the River Arac is a major tributary of the Salat, which in turn swells the Garonne. A pleasant river, its industry has been responsible for scouring the Gorges de Ker downstream of Massat.

④ The house with yellow shutters is set in an idyllic spot on the north bank of the Arac. A stream flows out of the woods, through the garden and beneath the house before emptying into the river.

WALK 54B: 7.5KM/ALLOW 3¹/₂-4 HOURS

The Cascade d'Ars

This climb to a classic viewpoint overlooking the Cascade d'Ars is moderately strenuous and steep in places. Much of it leads through woods where the path may be a little muddy in places. Walkers should be well shod. The descent is not difficult.

Route Directions

Start from beside the river in Aulus-les-Bains. Follow the road signposted Etang de Lers and Massat. The road curves to the left and is joined by another from the village. Bear right, and immediately afterwards take a path on the right (the GR 10 long-distance footpath) between meadows. At a crossing of tracks carry straight on to reach a bridge over the river. Cross this and turn left among trees. At a fork go right on a waymarked path through an avenue of hazel. Losing a little height, the path is joined by another, then forks again. Continue straight ahead on the right branch, still rising among hazel trees. The path goes uphill beside the river and passes some ruined huts ①.

The path forks again. Take the right-hand trail, still climbing. Eventually this emerges on to a broad track, where you turn left. After about 1km take a path branching ahead and to the left. Cross a bridge and climb in zigzags through steep woods to reach an obvious viewpoint overlooking the cascades ②.

Return downhill to the bridge. Cross back to the broad track and follow this as it winds down the hillside ③.

Remain on the track, at first high above the valley, then overlooking Aulus-les-Bains. When this reaches a surfaced road follow this road down to Aulus in the Vallée du Garbet ④.

Points of Interest

① In the Bois du Pouech et l'Artigue the path leads to a collection of ruined huts, typical of the many crumbling ruins throughout the region, as hill farms are deserted in favour of more lucrative work in lowland towns.

② The Cascade d'Ars bursts over a rocky lip, at first in a single fall, then in wide tresses, funnelling to a third and final cascade among the trees. At the end of winter, when the snows are melting, it plunges in one massive cataract of more than 100m.

③ From the woodland track there are fine views over the valley to isolated farms and barns on the opposite hillside. Beside the track aquilegias and asphodels brighten the way, as do wild raspberries and tiny alpine strawberries in season.

④ The Vallée du Garbet was widely known in the 19th century for its bear trainers. Once plentiful, the unfortunate brown bears were captured from the neighbouring forests and taught to perform at the end of a lead. The most successful trainers preferred to import their animals from Hungary, however, claiming that those indigenous to the Pyrenees were bow-legged and ungainly.

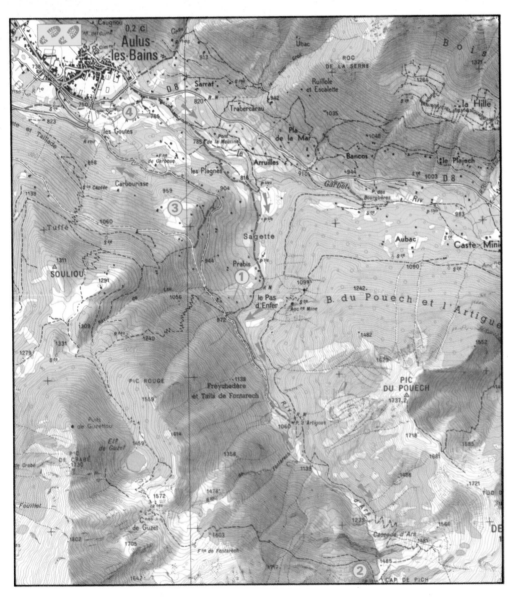

The Cerdagne and the Capcir

To the east of the Carlit massif, Col de la Quillanne links the Cerdagne, the sunniest valley in France, with the Capcir, a high plateau exposed to cold northerly winds. This tour explores both areas, and in addition crosses two other high cols – the busy Col de Puymorens near Andorra, and the little-known Port de Pailhères, in one of the loneliest districts of the Pyrenees. The roads are mostly good, except for the one between Quérigut and Ax-les-Thermes, which is narrow and tortuous.

Route Directions

The drive starts from Ax-les-Thermes ①.

Follow the Andorra road, the N20-E09 heading south, at first through wooded gorges then, above Mérens-les-Vals, into a more open valley. After 18km the road reaches l'Hospitalet-près-l'Andorre, above which a road tunnel through Col de Puymorens is due to open in 1994. Continue for 7km to a major junction and turn left, with care, for Perpignan. After 3km the road reaches Col de Puymorens ②.

Descend on the south side for 7km to Porté-Puymorens. The first walk begins in the valley of Lanous ③.

Continue down the valley, past Porta and the Tours de Carol ④.

Beyond Latour-de-Carol, 12km from Porté, enter the Cerdagne ⑤.

About 5km later, in the village of Ur, turn left on to the D 618 towards Font-Romeu-Odeillo-Via and drive through Villeneuve-des-Escaldes and Angoustrine, then among the rough granite blocks of the Chaos de Targasonne. Follow signs for Mont-Louis, and 13km from Ur pass the large 'solar oven' of Odeillo ⑥.

Go through Odeillo and keep on the D 618 until a junction with the N116. Continue ahead for Mont-Louis ⑦.

Return to the N116, and at a road junction by a large monument on the edge of Mont-Louis turn right, signposted Font-Romeu, and about 400m later bear right again on the D 118 for Quillan. The road winds uphill for about 6km to reach Col de la Quillanne ⑧.

Descend northwards into the Capcir, passing the dammed lakes of Matemale and Puyvalador. (The second walk starts from Puyvalador village.) After the lake at Puyvalador, fork left on to the D 32, which becomes the D 16, to Quérigut. The road winds through a forest before descending in a series of hairpin bends to the village of Quérigut ⑨.

About 2km later the road forks again outside le Pla. Bear left for Mijanès and Ax-les-Thermes, and left again in Mijanès, on to the D 25, to begin the climb to Port de Pailhères. The road narrows on the approach to the pass, but there are good views. After some tight hairpin bends it reaches Port de Pailhères ⑩.

Descend past chalets and a small ski area and continue for 14.5km to a T-junction just beyond Ascou. Turn left and wind downhill for 3.5km to reach Ax-les-Thermes.

The Cerdagne valley ▶

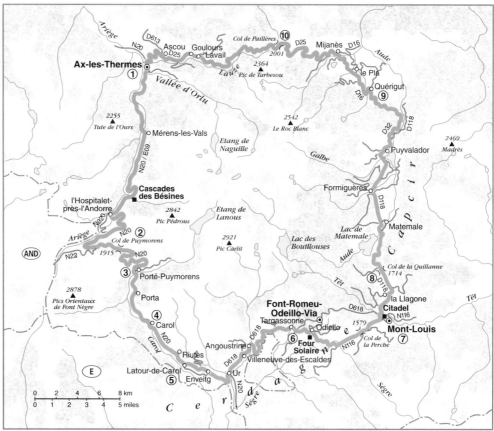

THE LITTLE YELLOW TRAIN

On its journey from Villefranche-de-Conflent, deep in the valley of the Têt, to Latour-de-Carol, where the Carol valley joins the Cerdagne, the *petit train jaune* rattles along 63km of electrified track.

To overcome the severe incline of the Têt's narrows below Mont-Louis, engineers who planned the line had to build two particularly airy bridges. The first of these is Pont Gisclard, a magnificent suspension bridge slung some 80m above the river and named after the army officer who designed it, and who was tragically killed in an accident during trials. The other is a huge viaduct, Pont Séjourné: a graceful piece of engineering with 16 arches measuring 200m end to end, the central section of which is delicately bold and has a single pointed arch.

This romantic and somewhat eccentric little railway once formed a valuable service in linking the many remote villages of the Cerdagne, but is now seen more as a tourist attraction with a number of unscheduled stops where would-be passengers need to catch the driver's attention.

By virtue of the international status of the station at Latour-de-Carol the 'little yellow train' makes a convenient connection between Perpignan and the main Paris-Toulouse-Barcelona line. As its name suggests, the train is decked out in a livery of yellow with a red trim. In summer there are one or two open carriages.

wall show ample evidence of the glaciers that poured down to it. The Cerdagne is noted for the attractive small villages that line its southern slopes, and for the abundant flora of its tributary valleys.

⑥ On the outskirts of Odeillo stands a huge solar oven, or *four solaire*, developed as an experimental power station to generate energy directly from the sun. A large concave wall of mirrors (nearly 10,000 of them) concentrates the sun's rays into a central area with the aid of 63 movable reflectors. Power equivalent to 1000kw is produced, and temperatures of

The four solaire, solar oven, at Mont-Louis ▶

▲ *The solar oven near Odeillo has achieved temperatures in excess of 3500°C by concentrating the sun's rays by using almost 10,000 small mirrors fixed to a movable concave surface. The device was first used in 1969*

Points of Interest

① The spa town of Ax-les-Thermes is a neat little resort at the confluence of the Rivers Ariège and Oriège. Numerous hot springs serve the thermal establishments, and in Place du Breilh a stone tank of steaming water (78°C) was long used by local women as a public wash-place. In 1260 Louis IX sent members of his crusading army who had caught leprosy in Palestine to Ax for treatment.

② Col de Puymorens (1920m) is located on a bleak, high, moorland-like plateau lying on a bald ridge of mountains that form a watershed between the Garonne (via the Ariège) and the Ebro (via the Carol and Sègre).

③ Draining the western slopes of the Carlit massif, the Lanous flows through a delightful valley of pastureland and mixed woods, with stands of wild cherry lining its tributary streams. Near the head of the valley lie two small lakes, with the larger, dammed Etang de Lanous caught in an upper valley surrounded by wild mountains.

④ It seems hard to believe that the small hamlet of Carol on the left bank of the river that shares its name was once the most important place in the valley. But in the 13th century the King of Aragon built a castle here to defend the Cerdagne

against invasion from the north. All that remain of this castle today are two towers, the Tours de Carol – not to be confused with the village of Latour-de-Carol, 5km down the valley.

⑤ With an enviable sunshine record the broad valley of the Cerdagne makes a first-class base for touring or walking holidays. This high, gently sloping plain is half-French and half-Spanish. It occupies the bed of a former glacial lake, and the mountains that form its northern

The medieval town of Mont-Louis was fortified by Vauban in 1679 to protect the French border and is still a garrison town, now used by commandos ▼

around 3800°C have been recorded. A smaller solar oven at Mont-Louis preceded that at Odeillo in the 1950s.

⑦ Created by Vauban on behalf of Louis XIV following the Treaty of the Pyrenees, Mont-Louis is a sturdy-looking township of medieval streets, with a moat surrounding the fortified walls. The citadel is now a garrison for commandos who exercise in the Carlit mountains behind. The main gateway to Mont-Louis looks south across the Cerdagne.

⑧ Col de la Quillanne (1714m) tops a wide, level plain with a fine panorama south to the rolling Puigmal hills.

⑨ Quérigut was once the capital of the tiny Donézan district, part of the Comté de Foix. The ruins of the Château du Donézan dominate the village from a stub near the church.

⑩ Port de Pailhères (2001m) links the Capcir with the Ariège valley. Fine views look south to Pic de Tarbesou.

The Estany de Font Viva

This circular walk offers a variety of captivating mountain scenery: lakes, streams, cascades, forest and pasture and grand distant views. Paths are a little obscure in places and there is a short, steep section to tackle, but nowhere is the route too demanding.

▲ *In springtime the meadows of the Lanòus valley are a delight*

Route Directions

Start from the end of the road leading from Porté-Puymorens up the Vallée de Lanòus. Follow a footpath to be found 50m north of an electricity works building ①.

The path leads among pine trees and alongside a small stream, soon climbing steeply in places. Alternative trails abound: if in doubt keep to the left of overhead cables, in order to emerge on to a pleasant open meadow. Skirt the meadow's right-hand edge and climb up a hillside bright with juniper and broom to reach a second high stretch of meadowland. Bear right and follow a path with yellow waymarks leading to the Estany de Font Viva ②.

Walk round the left-hand shore, passing a simple hut, and at the far end leave the lake and head east across a rich green pasture. Go through a grassy col at the far end and descend among pine trees into the head of the valley.

Cross over a wooden bridge below a series of cascades and turn right as the path forks. The way meanders above the Lanòus stream and is marshy in places. Veer left when the stream enters a ravine and climb to a grassy saddle to find a few cairns. Continue along the path, now losing height, with views ahead to the mountains bordering Andorra ③.

The way descends among mixed vegetation including sprays of *Daphne mezereum* ④.

Passing through walled meadows and pinewoods continue down to a broad track, turn right and soon afterwards cross a bridge over the Lanòus stream again to reach the parking area at the roadhead.

Points of Interest

① The works building and *téléphérique* at the roadhead are part of an electricity development focused on the dam at the Estany de Lanòus, about 600m above to the north-east, on the edge of some wild but scenic country.

② The Estany de Font Viva lies in a high, rough pastureland. A refuge on its northern shore provides basic shelter for anglers fishing the lake for trout.

③ From the valley head there are views westwards to the mountains on the Andorran border. Partially hidden by the Pics Orientaux de Font Nègra is Pic Nègre d'Envaliva, with a saddle below on which the frontiers of France, Spain and Andorra converge.

④ *Daphne mezereum*, much prized in British gardens, is the most fragrant of all plants found growing wild in the Pyrenees. Clusters of pink, mauve or sometimes white flowers adorn woody stems 30-100cm long, and the sweet scent is so heady that it is often detected before the plant is seen. At the end of summer bright-red berries replace the flowers.

The Estany de Font Viva is a high-lying lake much frequented by trout anglers ▼

55B

THE PYRENEES

Villages of the Capcir

a driveway leading to a house. Take a path cutting off at a bend to go down to the dam ②.

Cross the dam to reach the eastern side, where stands a lofty memorial to Joachim Estrade. Walk ahead on a broad path which bears right to

▲ *An abandoned cart near Réal recalls old farming methods*

head south alongside the lake, giving views of the whole Capcir plateau ③.

At the southern end of the lake the path joins a narrow road leading to the small village of Réal ④.

The road forks by the town hall. Bear right and walk ahead between meadows. Pass a junction where a second narrow road comes in from Réal to reach a gravel track on the left 200m later. Follow this as it winds up terraced slopes, then cuts back to the north. Above Réal the track forks. Continue straight ahead, soon passing a timber barn and a house set below on the left. When it makes a hairpin bend to the right, leave the track and take a narrow grass path heading left.

A renovated farmhouse in Réal suggests economic stability ▼

This path leads over a stream and along the foot of pine woods before coming to a broad grass terrace, where it disappears. Carry on straight ahead to reach a second stream. Bear left, cross the stream and walk straight on, now on a lower terrace, to gain a crossing track. Turn left to reach a narrow road soon afterwards which goes to Odelló.

At the edge of Odelló bear left on a surfaced track leading to a farm. Leave the track when it turns into the hamlet, and continue now on an unmade farm track leading downhill through meadows to the barrage at the end of the lake. Cross the barrage to return to Puyvalador.

Points of Interest

① The small farming village of Puyvalador sits on a knoll overlooking the lake. Its ski station lies to the north, with 20km of pistes.

② Rising in the Carlit mountains, the River Aude is dammed at Matemale and Puyvalador to feed hydroelectric power stations. When the water level is low the lakes reveal banks of silt brought down from the mountains. Similar deposits once built the plain of Narbonne.

③ The Capcir is a glacial plateau with some of the highest permanently inhabited villages in France. Bare and flat, it provides first-class cross-country skiing in winter.

④ Réal is a village in transition, being resurrected from near-decay. A stream flows through it, with water troughs at almost every corner and moulded animal heads forming the spouts.

A**n easy walk on farm tracks and footpaths, this circuit explores the villages overlooking the Puyvalador lake amid the peaceful landscapes of the Capcir. There should be no difficulties, although for one short section the footpath disappears completely.**

Route Directions

Start from beside the church in Puyvalador ①.

Walk through the village and down a slope towards the lake. Bear left on

The Côte d'Azur and the Parc National du Mercantour

There could hardly be a greater contrast than that between the Côte d'Azur coast and the Parc National du Mercantour. The one is glitter and noise, the other peace and unspoilt beauty. This tour combines the two, starting in Menton, one of the most pleasant of the Côte d'Azur towns, and then heading north into the hills of Haute-Provence, the foothills of the Alpes Maritimes. The roads to the north of the Côte d'Azur tend to be winding and slow.

Route Directions

The drive starts from Menton ①.

From the town centre take the road signposted Autoroute (Nice, Italia) and Sospel. Follow signs for Sospel on the D 2566, going under the A8 and passing through Castillon-Neuf. A new road is being driven under Col de Castillon, but at present you must go up and over the pass. Enter Sospel, go over the railway crossing and then turn left following signs for Moulinet and Col de Turini. Pass through Sospel ②.

Bear left at a bend on to the D 2204 and climb up to Col St-Jean, from where there are superb views back down to Sospel.

Go over Col de Braus (1002m) and descend around hairpin bends to l'Escarène. Just after a railway bridge take a right turn, signposted Lucéram and Peïra-Cava.

Drive through Lucéram ③.

At the next junction, which is isolated and on a steep hill, bear left (still on the D 2566), following signs for Turini. The road climbs around 16 hairpin bends and passes through Peïra-Cava ④.

Continue to Col de Turini ⑤.

Turn left on to the D 70, signposted la Bollène-Vésubie and Nice, carefully descending the long, winding road from the pass. After about 10km, and inconveniently placed on

a bend, there is a chapel on the left, just after the Chapelle-St-Anorat tunnel. There is a parking place here, and superb views over la Bollène-Vésubie. Continue through la Bollène. At a T-junction turn left on to the D 2565, signposted Nice and St-Martin-Vésubie, to reach a valley bottom. There, follow signs for Lantosque and Nice, going straight on at first, then turning left along the main road. After 1km you can either go right and drive through Lantosque village, or take the bypass. The road through the village rejoins the main road. If you go that way turn right (signposted Nice). Continue through St-Jean-la-Rivière.

The Roman Trophée des Alpes at la Turbie was blown up by Louis XV but restored in the present century ▶

Rising to over 1600m, Col de Turini provides fine views ▼

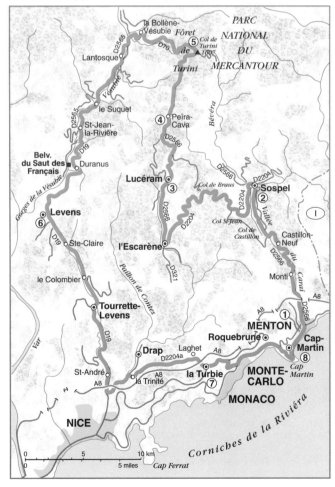

About 1km beyond St-Jean take the left fork, the D 19, signposted 'Nice par Levens'. (Be sure to follow this sign since both directions are signposted Nice.) The road narrows and climbs up the side of the Vésubie valley. After you leave the tunnel just before Duranus, there is a viewpoint to the right, the Saut des Français, set above sheer cliffs. Continue along the road into Levens ⑥.

The first walk starts from here. Leave Levens on the D 19, signposted Nice. Continue for about 16km, passing through Tourette-Levens. Just after St-André you will pass under the A8. Take a left turn at the traffic lights here, signposted Sospel, cross a river and go straight over at the next set of traffic lights to go back under the A8. Take the next right turn, signposted Route de Turin, crossing the river and a level crossing. Take a left turn at the traffic lights, signposted la Trinité and Drap, and leave the roundabout by the exit on the right, signposted la Turbie and Laghet. Follow the D 2204a up a winding valley to the Sanctuary at Laghet. There a hairpin bend takes the road sharply to the right. Pass under the A8 again, and turn left at the next junction (a

▲ Menton enjoys an attractive setting backed by mountains

motorway slip road, signposted Menton). Turn left again at the next junction on to a road signposted la Turbie and Monaco. Continue to la Turbie ⑦.

Drive through la Turbie and bear left past a hotel, following signs for Roquebrune and Menton, and then go downhill. At the bottom take a right turn at the traffic lights, signposted Nice and Beausoleil. Take a left turn at the next set of traffic lights, signposted Cap Martin. As it leaves the village centre the road veers sharp left. Go straight ahead here, signposted Mayerling and Cap-Martin ⑧.

This road soon reaches the sea. Park here for the start of the second walk. Rejoin the road you were on to return to Menton.

Points of Interest

① Menton describes itself as the warmest town on the Côte d'Azur, and the citrus orchards seem to reinforce this claim. It is a picture-postcard Italian town set down in France. The Musée Jean-Cocteau, at the southern corner of the port, has a collection of the artist's work.

② The old bridge in the pretty village of Sospel is of 11th-century design, complete with a central tower, but 20th-century vintage. The original bridge was destroyed in World War II.

③ The old village of Lucéram, what was the medieval town, is a haphazard collection of alleys, some vaulted, in which getting lost is a joy.

④ Peïra-Cava is one of the best viewpoints on the route, offering superb views to the Parc National du Mercantour.

⑤ At an altitude of 1607m, Col de Turini provides fine views of the Parc National du Mercantour, and has a hotel, café and restaurant.

⑥ See page 229.

⑦ The ancient village of la Turbie sits astride the Via Julia, a Roman road built by Julius Caesar to link Genoa with Cimiez, on the northern outskirts of Nice. It is an interesting place, but it is for the Trophée des Alpes that most visitors come. This triumphal arch was built by Augustus Caesar in or around 6 BC to celebrate local supremacy.

⑧ See page 230.

PARC NATIONAL DU MERCANTOUR

Created in 1979, the Parc National du Mercantour is the most recent of France's Parcs Nationaux. It covers parts of both the *départements* of Alpes-Maritimes and Alpes-de-Haute-Provence and adjoins Italy's Argentera National Park. Mercantour consists of high, rocky peaks and lush valleys, but was created mainly to protect the Bronze Age rock engravings around Mont Bégo, which is reached from the Tende valley.

The Park's flora is especially interesting, as it includes both alpine species, such as saxifrage, and Mediterranean species, such as the olive tree. About half of France's native flowers grow in the Park, some 40 species being unique to it. On these flowers feed a variety of insects, including a large number of Europe's more exotic butterflies.

The Park's bird life is also excellent, with the golden eagle and Tengmalm's owl being especially sought after by bird lovers. The wildlife includes chamois and ibex, but the animal most noticeable to the visitor is the marmot, even if it is more often heard than seen. When alarmed, this big, cuddly rodent gives a piercing whistle that carries a considerable distance. All visitors who leave their cars to walk in the Park should hear marmots, though patience and a little luck are needed for a good view of the furry whistler.

◄ Wildlife, including Tengmalm's owl, the golden eagle and the marmot, abounds in the green valleys of the Mercantour

Levens

The first tour of the area visits both coast and mountain, passing through several delightful towns and villages. It is appropriate, therefore, that the first walk should visit one of the towns, and one from which there are superb views to the mountains.

◄ *Humorous frescos depicting the powerful Masséna family can be seen in Levens' town hall*

swimming pool take a path on the left that goes towards the pool entrance. At the top take the road to the right (by the telephone), signposted Eglise (church), retracing your steps, then entering Rue Giraut. Turn right into Rue du Portal, following it into Place Victor-Masseglia. Retrace your steps, going downhill but turning left before the main square into Rue de la Terrasse. Go through an archway to the cafés

Levens, established as a village in medieval times, lies at a height of 600m. Its hilly terrain gives scope for creating terraced gardens ▼

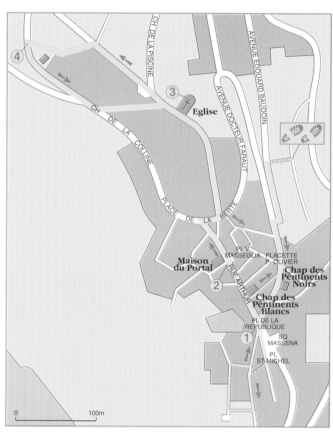

Route Directions

Start from the municipal car park, and climb the steps signposted Centre Ville. At the top go left into another car park, where there is a map of the town. From the far right-hand corner of the car park go down the road to Place de la République ①.

Follow the road and, as it starts to drop, cross a small square on the right, Place St-Michel. Leave the square at the far right-hand corner, climbing steps and turning right. Turn left and then right up tiny alleys to reach a shaded, grassy square with seats. Turn right and go down Rue de la Guérite. Take the next right and then turn left at a T-junction. On

reaching the square again go left up Rue Arthur M. Bear right at the top, and pass under an arch into Place Victor-Masseglia ②.

Continue uphill to reach another square. Turn right then left through an archway, up steps. Follow the Eglise (church) sign, taking the second turning on the right. Go up a path on the left side of the church entrance and pass the church's left side up a path ③.

Pass the swimming pool and follow the road to the left to a viewpoint near the World War I memorial ④.

Continue along the road (now going downhill), enjoying fine views over the town. When you are just past the

in Placette Paul-Olivier, just before the upper car park. Go across this car park and back down the steps to the lower car park.

Points of Interest

① The main square of Levens is a very attractive spot, with its shady gardens and excellent views to the south. On its northern side stands one of two old friaries. This is the Chapelle des Pénitents Blancs and dates from the late 18th century. The Chapelle des Pénitents Noirs stands to the east, but its fine baroque façade is less well preserved.

② To the left here is the Maison du Portal, the gateway itself being all that remains of Levens' castle. According to legend, in 1621 the

village folk of Levens rose up against the tyrannical rule of their feudal lord, one of the Monaco Grimaldis, and destroyed his castle. Only one stone, called the *boutau*, remained, kept as a memorial to the overthrow. Every year, on the festival of St Antonin, people come to the stone to recall that great day.

③ Inside the parish church are a fine statue of the Virgin Mary – the Virgin of Vows – and a 16th-century painting showing scenes from the life of St Antonin, a Roman martyr to whom the church is dedicated and who is also patron saint of the town.

④ From the viewpoint there is a magnificent view of the peaks of the Parc National du Mercantour, and of the valleys of the Rivers Var and Vésubie.

Cap Martin to Cabbé or Monaco

▲ Fishing off Cap Martin

This walk along the coast visits what many consider to be the most attractive section of the Côte d'Azur. It is a long, linear walk, the return being made by train, and is best undertaken during the afternoon, when the heat of the day has passed and the sun is at the best angle for the views.

Route Directions

Start from the car park at the seaward end of Avenue Winston Churchill in Cap Martin. Go back in the direction in which you came and then pass to the left of the hotel entrance, along a wide footpath at the edge of the sea. The path is marked at its start by a sign for Ville de Roquebrune-Cap Martin, and a list of times for walks, including 2 hours 20 minutes for Monte-Carlo, which is rather optimistic for all but

the dedicated walker. Follow the path past gardens and smart hotels, on one section going under a balcony that offers little headroom. The path heads west along the edge of Cap Martin ①.

There is a superb view of Monaco ahead, and the sea is to the left ②.

In several places there are steps leading up to the Cap, but the best route continues into Cabbé, from where trains run back to Carnolès. From Carnolès station head seaward and follow the coastal path back to the car park. Alternatively, to extend the walk, you can follow the path into Monte-Carlo ③.

From here also, trains serve Carnolès. This longer walk has the advantage of a glorious entrance to the Principality of Monaco, but the disadvantage that the route occasionally strays on to roads.

Points of Interest

① The thrusting headland of Cap Martin has long been a look-out, the old tower at its centre being the remains of a fortified medieval watch-tower. At the tower's base are the remains of an 11th-century priory. Legend has it that the prior had an agreement with the local folk that if the tower's bell were rung they would all hurry to the site to defend the monks. One night, just to test the system, the prior rang the bell, and was very pleased with the speedy response. The townsfolk were a good deal less pleased, however, and a few nights later, when the bell rang again, they did not bother to turn out. But this time it was no trial run, and the priory was sacked by pirates and all the monks killed. Today Cap

The sea batters the rocky shore below the villas of Cap Martin's wealthy residents ▼

▲ *Cap Martin is crowned by a telecommunications station and a ruined 11th-century priory*

Martin is a very rich suburb of Menton, its mansions set among sweet-smelling mimosas and clumps of olive trees.

② It is believed that Stephen Liégeard was the first to use the term 'Côte d'Azur' to describe the coast near Nice, in a poem in 1887. The name is truly descriptive of the colour of the Mediterranean when the sun is shining, which is most of the time. The walk, with rhododendrons, honeysuckle and huge cactus plants to the right, the turquoise sea to the left and coastal towns ahead, passes through an idyllic scene.

③ The Principality of Monaco comprises Monaco itself, with the Palais du Prince; la Condamine, the commercial centre: and Monte-Carlo, with its famous casino, hotels, marina, exclusive shops and restaurants. For many visitors it is fabled, glittering Monte-Carlo that is the main attraction. But to appreciate Monte-Carlo it is not necessary to be a wealthy player of the tables at the Casino, for the parks and gardens are a delight and the seafront and the views over the Mediterranean are superb.

Mont Ventoux

As the Rhône flows down towards Provence it swings to the west, avoiding Orange. To the east of the town are the hill ranges of the Dentelles de Montmirail and Mont Ventoux. From almost anywhere on the western edge of Provence, Mont Ventoux can be seen – a lone sentinel, its head usually in cloud, marking the entrance to Provence, with its pure light and warm sun. Our route climbs right to the summit of Mont Ventoux, but the roads should present no problem to the patient driver.

Route Directions

The drive starts from Carpentras ①.

From the town centre follow the road signposted Sault. At the first roundabout take the D 974, signposted Mont Ventoux, and follow signs for Bédoin and Mont Ventoux. At a crossroads with the D 70 turn left to Caromb ②.

Return to the main road on the D 55 via Modène and go on to Bédoin ③.

On leaving the village turn right, following signs for Mont Ventoux on the D 974. The road goes through St-Estève ④.

The same road then climbs across the flank of Ventoux, eventually reaching a junction with the main road (still the D 974) to the summit from Sault. Go left on a winding road that eventually reaches the summit of Mont Ventoux ⑤.

▲ *Vaison-la-Romaine blends Roman and medieval architecture*

The first walk starts from here. From the summit descend westward, with care, still on the D 974, towards Malaucène. At the junction just before the town turn right on to a road signposted Vaison-la-Romaine and go through Malaucène ⑥.

Follow the D 938 to Vaison ⑦.

In Vaison, go right over the old bridge and bear left to a car park, from where the second walk starts.

From the car park go back over the bridge and take a right turn on to the D 977, signposted Avignon. About 6km beyond Vaison turn left on to the D 88, signposted Séguret and Route des Vins. This follows the western side of the Dentelles de Montmirail ⑧.

Continue to Séguret ⑨.

At Séguret turn right on to the D 23, signposted Sablet. Turn left on to the D 7, signposted Carpentras and Gigondas, and pass through Sablet. Turn left to Gigondas ⑩.

Return to the D 7 and follow signs for Carpentras and pass through Vacqueyras. Between Vacqueyras and Aubignan a road to the left offers a short detour to Beaumes-de-Venise ⑪.

Rejoin the D 7 to Carpentras.

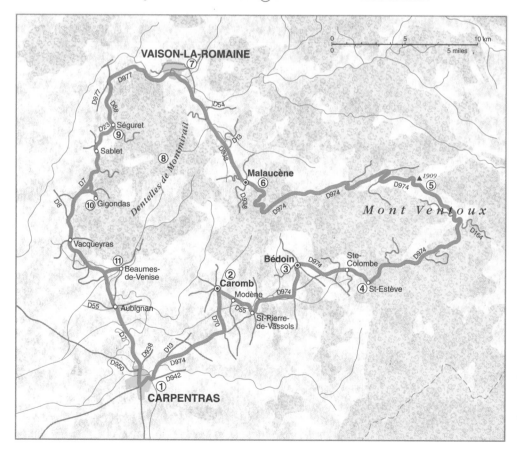

Points of Interest

① Carpentras is both the market town for the local market gardens and a light-industrial town. Of chief interest is the cathedral of St-Siffrein, a 15th-century Gothic building entered through the Porte Juive, the Jews' Door, which is in later, Flamboyant Gothic style. The door is so named because it was through it that Jews converted to Christianity entered the church for baptism. Carpentras had a thriving Jewish community and the town's synagogue is the oldest in France, dating from the 15th century. Visitors can see the ground-floor baths and kosher bakery, as well as the temple on the first floor. Until the Revolution there was a Jewish ghetto numbering over 1000 in Carpentras.

To the west of the cathedral, in Boulevard Albin-Durand, is a museum complex that includes a library of rare books collected by an 18th-century town bishop, and the Musée Comtadin. During the transhumance, when cattle and sheep were moved from winter to summer pastures, or vice versa, the animals wore bells to aid the herders. Bells of different sizes were made for rams, sheep, goats, donkeys and horses, and the chief bell makers were a Carpentras family called Simon. The Musée Comtadin houses many examples of their work.

② Caromb is an elegantly situated old wine village with a fascinating museum of historic craft tools.

③ Bédoin is an attractive little village, with a number of very picturesque streets and alleys, and a classical church with several fine altars.

④ Just after the delightful village of St-Estève is passed there is a sharp left-hand bend where you can stop to enjoy a magnificent view of the Dentelles de Montmirail and the plains of central Provence.

⑤ See page 233.

⑥ There can be few other villages in France that can equal Malaucène's claim to fame, the village church having been built by a Pope, Clement V, when he was resident here. Clement was the first of the Avignon Popes, and moved to Malaucène in 1309 in order to escape troubled Rome.

⑦ See page 234.

⑧ Geologically, the Dentelles de Montmirail are the last section of the Ventoux ridge. They would be rounded hills, topped with pines and

WINES OF PROVENCE

It is believed that the Greeks established vineyards in Provence as early as 600 BC, though it is with the coming of the Romans that Provençal wine enters written history, Julius Caesar mentioning them approvingly in his *Commentaries*. The Romans are also known to have imported different types of grape into the area, one of which, Syrah, was such a success that it is still grown today.

The next advance came in the 15th century, when the dukedom of Provence passed to René, who was also King of Sicily and Duke of Anjou. René is credited with introducing the Muscat grape to Provence, from Sicily, and also with importing the first silkworms. A statue of him, holding a bunch of grapes, can be seen at the end of Cours Mirabeau, the finest boulevard in Aix-en-Provence.

Despite this long history, the wines of the Côtes de Ventoux did not achieve AOC *(appellation d'origine contrôlée)* status until 1973. Most of the wine produced in the area is red, although there is also a little rosé and about one bottle in 20 is white.

▲ *The Porte d'Orange, the 14th-century gateway to the old quarter of Carpentras*

oaks, their flanks covered in vineyards, had not folding of the earth's crust pushed the limestone rock into a jagged line of points. Resembling the edge of lace, these give the range its name. The Dentelles de Montmirail are beloved of rock climbers and those seeking a hard day on difficult terrain. The best approach to the Dentelles is from Beaumes-de-Venise, via Suzette, on the eastern flank, though the western flank can be reached from Gigondas.

⑨ Séguret, a typical Dentelles wine village, nestles below a sheet of rock and would be worth a visit for the views it offers even if it lacked its fine 15th-century fountain, 12th-

century church, ruined castle and steep streets.

⑩ Gigondas is the home of Grenache, a wine described as a 'heady red' by those who know. Close by is the chapel of Notre-Dame d'Aubune, which is topped by an elegant belfry.

▲ *Vaison-la-Romaine's Roman ruins include a colonnaded street, a temple and a theatre*

⑪ Beaumes-de-Venise, a village of fine terraced houses on the narrow road to Suzette, is the starting-point for visits to the Dentelles de Montmirail.

On top of Mont Ventoux

The road up Mont Ventoux spoils the mountain for ever for the walker who feels that all peaks should be climbed the traditional way – on foot. For many visitors, by contrast, the road is a godsend, allowing the views from the summit to be enjoyed without having to spend hours on the ascent.

Near the summit of Mont Ventoux stands a modest chapel ▶

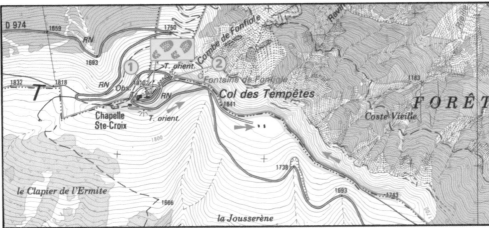

An observatory, a TV mast and a radar station crown Mont Ventoux ▼

Route Directions

Start from the car park at the summit of Mont Ventoux ①.

Walk down beside the road on which you drove up, and then down a path which follows a rock arête, to reach an old chapel. Often, even in summer, the chapel is filled with snow. Turn left at the chapel to pass in front of a café. Pass the café and go straight on down the main road off the peak, returning the way you came. At the first right-hand corner, Col des Tempêtes, leave the road and follow a path along the ridge, heading away from the top. After climbing for about 250m you reach a small peak which offers tremendous

Tom Simpson died on Mont Ventoux in the 1967 Tour de France ▼

views back towards the observation tower. You can continue along the path as far as you wish, but you will have to return the same way. Return to the road, but do not go along it. Instead, walk up the path that leads to the right-hand corner of the summit, where there is a viewing table ②.

Turn left from here to return to the car park.

Points of Interest

① The name Ventoux derives from the Provençal name for the peak: Ventour, meaning Windy Mountain. The name is apt at all times, but never more so than when the Mistral is blowing. Be sure to carry a coat or anorak when you start out on the walk, since the temperature is usually 10°C lower than that at the foot of the mountain, and the wind makes it feel cooler still. Ventoux also attracts twice the rainfall of the valleys.

In geological terms the Ventoux ridge is the final, western, peak of the Alps. The upper reaches of the 1909-m peak have been laid almost bare of vegetation by the scouring of the wind, the high rainfall and winter's cold. At one time forest clothed the peak, but this was cut down for ship building in medieval times. Today there are trees only on the lower flanks. The visiting botanist will be amazed to discover the Arctic poppy and a form of saxifrage that also grows on Norway's Svalbard Islands, which are only 1000km from the North Pole.

② On the summit of Mont Ventoux there are a weather observatory, a TV mast and a radar station. A viewing table helps the user to pick out the Cévennes, the Luberon hills, the Alpilles, the Montagne Ste-Victoire and Marseille from the impressive 360-degree panorama.

Vaison-la-Romaine

Route Directions

Start from the car park in Vaison-la-Romaine, which is reached by crossing the Pont Romain ①.

Walk back over the bridge. Turn right at the main road, then cross over and go up a road opposite, signposted Ville Médiévale. Go through an arched gateway ②.

Turn sharp left, backtracking a little, up a narrow road. Continue to climb, looking towards the clock tower that gives the road its name (Rue de l'Horloge). Follow the road around to the right, and turn left at a T-junction, following signs for the château. This is Rue de l'Eglise, the church of the name being reached soon on the left. There is also a viewpoint to the left here. Pass the church and carry on winding uphill to Plan Pascal and on again, up steps, to Rue de la Charité. This road narrows into a rubble track: at the end of the stone wall on the left turn left and climb to the ruins of the château ③.

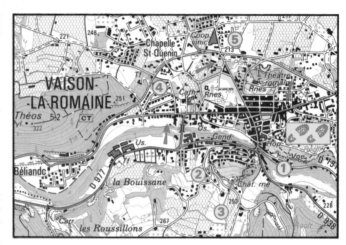

From here there is a fine view over the Roman remains and the lower town.

Return to the stone wall. Turn right and then left under an arch and descend rough-hewn steps. These lead to a beautiful square, with a fountain and the Hôtel de Prévôt.

Leave the square to the left, and go down Rue des Fours, one of the prettiest streets in old Vaison. When a road leads off to the right, keep straight ahead. Turn right at the next junction to reach a T-junction. Turn left, then take the next turning on the right, which opens up a view over the lower town. Descend steps on the left, and then more steps to the right, to reach Rue du Château. Turn left and follow the road to a main road junction. Bear right and cross the River Ouvèze by the Pont Neuf. Take the first turn right into Avenue Jules Ferry and then go left to reach the cathedral ④.

Return to Avenue Jules Ferry and turn left. Take the first left turn and follow it to a Y-junction. Bear left and after 120m turn right. Bear right at the next Y-junction and turn right again at the main road, Avenue du Général de Gaulle. Turn sharp left in Place Abbé Sautel, into Rue Bernard Noël, and then right into the Quartier Puymin ⑤.

Return to Place Abbé Sautel and continue down Avenue du Général de Gaulle. Cross into Grande Rue at the main junction, and turn right just before the Pont Romain to return to the car park.

Points of Interest

① As the name implies, the Pont Romain was constructed by the Romans and, apart from some

necessary repair work, looks as it did when it was built, perhaps 1800 years ago.

② After the Romans had left, Vaison-la-Romaine was destroyed by barbarian invaders. When the town was re-established, the more easily defended upper site was occupied at first. The arched gateway is a remnant of the medieval ramparts. Upper Vaison is an almost complete medieval town, with fine alleys of houses dating from the 14th century. The exquisite wrought ironwork on some of the houses is of later date. The hanging baskets are later still, and equally good.

③ The château dates from the initial rebuilding of the upper town in the 12th century, though it was much rebuilt in the 14th and 15th centuries. It is now ruinous, and access is not allowed.

④ The Cathédrale Notre-Dame-de-Nazareth was built in the 12th century on the ruins of a 6th- or 7th-century Merovingian church and has a fine altar beyond which is the old bishop's throne. St Quenin, a native of Vaison who was the bishop here from 556 to 575, is buried close to the throne. Beside the cathedral there are excellent 12th-century cloisters, restored in the 19th century, where there is a small but interesting museum of Christian art.

⑤ The fascinating Roman remains found in Vaison's Quartier Puymin include several houses and a fine 1st-century Roman theatre. The best items, including a superb marble head of Venus, can be seen in the site museum. The Quartier Villasse contains the baths, which were for a long time believed to be a temple, the main street and a colonnaded street, and two substantial town houses.

◀ *Vaison-la-Romaine has several fine medieval town houses*

Vaison is an interesting village

V aison is an interesting village which is split into two by the River Ouvèze, the halves being quite different. The lower half includes the 12th-century cathedral as well as the excavated Roman remains, while the upper half dates from the late Middle Ages, and remains unspoilt by cars. The walk has some steep climbs, but fortunately these are short and on a reasonable surface.

Haute-Provence

Give yourself a long day for this tour, on which you will see some wonderful mountain views, the more attractive for being no more than an hour or so by car from the Côte d'Azur. The route includes the whole of the Gorges de la Vésubie and the Gorges du Cians. Linking the two spectacular valleys at the southern end is the N202, the fastest road on the tour. The majority of the route presents a challenge, though not a daunting one, by following winding roads that rise and fall over mountain passes.

Route Directions

The drive starts from St-Martin-Vésubie ①.

Head north from the town on the D 2565, following signs for Col St-Martin. The road winds up to the Col, a ski centre lying at 1500m, and then drops down the other side through the villages of St-Dalmas and Valdeblore-la-Bolline. Beyond the latter the D 66, to the right and signposted Rimplas, leads up to an excellent vantage point near Rimplas itself. The route continues to the valley bottom. Turn right at the junction, on to the D 2205, signposted St-Sauveur-sur-Tinée. Continue to St-Sauveur ②.

Pass through the town and then turn left off the main road on to the D 30, signposted Roubion and Col de la Couillole. The road rises through a very pretty, twisting valley with small waterfalls, road tunnels and purple rock. Pass Roubion ③.

Go on to Col de la Couillole. Descend from the Col and arrive at a T-junction by bypassing Beuil-les-Launes ④.

Turn left for the Gorges du Cians, rounding a sharp right bend and then turning left again on to the D 28, signposted Gorges du Cians.

Both the upper and lower Gorges (Gorges Supérieures and Gorges Inférieures) are followed. Continue to the T-junction at the end of the Gorges du Cians. Turn left on to the N202, signposted Nice, following it for 19km to a junction with traffic lights. Go straight on here, but after about 7km take a left turn on to the D 2565, signposted Gorges de la Vésubie, to reach the Vésubie valley ⑤.

Pass through the Gorges and follow the road all the way back to St-Martin-Vésubie.

▲ *Near the southern edge of the Parc National du Mercantour, only about an hour's drive from the coast, are the fine Gorges Supérieures du Cians. The tour follows the Gorges Inférieures as well, which are also impressive*

Passes such as Col de la Couillole, lying beneath snow-covered peaks, form a striking contrast with the gentler coastal region to the south ▼

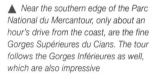

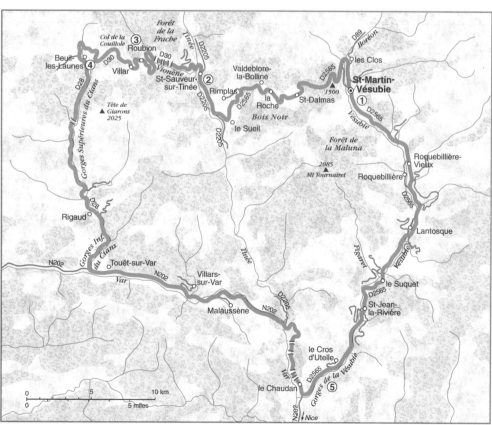

SKI RESORTS

The high ridge of the Alpes Maritimes forms the border between France and Italy, and on our route this frontier is just a few kilometres to the north. From the high ridge the Alps fall southward, dropping in height through the Parc National du Mercantour and towards the sea. On these south-facing flanks a new generation of ski resorts is springing up, hoping to make up in good weather and closeness to the Mediterranean for what they lack in altitude. As you drive westward along the road that links the heads of the south-draining river valleys, you will see ski lifts and tows standing out against the blue Provençal sky.

The best of the new resorts is Isola 2000, which has more than 20 lifts and tows for skiers. The name appears futuristic, but it refers to the resort's height in metres. Notable among the other towns passed along the way is Valberg, lying at 1669m. This is similarly well equipped with lifts and tows and has created cross-country ski runs.

now building a reputation as a winter-sports centre.

⑤ The lower section of the Vésubie valley was followed by the second tour (see pages 231-2). The upper section, followed by the present tour, is distinctly alpine, the meadows and forests being punctuated with rockier sections, high peaks and waterfalls. Some idea of the mountainous nature of the country here can be gained from the fact that the village of Roquebillière has been rebuilt six times following devastation by flood or landslide. The most recent reconstruction, in 1926, was on a new site, so that now there are two villages. The old village contains fine old houses, but, surprisingly, it is the new village that has the 16th-century church. The architects clearly knew a little about the local geography, building the church in a very safe spot, and in a curious mix of Romanesque and Gothic styles.

Points of Interest

① As a refuge from the heat of the coast, there can be few better places than St-Martin-Vésubie, set high on a ridge and ringed by mountains. The best part of the village is Rue du Docteur-Cagnoli, a narrow street of Gothic houses in which stands the 18th-century Chapelle des Pénitents Blancs. The village church, at the southern end of the same road, is a little older. Close by is the Place de la Frairie, from where the mountain views are magnificent.

② Set at the head of the fine Tinée valley, which the route crosses twice, St-Sauveur-sur-Tinée has a church with a 13th-century Romanesque campanile, and a number of picturesque old houses.

③ The tiny village of Roubion is set on an outcrop of red rock and still has part of its 12th-century defensive wall.

④ A wonderfully situated village, Beuil-les-Launes has a bloody history of strife between the Grimaldis of Monaco and the Dukes of Savoy, its position in the Cians valley making it strategically important. The village is

The village of la-Bollène-Vésubie is attractively situated on a hill surrounded by woodland in the beautiful valley of the Vésubie, a tributary of the Var ▼

The Maures coast

T he Massif des Maures is a long range of wooded hills backing the coast between Hyères and Fréjus. Despite the hilly terrain, the roads on this tour are good, and only on the short section between Bormes-les-Mimosas and Collobrières are they narrow enough to cause any difficulty. Furthermore, throughout the drive the views of both sea to one side and woodland to the other are superb.

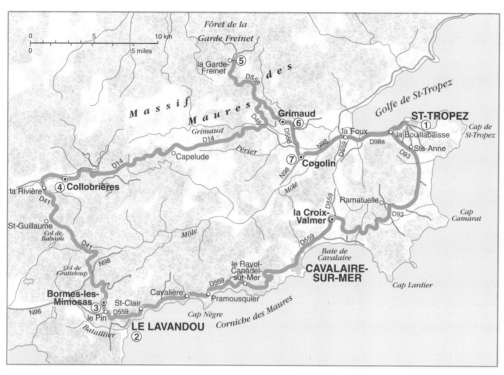

▲ *The pretty village of Bormes-les-Mimosas lies inland a little way, backed by the hills of the Massif des Maures*

Route Directions

The drive starts from St-Tropez ①.

Leave the town centre on the only available exit road. At the first major junction, where there are traffic lights, take the D 93 to the left, signposted Ramatuelle. At Ramatuelle the road, signposted la Croix-Valmer, bears left, and soon becomes very narrow. Continue to la Croix-Valmer and at the junction turn left on to the D 559, signposted Cavalaire-sur-Mer and le Lavandou. At a roundabout,

take the exit signposted Cavalaire-sur-Mer and le Lavandou. At Cavalaire-sur-Mer, at a small roundabout, take the exit signposted Centre Ville and Le Pont. The road follows the seafront and then sweeps right, through the centre of the town. Continue along the coast road, going through le Rayol-Canadel-sur-Mer and Cavalière, which has a confusingly similar name to the larger village passed through earlier. At Cavalière go straight over the mini roundabout, and take the exit signposted le Lavandou ②.

From le Lavandou follow signs for Hyères and then turn right, opposite a petrol station, towards Bormes-les-Mimosas. The road goes through le Pin to reach a T-junction. Turn sharp right and enter Bormes-les-Mimosas ③.

There is a good car park in the village, on the right-hand side. The first walk starts from here.

Leave the car park, pass through the village and continue to Col de Gratteloup. At the Col, go over the main road, the N98, and take the D 41, signposted Col de Babaou and Collobrières. This is a beautiful

but narrow road, and is designated a cycle-touring route, so take care, as cyclists have priority in France. Pass the entrance to an arboretum on the right, and at a T-junction take a right turn, signposted Collobrières,

Grimaud and Chartreuse de la Verne, and follow the road into Collobrières ④.

Leave the village and bear right at the first fork on to the D 14. Follow this road for about 20km and then fork left on to the D 48. Turn left at the next junction on to the D 558 and continue to la Garde-Freinet ⑤.

The second walk starts from here. The road bears left, then right, into the village square. Return on the same road, and follow signs for Grimaud and St-Tropez. Pass through Grimaud ⑥.

After Grimaud, at a roundabout, take the first exit, signposted Cogolin, and follow this road, which sweeps left into Cogolin ⑦.

Take the main street through the village, signposted Toutes Directions. At the junction with the N98, turn left, following signs for St-Tropez and Ste-Maxime. At the next roundabout go straight over, towards St-Tropez and Ste-Maxime, and at the next junction turn right on to a road signposted St-Tropez. At a fork bear right, following signs for St-Tropez, to return to the town centre.

For all its glamour, St-Tropez has a pleasantly simple port ▼

▲ Not far from Grimaud, named after the Grimaldi family of Monaco, lies the modern development of Port-Grimaud

An attractive hill village, Bormes-les-Mimosas is also blessed with three sandy beaches and a marina ▶

Points of Interest

① It is difficult to separate the real St-Tropez from the myth. Yet, once the yachts, the topless stars-in-waiting and the dream-seeking crowds have all left, it is revealed as a charming little village, bathed in the pure light that attracted Matisse, Braque and other artists in the days before it was notorious. Some of their work is in the Musée de l'Annonciade, but it will be ignored by many visitors, captivated instead by the port, the little squares, the view across the bay, indeed just about everything in this most delightful of coastal villages.

② Le Lavandou is one of the discoveries of the Var coast, a Provençal fishing port that is still just that, despite the growth of tourism all along the Maures coast from here to St-Tropez. Eastward from le Lavandou there are several more charming spots, many with excellent beaches: St-Clair, Cavalière, le Rayol-Canadel-sur-Mer and Cavalaire-sur-Mer. From the latter there is a summer boat service to the Ile de Port-Cros.

③ See page 240.

④ Collobrières, a charming village with picturesque houses grouped beside a humpback bridge, is a centre for the production of corks and sweet chestnuts (marrons glacés). The village is one of the biggest on the Maures Coast, and the drive to and from it passes through the forest that gave the hills their name, derived from the Provençal word for a dark forest.

⑤ See page 239.

⑥ The name Grimaud derives from the fact that the village once belonged to Monaco's Grimaldi family. The original château was destroyed by Louis XIII when he needed to stamp his authority on the area. From the village there are superb views of the sea and the Massif des Maures. Port-Grimaud, to the east, is a modern residential complex, marina and beach.

⑦ Cogolin is a centre for the making of carpets, and has a museum devoted to the craft. One of the most unusual museums in Provence, it is well worth a visit.

THE MISTRAL

When there are areas of high atmospheric pressure, winds are created, moving masses of air to regions of lower pressure in order to equalise the pressure. When a region of high pressure forms over the high Alps, a powerful wind, the Mistral, occasionally takes the cold Alpine air southward towards Provence. This wind usually blows in winter and spring, but once in a while makes itself felt in summer too. The Mistral is dry as well as cold, so that it both dries and chills the skin. These two effects, combined with the fact that the wind blows constantly, rather than in gusts, drive the local folk to distraction. The Romans claimed the wind was a god, a particularly malevolent one, while the folk of Avignon and Marseille talk of winds capable of pulling the tails off donkeys. Those cities experience the worst of the Mistral, as it is channelled down the Rhône valley, seeming to grow in venom until it bursts out at the coast. Those who travel along the sides of the valley will soon notice the positioning of the houses and the windbreak trees and fences – all done to diminish the impact of the wind.

A summer Mistral can be even more unwelcome if it follows close on the sirocco, a hot, dry wind that blows up from the Sahara. Either wind can fan a forest fire. To reduce the risk of fires the authorities are at present discouraging forest walking between July and September. Sadly, most forest fires are still caused by carelessness.

Above la Garde-Freinet

The Massif des Maures demands at least one high-level walk, if you are to enjoy the best of its views. This walk is that, although it is not strenuous. It also visits a site of great historical interest along the way.

Route Directions

Start from the car park close to the Croix des Maures above la Garde-Freinet ①.

Leave the car park on the right-hand side (facing the cross). There are already fine views over the roofs of the village. Follow the well-defined path to the Croix des Maures ②.

Continue along the path to the end of a rocky peak and the remains of an old fort ③.

Do not be deceived on this section: it is further than it first looks, but it does offer extraordinary views inland ④.

The fort is the limit of the walk, so return along the path to the Croix des Maures. Continue to a manhole cover. To extend the walk you may now turn left and walk down into the village. Otherwise, go over the first hillock to return by a more direct route to the car park.

If you have descended into la Garde-Freinet pass the church into the square in front of it, where there are several cafés. Turn right out of the square on to a road which leads uphill to the car park.

La Garde-Freinet's fort was probably built as a defence against Saracen invaders ▶

Points of Interest

① The fine village of la Garde-Freinet is a centre for the production of cork and chestnut. It is said that the Saracens who remained in the area after the French had reoccupied it (see ③) taught the locals the secrets of sweet chestnuts (known locally as *marrons de luc*) as well as how to make the typically flat Provençal roof tiles.

② The Croix des Maures is a mission cross – that is, one erected to proclaim the message of Christianity over a wide area. Near by, in season, the wild flowers make a beautiful display and are often alive with butterflies, including the spectacular swallowtail.

▲ *The Croix des Maures*

③ After the Romans had left Provence, and the barbarian hordes had dispersed, much of southern France was occupied by Saracens – the collective name for a mix of Arabs, Moors and other North African tribes. By the 8th century they had pushed into central France, but were defeated in a decisive battle at Poitiers in 732 by Charles Martel, the Merovingian leader. The Saracens were gradually squeezed south, but remained in the area around the Maures until the 10th century, when they were again defeated, this time by Guillaume, Duc de Provence. The fort is often claimed to be the ruins of a Saracen fortress, but it is almost certainly medieval, on Saracen foundations.

▲ *The walk gives a good view down to la Garde-Freinet*

④ The Massif des Maures stretches from Hyères to Fréjus, its crystalline rocks – mostly gneiss and some micro-schists – forming one of the oldest ranges of hills in Provence. It is a comparatively low range, rarely rising above the 700-m contour, but it is exposed to a fierce summer sun. On the coast the trees are pine, with sharp needles that reduce water loss, and there are many succulent shrubs. In the area covered by the tour pines give way to chestnut and oak, larger-leaved trees better able to cope with higher ground. The oaks are chiefly cork oak, supplying the raw material for la Garde-Freinet's wine-bottle cork industry.

WALK 59B: 7KM/ALLOW 1½ HOURS

Bormes-les-Mimosas

Bormes-les-Mimosas is a typically attractive Provençal hill village, alive with mimosa and camomile, and offers excellent views from its ruined castle. This walk, which is not demanding, follows the Circuit Touristique and is well signposted throughout.

Route Directions

Start from the town hall, which is a few metres from the car park. Pass a windmill without sails ①.

Cross the car park to reach the chapel ②.

Go to the right of the chapel and uphill, then take the first lane on the left ③.

Follow the lane to the old castle ④.

Turn right and climb up to the castle, then go left past a telephone box and down the road to the right to where a high wall ends. Zigzag down through alleys to reach a road ⑤.

Turn left and then right along the road. Go left through an alley, then zigzag through more alleys to reach the main square. Go back up the main street to the tourist office and turn left there, then turn right and right again to reach a large church. From there return to the car park.

Points of Interest

① The old windmill was once used to power an oil press, Bormes-les-Mimosas being a centre for olive oil.

② The fine chapel, dedicated to St François, dates from the 16th century. The dedication commemorates the saint's saving of Bormes from plague in 1481. In front of the chapel is a statue to the saint erected in 1720. The old cemetery beside the chapel includes the grave of Jean-Charles Cazin, a painter whose work can be seen in the village museum in Rue Carnot.

The walk threads its way through Bormes-les-Mimosas ▼

③ The view to the coast from here is breathtaking. The islands are the Iles d'Hyères. The largest island, the Ile de Porquerolles, is closest to Hyères itself, and has a small village, once a fishing port but now mostly given over to tourism. The next island, Ile de Port-Cros, is fascinating for being at the centre of one of France's six Parcs Nationaux. The other five Parks are all on the mainland, and in mountain areas. Port-Cros is a marine park, its treasures lying below the waters of the Mediterranean. The final island, Ile du Levant, has a naturist centre.

④ The castle was built by the Counts of Marseille in the 13th century. Later the building was taken over as a monastery, but has lain in ruins for many years.

⑤ The longest of the steep alleys has over 80 steps in its 150-m length. It is called Rue Rompe Cuou, a frank Provençal name attesting to its slipperiness, which is due to a small central stream that takes waste water from the houses on each side.

◄ *Mimosa, camomile, eucalyptus and oleander adorn Bormes*

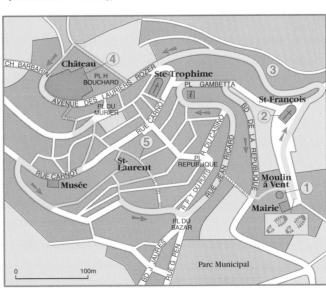

The heart of Provence

I n contrast to nearby Marseille, Aix-en-Provence is relatively peaceful, and of moderate size. From Aix we travel east to the Montagne Ste-Victoire – the mountain that inspired Cézanne – before turning south towards the Massif de la Ste-Baume. From the ridges of these hills there is a view to Marseille. The route does not take in Marseille, instead turning north to return to Aix. The roads are narrow in places and hilly in others, but not problematic, so that the drive is interesting rather than arduous.

Route Directions

The drive starts from Aix-en-Provence ①.

Leave Aix on the D 10, signposted St-Marc-Jaumegarde and Vauvenargues to reach, after about 8km, the Barrage du Bimont ②.

The first walk starts from here. Leave the car park and go back to the D 10, turning right on to it. Although there is a bypass around the village, most people will want to visit Vauvenargues ③.

If you do visit it, rejoin the bypass by driving straight through the village – there is only one road. The D 10 is now signposted Jouques and Rians, and runs along the northern flank of the Montagne Ste-Victoire ④.

Go straight on at the next junction, following the D 223, signposted Rians. The road narrows and climbs, but offers good views all the way. At the next junction take a left turn on to the D 23, signposted Rians and Manosque. This road ends at a T-junction with the D 3. Take a right turn, signposted Ollières and St-Maximin. St-Maximin is soon reached. At traffic lights turn left into the town. Bear right and left, and right and left again as you traverse St-Maximin ⑤.

The road divides as it leaves the town. Go straight on, along the N560, as the main road bears left. This smaller road goes under a railway bridge and is signposted Aubagne, Marseille and St-Zacharie. Continue for 100m, then bear left on to the D 83, signposted Rougiers. This road is a slip road that crosses the main road at a STOP sign. Again it is signposted Rougiers. This is a narrow road, and becomes narrower after Rougiers. To reach the village of Rougiers you cross the D 1. Go through the village. The road goes uphill towards a ruin and church seen on top of the hill ahead. It then bears sharp left and goes through an open barrier, before continuing up the valley. Go over a crest and down to a junction. Turn right on to the D 95 (only the back of the signpost is visible, so to check that you are on the right road make sure the wrong side says Plan-d'Aups). Go past

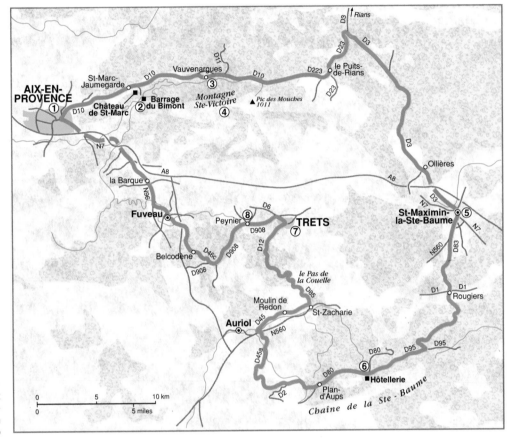

signs warning of deer, and continue to the Hôtellerie at la Ste-Baume ⑥.

The second walk starts from here. Continue on the D 80 through Plan-d'Aups, after which the road widens a little. At the next junction turn right on to a road signposted Auriol, which joins the D 45a to make a long, twisty decent around many hairpin bends. When the N560 is reached take a left turn, signposted Aubagne, Auriol and Roquevaire, and then immediately turn right (after the Citroën garage) back on to the D 45a. At the next crossroads take a right turn, signposted Moulin de Redon, on to the very narrow D 45, going towards St-Zacharie. At a crossroads go straight over into St-Zacharie. Turn left, then immediately left again in the village centre on to the D 85, following signs for Trets and Col du Petit Galibier. Stay on this road and the D 12, which climbs, giving fine views, to reach Trets ⑦.

In the centre of the town turn left on to the D 6, signposted Aix and Marseille. At the roundabout take the D 908, signposted Peynier ⑧.

Pass through Peynier, and climb up to pass a red and white communications tower on the left. Take the D 46c to the right, signposted Belcodène, and go through the village, following signs for Fuveau.

Go over the motorway and enter Fuveau. Turn left and right into the main square, then, almost immediately, take the first turning on the left, next to a chemist's. A little farther on the road is signposted Aix-en-Provence and Gardanne. At a roundabout with a central fountain, take the exit signposted Aix and continue to the N96. Turn right and follow this road and the N7 to Aix.

▼ St-Maximin's basilica is one of the treasures of Provence

▲ *Aix-en-Provence's 16th-century Clock Tower adjoins its town hall*

▲ *The Montagne Ste-Victoire rises to a height of 1011m*

Points of Interest

① The heart of Aix-en-Provence is Cours Mirabeau, named after a townsperson of the time of the Revolution, an ugly man of ugly habits who, nonetheless, was a superb orator and beloved of the common people. The boulevard is wide and airy, and each of its pavements is planted with a double row of plane trees that offer welcome shade from the summer sun. In the centre of the boulevard is a moss-encrusted hot-water fountain, its water coming from a source first tapped by the Romans in 122 BC. The water is mildly radioactive, as well as being a brew of mineral salts, and reaches the surface at 36°C.

Vieil Aix, the oldest and most charming section of the city, lies to the north of Cours Mirabeau. Some of the streets here are pedestrianised and lined with smart fashion shops, antique dealers and shops selling Provençal handcrafts. To get the old quarter's real flavour, take Rue Doumer from Cours Mirabeau and turn right into Rue Espariat, which leads into Place d'Albertas. This is the most delightful of the little squares of old Aix, cobbled and with fine terraced houses around a central fountain.

North again are the Tour de l'Horloge (Clock Tower) and the Cathédrale St-Sauveur. The former dates from the 16th century, though the lower statues of Night and Day are modern. The wooden statuettes of the four seasons higher up are each visible for three months at a time. The cathedral has a 5th-century baptistery and architectural styles of many different periods come together in this 16th-century Gothic building.

② See page 243.

③ The pretty village of Vauvenargues is famous for its Renaissance château, which was inherited by Picasso in 1958 and is where he died in 1973. The artist is buried in the extensive park, but neither park nor château is open to the public.

④ See page 243.

⑤ The basilica in St-Maximin-la-Ste-Baume is the best example of Gothic architecture in Provence. It was built on a 6th-century church that was itself the resting place for the remains of St Mary Magdalene (see page 244), and, later, St Maximin himself. Building of the new basilica started in 1295 and continued intermittently until the 16th century, though no belfry was ever built, a most unusual omission, and the west front was not finished. The building was due to be demolished at the time of the Revolution, but Napoleon's brother Lucien, who was stationed in the town, had the *Marseillaise* played on the organ every day and the Revolutionaries spared it. The organ is still in use today.

⑥ See page 244.

⑦ Originally a Roman town, Trets is now almost purely a medieval one, with the remains of old walls, square 14th-century towers, a castle that is 100 years older, and a 15th-century church.

⑧ The tiny village of Peynier has a pleasant Romanesque church.

CEZANNE

Paul Cézanne was born in Aix-en-Provence in 1839, at 28 Rue de l'Opéra. He was baptised in the chapel of Ste-Marie-Madeleine in the same year, and attended a primary school in Rue des Epinaux from 1844 until 1849. The family moved to 14 Rue Mathéron and Paul attended the Collège Bourbon – now the Lycée Mignet – in Rue Cardinale, where he was a pupil at the same time as Emile Zola. Cézanne's father acquired an estate about 4km south-west of the town, called Jas de Bouffan, but Paul went to Paris, intending to study law. There, however, he decided to fulfil his dream by becoming a painter. But he left Paris in 1881, disillusioned by what he saw as the limitations of Impressionism, and by the public reaction to his Impressionist friends, whose work he believed to be critical to the development of painting.

Back in Aix, Cézanne rented several rooms, most importantly in the Château Noir, on the D 17 to the west of the town, and at 23 Rue Boulegon, where he died in 1906. In 1902 he rented a studio at number 9 in the avenue that now bears his name. The studio is now the Atelier Paul Cézanne, a museum dedicated to his work.

Cézanne was by all accounts a modest man, but he was clear of his own position in art. 'A painter like me,' he said, 'there's only one every other century.' His idea was to create harmonious pictures, for he admired greatly the balance in the work of the great classical artists. He imposed this quality on his landscapes, creating paintings that appear to be patchworks or mosaics, blocks of colour whose patterns balance each other as well as portraying the subject. That subject was frequently the Montagne Ste-Victoire, which Cézanne loved above all local themes.

Barrage du Bimont

PROVENCE AND THE
CÔTE D'AZUR

◀ Fish abound in the lake formed by the Barrage du Bimont, below the Montagne Ste-Victoire

The vaulted Barrage du Bimont, which is situated some 5km east of Aix-en-Provence, has created a fine lake by damming the River Infernet ▼

This fine walk starts from an artificial lake set below the Montagne Ste-Victoire, and leads up to a low point on the ridge of that peak, from where there are views to the second hill range that this tour visits.

Route Directions

Start from the car park at the Barrage du Bimont. Leave through the gates in the left end of the car park, where a sign gives the opening times of the dam: 1 November-28 February: 9am-6pm; 1 March-31 October: 7am-10pm. Go along the road and cross the dam ①.

Look to the right here to see a collection lake feeding a system of canals that go through the mountains. On the left the Montagne Ste-Victoire is topped by a commemorative cross ② and ③.

At the end of the track go through a barrier against cars, passing a notice that warns of the risk of forest fires. Do not smoke on this walk.

The wide track continues uphill, then flattens out to reach a fork. Take the left fork to reach a viewpoint over the Ste-Victoire ridge and trees to the Massif de la Ste-Baume. Continue walking towards the Croix de Provence, on the summit, through country that opens out, to reach another clump of trees. Here the track bears right, with a smaller track going straight on. A sign on a tree to the left reads 'Chemin des Costes Chauds'. Go up this track through a very pretty stretch of mixed woodland with many different flowers. As the track flattens and then begins to go downhill, a smaller track merges from the left. Soon there is a more definite left fork. Turn left down this track, where you may be lucky enough to see green lizards among the flowers. At a T-junction of tracks, take the smaller one, which goes left. This leads to the lake. At the lake turn left up a rougher, narrower track that leads back to the dam. Go over the dam to return to the car park.

Points of Interest

① The Durance valley, and its tributary valleys, have been turned into a water system that supplies irrigation water to agricultural land, as well as hydroelectric power and drinking water. The lake here is part of this scheme, and some of the irrigation channels are visible from the walk. The dam creates a water head, and the lake it creates provides water to the local towns. The lake holds fish, but note that swimming is banned.

② When the Romans moved into this area of Provence they found the hot springs that still feed the Cours Mirabeau fountain and founded Aquae Sextiae Saluviorum – the future Aix – around them in 122 BC. Twenty years later, Roman historians record, a band of Teutonic barbarians invaded the area and were confronted by a Roman army on the flanks of the hill to the east of the town. In the battle 100,000 barbarians were killed and 100,000 more captured. The mountain above the battlefields was called Victory to commemorate the slaughter, and it still bears the name. It is a good story, even if the death toll is dubious. The mountain was beloved of Cézanne and inspired many of his greatest works.

③ The Croix de Provence, an 18-m cross, is the third to have been placed on the summit. Those who wish to see the Cross at close hand, and to obtain a breathtaking view that includes, on clear days, the Dauphiné Alps, can walk up. The best route is to follow GR 9 from les Cabassols, on the tour.

Woods near the Barrage du Bimont ▼

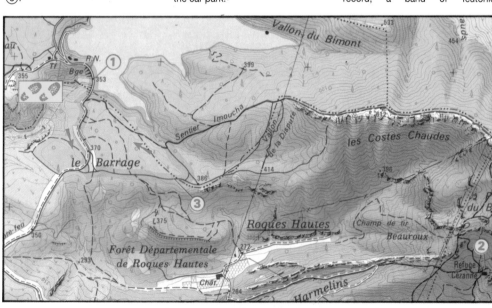

Grotte Ste-Marie-Madeleine

This walk, full of history and legend, involves about 280m of ascent, some of it up rock-cut steps, and so should not be undertaken lightly. However, even if it is not completed it is still worth while, since the woodland at the start is attractive.

Route Directions

Start from the Hôtellerie de la Sainte-Baume. Follow the Chemin des Pèlerins (Pilgrims' Way), which GR 9/98 also follows. The first GR arrows are on a huge oak tree. Go between two pillars, passing the old cemetery, and continue along an avenue of magnificent chestnut trees into a wood. The signposted route goes past rocks known as the Canapé to reach a chapel at the Carrefour de l'Oratoire, the Crossroads by the Oratory ②.

From here a wide path to the right – look for the brown waymarks – leads to about 160 steps cut into the rock face. Climb these to reach the Terrace ③.

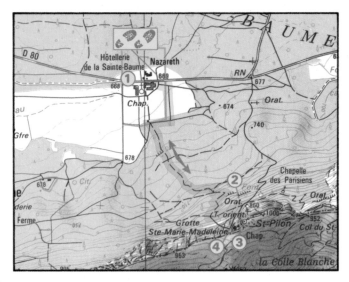

Continue to the cave itself ④.

From here there is no alternative but to return down the steps.

Points of Interest

① The Hôtellerie is a 19th-century restoration of a Dominican friars' pilgrim hostel, placed here to serve the needs of those who came to Ste-Baume as pilgrims in medieval times. The building is now an international centre for spiritual studies.

② The Oratory is a 16th-century chapel. Those who wish to extend the walk from here, by only about 50m of ascent, can climb to the summit of St-Pilon, the high point of the Ste-Baume ridge and named after a long-gone column that once stood at the top. To climb to the summit, pass the Oratory and follow signs for GR 9. The summit, where there is a small chapel and a viewing table, offers another quite remarkable vista, taking in both Mont Ventoux and the sea. Legend has it that angels brought St Mary Magdalene to the summit from her cave seven times each day so that she could hear the music of paradise.

③ The Terrace offers a view that is almost as expansive as that from the main summit, being only a few tens of metres lower. The dominant view, however, is to the Montagne Ste-Victoire, which was so often the subject of paintings by Cézanne, who lived at Aix-en-Provence.

④ A Provençal legend tells that about AD 40 St Mary Magdalene, together with Mary the mother of James and John, Mary the sister of the Virgin Mary, Lazarus and several others were cast adrift from Palestine in a boat. They landed at a Camargue fishing village, where two of the Marys decided to stay. That village, Saintes-Maries-de-la-Mer, still commemorates the event in name, and has a church that holds the remains of the two women. Lazarus and St Mary Magdalene did not stay, choosing to go inland. Lazarus went to Marseille to spread the word of Christianity, but Mary came here, to la Ste-Baume, in order to find peace, and took up residence in this cave. She lived in the cave for 30 years, and when she died angels took her body for burial to the town that is now St-Maximin-la-Ste-Baume. The present basilica at St-Maximin is said to have been erected over Mary's remains. The cave has now been turned into a votive chapel and contains some interesting statuary. The annual votive feast is on 22 July.

The early part of the walk follows the Chemin des Pèlerins through woodland ▼

▲ *St Mary Magdalene may have lived in this cave for 30 years (top)*
The Romanesque church of St-Maximin-la-Ste-Baume (above)

The Durance valley

From Grenoble two routes head for the heart of Provence. The N75 crosses Col de la Croix Haute, while the N85 goes over Col Bayard. Eventually the routes converge, because there is now only one way into Provence – along the Durance valley. The Durance carves its way southward into the region, then turns west to traverse it before reaching the Rhône at Avignon. Our route follows the more interesting part of the valley, and returns over the Montagne de Lure. The mountain section of the route is narrow, steep and twisting, but is easily negotiated with care and patience.

Route Directions

The drive starts from Sisteron ①.

The car park beside the tourist office in Sisteron is the starting-point for the first walk. Leave Sisteron, heading south on the N85, signposted Aix. After 6.5km turn right on to the D 951, signposted St-Etienne-les-Orgues. Bear right at Peipin to take the bypass, signposted Châteauneuf-Val-St-Donat and St-Etienne, and continue to follow signs to St-Etienne, going through Cruis before reaching St-Etienne ②.

Go into the centre of the town, and take the road to the left, signposted Fontienne and Forcalquier. After a few hundred metres turn right on to the D 13, signposted Limans and Forcalquier and follow it and the D 950 to Forcalquier ③.

Return to the junction with the N100 and turn left for Mane ④.

Pass through Mane, continuing on the N100, now signposted Apt, but leaving it soon after by going left on to the D 13, signposted Voix, Manosque, St-Maime and Dauphin. After about 5km, at a small roundabout, take the exit signposted Dauphin. Turn right on to the D 16, crossing a small river bridge, and left at the Dauphin sign. Pass a small car park to reach a junction. Take a left turn, signposted Manosque, and follow this narrow road, the D 5, over Col de la Mort d'Imbert and down into Manosque ⑤.

Leave the town centre, following signs for Apt, Pierrevert and Auves. Once you are out of the town follow signs for Apt on the D 907. After 8km turn right on the D 105, signposted St-Martin-les-Eaux. At the next junction turn left for St-Michel-l'Observatoire. When you reach the main road, the N100, turn right and left (it is a staggered junction) to continue on the D 105, signposted St-Michel-l'Observatoire and Banon. Turn left into St-Michel ⑥.

At the town square turn right for the Observatory if you wish to visit it. Otherwise, leave St-Michel by going straight past the square and taking the next left turn on to the D 5 (by the church and fountain), signposted Banon. On leaving the village you will be able to see the Observatory to the right. Continue on the D 5, following signs for Banon all the way to the town and then follow signs for Centre Ville to reach the heart of Banon ⑦.

Take a right turn on to the D 950, signposted St-Etienne-les-Orgues and Forcalquier, and after 1.5km turn left, then right, following the same signs. At a junction turn left and cross a river, then turn right on to the D 951, signposted St-Etienne. Just before you reach St-Etienne take a left turn, signposted Montagne de Lure ⑧.

This road climbs behind the town. Turn sharp left to reach the D 113, the winding road that climbs the mountains. The road passes the Refuge de Lure and, about 4km further on, reaches its high point, where there is a car park. The second walk starts from here.

From the car park descend carefully for about 25km to a T-junction. Take a right turn on to the D 946, signposted Sisteron. After about 6km turn left on to the D 53, signposted Sisteron. This climbs before dropping into the town.

▼ Forcalquier and its hilltop chapel

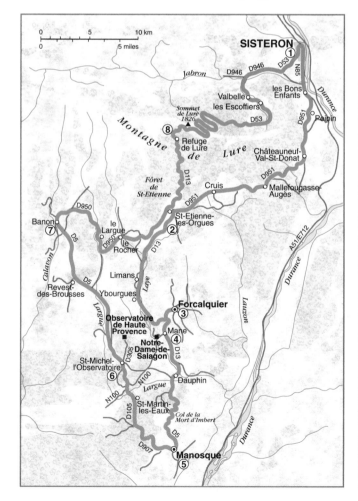

Points of Interest

① See page 247.

② See page 248.

③ Start your visit to Forcalquier by going to the Terrasse Notre-Dame-de-Provence, a chapel set on a high terrace from where the view to the town, and away from it, is excellent. In the town, the old quarter, below the chapel, is a huddle of narrow streets, each lined with tall houses to keep the Mistral at bay.

④ Mane is frequently overlooked by visitors hurrying by to find the church of Notre-Dame-de-Salagon, but in fact deserves to be seen, if only for a look at the two-tiered medieval walls of the castle on the outcrop beside the village. The famed 12th-century church was once a priory church, the last monks having left at the time of the Revolution.

⑤ The town is often called 'Modest Manosque', the name, now generally used disparagingly, dating from a visit by François I in the early 15th century. The loveliest of the town's girls presented the keys of the town to the king. He was much taken with her and decided that droit de seigneur should be added to his gifts. The girl's father, the town mayor, was horrified, and threw acid in his daughter's face to save her virtue. The king lost interest, the mayor was satisfied, and of the poor, mutilated girl, history knows no more.

To get the best from your visit to the 'modest' town, visit the old quarter, north of Place du Terreau, where there are fine old houses, and a section of the town's 14th-century gate, still defended by mantraps.

⑥ The village of St-Michel-l'Observatoire still has a few medieval houses, and an interesting church, but most visitors pass through on their way to the Observatory. The purity of the local air makes this one of the leading centres for the study of astronomy, and visitors can have a guided tour of the numerous domes.

⑦ Banon is a village with the remnants of medieval walls still intact. In this case they surround the old village, set on a rocky outcrop, and overlooking the newer village.

⑧ See page 248.

Mane is best known for its 12th-century former priory church, but the medieval castle walls are also worth seeing ▶

NAPOLEON

When he landed close to Antibes from Elba on 1 March 1815 Napoleon Bonaparte probably knew he would not receive a universal welcome from the French. He was disappointed to be rejected by the garrison at Antibes, where he had been the garrison commander in 1794, but at least he was not arrested. He learned that he could expect no better treatment in the Rhône valley and so he struck inland to reach the Durance valley, planning to use it to leave Provence and to penetrate the French heartland. He and his followers made for Grasse, continuing on a difficult path to Séranon. The following day they had to cross the River Verdon, and to do this they made for Castellane. There Napoleon stopped for lunch at 34 Rue Nationale.

Such details are known for all the points along the route to Grenoble where, on 7 March, Napoleon was met by shouts of 'Long live the Emperor'. Our route follows a section of the 'Route Napoléon', as the line of the Emperor's journey is called, from Sisteron to Digne. At Malijai, Napoleon spent the night of 4 March 1815 in the château. The next day he travelled through Volonne to Sisteron, where he had breakfast at 20 Rue Saunerie.

Sisteron

PROVENCE AND THE
CÔTE D'AZUR

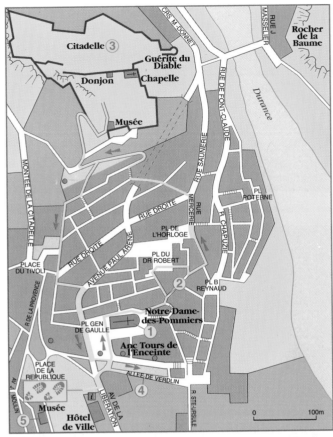

S isteron is one of the most interesting towns in Haute-Provence, with a fine old castle, narrow streets of medieval houses, and tremendous views of the cleft through which the River Durance enters Provence. The walk is straightforward, but has a couple of stepped sections which might inconvenience the less agile.

Route Directions

Start from the car park near the tourist office in Sisteron. Cross the main road, in the downhill direction, and pass the front of the church of Notre-Dame-des-Pommiers ①.

Go right down the side of the church, taking Rue Deuleuze ②.

Turn left down Traverse de Rieu, going under a tiny archway beneath houses. Turn right into what looks like a dead end, but leave it by going right again, and again go below houses and buildings. Take the next turning on the left, and follow white signs for Centre Ville and Tour Commerces. Go up and under an archway, then up steps into Rue Saunerie. Go straight across the road to reach a narrow alleyway signposted Citadelle. Go up and right, following signs for 'Visite Vieille Ville'. Turn right at a hairpin bend to return almost the same way as you came, going up steps and following the signs. In the next road pass a telephone box and go straight up to reach steps up to the Citadelle ③.

After your visit to the Citadelle, go back down the steps and turn left. Take the first turning to the right, going down steps into Rue des Poteries. Continue straight on into a square, Place du Tivoli. Go left down Rue Haute-du-Rempart, crossing over at the first junction to reach a main shopping street. Turn right here and follow the road back past the church. The road also leads back to the car park, but before reaching it, make a short detour to the left, down Allée de Verdun. There you will see a section of Sisteron's old walls ④.

Return to the main street, and go left, to return to the car park, which is near the town museum ⑤.

Points of Interest

① This church, formerly the cathedral, was probably built in the late 12th century and is in the Provençal Romanesque style. The Romanesque element can be clearly seen in the symmetric façade, a Lombardian element being the alternate black and white stones of the doorway. Inside there is a fine baroque altar, and several interesting canvases. The church is dedicated to Notre-Dame-des-Pommiers, though this has nothing to do with apples, the final word deriving from *pomerium*, meaning an area that must be left open, without buildings.

② Old Sisteron is a delightful place, with its narrow alleys – some of them very steep – arches and sudden views. The steep alleys are called *andrônes*, though some have more colourful names as well; Rue du Glissoir means Slippery Street, made more of a problem by the throwing out of waste water, and still a danger in winter. Some of the houses date from the 13th century, though most are a century or two younger.

③ Sisteron is cleverly set where a stream, the Buech, meets the Durance, and is built into the rocks on the west side of the Durance gorge. The strategic importance of the site was first recognised by the Romans, who named it Segustero. The Citadelle, a truly massive fortress, was started in the 11th century, but added to over many years, the major work being carried out in the 16th century. Unfortunately the building was badly damaged in 1944, but has been restored. Within the walls there is an open-air theatre and a panorama dial. From this point the view to the Rocher de la Baume is awesome. The rock folding of the vertical cliffs makes the Rocher a vivid lesson in geology.

④ The town walls were built in the 14th century. Originally there were five towers protecting the walls, and three of these can still be seen in Allée de Verdun.

⑤ The town museum illustrates the history of Sisteron from Roman times.

Sommet de Lure

Points of Interest

① The Montagne de Lure forms part of the Alpine chain that ends with Mont Ventoux. In form it is a rugged ridge, the high point being at 1826m. The ridge is followed by GR 6, one of France's fine long-distance footpaths, which runs from Sisteron to Tarascon. On the lower slopes of its southern face the Montagne de Lure is quite heavily vegetated, with cedar and oak, and lavender fields. The lavender grows in several forms, but an interesting change occurs at around 800m in altitude, when one form is almost entirely replaced by another. The upland, hardier, form disappears above about 900m. The lavender here is wild, though cultivation of the plant is widely carried out to the south-east and south-west of the Montagne de Lure. There, chiefly in the area around Grasse, a hybrid plant known as *lavandin* is grown for its perfume. The perfume essence is extracted from the plant and mixed with wax to form a solid mass that is then sent to the great perfume houses of Paris. The Provence perfume industry supplies not only lavender, but also jasmine and other scented blossoms.

Above about 900m the only plants found on the mountain are a few herbs and wild flowers, some of these persisting quite high in the sheltered spots. The herbs made the mountain famous in medieval times, and the pretty village of St-Etienne-les-Orgues became very prosperous from the sale of herbal medicines made from local plants.

The lower slopes of the northern flank of the mountain ridge are clothed in hardier trees: pine, spruce, beech and maple.

② The summit of the Montagne de Lure provides what is undoubtedly one of the finest viewpoints in Provence. From the top the peaks of the Cévennes, in the Massif Central, are visible to the west, beyond Mont Ventoux.

O our tour is a valley route, and only on the return route are the uplands of Haute-Provence reached. This walk goes up to the high point of the Montagne de Lure. It is a steep climb, finishing at a height of over 1800m. On top the wind blows almost continuously, so you should prepare yourself for a breezy walk.

Route Directions

Start from the car park at the high point of the road that crosses the Montagne de Lure ①.

Head northwards over the barren flank of the mountain ridge. There is a path, though one is hardly required. If you can see the way ahead it will be obvious that you are going in the right direction. If you cannot see very clearly, then the weather is too bad for your walk, and you should come back another day. At the top of the ridge turn right and then climb up to eventually reach the Sommet de Lure ②.

Return down to the path and follow it to a T-junction on the ridge edge. Now carry straight on along the obvious track to reach the next summit (1813m). Go over this and continue downhill to reach the road, following GR 6. Turn left and walk alongside the road to return to the car park.

The slopes of the mountain are graced by attractive clusters of primroses ▼

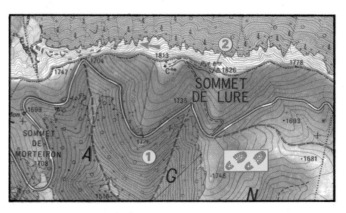

▼ *A wide variety of wild flowers, including orchids, abound on the Sommet de Lure*

Useful Information

Camping

There are over 11,000 camp sites throughout France. They have to be registered and are then graded (by the Fédération Française de Camping Caravaning, 78 rue de Rivoli, 75004 Paris) from one to four stars, depending on the facilities provided. A four-star site would have communal indoor recreation areas, hot water, washing machines and security for valuables; one-star sites are more crowded and sometimes have only cold water. Local farmers often let out their fields to campers – *camping à la ferme* – but such sites tend to be fairly basic.

A camping *carnet* is useful as some sites won't let you in without one, and includes some third-party insurance cover. They are obtainable by members from motoring organisations and caravan and cycling clubs affiliated to either the AIT or the FICC. One *carnet* covers up to 12 people.

The Camping Traveller in France, published by the FGTO, has up-to-date information.

Customs Regulations

The following quantities of goods may be imported into France. The lower figure in brackets applies to goods purchased duty free at the airport.
300 cigarettes (200) or 150 cigarillos (100) or 75 cigars (50) or 400g tobacco (250g).
Spirits over 22 per cent vol (38.8 proof), 1.5 litres (1 litre) alcohol under 22 per cent vol or sparkling wine 3 litres (2 litres). You can also import 5 litres table wine (2 litres).
Perfume 75g (50g) and toilet water 375cl (250cl).
Real coffee 1kg (instant 400g, essence 80g); tea 200g (instant 400g).

Children aged 16 and under may not import alcohol or tobacco.

Visitors may export from France duty-free goods up to the value of 2800FF (for children under 15, the value is 700FF).

Cycling

Remember to ride on the right-hand side of the road unless there are cycle paths.

Cycles can be hired from many cycle shops (local information from tourist offices) and also from French Railways (SNCF). Two hundred railway stations offer the service Train + Vélo; travellers can pick up their cycle from one station and return it to another. If you want to take your cycle on a train you must register it, but as it will not necessarily travel with you, try to send it a few days in advance. For short journeys it can travel in the luggage van; this service is free. The leaflet *Guide du train et du vélo* lists stations and prices.

More information from Fédération Française de Cyclisme, Bâtiment Jean Monnet, 5 rue de Rome, 93561 Rosny-sous-Bois (tel: 49 35 69 00).

Disabled Travellers

Facilities for the disabled have improved greatly over the past few years, and now many hotels and public buildings, airports and the railway system (SNCF) have been modified to provide help.

The book *Touristes quand même! Paris* (in French) covers the French capital only, listing the facilities accessible to wheelchair travellers and amenities provided for blind and deaf visitors in museums, main sights, parks, shops, places of worship and theatres. The publishers are at 38 boulevard Raspail, F-75007 Paris (tel: 45 48 90 13).

Useful addresses Australia: ACROD, PO Box 60, Curtin, ACT 2605 (tel: (06) 282 4333).
Canada: Canadian Rehabilitation Council for the Disabled, 45 Sheppard Avenue, Toronto ON M2N SW9 (tel: (416) 250 7490).
Eire: The Disabled Drivers' Association of Ireland and the Irish Association of Physically Handicapped People, Ballindine, Co Mayo (tel: (094) 64 054).
New Zealand: Disabled Citizens' Society Inc, PO Box 56-083, Dominion Road, Auckland 3, (tel: (9) 688 153).
UK: RADAR (the Royal Association for Disability and Rehabilitation), 25 Mortimer Street, London W1N 8AB); Tripscope, 63 Esmond Road, London W4 1JE (tel: (081) 994 9294); Holiday Care Services, 2 Old Bank Chambers, Station Road, Horley, Surrey RH6 9HW (tel: (0293) 774535).
US: Information Center for Individuals with Disabilities, Fort Point Place, 27-43 Wormwood Street, Boston MA 02210 (tel: (617) 727 5540).

Embassies and Consulates

Only in extreme circumstances do you contact your country's embassy. It is the Consul who issues emergency passports, contacts relatives and advises how to transfer funds.
American Embassy: 2 avenue Gabriel, 75008 Paris Cedex 08 (tel: (1) 42 96 12 02). There are Consuls-General in Bordeaux, Lyon and Marseille.
Australian Embassy: 4 rue Jean-Rey, 75015 Paris Cedex 15 (tel: (1) 40 59 33 00).

British Embassy: 35 rue du Faubourg-St-Honoré, Paris 8e (tel: (1) 42 66 91 42); British Consulate-General is at 16 rue d'Anjou, 75383 Paris Cedex 08 (tel: (1) 42 66 91 42). There are British Consuls-General in Bordeaux, Lille, Lyon and Marseille and Honorary Consuls (who work restricted hours) in Biarritz, Bordeaux, Cherbourg, Le Havre, Nantes, Nice, St Malo/Dinard and Toulouse.

Irish Embassy: 12 Avenue Foch, 75116 Paris (tel: (1) 45 00 20 87). There is an Honorary Consul in Antibes and Monaco.

Canadian Embassy: 35 avenue Montaigne, 75008 Paris Cedex 08 (tel: (1) 47 23 01 01). There are consulates in Lyon, Strasbourg and Toulouse.

New Zealand Embassy: 7 *ter* rue Léonard de Vinci 75016 Paris (tel: 45 00 24 11).

Money Matters

To change foreign currency into francs, find a bank displaying a *Change* sign or go to foreign exchange bureaux; avoid changing money at hotels, as the rate is poor. Eurocard (Access/ Mastercard) and Carte Bleue (Visa/Barclaycard) and charge cards (Diners and American Express) are widely accepted in larger hotels and restaurants and many shops.

Museums

National museums usually charge an entrance fee but allow free entry for children and young people under 18, and half-price entry for those aged between 18 and 25 or over 60. Everyone is entitled to half-price entry on Sundays. Municipal museums offer free entry to their permanent collections every day to children under seven and people over 60 and to everyone on Sundays.

Opening Hours

Banks Hours vary, but banks are generally open 09.00-noon and 14.00-16.00hrs. They are closed on Sundays and either Monday or Saturday. Banks close early the day before a public holiday.

Museums National museums are closed on Tuesdays, except Versailles, the Trianon Palace and the Musée d'Orsay, which are closed on Mondays. Municipal museums are closed on Mondays. Most museums close on Easter Sunday and Monday, Christmas Day and public holidays. Opening hours may be longer in summer.

Shops Hours vary depending on the type of shop, location and season. For example, lunchtime in summer in the south of France may extend to 16.00hrs and the shops then stay open later in the evening.
Food shops are open Tuesday to Friday 07.00/08.00-18.30/19.30hrs. Most close all day Monday but some may open in the afternoon. On Saturday and Sunday they may open mornings only. Smaller shops may close at lunchtime (noon-14.00hrs). Bakers are open on Sunday mornings. Supermarkets and hypermarkets open from about 09.00hrs until 21.00 or 22.00hrs. They are closed on Sunday and some hypermarkets also close on Monday mornings.

Telephones

The coins which payphones accept are 50 centimes, one, five and 10 francs. But some phones accept only *jetons* worth 50 centimes: small metal discs sold at bars, *cafés-tabac* and post offices. You can receive a call in a phone booth if a blue bell sign is shown. Many booths accept phone cards (*télécartes*): buy them from post offices, tobacconists and railway stations.

National and international dialling

Every French phone number has eight digits and the country is not divided into area codes for phone calls: only Paris differs from the rest of the country. If you're phoning Paris from the provinces dial 161 before the eight digits; to dial the provinces from Paris, dial 16 first.

If you're phoning France from abroad, dial the international code, then 33 (for the provinces), then the eight digits; for Paris, dial 331.

To dial abroad from France, dial 19, then dial the following code for each country:

Australia: 61	New Zealand: 64
Canada: 1	UK: 44
Eire: 353	US: 1

Then dial the area code (omitting the first 0), followed by the number.

Tourist Offices

There are over 5000 tourist offices in France, called either *Offices de Tourisme* or *Syndicats d'Initiative*. Larger towns have tourist offices called *Acceuil de France*.

The French Government Tourist Office (FGTO) publishes a great deal of literature in English, available from the following addresses:

Australia: French Tourist Bureau, BNP Building, 12th Floor, 12 Castlereagh Street, Sydney NSW 2000 (tel: 2 231 5244).

Canada: Représentation Française du Tourisme, 1981 Avenue McGill College, Suite 490, Montréal, Québec H3A 2W9 (tel: 514 288 4264).

Eire: FGTO, 35 Lower Abbey Street, Dublin 1 (tel: 1 77 1871).

UK: FGTO, 178 Piccadilly, London W1V 0AL (tel: (071) 491 7622).

US: FGTO, 610 Fifth Avenue Suite, New York, NY 10020-2452 (tel: (212) 757 1125).

INDEX

One of the pleasures of Provence is to buy fruit in markets like this one in Aix. After the sprawling port of Marseille, Aix is the second city in Provence and was once the regional capital ▶

D

E

F

G

Elaborate wrought-iron gates adorn Lons-le-Saunier's 18th-century Hôtel-Dieu ▼

Changing the guard at the royal palace in Monaco ▼

ACKNOWLEDGEMENTS

The Automobile Association would like to thank the following photographers, libraries and associations for their assistance in the preparation of this book.

P ATTERBURY 41a, 41b, 42a, 45a, 46a, 46b, 63b, 65a, 65b, 66a, 66b, 69a, 69b, 70a, 71a, 73a, 77a, 77b, 78a, 78b, 81a, 81b.

A BAKER 255

P BENNETT 207a, 208a, 208b, 208c, 211a, 211b, 212a, 212b, 223a, 223b, 224a, 224b

CDT CANTAL 136b

CHAMONIX TOURIST BOARD 170b

J EDMANSON 61a, 61b, 62a, 62b, 62c, 64a, 68a, 68b, 73b, 74a, 74b, 75a, 76a, 76b, 76c, 80a, 82a.

HAUTE SAVOIE 165a, 166b.

INTERNATIONAL PHOTOBANK 4a, 8a.

P KENWARD 12a, 115a, 115b, 116a, 116b, 116c, 119a, 120a, 120b, 120c, 123a, 124a, 124b, 127a, 128a, 128b, 128c, 187a, 188a, 188c, 191a, 192b, 192d, 195a, 195b, 196b, 196c, 200a, 203a, 203b, 204a, 204b, 205a.

J LLOYD 11a, 93a, 93b, 94a, 97a, 97b, 98a, 98b, 101a, 101b, 102a, 102b, 105a, 106a, 106b, 106c, 159a, 159b, 159c, 160a, 160b, 161a, 162a, 162b, 163a, 163b, 164a, 164b.

NATURE PHOTOGRAPHERS LTD 185a (P R Sterry), 185b (B Burbidge).

R NEILLANDS 15a, 15b, 16a, 16b, 17a, 19a, 23e, 24a, 24b, 30a, 33a, 34a, 34b, 34c, 37a, 38b.

D NOBLE 83a, 83b, 84a, 84b, 84c, 87b, 88b.

T OLIVER 44a, 58b, 60b, 131a, 132a, 132b, 133a, 133b, 134b, 135a, 135b, 136a, 137a, 137b, 138a, 139a, 140a, 140b, 141a, 141b, 142a, 143a, 143b, 144a, 144b, 145a, 145b, 146a, 146b, 147a, 147b, 148a, 148b, 148c, 149a, 150a, 150b, 151a, 151b, 152a, 152b, 152c, 153a, 154a, 154b, 154c, 155a, 155b, 156a, 156b, 229a, 229b, 230a, 230b, 230c, 233a, 233b, 234a, 235a, 235b, 236a, 239a, 239b, 239c, 240a, 240b, 243a, 243b, 243c, 244a, 244b, 244c, 248a, 248b, 248c.

I POWYS 51a, 52a, 53a, 54b, 55b, 56a, 59a, 85a, 85b, 86a, 88a, 89a, 89b, 90a, 90b, 107a, 109a, 110a, 113a, 114a.

M RATCLIFFE 189a, 189b, 189c, 190a, 190b, 190c, 193a, 193b, 194a, 194b, 194c, 197a, 201a, 202a, 202b, 202c, 206a, 206b.

K REYNOLDS 209a, 210a, 210b, 213a, 213b, 213c, 213d, 214a, 214b, 214c, 218a, 218b, 218c, 218d, 221a, 221b, 221c, 222a, 225a, 225b, 226a, 226b.

D ROBERTSON 39a, 39b, 40a, 40b, 43a, 44b, 47a, 47b, 48a, 48b, 48c, 48d, 50a, 54a, 55a, 57a, 58a, 58c, 60a, 60c.

C SAWYER 27a, 28a, 28b, 29a, 31a, 31b, 32a, 32b, 32c, 35a, 35b, 36a, 36b, 38a.

SCOPE 199a, 200b, 200c, 215a, 215b, 216b, 216c, 219a, 219b, 220a, 220b, 220c.

M SHALES 123b, 125a, 125b, 126a, 126b, 127b, 129a, 129b, 130a, 130b.

M SHORT 91a, 92a, 92b, 95a, 95b, 96a, 96b, 96c, 99a, 100a, 100b, 100c, 103a, 104a, 104b, 104c, 107b, 108a, 108b, 108c, 111a, 112a, 112b, 112c, 253.

B SMITH 14b, 23a, 23b, 23c, 23d, 63a, 64b, 67a, 87a, 91b, 134a, 166a, 170c, 175a, 175b, 176a, 176b, 179a, 179b, 180a, 188b, 191b, 192c, 216a, 224a, 227b, 237a.

R STRANGE 2/3a, 9&10, 169a, 169b, 170a, 183a, 183b, 184a, 184b, 227a, 228a, 228b, 231a, 232a, 232b, 232c, 233c, 237b, 238a, 238b, 241a, 242a, 242b, 242c, 245a, 246a, 247a, 252, 252, 254.

R VICTOR 14a, 18a, 18b, 19b, 21a, 22c, 25a, 26a, 26b.

R WEIR 22b.

J WHITE 167a, 167b, 168a, 168b, 171a, 171b, 172a, 174a, 174b, 177a, 178a, 181a, 182a, 186a, 186b.

WORLD PICTURES 1a.

ZEFA PICTURE LIBRARY (UK) LTD 13a, 22a.

Cover photograph: **INTERNATIONAL PHOTOBANK**
Background photograph: **BARRIE SMITH**